Economics and Social Interaction

Economics and Social Interaction is a fresh attempt to overcome the traditional inability of economics to deal with interpersonal phenomena that occur within the sphere of markets and productive organisations. It makes use of traditional economic concepts for understanding interpersonal events, while venturing beyond those concepts to give a better account of personalised interactions. In contrast to other books, *Economics and Social Interaction* offers the reader a rigorous effort at extending economic analysis to a notoriously slippery field in a consistent manner, sensitive to insights from other behavioural and social sciences. This collection represents an important contribution to a growing research agenda in the social sciences.

BENEDETTO GUI is Professor of Economics at the Università di Padova, Italy.

ROBERT SUGDEN is Professor of Economics at the University of East Anglia, Norwich.

T0323720

Economics and Social Interaction

Accounting for Interpersonal Relations

Edited By

Benedetto Gui and Robert Sugden

CAMBRIDGE
UNIVERSITY PRESS

CAMBRIDGE UNIVERSITY PRESS
Cambridge, New York, Melbourne, Madrid, Cape Town, Singapore,
São Paulo, Delhi, Dubai, Tokyo, Mexico City

Cambridge University Press
The Edinburgh Building, Cambridge CB2 8RU, UK

Published in the United States of America by Cambridge University Press, New York

www.cambridge.org
Information on this title: www.cambridge.org/9780521169554

First published 2005
Reprinted 2006
First paperback edition 2010

A catalogue record for this publication is available from the British Library

ISBN 978-0-521-84884-8 Hardback
ISBN 978-0-521-16955-4 Paperback

To our wives, Marina and Christine, who tolerantly accept the discrepancies between righteous theorising about social interaction and its domestic practice.

Contents

Illustrations

Figures

Tables

Notes on contributors

ANGELO ANTOCI holds a Ph.D. in political economy from the University of Siena, Italy (1993), and is currently Associate Professor of Mathematics for Economic Decision Making at the University of Sassari, Italy. His main research interests are economic growth, environmental economics, evolutionary game theory and its applications. He has published in international journals on partnership formation, corruption in public contracting in an evolutionary framework, and the dynamics of cooperative strategies.

NICHOLAS BARDSLEY is a research fellow at the School of Economics in the University of Nottingham. His fields of interest comprise experimental economics, methodology, and philosophy of economics. He currently researches artificiality arguments against experimental economics and is conducting a meta-analysis of preference reversal experiments. His most recent publication is, with Robert Sugden, 'Human nature and sociality', in *The Handbook of the Economics of Gift-Giving, Altruism and Reciprocity* (forthcoming).

CARLO BORZAGA is Professor of Economic Policy and Director of ISSAN (Institute for the Development of Non-profit Organisations) at the University of Trento, Italy. He has published extensively – in Italian, English and French – theoretical and empirical research on the economics of labour, welfare services, and non-profit organisations. He has recently edited *The Emergence of Social Enterprises* (2001), with Jacques Defourny, and *Capitale umano e qualità del lavoro nei servizi sociali: un'analisi comparata tra modelli di gestione* (2000).

LUIGINO BRUNI is Assistant Professor of Economics at the University of Milano Bicocca. His principal fields of interest are the history of economic thought, the ethical and anthropological foundations of economic discourse, and social and non-profit economy. His publications include several articles in international journals, chapters of edited volumes, and several books. Among these are *Vilfredo Pareto and the Birth of the Modern Microeconomics* (2002) and *Economics and the Paradoxes of Happiness* (edited with Pier Luigi Porta, 2004).

SARA DEPEDRI is a Ph.D. student in law and economics at the University of Siena. She lectures in political economy at the University of Bolzano, and is a researcher in non-profit organisations at ISSAN, University of Trento.

BERNARD GAZIER is Professor of Economics at the University of Paris 1 (Panthéon–Sorbonne). His fields of interest comprise labour economics and policy, social justice and non-market-oriented behaviour. He currently explores 'transitional labour markets', a European perspective on the reform of labour market policies aiming at reintegrating the long-term unemployed and promoting full employment. Recent publications are *Tous 'Sublimes': vers un nouveau plein emploi* (2003) and *The Dynamics of Full Employment: Social Integration through Transitional Labour Markets* (2002).

BENEDETTO GUI is Professor of Economics at the University of Padova. His research has mostly focused on labour economics, and the economics of self-managed and non-profit organisations. He has authored a book in Italian on marginal employment subsidies (which received the Tarantelli Award in 1990) and a number of book chapters and articles in international journals. He has co-edited with Avner Ben-Ner *The Nonprofit Sector in the Mixed Economy* (1993). More recently, he has concentrated on the new field of economics and interpersonal relations.

SHAUN HARGREAVES HEAP is Professor of Economics at the University of East Anglia. His current research is on rationality in a historical and social context, and on the economics of television and film. Recent publications are, with Yanis Varoufakis, in *The Economic Journal* (2002) on the evolution of cooperation and discrimination in an experimental setting, in *The Cambridge Journal of Economics* (2004) on participatory decision making and, with Yanis Varoufakis, the second edition of *Game Theory: A Critical Text* (2004).

SERGE-CHRISTOPHE KOLM, formerly Director and Professor at EHESS (Institute for Advanced Studies in the Social Sciences) in Paris, has made important contributions in several branches of economics and the social sciences, including welfare economics, economics and ethics, economic philosophy and the theory of justice. He is the author of several hundred scientific articles and over thirty books, including *The Good Economy*, *Justice and Equity*, *Modern Theories of Justice* and, most recently, *Macrojustice: The Political Economy of Fairness*.

JULIE A. NELSON is a Senior Research Associate with the Global Development and Environment Institute at Tufts University, Massachusetts. Her writings on household behaviour and on feminist theory have appeared in many leading journals, including *Econometrica*, *The American Economic Review*, *The Journal of Political Economy* and *The Journal of Economic Perspectives*. Nelson is the author of *Feminism, Objectivity, and Economics* (1996) and has recently co-edited *Feminist Economics Today: Beyond Economic Man* (2003).

VITTORIO PELLIGRA is Assistant Professor at the University of Cagliari, Italy, where he teaches economics, game theory and behavioural finance. His research, theoretical and experimental, is focused on the role of trust in strategic interaction and its consequences for institutional design. He has published on trust and happiness, social economy, intrinsic and extrinsic motivations, consequentialism and path dependency. He has edited, with Luigino Bruni, *Economia come scienza sociale* (2002).

LOUIS PUTTERMAN, Professor of Economics at Brown University (Providence, Rhode Island), is the author of numerous articles and books on economic systems (including those of Africa and China), organisations, incentives, economic behaviour and the historical roots of economic growth. Among these are *Economics, Values and Organization* (edited with Avner Ben-Ner, 1998), and *Dollars and Change: Economics in Context* (2001). Recently he has conducted experimental research on reciprocity and cooperation, and at present he is investigating trust, communication and costly contracting, as well as distribution preferences.

PIER LUIGI SACCO is Professor of Economics at the IUAV (University Institute of Architecture) in Venice. He has published widely in international refereed journals and books, mainly on the evolution of game theoretic models, the dynamics of norms, bounded rationality and learning issues, the economics of crime and corruption and the economics of art and culture. Recently he has co-edited with Stefano Zamagni a book in Italian on relational complexity and economic behaviour.

ROBERT SUGDEN is Professor of Economics at the University of East Anglia, Norwich. His research uses theoretical, experimental and philosophical methods to investigate issues in welfare economics, social choice, choice under uncertainty, the foundations of decision and game theory, the methodology of economics and the evolution of social conventions. Among his numerous publications, especially well-known is *The Economics of Rights, Cooperation and Welfare* (1986). His recent work includes explorations of ways in which sociality can be represented in economic theory.

ISABELLE THIS SAINT-JEAN is Lecturer in Economics at the University of Paris 1 (Panthéon–Sorbonne). She has published in refereed journals on economic epistemology and methodology (especially the frontiers between economics and its sister social sciences), self-fulfilling and rational expectations, empirical validation in economics, and rationality.

PAOLO VANIN received a doctorate in political economy from the University of Pavia, Italy, in 2002 and is currently a Ph.D. student in economics at the Pompeu Fabra University of Barcelona. His research interests include social capital, growth, social interaction and network dynamics, and are now extending to the relationship between trade policy, regulation and innovation. He has published 'Network interaction with material and relational goods: an exploratory simulation' (2000), with Pier Luigi Sacco.

Preface

While searching for a suitable example for this preface one of the editors of this book had the opportunity of hearing a senior manager reporting on an executives' training course, and was particularly struck by one image. Participants in their forties and fifties were asked to engage in groups in a game. At one point they had to pass through a network of cords without touching them. After a while they were playing so excitedly that, in order to ease the passing, not only was everybody's clothing reduced practically to underwear but somebody's protrusive stomach was pressed by mates' hands during the most crucial phases. Interestingly, this unconventional session ignited a fruitful communication among participants that contributed positively to the course's educational outcome.

We are not advocating that our readers should be involved in similar learning procedures. What we claim is that invisible and hardly definable interpersonal elements – such as those that made training more effective after that bizarre game than before it – do matter in economic life, even though this is usually viewed as the province of the material, the measurable, the objective. And, secondly, that this has momentous consequences for how we depict, conceptualise and manage economic life.

According to conventional interpretations of the thematic and methodological boundaries of economics, interpersonal relations seem not to be the business of economists at all. However, we feel supported by evidence such as the example above, and by considerations that we present in the introduction below, in thinking that a book on economics and interpersonal relations need not trespass unduly beyond the competence of our discipline. We hope to convince our readers of this statement, and of the significance of the 'relational' domain for both economic facts and ideas.

The project of this book began in April 2001 in the quiet atmosphere of Praglia's abbey conference centre, at the foot of the Euganean hills, not far from Padova. The British editor had been invited there by the native to comment on the special issue the latter had edited the year before for *Annals of Public and Cooperative Economics*, devoted to economics and interpersonal relations (issue 2 of 2000). The dialogue was fruitful. The result is that two of the chapters of this book, by Bardsley and Kolm, come directly from that special issue; two more, by Bruni and Gui, have their roots there, but have been heavily revised; one is a new piece of work by contributors to the special issue (Sacco and Vanin, with co-author Antoci); three are by other invited speakers at that conference (Borzaga and Depedri, Gazier and This Saint-Jean, Sugden); another two are by authors whose research has intersected with the editors' (Pelligra, Hargreaves Heap); and, last, the two commentaries at the end are by American scholars who have reacted from the other side of the Atlantic to this otherwise strictly European book. Wait a moment; we were forgetting the introductory chapter, which has forced us actually to confront each other's views, in the spirit of the book's title.

Many people gave moral support and useful suggestions for the completion of this book. Some are mentioned in individual chapters. Many others are collectively thanked here.

Furthermore, we cannot help expressing our gratitude to: Luca Clerici and Chiara Possia, who provided precious editorial aid; Mary Gabriel Walton, who took care of the final revision of the English style of some chapters; Blackwell Publishing, which allowed us to reprint previously published material; and, finally, the Italian Ministry for University and Research, for financial support.

1 Why interpersonal relations matter for economics

Benedetto Gui and Robert Sugden

1. Introduction

Is sociality decaying? Are the hidden foundations of society silently crumbling beneath the ever more complex institutional buildings we are busy constructing or repairing on top of them? That many people are concerned about these questions is obvious from the response evoked by Robert Putnam's (1993b, 1995, 2000) recent claims that, at least in the United States, the last thirty years have seen a steady downward trend in many different kinds of formal and informal social engagement. An explosive number of articles, books, speeches, conferences and Web pages witness that Putnam has touched a sensitive nerve.[1] Many social scientists and politicians have taken his arguments very seriously. Others have rejected them in ways that suggest that something more than intellectual disagreement is at stake (see, for instance, Fine, 2001). Among some of Putnam's opponents, there is a fear that he is providing ammunition for a conservative or communitarian backlash against the liberal social trends of the late twentieth century. But, even if this fear is understandable, it seems to betray an uneasy sense that Putnam's arguments have some credibility.

In trying to understand these concerns about trends in social engagement, it is useful to compare the environmental concerns that began to assume salience in public debate in the 1970s. People gradually came to realise that many of the processes through which economic wealth is created – more generally, many of the processes that contribute to human well-being – depend on inputs from the natural environment; in economic and political analysis, these inputs were being treated as permanent background features of the world, but their sources were being systematically degraded by the wealth-creating processes that ultimately depended on them. Current concerns about sociality have a

---

[1] See, for instance, Durlauf (2002) and the 'Symposium' in *Contemporary Sociology* (2001, no. 3).

similar character. Do certain forms of social engagement provide essential inputs to economic processes, and are these not being accounted for in conventional economic analysis? Is social intercourse an important source of well-being in its own right? And could it be that the social environment we are used to is not a permanent background feature of the world, but something that is being degraded by economic developments?

The starting point for this book is our shared sense that these are important questions, and ones that intersect with the domain of economics – the discipline to which we both belong. Our aim is to explore some of the connections between social interaction and economics. In taking this as our objective, we are contributing to an already large literature (see the brief review by Gui in chapter 2). The principal new concepts we find in (and draw from) this literature are 'social capital' and 'social interactions'. The former is a very insightful concept, although its being interpreted in many different ways makes it too loose a theoretical tool.[2] The latter has been defined more sharply, to include agents' non-contractual influences on others' preferences, information or constraints.[3] However, what we do not find sufficiently stressed are some peculiar elements that come into play when interactions are highly personalised. This is why we make recourse to the concept of *interpersonal relations* to refer to forms of human interaction in which the identity of the participants *as particular human beings* has affective or cognitive significance. In doing this we refer not only to informal interactions occurring in contexts such as families, neighbourhoods, associations or churches, but also to personalised interaction connected with (or entailed by) the performance of typical economic roles in contexts such as firms or markets.

For example, if you buy a travel package by going to an airline Web page, clicking the right button and entering your credit card number, you are initiating a transaction that has consequences for other people (other would-be customers who may have wanted to use the flights that you have booked on, shareholders in the airline, and so on); but there is no interaction with specific people as specific people. If instead you go to your local travel shop, and, while booking a travel plan from one of the agents, exchange views about the current state of congestion at your local airport, or perhaps just chat about the weather outside, you are

---

[2] Martin Paldam (2000) provides a useful survey of the social capital literature. The looseness of the concept of social capital is criticised by, among many others, Samuel Bowles (1999) and Edward Glaeser, David Laibson and Bruce Sacerdote (2002).

[3] See Manski (2000) and Blume and Durlauf (2001).

engaging in a minimal form of interpersonal relation. The more so if you go there to discuss a less routine matter, such as the proposal of a group tour, which requires explanations, a discussion of alternatives and bargaining. A similar distinction is made by Putnam (2000, pp. 48–64) when he contrasts the *membership* of voluntary organisations with *participation* in meetings or other events in which members come into face-to-face contact with one another. According to Putnam's data, there has been little change in overall rates of membership of voluntary organisations, but there has been a very marked decline in participation. The trend is towards voluntary organisations such as Greenpeace or the (American) National Rifle Association, organised on a national or even international scale, with large numbers of members whose engagement takes the form of contributing money in response to mailshots, reading newsletters and expressing their attachment to the organisation's ideals by buying affinity products such as T-shirts and car window stickers. It goes without saying that such organisations are a significant form of social capital (one has only to think of the disparate impacts of Greenpeace and the National Rifle Association on political decisions); but a response to a mailshot is not a full-fledged interpersonal relation.

According to conventional interpretations of the thematic and methodological boundaries of economics, interpersonal relations may seem not to be the business of economists at all. So – some could legitimately wonder – are we trespassing beyond our disciplinary competence? We think we are not, as we explain below. And, at the same time, we want to reassure the reader that our project is not one of scientific imperialism. Our aim is not to explain interpersonal relations by the straightforward application of conventional modes of economic explanation. As our choice of title – Economics *and* (not *of*) Social Interaction – is intended to signal, the aim is to shed light on how the interpersonal realm intertwines with the economic realm.

We do not presuppose that any particular form of theorising is *the* way to understand these interrelationships. Indeed, one fruitful strategy is to represent and analyse some of the components or features of interpersonal relations, and how these are affected by standard economic choices, within the established conceptual framework of economics; this is the theme of section 3 of this introductory chapter, and the approach of choice for some of the contributions in this book. On the other hand, however, the inability of conventional economic theory to provide a satisfactory account of how personalised interaction affects economic variables points to the need for far-reaching methodological changes, supported by the insights of other disciplines; this strategy, sketched in section 4 below, is also adopted in several chapters.

Nor do we presuppose here any judgements about the ultimate value of sociality. On some philosophical accounts – particularly those influenced by utilitarianism – social relations, like any other thing that might be supposed to be good for people, are valuable only to the extent that people actually desire them: to the extent that trends in patterns of social interaction simply reflect changes in preferences, they are to be neither approved nor disapproved. Viewed in other philosophical perspectives, rich interpersonal relations are essential for human fulfilment: a major decline in their intensity, continuity and degree of involvement, if real, is necessarily a matter for concern. We are not at all indifferent to these fundamental questions, as our own chapters reveal, but we recognise that we cannot contribute much to their debate as economists. Thus, when jointly undertaking the editing of this book, we gave ourselves the preparatory task of contributing to a better understanding of how interpersonal relations connect with economics.

In what follows we begin, in section 2, with an overview of the various connections between the economic and the relational realms. Successively, in section 3 we utilise three established categories – namely non-rivalry, excludability and non-contractibility – for discussing whether recent trends in spontaneous sociability are really a reason for concern. In section 4 we observe that something extraneous to established economic theory is also involved, namely communication at the emotional or affective level, and show that this has implications to which economics needs to give attention. In doing so we make reference to the works of authors who have ventured into these unsettled territories. These include the contributors to this book, whose chapters are briefly presented and situated in section 5.

2.   How interpersonal relations connect with the economic sphere: an overview

In the scientific excavation to which this book is devoted, not only do different authors have different ideas as to the most promising tunnelling pattern (as we mentioned above), but they also employ different technologies and, furthermore, work at different parts of the field. In this section, we try to convey a sense of the third type of diversity in the analysis of economics and social interaction. For the sake of brevity we proceed schematically, pointing out the most important causal links that connect interpersonal relations with the economic sphere (and vice versa), each of which deserves careful investigation. In so doing we make reference to examples mentioned in the still-thin literature that examines these links.

For a first overview of the terrain of economics and social interaction, we draw a distinction between the 'economic' and 'non-economic' spheres of social life. In reality, however, there is no sharp divide between those parts of the social world that are economic and those that are not. To the contrary, the more one thinks about how interpersonal relations impact on economics the more artificial this distinction comes to look.

(i) *Interpersonal relations inside the economic sphere can affect economic performance.* Good interpersonal relations among economic actors may reduce transaction costs and facilitate mutually beneficial interaction. For example: habits of cooperation allow some agricultural communities to manage common-pool water resources effectively, without recourse to costly technological devices (Ostrom, 1990, ch. 6); enmity is a barrier to trade (Schmid, 2000); groups of workers with favourable mutual feelings can better solve dilemmas of collective action (Rotemberg, 1994a); mismanagement of interpersonal rapport has a distinct negative effect on the continuation and fruitfulness of inter-organisational collaborations (Jap and Anderson, 1998).

(ii) *Economic choices can affect interpersonal relations inside the economic sphere.* Intra- and inter-organisational practices can impact on interpersonal relations among the actors involved. For example: incentive, consultation and monitoring arrangements affect relations among peers and between superiors and inferiors within enterprises (Aoki, 1984; Barkema, 1995; Gibbons, 1998); the design of development projects may promote or hinder the creation and maintenance of patterns of collaboration among members of rural communities (Fox and Gershman, 2000).

(iii) *Interpersonal relations inside the economic sphere can affect well-being.* Positive interpersonal relations among economic agents may provide intrinsic benefits (and negative relations may cause direct welfare losses). For example: ties of solidarity improve employees' satisfaction with the social aspects of their jobs (Flap and Volker, 2001); bullying and sexual harassment significantly affect job satisfaction (Laband and Lentz, 1998); shopping in local stores is associated with intangible benefits stemming from involvement in meaningful relations (Miller, 2001).

(iv) *Interpersonal relations outside the economic sphere can affect economic performance.* Mutual familiarity, norms of cooperation and other features of interpersonal relations can bring instrumental benefits, in both formal and informal economic contexts. For example: in closely knit neighbourhoods, bystanders tacitly cooperate in looking after the children playing in the streets, relieving mothers from a time-consuming engagement (Coleman, 1988, p. 99); strong social networks provide material and emotional support for starting entrepreneurial initiatives (Allen,

2000); attitudes of trust among citizens can lead to faster economic growth (Zak and Knack, 2001). Informal interpersonal relations may also act as channels for the transmission of economically valuable information. This helps explain differences in unemployment rates among socially separated, although geographically contiguous, neighbourhoods (Topa, 2001).

(v) *Economic choices can affect interpersonal relations outside the economic sphere.* The creation and consolidation of personal relationships can be facilitated or hindered by individual and collective economic choices. For example: the integration of markets across geographical space induces high job and residential mobility, making long-term relationships more difficult to sustain (Gui, 1996; Folbre and Nelson, 2000); innovations in consumer goods may substitute individual for collective forms of consumption, shrinking the social spaces in which personal relationships can be formed and sustained (see section 3 below); the location of service facilities such as schools has an appreciable effect on patterns of informal relations (Bogart and Cromwell, 2000); fiscal decentralisation appears to favour social cohesiveness and the strengthening of associative life (de Mello, 2000).

(vi) *Interpersonal relations outside the economic sphere can affect well-being.* Family, friendship and associative relations may bring intrinsic benefits. For example: even though migrant workers often earn greater income than those who stay behind, their quality of life suffers from poor interpersonal relations (Schiff, 2002); the characteristics of the networks of personal relations in which people are involved have significant welfare effects (Diwan, 2000). Such effects have economic significance if networks of interpersonal relations are themselves affected by economic variables.

3. Economics and interpersonal relations: social engagement as a special kind of economic good

If, in the light of all these connections, we want to take account of interpersonal relations in economics, we immediately face a fundamental problem: in terms of the conceptual structure of economics, what do interpersonal relations consist of? Are they forms of production, or of exchange, or of consumption? And, if they are any one of these, just what is being produced, exchanged or consumed? To frame these questions and to explain their significance, we begin by considering how the evidence of trends in patterns of social interaction might be interpreted within economics. One possible interpretation of the evidence marshalled by Putnam is that it documents some of the many changes in production and consumption patterns over time that characterise all market economies. Improvements in technology, retailing and transport are making it more feasible to separate production from consumption, and to separate one person's consumption from another's, with the result that interpersonal interaction occurs less commonly as a by-product of ordinary production or consumption activities. For example, developments in electronics have made it much easier for individuals to choose their own forms of entertainment. A hundred years ago musical entertainment within the home required a collective act of production and consumption, perhaps around a piano; more complex musical experiences were possible only in public concerts or shows, often organised by voluntary societies. The development of the gramophone allowed production and consumption to be separated; the development of personal tape and CD players has allowed consumption to be further separated between individuals. Similarly, the development of microwave ovens and pre-cooked meals has made it possible for individuals to choose their own dishes and mealtimes, rather than, as members of families, eating common meals prepared just for the occasion. And new technologies and organisational practices in service delivery – for example, on-line consulting, Internet shopping and telephone banking – are separating the consumption of services among people and from their production in much the same way that the new technologies and organisational practices of the Industrial Revolution separated the consumption and production of many manufactured goods.

The market, it might be said, has expanded individual choice by unbundling what previously were indivisible packages of private and social characteristics of goods and services. As part of this unbundling, we should expect to find that interpersonal relations, to the extent that they are desired, are increasingly supplied on the market as distinct entities: think of the growth of dating agencies and of psychological and body care services. Similarly, we should find that interpersonal relations are bundled with the goods and services with which they are now most complementary – for example, organised travel for specific affinity or age groups, and training courses the value of which depends considerably on the professional prestige of the fellow students with whom a participant will interact. It could also be said that the reluctance to purchase social opportunities in these forms tends to fade as they become more widespread. When market transactions first enter any sphere of human life, they tend to be seen as incompatible with the ethos of that sphere; but this perception often dissipates with experience – think of the erosion of the distinction between professionals and amateurs in sport, or of the changing attitudes to the practice of entertaining guests by taking them out to restaurants rather than preparing a meal for them in one's home.

A similar interpretation might be offered of a decline in the role of interpersonal relations as channels for the generation and communication of valuable information. A common theme in the social capital literature is that dense networks of civic engagement provide the preconditions under which individuals have the incentive to build reputations for reciprocity and trustworthiness. The idea is that information about individuals' trustworthiness is transmitted through interpersonal interaction in civic society; the more social engagement there is the more valuable reputations become, and the greater the rewards for individuals who are trustworthy (Coleman, 1990; Putnam, 1993a). It might be argued, however, that new organisational and information technologies have led to new, market-based methods of monitoring reputations; these developments have been made necessary by (and have helped to make possible) the ever-increasing geographical integration of markets. For example, the use of brand names for manufactured goods (an innovation that diffused widely in the late nineteenth century) has allowed the reputation of a product to be separated from the personal reputations of its manufacturers and retailers. Assessing the creditworthiness of potential borrowers was once a task for local bank managers, who could make use of knowledge gathered through participation in civic life; this work is now done largely through computer-based credit ratings, using international data sets. The cumulative effect of such developments is to unbundle the transmission of information from a range of civic activities based on social interaction.

If declining trends in social engagement and involvement are attributable to improvements in technology and the expansion of the market, should we be concerned about them? Why should we *want* social interaction to be bundled with other forms of production and consumption? Why should we regret changes that make it easier for individuals to choose when and how they interact with one another?

Received economic theory offers some possible responses. The first is to ask whether sociality is a sufficiently private good for markets to be capable of supplying it efficiently. If, to the contrary, sociality is more appropriately understood as a *public* good then economic theory gives us reason to expect that it will be under-supplied in a competitive market: a peculiar instance of a well-known sort of market failure. In economic theory, a public good has two essential characteristics: non-rivalry (one person's consumption of the good does not prevent others from also consuming it), and non-excludability (if the good is supplied to one person, it is difficult to exclude others from consuming it too). Clearly, social engagement has at least some of the first of these characteristics: by its very nature, it is consumed jointly by more than one individual. Indeed, one could go further and say that, in this respect, interpersonal relations are public goods par excellence, since, in contrast to all other goods, no conceivable technological innovation can ever make it possible that they are individually 'consumed'. Another characteristic that adds to the nature of personalised interaction as a public good is the need for coordination among people involved (see, among others, Sobel, 2002). Appropriate behaviour (e.g. showing up at the right place and time) on the part of each is needed for the interaction to occur, so individual compliance has the nature of a voluntary contribution to an event from which others also expect to benefit.

It is not quite so obvious that interpersonal relations are non-excludable. Some forms of social engagement are naturally analysed as *club* goods – that is, goods that, though non-rival in consumption, can be supplied in ways that prevent those who do not contribute to the costs of provision from enjoying the benefits. Such goods can often be supplied quite effectively in response to private incentives. Indeed, social intercourse is one of the forms of joint consumption that is most characteristic of the real clubs that provide the story behind the economic model of 'club goods'. Exclusive sports clubs provide an example of how the benefits of certain kinds of social engagement can be 'internalised' to organisations that can control access to those benefits. Similar mechanisms can work in organisations that are not so obviously clubs. For example, if people prefer to work in jobs that offer more opportunities for social interaction (and are willing to sacrifice income in return), employers have an incentive to adopt forms of workplace organisation that satisfy those preferences. (The empirical work by Borzaga and Depedri, chapter 6 in this book, documents that the trade-off between the wages and desirable social features of a job is exploited by real economic organisations.)

However, social engagement can have other, more genuinely public, benefits. For example, institutions that increase people's propensity to trust others *in general* to keep their commitments (and not just to trust *particular* others to do so) are classic examples of public goods. The maintenance of such a 'climate of trust' may depend not only on the formal institutions of civil and criminal law, which everyone recognises to be public goods, but also on norms that are reproduced in the interpersonal relations of civil society (Putnam, 1993a; Gambetta, 1993). Similarly, sentiments of approval and disapproval, conveyed in personal interactions, may play an important role in maintaining prohibitions on anti-social behaviour, such as shoplifting, tax evasion and driving while drunk. To the extent that it is a source of these kinds of diffused benefits, social engagement is a public good in the classic sense, and we should expect it to be under-supplied if decisions are made according to individual advantage. (The possibility of prisoner's-dilemma-like traps of 'relational poverty', ensuing from individuals allocating too much time to the production of private goods, is the main theme of Antoci, Sacco and Vanin, chapter 7).

If interpersonal relations are public goods, technological constraints that prevent their being unbundled from private goods may work in everyone's interests, since bundling counters the tendency to under-provision that characterises public goods. As an analogy, think how voluntary organisations finance activities that generate public goods. One of the commonest strategies is to provide donors with some private benefit as a partial return for their contributions. For example, political fund-raisers offer donors opportunities to meet leading politicians in exclusive social occasions; wildlife organisations allow their members special access to nature reserves; professional associations publish informative journals that are supplied free of charge to their members. By means of these devices, voluntary contributions to public goods are bundled with private goods (Olson, 1965; Cornes and Sandler, 1986). Of course, such mechanisms for the supply of public goods are potentially vulnerable to unbundling. Thus, many of the direct consumption benefits that visitors gain from a nature reserve might be supplied by a private firm (perhaps as a form of theme park), without its engaging in the full range of activities of a wildlife charity; a private publisher might supply technical journals without taking on the other activities of a professional society. But, whatever the various frictions are that resist the unbundling of private and public characteristics of goods, they are not simply deadweight costs; by providing a mechanism for the supply of the public characteristics, they allow common preferences to be satisfied in ways that would not be possible in a frictionless market.

Thus, an important question is placed on the agenda of economics and social interaction: is a social context that favours interaction a public good that is most effectively supplied as a joint product alongside other goods? Indeed, the idea that, in the economic sphere, goods of a 'relational' nature are produced jointly with more conventional outputs is just the starting point of Gui's (chapter 2) representation of economic interactions as 'encounters' – a concept that is broader than that of an exchange, or a transaction.

Intrinsic benefits from social intercourse may differ from more conventional market goods, not only by virtue of non-rivalry and non-excludability, but also because of the special difficulties that are involved in making *contracts* for their supply. The affective components of interpersonal relations ('relational goods', in Gui's terminology) are usually perceived as having value through their *sincerity* or *genuineness* – properties that are liable to be lost if the behaviour of one party is dictated by a contract. A smile or a friendly remark has value, not as a pleasing sight or sound but as an *expression* of an underlying attitude of friendship; and it seems intrinsic to friendship that it is not pursued in a purely instrumental way. This feature of relational goods does not necessarily prevent their being created in a market context, but it does work against their being obtained through wholly instrumental motivations. For example, for shop assistants and bar staff a friendly disposition is an important qualification, for which employers are willing to pay, and which, like other job skills, can to some extent be learned. As customers, we all know that the people who serve us are paid to do so, and that their apparent friendliness to us is in part a response to those incentives. But, still, if it becomes obvious that the shop assistant's remarks have been pre-scripted – rather than emerging spontaneously in a particular interaction with us and not others – part of their value is lost: we are looking for genuine affective qualities. Similarly, we want the nurse to be genuinely caring – acting not only on professional standards, but also out of sympathy for us, distinct persons. Such things cannot be bought and sold directly without being transformed into something else, and so losing much of their value.[4] For this reason, relational goods are often most effectively obtained as by-products of other economic activities. That is, the interactions in which these goods are created and 'consumed' are understood by the participants as having other purposes. Earlier, we pointed to some of the ways in which opportunities for social interaction, previously secured through families, friendship groups and civic associations, are now being supplied by markets. But even these new forms of provision often retain significant aspects of indirectness. For example, in selling packaged holidays for affinity groups, travel agents are in a sense selling 'companionship'; but each purchaser is buying not the courtesy of the vendor but the opportunity to engage in friendly relations with fellow customers; and that opportunity is not sold as such, but as a characteristic of a journey. Because of the delicacy of these distinctions, and because of their social contingency and their capacity to evolve over time, it is hard to define the limits of the market's ability to respond to desires for relational goods. Still, it seems clear

---

[4] This is a distinct variety of market failure: see Kolm, chapter 8 of this book. At the same time, however, it is also an instance of 'government failure', since command cannot do any better.

that, for the value of relational goods to be realised, there need to be some areas of economic life in which individuals are not motivated in a wholly instrumental way. (This idea is developed by Hargreaves Heap, chapter 9.)

Received economic theory offers a further possible response to the question of why society should be concerned for the effects of current technological and organisational trends on interpersonal relations. This response focuses on the *distributional* consequences of changes in patterns of social engagement. If there is a general decline in the frequency and intensity of social interaction, if there is a general tendency for previously public goods to be privatised, do some people systematically lose out? If so, concern about such a decline might be driven by ideas of social justice and social inclusion. In fact, there is reason to expect any losses to fall particularly on the relatively poor, since the benefits of non-excludable public goods are available free of charge, while both market-supplied private goods and exclusive club goods have to be paid for. For example, the higher a person's income the more freedom he/she[5] has to choose where to live; so, if crime and anti-social behaviour cause the social environment in a neighbourhood to decline, the well-off can avoid having to live there. Although the poor are not excluded from family and friendship relationships they can create themselves, since these can be seen as club goods admission to which is not related to wealth, the maintenance and recreation of these relationships in the face of increasing mobility also depend on the availability of human and material resources. This is why we might expect losses to be concentrated among the oldest age groups: the very old are particularly vulnerable to increases in the rate at which social capital turns over, since physical frailty makes it difficult for them to establish new social relationships.

4.   Economics and interpersonal relations: the communication of dispositions, sentiments and motivations

In section 3 we considered interpersonal relations in terms of the established conceptual structure of economics. We must now ask whether that framework is too constricting. Is the invisibility of interpersonal relations in economics something more than a failure to take account of a particular class of public goods? Do interpersonal relations involve some ingredient that is not recognised in the standard rational choice

---

[5] As a rule, future references to 'he' can be taken as referring to both sexes.

approach, but which impacts on the behaviour that that theory sets out to explain?

Conventional economic theory models the behaviour of rational agents, characterised only by, and motivated only by, their preferences and beliefs; in consequence, it recognises only the cognitive dimensions of interactions between its agents. This methodological strategy, one might say, treats all interaction as *impersonal*. In contrast, a recurrent theme in recent work on economics and social interaction is the idea that interpersonal interaction involves the communication of dispositions or sentiments that are affective or visceral in nature.

This strand of literature can be seen as part of a recent tendency in economic theory to question whether rational choice models adequately capture the behaviour of economic agents. For example, the research programme of *evolutionary game theory* models the behaviour of economic agents as the product of trial-and-error learning or blind selection mechanisms. The programme of *behavioural economics* seeks to explain economic behaviour by using hypotheses about human psychology. One branch of this programme, in which Herbert Simon and (later) Daniel Kahneman and Amos Tversky were pioneers, recognises the limited cognitive capacities of human beings, and investigates the heuristics that people use in processing information and in tackling decision problems (see Simon, 1978, and Kahneman and Tversky, 2000, for overviews). Another branch, developed by researchers such as Paul Slovic (see Slovic et al., 2002) and George Loewenstein (2000), explores the affective components of decision making. This is the approach that prevails in the work we discuss in this section. One hypothesis, advanced by Robert Frank (1988), is that human emotional states are expressed through many signals – tone of voice, speed of speech, facial expression, body posture, blushing, and so on – that are not under the conscious control of the sender of the signal, and recognisable (perhaps subconsciously) by others. Thus, personalised interactions activate mechanisms of information transmission that are not recognised in rational choice theory. In some cases, these may allow human beings to solve what for the ideally rational agents of game theory are insoluble problems of cooperation and coordination. For example, in face-to-face interaction, credible promises can be made by human beings who are known to blush when they lie; and credible threats can be made by human beings who are known to be susceptible to anger.

A related hypothesis is that personal interaction facilitates the communication of sentiments. One example of this mechanism is described by Julio Rotemberg (1994a): the formation of altruistic bonds in a workplace in which each interactant recognises the other's altruism by perceiving his sentiments. The mutual perception of sentiments is an ingredient of Sugden's (2002) rediscovery of Adam Smith's analysis of *fellow-feeling*. On this account, individuals' mutual awareness of a common sentiment is a source of pleasure for them. This hypothesis might help to explain how interpersonal relations can be a source of value, even when (in the cognitive perspective of economic theory) no joint *action* seems to be involved: think of two people watching a movie together rather than each watching it alone. Also part of this complex of ideas is the hypothesis that preferences and norms are transmitted from person to person through involuntary processes of mutual adjustment, prompted by the unease and dissonance caused by perceptions of disparities of sentiment. Such mechanisms of conformism or 'emotional contagion' may be important in explaining how negative attitudes towards education and paid employment are sometimes reproduced among youngsters in deprived communities (George Akerlof, 1997, is among those who have brought these phenomena to be part of economists' concerns).

Specially interesting for our discussion is the growing literature that aims at explaining observations of non-selfish behaviour. In large part, this enterprise responds to a body of evidence from controlled experiments in which participants are found to act contrary to their own interests in ways that, intuitively, can be interpreted as 'altruistic' or 'socially oriented'. A striking feature of this literature is a progressive relaxation of the assumptions of rational choice theory, and their replacement by hypotheses about how the motivations of different individuals interact with one another. (This point is brought out in Bardsley's review of this literature, in chapter 4 of this book.) This shift in focus can be interpreted as an attempt to expand the set of entities that economics takes into consideration, bringing in some of the characteristic elements of interpersonal relations.

Within rational choice theory, the traditional method of taking account of non-selfish motivations is to represent them as properties of individuals' preferences, and to maintain the assumption that each individual's motivation is to satisfy his own preferences. In a model of this kind, individuals may be *altruistic* (that is, they prefer that other individuals' outcomes are better rather than worse) or *inequality-averse* (that is, they prefer that outcomes for different individuals are more equal rather than less); but there is no interaction at the level of motivation. Each individual acts on his own pre-defined objectives; he treats other individuals merely as instruments for, or as obstacles preventing, the pursuit of those objectives, even when those objectives give weight to the welfare of just those others. Martin Hollis (1998) calls this kind of motivation 'philosophical egoism' (as distinct from 'substantive egoism' – that is, plain self-interest).

In contrast, theories of *reciprocity* are concerned with causal links between motivations. On one construal, the core idea of reciprocity is a relationship between individuals in which each is motivated to return kind behaviour for kind behaviour, and unkind for unkind. Matthew Rabin (1993) models this form of motivational connection in a two-person game, in which each player interprets the other's action in terms of its implied degree of 'kindness' towards him, and then reciprocates that motivation.[6] Such reciprocity, even in the positive sense of returning good for good, is more than an implicit exchange, because a reciprocating action expresses motivations that cannot be bought (Kolm, chapter 8). Alternatively, reciprocity can be construed as a relationship between the members of a group of individuals who share some common interest that can be pursued by collective action; each member is motivated to make a fair contribution to the collective action if the others do so too (Sugden, 1984). This latter form of reciprocity is closely connected with the idea of *collective agency* or *team reasoning* – that individuals interpret themselves as members of a collective agent or team, each doing his part in whatever joint action best achieves the collective objective (Bacharach, 1999; Sugden, 2000a). In some versions of this kind of theory, a sense of group identity is a precondition for the perception that a decision problem calls for team reasoning. In other versions, each individual's motivation to reason as a member of the collective depends on his perception that enough other individuals are reasoning in the same way. In each case, there is an implication that socially oriented behaviour may be most capable of reproducing itself in those social environments that give most scope for the communication of sentiments of solidarity and group identity.

Another strategy for explaining non-selfish behaviour is to assume that individuals have some motivation to meet other people's expectations about them. This gives rise to a different kind of endogeneity of motivations: one person's motivation depends on another person's beliefs. In theories of *normative expectations*, social practices that work contrary to the self-interest of some participants can be sustained by each person's desire not to induce other people's resentment by imposing unexpected losses on them. In a population of individuals who interact recurrently, repeated experience of a pattern of behaviour can induce expectations

---

[6] Theoretically, this involves a departure from the usual conventions of game theory, since motivations are endogenised. The innovation is to use the concept of a 'psychological game', due to John Geanakoplos, David Pearce and Ennio Stacchetti (1989).

that it will continue, which, through the mechanism of normative expectations, motivate people to continue it. For example, a social practice
of giving tips to service providers, if once established, may be sustained
through donors' perceptions of the expectations of would-be recipients
(Sugden, 2000b). Expectations may also be communicated by one-off
actions that signal the actor's beliefs about how another person will
respond; the other's perception of that belief may then motivate him to
respond in a way that confirms the expectation. Thus, actions that
express trust in another person may elicit trustworthy responses – the
mechanism of *trust responsiveness* (see Pelligra, chapter 5). Objectives
may also be endogenous because agents care about other people's consideration, or admiration. These feelings are communicated in personal
interactions, as are the preferences or convictions that lie behind them
(the relevance of these processes for both individuals and society is
discussed by Hargreaves Heap, chapter 9). For instance, in the theory
of *esteem* proposed by Geoffrey Brennan and Philip Pettit (2000) individuals are motivated to behave in ways that other people deem to be
meritorious. Because esteem is a 'positional good', the esteem that
can be earned by any given action depends on how that action compares
with the actions chosen by others.[7] Thus, in a society that applauds
philanthropy one gains esteem by being more generous than one's
fellows.

The introduction of motivations, sentiments and dispositions into
economic theory brings in further complexity. A neat example in this
regard is an ultimatum game: in deciding whether to accept or reject a
proposed division of a pie (in the latter case the whole pie gets lost), the
respondent does not care only about the amount that is offered, as
simple rational choice arguments would suggest. His reaction also
depends on the set of alternatives from which the proposer has chosen
that offer. This information is necessary to assess the degree of 'kindness'
(or 'grimness') of that offer, which affects the responder's reaction
(see the experimental evidence presented by Ernst Fehr and Urs
Fischbacher, 2002). Observe that this complication has a close parallel
in some advances brought about by the economics of information, which
nowadays are part of economists' professional stock. For instance, in
analysing the reaction of the owner of an old piece of furniture to an
unsolicited bid, it is not sufficient to consider the price that is offered;
one also has to consider what information the bid itself conveys to the

---

[7] A good is positional if each individual values being placed above others in some ranking;
think of golf players who judge their relative status by comparing handicaps, or academics
who do so by comparing citation counts. The idea of positional goods is due to Fred
Hirsch (1976); see also Robert Frank (1985).

owner. A price that may seem attractive – and be happily accepted – if it is offered by an unsophisticated friend may be refused if it is offered by an antiques trader, since the fact that a specialist shows interest in that piece shifts to the right the owner's probability distribution of the best price he could get by selling the piece carefully. A delicate but momentous consequence of the recognition that sentiments, motivations and dispositions play a role in economic affairs is their becoming a legitimate part of economists' normative considerations, in much the same way that information has now become.

We do not intend to suggest that the communication of information about motivations, dispositions, sentiments, expectations and judgements takes place *only* in face-to-face interaction. For example, we have already referred to the increasing tendency for charities to raise funds by mailshots rather than through the activities of local networks of volunteers. Charities' postal appeals may also trade on normative expectations (by expressing confidence that the person approached will respond generously), reciprocity (by expressing confidence that other people will support the appeal), a desire for esteem (by promising various forms of public recognition for sufficiently generous donors), and so on. Indeed, all forms of post and telecommunication (letters, telegrams, telephone messages, e-mails, etc.) share some of the peculiarities of face-to-face relations that we have just been discussing. Still, face-to-face interaction does seem to provide particularly effective channels for the communication of dispositions and sentiments. (Useful experimental results are provided by Norman Frohlich and Joe Oppenheimer, 1998, who find that e-mail communication before the play of a prisoner's dilemma significantly increases the proportion of cooperators, but not so much as communication in person.)

Much more might be said as to the reciprocal influences of social interaction and economic variables than can find a place in this introduction. For example, we have focused for simplicity on elementary instances of 'horizontal' interactions among peers, but we have not mentioned personalised interactions in complex hierarchical organisational contexts; however, see Gazier and This Saint-Jean (chapter 11). Another important theme we have neglected is how idiosyncratic behaviour at the micro level may relate to sizable and lasting effects at the macro level (see, for instance, Turner, 1999). Still, we hope that we have said enough to convince the reader that interpersonal relations are relevant for economics, and that economics is at least beginning to develop the theoretical resources to allow it to take account of them. It is undoubtedly true that, over many years, economics has managed to relegate interpersonal relations to the sidelines. (The various ways in which, over the last two centuries, economics has done this are discussed by Bruni, chapter 10.) Perhaps – as Gazier and This Saint-Jean, chapter 11, argue – we economists are still too prone to ignore the insights of other disciplines, and to project the traditional conceptual structures of economics onto our understandings of sociality. Still, on our reading of the recent economic literature, we detect an increasing awareness of the importance of sociality – both within and outside the economic sphere – and an increasing openness to new ways of thinking about it.

It is time now to turn to a brief presentation of the chapters that follow.

5.   In the following chapters

In chapter 2 Benedetto Gui addresses in its entirety the challenge of accounting for the communicative/affective side of face-to-face inter-actions, starting with a review of the various proposals that economists have advanced for doing this. Then he proposes to view such inter-actions as 'encounters', i.e. as peculiar productive processes in which agents – besides possibly exchanging ordinary goods or delivering ser-vices – create and get pleasure (or displeasure) from 'relational con-sumption goods'. He stresses the fact that the inputs of these processes include 'relational capital goods', i.e. durable, relation-specific intan-gible entities, which in turn accumulate (or decumulate) over successive encounters. After discussing these concepts, he provides examples of how this conceptual framework can be used for obtaining new insights into various phenomena, ranging from migration patterns to financial markets.

Chapter 3, by Robert Sugden, addresses the same theoretical chal-lenge, but rather in depth than in breadth. His concern is with the processes by which the affections of different individuals interact with one another in face-to-face interactions, and with the significance these processes have for both economic life and economic analysis. In doing this he re-examines Adam Smith's concept of fellow-feeling in the light of recent contributions to the psychological literature on empathy, and claims that mainstream economics has defined its own field in a way that is incompatible with consideration of such a concept. He then connects this debate to current work by economists on relational goods, stressing that interpersonal relations may generate affective states that are valued by participants, play a role in the formation of moral judgements and nurture norms of cooperation.

In each of the three general chapters that open the book, examples and applications of theoretical claims are presented, but these are necessarily brief. So, our readers may justifiably wonder whether interpersonal relations have an appreciable bearing on behaviours that economists are used to investigating. The three following chapters witness that they do. In chapter 4 Nicholas Bardsley re-examines one of the classic puzzles of economic behaviour: voluntary contributions to public goods. He starts from data – both experimental and from the field – that confirm that people obstinately contribute more than is predicted by models based on conventional motivational assumptions. Then he examines several alternative accounts of givers' behaviour; some of these are compatible with the standard model of rational choice, while others require different conceptions of rationality and/or more radically social agents. Among the alternatives that survive the theoretical and empirical objections raised by the author, three are of special interest to students of interpersonal relations: expressive rationality, for focusing on the communication of attitudes, or of adherence to principles; collective rationality, for recognising that people may reason as part of a team; and conformism, for making evaluation of own behaviour depend on the behaviour of others.

The focus of Vittorio Pelligra's chapter 5 is, among interpersonal phenomena, the one that has attracted most attention on the part of economists: trust. Pelligra first defines trustful and trustworthy behaviours in rigorous terms, fit for studying them in the framework of game theory. Then he proposes and substantiates from a philosophical viewpoint a truly 'relational' explanatory principle, which he calls 'trust responsiveness': in some circumstances people are motivated to behave trustworthily by the tacit message that is conveyed by the very fact of being trusted. Pelligra discusses the similarities and the differences between this principle and the other logics of action that have been considered in the literature for explaining trust, in particular altruism, reciprocity, inequality aversion and team thinking.

Chapter 6 – by Carlo Borzaga and Sara Depedri – deals with work environments, probably the most promising field for students of interpersonal relations. Borzaga and Depedri study the effects of relational aspirations and satisfaction on overall worker satisfaction and quit intentions, drawing from a large data set on Italian social service providers. They find a double indication that workers really value the relational goods they 'consume' on the job: the opportunity to create new relations is an important element in decisions concerning jobs; and, above a threshold wage, workers' satisfaction and intentions to quit are significantly affected by indicators of the quality of interpersonal relations on the job – with clients, colleagues, managers and volunteers – but not by the wage level. They also obtain interesting results by comparing for-profit, non-profit and public service providers, finding that non-profit providers have a competitive advantage in their ability to provide relational incentives.

Other readers, instead, may be more concerned with another objection to this novel interest in interpersonal relations on the part of economists: can such relations be captured in formal models, and so become the object of rigorous economic analysis? Chapter 7, by Angelo Antoci, Pier Luigi Sacco and Paolo Vanin, shows that at least some features of interpersonal relations can be modelled. These authors investigate if and how the pursuit of ever-increasing material output may conflict with the enjoyment of rich social interactions, as the two draw on the same scarce resource: time/effort. The presence of a trade-off would not concern economists were it not for the fact that relational goods share some features of ordinary public goods – in particular that individuals who contribute to their production do not reap the full social value of their contribution. Indeed, their dynamic model shows that convergence towards a fixed point characterised by material plenty may be not the manifest sign of allocative efficiency but one facet of a sub-optimal 'social poverty trap'. In fact, satisfaction of citizens' objectives depends on the accumulation of both ordinary private capital and social capital, in suitable proportions. For the sake of tractability, the model cannot include some important links, such as the effects of social capital on material production. Still, it shows that well-being is the outcome of a complex interplay between its private and social components, thus raising serious doubts as to the soundness of widespread policy recipes.

If in the chapters presented thus far the main messages of the book are presented, substantiated with applications or empirical evidence and incorporated into formal analysis, the role of the following two chapters is, rather, to refine and extend the study of the subject matter.

In chapter 8 Serge-Christophe Kolm, a distinguished pioneer of the economics of reciprocity, examines the implications of an apparently minor fact, often disregarded in economic theorising: people care not only about which goods they end up obtaining, but also about the procedure by which they get to obtain them, and in particular about the motivations of other people involved in that procedure. Favourable attitudes on the part of others cannot be bought, as they are in the nature of gift-giving (this holds true even when the underlying economic relation is an exchange or a hierarchical one). The author examines several possible preference structures over one's own and others' attitudes towards opposing players in a game representative of economic interactions, and finds that the only candidate equilibria of the game are 'generalised keeping' and 'generalised giving'. That the latter outcome is more efficient than the former, however, is not enough to license the conclusion that people would be better off by adopting the preference structure he calls 'conditional altruism' (the least demanding preference structure that is likely to secure a 'generalised giving' equilibrium). To address this issue, Kolm conducts a subtler 'inter-preference comparison' and concludes that the adoption of other-regarding preferences is liable to benefit all members of society.

Chapter 9, by Shaun Hargreaves Heap, deals with one function of interpersonal relations that, until recently, would have been very unlikely ever to be discussed from the viewpoint of economics, despite its great practical import for economic lifestyles: the 'mutual validation of ends'. While in the conventional economic approach agents have well-defined pre-existing systems of preferences, real humans have doubts as to whether their goals and convictions are really worthy. So, Hargreaves Heap observes, one of the effects of dialogue with others is to provide confirmation, or refutation. However, the socio-economic system tends to be structured so as to favour the satisfaction of ordinary consumption preferences. This may run counter to people's need for personal interactions as opportunities for verifying their convictions, developing individual and collective identities, and so gaining a sense of self-worth. The author claims that such opportunities, and the institutions that help create them, have not only an intrinsic value for the individuals directly involved but also an instrumental value for society, in maintaining norms of cooperation.

The next two chapters provide a sense of perspective. In chapter 10 Luigino Bruni contributes to this aim by looking back. He asks which philosophical and methodological choices of the past have shaped the current economists' attitude of neglect towards interpersonal relations. Although the Adam Smith of *The Theory of Moral Sentiments* and his Neapolitan contemporary Antonio Genovesi both put great stress on sympathy and its contribution to happiness, classical – and, even more, neoclassical – economics took another route, one that led it to delegate the exploration of the relational realm to other social sciences. Nearly all great economists repeatedly declared the importance of friendly relations and favourable reciprocal attitudes for human happiness, but for one reason or other in the end 'sacrificed' this theme – either by framing it as orthogonal to the analysis of productive and allocative processes, or by opting for continuity with their predecessors, or else by defining their discipline in a way that left out 'non-logical' actions. The effects of all this, Bruni maintains, are clearly discernable in today's economics.

The value added of chapter 11 by Bernard Gazier and Isabelle This Saint-Jean is in its enlarging the perspective of today's economists, not by looking back but rather by looking aside, at the contribution of sister social sciences. The first message they send to students of interpersonal relations is a warning against their adhering to an optimistic or a simplistic view of features and effects of personalised interaction. In particular, they introduce into the picture authority and power. After discussing the various forms of influence of one interacting party on another, they compare four economic and sociological approaches to the study of 'vertical relations' in the workplace, distinguishing between 'weak' and 'strong' notions of authority. Despite the useful hints derived from these approaches, they look for something broader, and find it in the concept of the embeddedness of economic relations within social and political relations, as developed by Mark Granovetter and Pierre Bourdieu. They end by inviting economists interested in interpersonal relations to look for inspiration not only in the psychological but also in the sociological literature.

The book also includes two commentaries by scholars who have thought and written extensively on the matter of the previous chapters but have not been involved in the process of communication and dialogue that led to this book. Although certainly sympathetic to the project that is behind it, they take advantage of the opportunity to raise objections to some of the arguments and claims made in the book, and to introduce additional themes and insights. In particular, in chapter 12 Julie Nelson, drawing from a feminist literature to which she has significantly contributed, presents a view of *individuals-in-relation* that allows her to find common elements across situations that are usually viewed as opposed: on the one hand, 'vertical' versus 'horizontal' relations; on the other, service relations that are mediated by the market versus others that imply unpaid care. Louis Putterman in chapter 13 draws on the experimental literature on social preferences and offers an evolutionary interpretation of what it shows. Social preferences do exist and matter for both positive and normative economics – he claims – but do not lend themselves to drawing simplistic conclusions about human natural kindness.

The book is completed by a brief postscript by the editors, who cannot resist the temptation to have the final word.

2 From transactions to encounters: the joint generation of relational goods and conventional values

Benedetto Gui

1. Introduction

'Welfare economics should be concerned not only with the efficient allocation of material goods, but also with designing institutions such that people are happy about the way they interact with others.' This sentence by Matthew Rabin (1993, p. 1283) evokes not only Serge-Christophe Kolm's (1984, p. 18) pioneering stance in these matters but also some voices from the mainstream that point to a novel area of concern for economic analysis: interpersonal relations. Take the lucid admission by Jack Hirschleifer (1978): 'Perhaps the grossest flaw in the economist's traditional view of the human being is illustrated by the attention we devote to his "man-thing" activities as opposed to "man-man" activities. Our textbooks talk of tastes for cheese or shoes or automobiles, rarely of desires for children or mates or subordinates or fraternal associates. Other social scientists ... have just scorned this view of man as rational unaffiliated thing-consumer, interacting with others only through market exchange.'

As an increasing number of similar statements confirm,[1] there exists a largely unexplored 'interpersonal dimension of economic reality' that encompasses the innumerable reciprocal influences between the entities or actions we commonly identify as 'economic', and the interpersonal occurrences of a communicative/affective nature.[2]

One way of discerning the economic significance of this interpersonal or relational dimension is to measure the monetary amounts that are

---

[1] See, among others, Ben-Ner and Putterman (1998a) and Ash (2000).
[2] With reference to events occurring in a personal relationship, Harold Kelley (1986, p. 12) writes: 'Their affective consequences derive partly from the specific rewards and costs they entail but also partly from what the events reveal about each person's underlying dispositions...' The expression 'communicative/affective' refers to the latter component.

involved – for instance, the expenditure in two inputs for the satisfaction of relational needs: the travel costs people undergo for spending the weekend with those they love or like, despite the natural or historical attractions of the regions where they may happen to be working; or the expenditure in telecommunications that is imputable to mere relational exchange.

Another confirmation is found in psychologists' statements on the importance of the social environment for both workers' happiness and productivity (see, for instance, Lea, Tarpy and Webley, 1987, p. 170).

A third source of corroborating evidence is experimental games. In public good provision games – a typical instance of a prisoner's dilemma, where usual rational choice considerations go against contributing – cooperation rates are higher when participants can socialise before the experiment, even when the procedure is anonymous (Sally, 1995).[3] Likewise, costly face-to-face staff meetings continue to be encouraged by companies, since greater affective involvement facilitates information exchange and trust creation (*The Economist*, 2002).

Economic theory is doing a lot to shake off the deep-rooted bias described by Hirschleifer and to incorporate further interpersonal elements into its account of human interaction (see Bruni's historical overview, chapter 10). Apart from pioneering and isolated works by both 'heterodox' and 'orthodox' writers (see, among others, Arrow, 1974; Ng, 1975; Hirsch, 1976; Ben-Porath, 1980; Cauley and Sandler, 1980; Prescott and Visscher, 1980; Hansmann, 1986; Hollander, 1990), a few strands of the literature that take personalised interactions seriously can be tentatively identified. One focuses on 'positional goods', the consumption or possession of which confers prestige in the eyes of neighbours, colleagues, etc. (see Ireland, 1994; Frank, 1997). A second strand studies unselfish behaviour – in particular positive and negative reciprocity – in experimental 'social dilemmas', and explores the underlying 'other-regarding' or 'social' preferences (see Hoffman, McCabe and Smith, 1996; Fehr and Gächter, 1998b). A third group of papers investigates 'peer effects' – i.e. the influences of mates, neighbours and associates on economic behaviour and performance (Glaeser, Sacerdote and Sheinkman, 1996; Akerlof, 1997; Topa, 2001); this is an instance of 'social interactions' or 'non-market interactions', in which agents exert non-contractual influences on each other, as occurs when the value of a good for a consumer depends on who else consumes it (Cowan, Cowan and Swan, 1997; Glaeser and Sheinkman, 2000; Manski, 2000).

---

[3] On personal interactions and contributions to public goods, see Bardsley (chapter 4, this book). See also Bohnet and Frey (1999).

Informational and other spillovers also characterise work on 'social networks', a notion that carries an additional message: agents do not operate in a homogeneous social space but within structured environments where links between specific pairs of agents facilitate business or other interactions (Kirman, 1997; Kranton and Minehart, 2001). Overlapping with some of the previous strands, there are then a number of papers revolving around the notion of 'social capital' – i.e. the fabric of informal relations between actors that represents an invisible resource of well-functioning communities, with an impact on economic performance (Johnson and Temple, 1998; Dasgupta and Serageldin, 1999).[4]

I will not proceed much further, out of respect for the reader, apologising for the numerous authors and themes I have neglected. I mention only a few writings (Gui, 1988, 1996; Uhlaner, 1989; Zamagni, 1999) that introduce the notion of 'relational goods' – i.e. intangible entities that are inextricably associated with personalised interactions – upon which this chapter focuses.

In developing the framework I present below, I have been inspired by a brief sentence by Mark Casson, who broadens the prevailing view of economic relations by proposing that 'the concept of a trade [be] replaced with the concept of an encounter, which can also include teamwork, public assembly, chance meetings, and so on' (1991, p. 25). I found there a suggestion for investigating human interaction in the economic sphere from a perspective that Harvey Leibenstein (1979) would call 'micro-micro', in the attempt to incorporate 'relational goods' coherently into economic discourse. Indeed, in real-life 'encounters' much more takes place than is captured by the variables usually considered for studying economic interactions: the quantities and characteristics of goods and services, property rights, financial assets and objective information, all of which are contributed or received by each party. According to Uriel Foa's (1993) classification of 'interpersonal resources', those above can be categorised as goods, money, services or information. All these are, to some extent, universalistic and concrete. There remain two often disregarded categories of resources, which are rather particularistic and symbolic: status (defined as 'prestige, regard, or esteem'; see p. 15), and love (i.e. 'regard, warmth, or comfort'). Indeed, Foa's 'status' and 'love' categories are the primary ingredients

---

[4] Authors such as Edward Glaeser, David Laibson, José Sheinkman and Christine Soutter (2000) and Marcel Fafchamps and Bart Minten (2002) view social capital rather as part of an individual's human capital. So does Gary Becker, who, however, turns social capital from a tool for more effective action into something that affects agent's choices: 'I incorporate the influences of others on a person's utility through the stock of social capital' (1996, p. 12).

of relational goods, the rest being made up of 'local' information (i.e. information that is hard to define objectively and to transmit beyond the direct interactants).

In the following, after a brief exploration of the relational side of economic interactions (section 2) and of the theoretical alternatives for taking it into account (sections 3–5), I propose to view an 'encounter' as a peculiar productive process that generates, besides conventional values, 'relational' goods (sections 6–11). Section 12 presents some sketches of applications. A few concluding remarks are presented in section 13.

2.   From impersonal exchange to real-life personalised interaction

Were agents' human capital unaffected by contact with others, and the economic environment a complete set of perfect markets, personalised interaction between economic agents would be irrelevant for resource allocation, so economists would be right in neglecting interpersonal phenomena in their analyses. These assumptions have traditionally been adopted in general equilibrium theory, which has strongly influenced how economists view their object of study.[5] Indeed, if goods are homogeneous and contracts are fulfilled with certainty at no cost then each transaction is independent of the others (past, present or future) and buyers are indifferent between sellers offering the same price (and vice versa). Secondly, due to the centralised clearing of transactions, the only communication involving agents is an exchange of codified information through the 'auctioneer'. Third, agents are plunged into an all-embracing set of markets, so these price all their actions and mediate all their interactions.

Starting from such an aseptic description of economic interaction, three paths bring us back towards real-life interpersonal events. The first is the recognition that exchanges are complex, due to information asymmetries, the heterogeneity of goods, bounded rationality, spillovers and other market failures. Insurance, franchise or employment contracts are eloquent examples. All this leaves ample room for transactants to communicate with each other in order to elicit or transmit information, negotiate, or enforce agreements once made. In so doing, exchanges are often transformed into full-fledged interpersonal relations. In Ian Macneil's (1987) language, virtually all real-life contracts are to some extent 'relational', rather than 'discrete', as they imply durable threads of reputation and interdependence, even of friendship (p. 276).

[5] Samuel Bowles and Herbert Gintis (2000) blame just the success of the Walrasian over the Marshallian approach for the long neglect of relational and other themes.

As seen from the viewpoint of Oliver Williamson's 'transaction cost economics', real contracts are not the place of pleasant socialisation but, rather, the habitat of a 'contracting man [who] is given to self-interest seeking of a deeper and more troublesome kind than his economic man predecessor' – i.e. to self-interest with guile (1996, pp. 55–6). However, here too man is acknowledged to be, after all, a 'social animal' (p. 267), capable of trust, under certain circumstances. Furthermore, real trans-actants differ as to the strength of their opportunistic tendencies and the external constraints to which such tendencies are subjected, and so the identity of parties to a contract matters (p. 370). Lastly, 'the social and organisational context within which contracts are embedded' also counts (p. 275).

A convergent perspective is found in those authors who emphasise intangible relation-specific capital. Becker's (1975) specific human capital is the most well-known instance: over time the worker accumulates a stock of firm-specific knowledge that would become useless in the event of separation. Less often mentioned, but not less real, is another relation-specific capital asset: the knowledge that managers acquire concerning the strengths and weaknesses of an employee, and how these relate to possible tasks.[6] Intangible relation-specific capital is also formed in connection with other recurrent transactions – e.g. between a customer and a supplier (see Ben-Porath, 1980).

The second path is the consideration of modes of carrying out trans-actions other than exchange.[7] The most obvious non-market mode is administrative allocation within an authority structure that covers both the supplier and the receiver of a good or a service. Another possibility is what Henry Hansmann (1989) calls 'politics'. In joint-stock companies, condominiums, cooperatives, etc. important choices are left to 'political' procedures, in particular collective decisions by assemblies or commit-tees.[8] A third – albeit informal – mode of managing transactions is reciprocity – i.e. non-contractual transfers in cash or kind occurring

---

[6] See Prescott and Visscher (1980) and Tomer (1987). Kenneth Arrow's (1974) commu-nication channels, team human capital (Chillemi and Gui, 1997) and Becker's marital-specific capital (1981) are other instances.

[7] For Oliver Williamson (1996, p. 58), a transaction occurs when that 'good or service is transferred across a technologically separable interface'.

[8] Interestingly, the famous institutionalist John Commons categorises transactions into 'Bargaining, Managerial, and Rationing transactions': '[T]he transfer of legal control is the outcome of a Bargaining transaction ... the assumption back of Managerial transac-tions is that of superior and inferior ... Rationing transactions ... are the negotiations of reaching an agreement among several participants who have authority to apportion the benefits and burdens to members of a joint enterprise' (1934, p. 58). I thank Antonin Wagner for this citation.

within a group or a community according to a logic of fairness, solidarity or mutual insurance. Examples are numerous in traditional economies – e.g. informal insurance (see Coate and Ravallion, 1993) or group harvesting of individual plots (see Geschiere, 1995) – but reciprocity has a role to play even in modern economies. What matters here is that non-market transactions typically require face-to-face interactions, so agents find themselves in highly personalised contexts where attitudes, feelings and other relation-specific elements enter into play.

The third path from impersonal market exchange towards personalised interactions brings us to situations where, according to usual definitions, no transaction occurs. Take fellow workers, who are continuously involved in chatting, explaining, deriding, encouraging, disapproving, and so on. Such interactions – which might seem irrelevant for economic analysis – impact on two important magnitudes: employees' satisfaction and the firm's productivity. Similarly among neighbours, social interactions without apparent transactions contribute to the perceived quality of life and well-being (Diwan, 2000).

3.   How to account for the communicative/affective side of economic interactions?

If the communicative/affective side of economic interactions that was pruned off by the Walrasian razor is worthy of consideration within economic analysis, how can it be conceptualised? Answering this question requires two steps: first, one has to define some conceptual entity that may host relational phenomena conveniently; secondly, one has to consider agents' preferences or motivations concerning such entities. Below, I focus most on the former, more difficult step.

Skipping it may lead to misleading results, as is shown by Douglas Bernheim and Oded Stark's (1988) discussion of couple formation based only on a feature of preferences: altruism. Excluding income transfers, for simplicity, a woman is best off choosing the partner with whom the utility interdependence created by altruism works best for her. Thus, if her individual characteristics grant her little happiness, she had better choose a less altruistic partner, so he will suffer less from her unhappiness, and so will be less unhappy, and therefore the negative feedback on her utility will be smaller. So we are taught that, when one is hurt by misfortune, the recipe for happiness – or less unhappiness – is having at one's side an unconcerned, and therefore content, partner. The disregard for the genuinely relational aspects of the interaction is complete: the partner's sympathy, the very fact that he shares her concerns, is irrelevant for the heroines of this novel.

Therefore, relational entities must be introduced into the economic discourse; but how?

4.   Not only externalities or goods' characteristics

The first notion that comes to an economist's mind when discussing non-contractual reciprocal influences is externality. And rightly so. Indeed, one can identify quite a long list of 'interpersonal externalities' – i.e. externalities that (unlike pollution or road congestion) do not operate through physical mediums but rather through interpersonal communication (both verbal and visual) or emotional links.[9] These include not only 'positional externalities' (Frank, 1991) and 'human capital externalities' (Borjas, 1995), which have been mentioned above, but also the additional satisfaction that spectators derive in the presence of a large and enthusiastic audience (Rothschild and White, 1995), or the benefits that restaurant-goers receive from the atmosphere created by other customers (Becker, 1991; see also Corneo and Jeanne, 1999a, who consider a similar but 'type-specific' externality).

However, the notion of an externality is most useful when the unpaid/ uncompensated effects on other agents are unintentional, a by-product of actions having other purposes.[10] I do not find it illuminating to categorise as an externality a punch on the nose of a rival, or the secret poisoning of cans sold by a competitor, despite the fact that these actions satisfy the condition that the affected party did not consent to them.[11] Coming to an example more relevant to our discussion, take a wealthy manager chatting about his yacht in the presence of a penniless, unnoticed clerk. The fact that the listener may feel humiliated is typically an externality: his presence or absence neither adds to nor detracts from the value of the conversation for the manager, in the same way as the presence or absence of damaged inhabitants in the vicinity of a polluting plant does not affect its profitability, as long as no internalisation mechanism is at work. However, if the manager walks closer to the clerk so that he can listen, or if he directly addresses the clerk, for instance expressing a positive or negative judgement about the accomplishment

---

[9] A related expression is 'social externalities', as distinct from 'physical externalities'. Unfortunately, its meaning is not univocal: see, for instance, Anne Preston (1989) and Isabel Grilo and Jacques Thisse (1999); Roland Bénabou (1996, p. 237) prefers 'sociological spillovers'.

[10] There is no agreement as to the role of intentions in the definition of externality. I strongly support the position of Sara Connolly and Alasdair Munro, who clearly state that 'it also excludes situations where the damage (or gain) is deliberate' (1999, ch. 5).

[11] This condition is the only one required, for instance, by James Meade (1973); see Cornes and Sandler (1986, p. 29).

of a task, the logic of these actions stands outside the range of fruitful application of the notion of externality: the clerk's presence and attention are indispensable for the action to attain its goal. The clerk is no more an 'external party'.

The second notion that permits the communicative/affective aspects of economic interactions to be captured to some extent is the characteristics of goods. This notion fits a shopkeeper politely counselling a customer: the intensity of this service can make an item bought in a boutique different from the same item bought in a department store. However, in some interactions – e.g. among colleagues – no (even implicit) sale of goods occurs; furthermore, usually communicative/affective entities are not 'supplied' by one party and 'consumed' by the other, but both parties contribute to their creation.

5.   Extending the exchange paradigm

Another option that comes immediately to the economist's mind for conceptualising the communicative/affective side of personal interactions in economic terms is to extend the definition of a good to include such entities as a pleasant message, a story told during a boring wait, a nice smile; and, similarly, to include among 'bads' abusive invective and other unpleasant communicative acts. In this way the communicative/affective side of an interaction would be likened to a set of transfers of unusual 'articles of trade'. Taken literally, this option sounds a bit naive, as it crystallises as 'goods' entities the meaning of which crucially depends on the context and on irreducibly subjective elements.

Not surprisingly, the authors who describe human interaction as 'social exchange'[12] – or, like Foa (1993), 'interpersonal exchange' – interpret the expression 'exchange' loosely, as a non-contractual combination of reciprocal contributions. Moreover, they refer to the intangible items being traded off, not as individual acts objectively described but, rather, as sets of acts identified by their interpersonal meaning; after all, a bow – or a given sentence – can express deference, but it can also express derision, and this is what matters.[13]

---

[12] Among economists who have utilised the notion of social exchange, see Chadwick-Jones (1986), Hollander (1990) and Gächter and Fehr (1999).

[13] Giacomo Corneo and Olivier Jeanne (1999b) and Philip Pettit (1995) do not speak of 'social exchange' but they do take a similar stance. According to the former, agents also consume 'goods that are directly obtained ... from their own social environment. [...] Examples include ... receiving deference, sympathy, approval, and courtesy... [S]uch goods are not allocated by the market but through a process of social interaction ...' (1999b, pp. 711–12). Interestingly, Pettit distinguishes between conventional services, which he dubs 'action-dependent goods', and goods (such as 'being loved, being

The social exchange approach brings to light economic phenomena such as implicit barter (money for gratitude and care), which is hidden behind apparently unilateral intergenerational transfers that occur within families (see Cox and Rank, 1992). However, the exchange analogy also reveals strong limitations. First of all, it turns the spotlight towards the private-good component of acts that make up personal interaction, and so leaves in the shade the public-good components that are also present. Indeed, benefits and costs are often shared among direct interactants (let's assume they are two), as when a joke makes both laugh, or an inadvertent sentence transforms a quiet talk into an odious row. Furthermore, there may be spillovers on bystanders, as when a conflict between two colleagues damages the atmosphere of the whole workplace. Secondly, the idea of social or interpersonal exchange depicts agents entering an interaction as having an endowment of resources that are, subsequently, transferred to (or spent for the benefit of) the other party. This obscures the fact that personal interaction generates something that did not exist before, and that interactants act as co-producers of this something. Notice the parallel with the practice of depicting services such as consulting as the exchange of valuable knowledge against a payment, which obscures the fact that a restructuring plan is typically the outcome of cooperation between consultants and a company's managers.

6. Personal interaction as a productive process generating relational goods

The discussion above of the alternative theoretical options for conceptualising economic interactions having a communicative/affective component leads us to what seems a more promising route: to view this component as a set of peculiar outputs – 'relational goods' – generated by a 'productive' process called an 'encounter'.[14]

Examples of encounters are: an estate agent and a customer engaged in a deal; a physician visiting a patient; a foreman explaining a new task to a worker; a non-profit manager and a wealthy philanthropist examining a new project; a board meeting; a group of secretaries chatting in a corridor.

---

liked, being acknowledged, being respected, being admired'), which he calls 'attitude-dependent'.

[14] This acceptation of the term 'encounter' is aligned with its use in marketing literature, where a 'service encounter' is defined as 'the dyadic interaction between a customer and a service provider' (see Bitner, Booms and Tetreault, 1990). On the provider's side there is more to the service encounter than personnel behaviour (facilities and procedures also enter into play), but usually the focus is on personal interaction between employees and customers.

A common characteristic of all these examples is face-to-face interaction, which is almost a defining element of an 'encounter'. Other forms of interaction – in particular teleconferences and telephone conversations, which entail simultaneity – can also be seen as encounters, albeit with different 'productive technologies' (this expression is used by Sugden, 2002, and chapter 3 of this book). Communication via e-mail or letter also has some of the elements that make up an encounter.

I now turn to a description of encounters as productive processes.

The most obvious outcomes – or 'outputs' – of an encounter are:

(O1) transfers of property rights (for instance, the sale of a house, in the estate agent example; but also a donation from the philanthropist to the manager's organisation);

(O2) the provision of a service (e.g. the physician's diagnosis);

(O3) the performance of a task within an organisation (a collective decision, in the example of the management board; the implementation of a plan, in the case of the job assignment).

All of these can be called, broadly speaking, transactions (see, once more, Williamson, 1996, p. 58). As the transaction cost literature has made clear, transactions require the employment of some inputs. These can be divided into the following two large classes.

(I1) Ordinary goods and services.

Examples are: transportation and telecommunication services; the use of a meeting room; and legal advice about a contract's clauses.

(I2) Interactants' human inputs.

These can be seen as flows of services of interactants' stocks of human capital. Their quantity and quality depend on the stocks themselves, and the intensity of their use – i.e. the time devoted and effort exerted. Here 'human capital' is understood very broadly, so as to include: personal characteristics, such as physical appearance or psychological strength; the accumulation of previous investments in education and work experience; behavioural habits, convictions, tastes, general interpersonal skills; charisma, status and reputation.[15]

---

[15] This acceptation of human capital brings together elements mentioned in different contexts by various authors who have discussed personal aspects of interactions. In particular: Jon Cauley and Todd Sandler (1980) include personal characteristics among the capital inputs of a couple's household production function that supplies final commodities (such as 'respect, warmth, knowledge, and inspiration'), which then enter the utility functions of at least one of the two; Becker (see, for instance, 1996, introd.) includes in human capital 'personal consumer capital', which is behind the agent's apparent tastes; Glaeser, Laibson, Sheinkman and Soutter (2000) define an individual's social capital as 'the individual's social characteristics – including status, charisma and access to networks – that enable that person to extract private returns from interactions with others'.

In the following I will try to adhere to a 'technological' conception of capital, as a collection of entities that can impact a productive process over an extended period of time by affecting the transformation of inputs into outputs. This conception is distinct from the notion of an asset – i.e. a property right or another claim that ensures its owner an expected stream of revenues or benefits – despite the fact that most entities that qualify for the former definition also satisfy the latter, and vice versa.[16] The reason for keeping this distinction is that, in encounters, both cooperation and conflict take place, in non-obvious blends. So an input contributed by one interactant can be directed to enlarging his own share, even if the pie shrinks, rather than to increasing the 'size of the pie'. Take the legal advice example: the aim of the lawyer's client can be a smoother post-contractual relation, with beneficial effects for both parties, but can also be expropriation of the opponent, a privately beneficial manoeuvre that is likely to reduce social surplus through greater litigation costs.[17]

The same occurs with interactants' human stocks. Within the class of relation-specific information, the salesman's knowledge of the customer's preferences may benefit both parties, as it can direct the former's efforts straight to the items the latter likes most; however, a salesman who knows that a customer is unaware of competitors' offers can be successful if he attempts to sell at above-market prices. So some pieces of relation-specific capital represent an asset for the interactants as a whole (i.e. seen as a cooperating team); others, instead, are such for individual parties (i.e. they are private assets).[18] Which item falls into which category does not depend only on its nature but also on interactants' intentions: in the hands of an altruistic agent, information that can bring him a certain benefit but would confer on the other party much greater damage has zero private value; instead, were a selfish agent in

---

[16] According to the technological conception, a piece of machinery can be called 'capital' if it is capable of performing a certain productive function, despite the fact that lack of authorisation may forbid its actual use, thus reducing or zeroing its value as an asset.

[17] Another example is a luxurious country cottage freed by one party for the purposes of holding a meeting there; its comfort may facilitate communication, but the guest may also feel inferior, and therefore behave differently from in another context – an effect that may be the main purpose of the host's offer.

[18] To sketch a physical analogy, a relation-specific capital good may be a pipeline connecting a producer's chemical plant to the plant of a user. If the tap that regulates the flow is under the control of a technician charged with optimising the operation of the whole complex, it represents an asset for the two parties taken together. If instead the tap is controlled by the producer, it is an asset only for him, as he can extract a greater share of the joint surplus from the pipeline, despite efforts by the user to protect himself, which may reduce the joint surplus.

the former's shoes, that information might be a highly valuable asset. Observe that a piece of information may also represent a 'relational liability' for an interactant. An example is when the memory of an unpleasant event that occurred in the presence of a person is revived by the sight of that person, so fruitful interaction with him is hindered.[19] In conclusion, the specification of how it is directed is a necessary step for identifying who a piece of relation-specific capital is an asset for.[20]

A characteristic of relation-specific capital that depresses its asset value for the persons involved is lack of appropriability. Consider two lawyers with complementary skills, who possess abundant 'local' information about each other and share friendly feelings, so their professional cooperation generates more income than that of two equally skilled random replacements. This collective asset is liable to the usual drawbacks of public goods. Take in particular individual mobility decisions, which drastically reduce the future flow of returns from relation-specific capital, not only for the 'movers' – who are in a position to weigh this loss against the expected benefits from the move – but also for the 'stayers' (be they partners, relatives or neighbours). Compensation of the latter is conceivable, but seldom implementable, for a host of reasons.[21] This makes it possible that each member of society considers moving preferable to staying, and that as a consequence the welfare of everybody drops (see Schiff, 2002).

In order to improve our understanding of encounters, in particular their communicative/affective side, two additional categories of outputs should be considered:

(O4) *changes in interactants' human capital, in particular its relation-specific component*;

(O5) *'relational' goods 'consumed' in the course of the interaction.*

This will be done in the next two sections.

---

[19] Similarly, an affective bond (which can also be seen as a piece of relation-specific capital, as will be discussed below) can represent a liability as well. An example is psychological dependence on a charismatic superior, which may prevent an executive from taking autonomous initiatives.

[20] Notice that third parties may also gain (or lose) from encounters. George Mailath and Andrew Postlewaite (1990) discuss the splitting between a firm's owners and workers of the excess productivity created by workers' ability to cooperate effectively. With reference to social clubs, Benjamin Klein, Robert Crawford and Armen Alchian (1978) suggest that a possible individual owner would end up appropriating the value of personal bonds created over time by members themselves.

[21] In particular, asymmetric information and reluctance to make recourse to contracts in social relationships.

7.   The accumulation/decumulation of relation-specific human capital

Interactants' human capital is modified by encounters in several ways. In nearly all encounters there is a passage of information from one interactant to another, or the generation of new information through their dialogue. Some of the information acquired by one party will impact on future individual activities, or on encounters with many parties. An obvious example is a foreman giving orders to a junior worker. The latter acquires knowledge of widely used techniques, as a side effect of a job assignment; conversely, the foreman may also learn something from a smart objection raised by the worker. The acquisition of such information is then to be classified as a change in interactants' general human capital.[22]

Instead, when a piece of information obtained during an encounter affects only the ability to derive outputs of various types from future encounters with the same interactant, it constitutes 'relation-specific human capital' (or, more simply, 'relational capital').[23] Indeed, this capital is made up, first of all, of *information*. One can distinguish between (i) 'local' information about one party possessed by the other,[24] and (ii) information that is common knowledge for those specific interactants but not for others.[25]

The second ingredient of relation-specific human capital is the 'state of feelings' of one party towards the other. Its inclusion captures the well-recognised fact that reciprocal feelings impinge on an encounter's outcome (e.g. reciprocal resentments obstruct interactive decision-making processes); furthermore, it stresses that these feelings have an

---

[22] That information possessed by an actor can be seen as a stock continuously modified by new messages is affirmed, for instance, by Jack Hirschleifer and John Riley (1992, p. 167). Note that, by including among the outputs of an encounter both the provision of a service and the change in the interactants' state of information, there is a danger of double-counting. This holds especially for services such as education or training, which consist largely of information transmission. A little care can obviate such problems. However, this suggests that including changes in human capital among encounters' outputs is important in the other cases, when the fact that interactants are learning something new is not formally recognised, and therefore is at risk of being overlooked.

[23] This expression 'relational capital' is being used by more and more authors, both in the business management and in economic literature (see, for instance, Frijters, 2000).

[24] An example is a physician who possesses more local information (i.e. information that can hardly be codified and transferred to others) about a specific patient, so on average makes a better or quicker diagnosis than another equally skilled physician who has access to the patient's written records.

[25] Noteworthy examples are: the ability of a proven pair of engineers charged with dangerous repairs to coordinate their actions in emergencies; and, in the case of two businessmen involved in complex contractual relationships, the shared conviction that, should an unanticipated event occur, both will react cooperatively.

inertial component. That reciprocal feelings are largely moulded in direct interactions is quite evident. Long-lasting mutual dislike among colleagues is typically the result of face-to-face events, such as a quarrel, that cause a 'decumulation' of reciprocal feelings.[26]

As remarked above, general human capital is also affected by past encounters.[27] However, as the number of events affecting human capital specific to one particular relationship is much smaller than those affecting general human capital, it is especially on the former that one single encounter can exert a noteworthy impact. This is why in this chapter I put more stress on relation-specific capital than on general human capital.

Notice that between the specificity of human capital to a two-person relationship and full generality there exists a wide spectrum of intermediate cases – i.e. specificity to a small group. An example is the greater productivity that a work team can acquire over time with respect to a group of workers who are individually equally skilled and experienced – thanks, for instance, to their development of specialised jargon, so that brief expressions can convey shared meanings, freeing group members from long explanations and costly misunderstandings (see Chillemi and Gui, 1997, who speak of 'team-human capital').

Enlarging the number of the group causes the notion of relational capital to overlap with the notion of 'social capital', which – in its prevalent 'meso-economic' usage – refers to a collection of intangible durable resources that are specific to a community: the respect of norms of cooperation (which requires, first of all, knowledge of the norm, and, secondly, a convergence of beliefs that it will be followed); mutual familiarity and trust among members of networks along which information flows easily (so research costs are contained); and so on. Indeed, social capital and what I call relational capital are made of roughly the same 'substance'. There are authors – such as Jonathan Turner (1999) – who refer to the latter as a micro-level instance of the former.[28] My using the adjective 'relational' – rather than the more generic 'social' – in reference to both consumption and capital goods associated with dyadic

---

[26] Frans van Dijk and Frans van Winden (1997) treat an agent's altruism towards one's opponent in a contribution game as a state variable modified over time by the latter's behaviour. Sacco and Vanin (2000) also study a repeated game and consider – for each pair of players – their 'relational intensity'; this too varies over time depending on the outcomes of the game.

[27] An instance worth mentioning is the possibility of damage to an interactant's psychological health.

[28] Interestingly, Turner, a sociologist, also uses the notion of encounter – previously investigated by Erwing Goffman (1961) – and stresses the role of the emotional side in discussing economic behaviour.

or small group interactions is to emphasise the peculiarity of face-to-face encounters – in particular, the significance of the affective component.

8.   'Relational' goods 'consumed' in the course of the interaction

Consider a member of an association on his way home, weighing the results of a meeting of the steering committee: the decisions he was most interested in may have been delayed; he may have obtained no valuable information from listening to the others; still, he may have liked the opportunity to talk with fellow members during the breaks.[29]

Or take an elderly person who spends the morning at a neighbourhood market, chatting with sellers and other customers. The outputs of the series of encounters he carries out include some purchases, information about new products, and the maintenance of personal relationships (provided he is going to meet the same people again). However, the very fact that he is engaged in conversations, in addition to the quality of these conversations, may have a significant direct impact on his quality of life, independently of the value of those other 'outputs'.

These examples are attuned to the statement by Kenneth Arrow that 'much of the reward from social interaction is intrinsic' (1999, p. 3). In other words, one of the outcomes of social interaction does not reside in what this can be instrumental to (advantageous transactions, or the accumulation of human capital of any sort) but in what is enjoyed (or suffered, if the communicative/affective side of the interaction is unpleasant) during the interaction itself – a peculiar form of 'consumption'. I refer to this – otherwise unaccounted-for – class of outputs of encounters as 'relational consumption goods'.[30] (Although in some instances 'relational consumption bads' would be a more appropriate expression, most of the time I will stick with 'goods', while admitting that they may be disliked by one or more interactants.)

I admit that recourse to the consumption paradigm for expressing the intrinsic value of human interaction is reductive. Indeed, I fully agree

---

[29] According to Henry Hansmann (1980, pp. 890–91), this sort of benefit contributes considerably to the success and continuation of participatory organisations such as cooperatives and non-profit organisations.

[30] Viewing relational consumption goods as outputs of encounters is reminiscent of Becker's (1965) 'household production function' theory of consumption. This theory stresses that most 'commodities' – e.g. a meal at home – are not bought, as such, but are produced by means of material inputs and family labour. Furthermore – Robert Michael and Becker (1973) add – this approach also encompasses commodities such as 'good health' or 'intercity visits', and even 'envy, prestige, physical and psychological health ...' (pp. 394–95).

with Nelson's (1994, p. 128) statement that 'affiliation with other persons ... is not just a choice issue, or a feel-OK issue, but rather a developmental necessity ... a psychological necessity for full human functioning'. She then asks how this recognition can affect economic theorising. The modest answer I implicitly give to her question in this chapter is to grant interpersonal relations a non-secondary place in our conceptualisation of economic processes. I hope that better ones will come.

Faced with the examples of relational goods described above, the reader might be doubtful as to whether they should really become the object of economic investigation. In fact, one could say, the association's committee example lies at the margins of what we usually consider 'economic'; and, as far as the neighbourhood market example is concerned, most economic agents – those who produce and spend most of a nation's income – have many other things to do with their mornings!

I am convinced that this is not the case. For most people, encounters in the economic sphere represent a large fraction of their social interactions. So, if relational goods matter at all, those generated in circumstances that fall within the domain of economic analysis must also matter. Empirical evidence in support of this statement refers especially to work environments. The literature on mobbing, bullying and sexual or racial harassment provides extreme examples in this regard. For instance, according to Michael Shields and Stephen Price (2002), colleagues' interpersonal behaviour appears to rank high among the determinants of intentions to quit and the job satisfaction/dissatisfaction of nurses in British hospitals (see also the survey by Einarsen, 1999).

Relational consumption goods/bads also result from interactions between employees and clients. Not surprisingly, the relational quality of such interactions also affects job satisfaction, and, consequently, effort, absenteeism and turnover as well (see the empirical analysis by Borzaga and Depedri, chapter 6 of this book; see again Shields and Price, 2002). In the same spirit, Mara Adelman, Malcolm Parks and Terrance Albrecht (1987) find that for urban citizens the psychological importance of personalised interactions connected with the purchase of services is greater than their apparently trivial content might suggest.

The presence of relational consumption goods (or bads) in an economic interaction can be identified through an easy mental test. Compare a personalised interaction with an unmanned procedure (real or fictitious) that secures an agent the same objective outputs, with exactly the same objective characteristics (be they prices, timing, location, quality, etc.). Examples are: being served by an automatic coffee machine, rather than by a barman with whom one can comment about recent sports events; being instructed by a software package, rather than by a colleague worker; or being nursed in a hospital bed by a smart robot, rather than by a human. Let us assume, for better comparability, that the two procedures also ensure the agent the same pieces of information (imagine, for instance, that the coffee machine is programmed to give road instructions); and, furthermore, that the accumulation of human capital is negligible in both cases. We can imagine then that the agent will sometimes prefer the manned procedure and sometimes the un-manned (e.g. since he wants to avoid the barman's curiosity). What interests us here, however, is that usually agents are not indifferent between the two procedures, and sometimes value one of them much more than the other. The entities responsible for that divergence are relational consumption goods.

There are a few subtle questions to be discussed that concern the notion of a relational consumption good. First of all, is it theoretically justified that the communicative/affective entities generated within per-sonalised interactions be regarded as goods, rather than just 'spillovers'? Among the implicit requirements for this attribution, the hardest to satisfy is that the candidate entity be distinguished from the impact that its consumption exerts on consumers. This requirement is not problem-atic for a material good such as butter, or even for a service such as nursing care: the former can be seen, touched, weighed, etc.; the latter cannot, but at least can be described (e.g. in written form, possibly with the help of figures) as a set of actions that can be performed on any patient. Instead, the communicative/affective occurrences that make up relational consumption goods are inextricably tied to the personality of the interactants, which makes them irreducibly subjective. Still, one can conceptually distinguish the emotions experienced and mutually com-municated in an encounter from the evaluation of those emotions by interactants. For instance, a subordinate worker asking for a further exception to current rules may perceive some contempt behind the superior's reaction, but give this unpleasant feeling less weight than the concession of a day off; another worker in exactly the same situation may give it more, to the point of refusing. This thin distinction between the affections experienced and their appreciation by the persons affected – the former being relatively objective, the latter subjective – allows one to extend the notion of good to the communicative/affective side of per-sonalised interactions, and then to employ it for studying interpersonal events.

Secondly, in order to keep the meaning of the expression 'relational consumption goods' as precise as possible, I propose that the adjective 'relational' be used only in a predicative, not an attributive, sense: for an entity to be called such it is not enough that it be somewhat connected with personal relations; it must be made of a relational (i.e. communicative/affective) 'substance'.[31] So, resisting a temptation that is widespread among those who find the notion of relational goods insightful, I advise against having as an example of a relational good a departmental party in which each participant brings some food. I rather view it as an encounter where among its various outputs – these include the implicit food exchange between participants, and the possible changes in their human capital – a prominent role is occupied by the 'good company' (hopefully) enjoyed by participants (this is the relational consumption good!).[32] Similarly, in the nursing of a patient, or the tutoring of a pupil, the communicative/affective outcome of the interaction is important, but can – and sometimes must – be distinguished neatly from the provision of health care or teaching services.[33]

Thirdly, Carole Uhlaner (1989) observes that relational consumption goods are (local) public goods. The criterion she uses is that they affect two or more persons at the same time. Examples that clearly support this position are not hard to find. One is a group of patients in the waiting room of a doctor's practice: chilly silence (broken from time to time by an embarrassed cough) or a relaxed atmosphere in which some people chat while others read is 'consumed' by all those sitting there. In reference to this example, acceptance of Uhlaner's claim is favoured by the fact that interactants are more than two, their roles are identical and their appraisal of the event is symmetrical. Instead, intuition is less clear when the interactants are just two, they play different roles and the affective impact of the interaction is strongly asymmetric – as when during an encounter a superior rebukes an inferior, so the latter feels humiliated, while the former may feel gratified by reaffirmation of his power. Still, interactants share the same communicative event, and consumption by one interactant cannot be separated from simultaneous consumption by the other.[34] Instead, that some consumers like it while others dislike it is not a definite objection to a good being

---

[31] Observe for comparison that, in Fred Hirsch's (1976) use of the expression 'positional goods', the adjective 'positional' has an attributive sense (otherwise a prestigious mansion could not be one, but only power or prestige would).

[32] A (remediable) danger of double-counting also exists with regard to relational consumption goods, in particular when the service one party purchases includes social support or entertainment (obvious examples are psychotherapy and disc jockeys hired for private parties).

[33] However, 'distinct' does not mean 'unrelated': the quality of teaching, measured in terms of notions learned by the pupil, may be boosted by a playful atmosphere during tutoring.

[34] In fact, being in each other's presence is indispensable for their production, and, secondly, production and consumption are simultaneous.

considered public (this also happens in reference to more conventional public goods, such as a modern sculpture in a square or a sketch by a comedian).[35]

As an immediate consequence of their being by nature public goods, relational consumption goods are subject to market failure, but with two special features. First, complete free-riding is not possible. In fact, in order for an individual to consume the relational goods generated in an encounter, he has to contribute at least some of the resources needed for its production: a portion of his time – the duration of the encounter, gross of transportation and preparation – coupled with the effort needed for interacting. Of course, as to who bears the costs of other inputs, free-riding continues to be a possibility. In the departmental dinner example, free-riding may occur in the buying or cooking of food, or the transport to the meeting place. Still, in these cases social incentives may make up for the scarcity of economic incentives. The categories of costs that are the hardest to be shared include those related to devising, promoting and organising the event, as well as taking responsibility for unplanned occurrences: first, they are hard to define and quantify, and, secondly, the very fact of measuring – not to mention bargaining – conflicts with the spirit of fellowship that should characterise a friendly meeting.

This remark introduces us to the second feature of relational goods that makes them especially vulnerable to the 'tragedy of commons': non-contractibility. Even if one interactant were willing to pay for all the resources devoted to an encounter – including the other interactants' human resources – an adequate supply would not swiftly follow; genuinely favourable reciprocal dispositions – which are key ingredients of the communicative/affective side of an interaction – cannot be effectively secured through monetary incentives.

The examples presented up to this point refer to encounters that either have an explicit economic content (a transaction) or, at least, occur in a context that everybody regards as economic (a firm, a market, etc.). However, economics cannot totally disregard relational consumption goods that are generated in non-economic contexts, even in the absence of transactions – for instance, in informal gatherings of friends, or in family or associational life. The reason is that the frequency and characteristics of these encounters are significantly influenced by choices that fall within the economic domain, in particular work schedules and occupational mobility.

---

[35] Assessing non-excludability is also controversial in the case of relational consumption goods: while it is possible to exclude someone from a party, it can be hard to exclude participants from 'consuming' jokes or exchanging gossip 'produced' during the party.

9.   Relational consumption goods and relational capital

First of all, a remark about the vocabulary adopted above is required. The distinction between communicative/affective outputs being 'consumed' within interactions, on the one hand, and relational capital that is first accumulated and then put to use in further interactions, on the other, was introduced in Gui (2000a), where I reserved the expression 'relational goods' to the former. While reaffirming the value of the distinction, I find it more convenient that 'relational good' may span both – so they can be jointly identified by a common name – and that specification of whether it is a consumption or a capital good be left to a subsequent refinement. In favour of this option stands the fact that there are expressions that are used with reference to both. Take, for instance, 'a good interpersonal climate', a phrase that can refer to a flow of relational benefits enjoyed during a one-off event (a consumption good) but also to a lasting feature of a workplace, built up over time at a cost and capable of increasing productivity over an extended period (a capital good). So, the choice of vocabulary I am advocating aligns the expression 'relational goods' with, for instance, the term 'public goods', which refers to both a park and an open-air concert in that park, despite the former being a capital and the latter a consumption good.

Up to now, in considering the role of relational capital within an encounter, I have explicitly mentioned only its impact on transaction costs – e.g. reducing the requirement of ordinary inputs for successful completion. I must add, however, that relational capital also impacts the generation of relational consumption goods. A straightforward example is an encounter between a client and a service provider – e.g. a therapist, or a lawyer: if the two parties are acquainted and sympathise with each other, it may help transform a dull duty into a lively dialogue. In other words, relational capital is also instrumental to the achievement of intrinsic benefits from interactions.

In order to sum up and clarify the connection between relational consumption goods and relational capital, consider an analogous connection drawn from the realm of 'tangibles', that between outings and footpaths. Outings are events produced and consumed (or 'pro-sumed': see Alvin Toffler, 1980) by country-lovers. We might call them 'recreational consumption goods', to establish a parallel. The list of inputs employed for 'producing' an outing includes not only time, effort and the use of outdoor clothing and equipment but also the utilisation of footpaths to cut across the country side. As footpaths provide recreational benefits over extended periods of time, we can call them

'recreational capital goods'. However, observe that footpaths also provide non-recreational benefits – e.g. they facilitate the transport of
timber – in the same way that relational capital also provides non-
relational benefits; in particular, they help in conducting transactions.
(Indeed, unlike relational consumption goods, relational capital is only
partly of a communicative/affective nature, the rest being made up of
information.) Finally, in the same way that relational capital is modified
by successive encounters, a footpath is to some extent modified by
successive outings, as the passage of hikers can both damage it (e.g.
unsteady stones may be displaced) but can also help maintain it (e.g. by
hindering the growth of foliage).

10.   Affecting factors

In order to complete the description of the productive process occurring
in an encounter, two classes of 'affecting factors' are to be considered.

The outcomes of an encounter are influenced by *(A1) the external
environment*. That the unfolding of other interactions taking place all
around exerts a conditioning effect is well illustrated by job search
theory, which describes wage setting and unemployment as the outcomes of a large number of firm–worker contacts. The outcome of each
contact is either further search or the signing of a labour contract, the
conditions of which cannot diverge much from comparable contracts. In
turn, the outcome of each contact exerts an influence on the external
environment. Similarly, a community's social capital can be seen as the
result of myriad encounters among its members.

The external environment also includes features of the organisational
or societal structure that put one interactant in a position of inferiority or
superiority. Indeed, despite the fact that the most obvious reference is
to interactions among peers or independent transactors, the approach
presented here also encompasses situations in which power plays a role
(see in this regard Gazier and This Saint-Jean, chapter 11). Other
environmental influences have to do with laws, culture and habits.

The second affecting factor is *(A2) interactants' attitudes and moods*.
The role of this item is to complement the interactants' reciprocal 'state
of feelings' in the determination of the actual ends pursued – consciously
or unconsciously – in an encounter. Indeed, besides the affective legacy
of past events, a host of transitory motives enter personal interactions,
with intensities depending on momentary inner states. Among them:
the desire for self-affirmation, the search for social approval and the
desire to behave according to values and ideals. Interestingly, actors

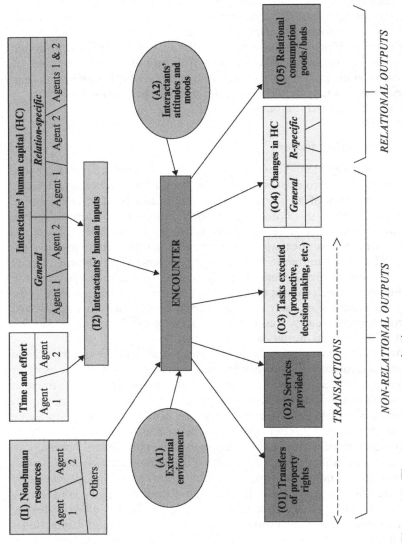

Figure 2.1. The encounter as a productive process.

can exercise some influence upon these motives through self-control efforts.[36]

As has already been said, intentional elements affect the outcomes of encounters by orientating the contribution of an interactant's inputs, for instance, for the maximisation of the parties' joint surplus rather than for the gain of just one, or the encouragement rather than the humiliation of an inferior, and so on.

Intentions have not been given great attention within microeconomics, partly because their content was considered obvious (the maximisation of a self-regarding utility function) and partly because their variability was deemed either to be irrelevant in market competition or to constitute a 'white noise' disturbance. Only recently have some economic models included intentions – as interpreted by opponents – among the elements influencing the outcome of a strategic situation (see Rabin, 1993; Falk and Fischbacher, 2001).[37]

11.   A graphic representation of an encounter

The 'production' process taking place in an encounter can then be portrayed as in figure 2.1. The upper row of boxes represents categories of inputs, or their determinants. In each box lines separate resources supplied by agent A from those supplied by agent B (in the case of non-human resources – the left box – the possibility that some inputs are contributed by third parties is also considered; instead, in the box representing relation-specific human capital (the one to the right), the possibility that some items are jointly attributed to both interactants is considered, in particular local information that is common knowledge for them). The two ellipses indicate the two sets of affecting factors (environmental and motivational) that condition the unfolding of the encounter. The lower row of boxes stands for the five categories of outputs: the three types of transactions, changes in interactants' human capital – both general and relation-specific – and relational consumption goods. The relation-specific component of the change in human capital together with relational consumption goods constitute the 'relational outputs' of the encounter. Last, the central box represents the process.

---

[36] Note that psychological or spiritual training, the use of which is spreading among the business community, can enhance self-control.

[37] See also Hirsch, who points out that a crucial component of the quality of a service such as nursing care is the sincerity of the caring attitudes that patients identify behind doctors' and nurses' objective behaviour (1976, p. 86).

12.   Using the framework presented above: sketches of possible applications

Consideration of relational goods helps push the economic discourse deeper into numerous important phenomena that cannot be adequately described by means of the usual economic concepts.

Take, for instance, the tendency for migrant workers to go back to their birthplace. As such behaviours are hard to explain in terms of job opportunities, relative wages or relative prices, some authors have assumed that, *ceteris paribus*, the utility from consumption is greater at home than elsewhere (see Dustmann, 1997, pp. 298–9), or that utility is an increasing function of both (material) consumption and the number of friends or relatives in whose presence consumption occurs (see also Djajic and Milbourne, 1988, pp. 337–8). However, these ad hoc assumptions do not fit other mobility patterns, such as Australia's internal migration towards the east coast, the main driving force of which apparently is not job availability (see Stimson and Minnery, 1998, pp. 203–7). Taking account of relational goods helps rationalise such a variety of trends. In the former case, upon their return migrants can again put to use relational capital regarding friends and relatives who stayed, thus obtaining both instrumental benefits (low-transaction-cost mutual help) and intrinsic benefits (relational consumption goods). In the second case, the high mobility of friends and relatives reduces the home attraction effect, and demand for relational goods is better satisfied by pursuing new relationships in a favourable social environment.[38]

The framework developed above also adds new hints to the usual explanation that volunteering is partly an opportunity for investing in new skills or reputation, and partly a consumption activity (see Menchik and Weisbrod, 1987). Indeed, by participating in a volunteer group people invest in human capital specific to other volunteers, who are self-selected as to pro-social dispositions and intentions. This makes interaction especially productive of relational consumption goods, either during the very accomplishment of service or in formal and informal meetings. Furthermore, encounters with beneficiaries can also bring, apart from the satisfaction of doing good, the benefit of intense interpersonal communication.[39]

---

[38] Studying mobility patterns through a game of investment in dyadic relationships where players can later seize random opportunities for spot interactions, Gui (1996) finds two equilibria: when the other's investment is high, high investment in the relation is profitable, as the resulting probability of separation is low; vice versa, if the other invests little, low investment is preferable, since early termination of the relationship is expected with a high probability.

[39] One may rightly wonder whether people are really so sophisticated when they consider volunteering. However, after experiencing it, people usually understand – or at least

Next consider scientific research. Relational capital goods such as mutual familiarity and understanding help in obtaining advice from colleagues for individual research projects, and increase the effectiveness of cooperation in carrying out joint projects, not to mention their favourable effects on the fruitfulness of seminar discussions. Moreover, relational capital may also contribute to the production of relational consumption goods (such as good humour during meetings and seminars), which add to the whole compensation package, thus contributing to discouraging quitting.

Associations are a different domain where relational goods count for a lot, especially those with social and recreational purposes (see Iannaccone, 1992). Indeed, member cohesiveness is often their most precious capital asset: the departure of a few key senior members, who share specific information and affective bonds with most other members, may be very difficult to remedy by admitting new members. Moreover, relational consumption goods typically account for a large share of the benefits that involvement in an association ensures its members.

As already hinted at, depicting all parties in an interaction as co-producers is especially insightful in the case of services. On a guided tour clients' behaviour impacts on the success or failure of the experience, not only by keeping to time schedules but also by contributing to the social environment they find themselves in – a crucial determinant of satisfaction. Similarly, the patient's cooperation in supplying information and complying with instructions is a precious input in health care. Observe that the patient's satisfaction largely depends on communicative/affective interaction with the nursing personnel; or, in other words, on the set of relational goods produced and consumed during the provision of medical care (thanks to contributions from both sides). Furthermore, in personal care relational capital often plays a key role in the perceived quality of services delivered and the intrinsic value of interaction; just think of frequently moving a child (or an elderly person) from one nursery school (one nursing home) to another.

Another use of the framework presented above is to discuss the goals that economic agents may have in mind when entering an encounter. In the case of an estate agent who is interested in striking only the best deal in selling a certain property, in order to compute the net benefit he obtains from encountering a customer one has only to subtract from the agreed intermediation fee the cost of carrying out this deal (e.g.

sense – most of the elements at stake. Richard Freeman (1997) does not make the distinction between starting and continuing to volunteer; so, since most people start volunteering on request, he likens volunteer labour to a contribution to public goods under social pressure.

transportation costs, plus the reservation value of the services of his human capital). In general, however, an interactant values an encounter according to all its inputs and outputs (certainly those contributed by – or accruing to – himself, but possibly also those concerning others, whether out of fairness considerations, or benevolence, or envy, etc.). In particular, when deciding to encounter someone else, an agent can also have in mind: the consumption of relational goods (e.g. chatting with a friendly person while being served by that hairdresser with whom one shares so many views);[40] and the accumulation of relation-specific human capital (so an otherwise unprofitable transaction – for example, because the travel costs for meeting the seller are high relative to the quantity purchased – may allow the buyer to know more about a supplier who seems fit for becoming an important source of parts in the future; or volunteering to represent the company at a meeting may be an opportunity for improving one's image in the eyes of that important businessman who is going to be present).[41]

Finally, consideration of the purposes and characteristics of economic interactions helps with the discussion of institutions that are used to host them. For instance, impersonal electronic exchange fits security markets, since – thanks to the standardisation of contracts, precautionary deposits, etc. – traders do not need to accumulate relation-specific human capital in order to make satisfactory transactions, so real encounters (i.e. personalised interactions) are not required. Instead, in industrial districts producing fashion goods, the numerous contracts among independent firms, which secure completion of the various steps in the production chain of ever-changing models, are potentially very costly. Not surprisingly, here enduring personalised business relationships prevail, and significant relational capital is accumulated, thanks to opportunities for interaction provided by business and other associations, wine bars and family or friendship links (see Pyke, Becattini and Sengenberger, 1990). If all this sounds too traditional, consider the fact that the venture capital industry displays equivalent features in the surroundings of Palo Alto. Interestingly, the relational characteristics of a trade are liable to change over time. When, once upon a time, stock traders met in Wall Street under a tree, modern security markets were

---

[40] The latter example is mentioned by Mara Adelman, Aaron Ahuvia and Cathy Goodwin (1994, p. 143) as one where high customer satisfaction is associated with service providers being ready to transcend their role definitions to become confidants.

[41] Or else, the main goal of an interactant can be a change in the human capital of another interactant (in particular, his convictions and preferences). This is one of the ways in which lobbying efforts affect policies.

quite similar to today's venture capital or investment banking businesses as to the importance of personally transmitted information and personal ties for carrying out transactions safely.

13.   Conclusions

In this chapter, after a brief overview of the growing literature of 'social economics', I have proposed viewing personalised interactions as veritable productive processes that are at the centre of economic life. This perspective assigns a key role to the notion of relational goods – i.e. intangible valuable entities that are inextricably associated with face-to-face 'encounters'. Relational goods comprise 'relational consumption goods' – i.e. the intrinsic rewards that interactants derive from and 'consume' during an interaction – and 'relational capital goods' – i.e. various forms of relation-specific human capital that impact not only on the outcomes of conventional transactions conducted by the parties but also on the communicative/affective side of the interaction.

To this end I have sketched a scheme of an 'encounter' that is intended to serve as a semi-finished theoretical basis for modelling coherently the relational aspects of economic interactions (an example of this modelling is given by Antoci, Sacco and Vanin, chapter 7 of this book). I have deliberately avoided specifying not only the preference structure of agents but also their logic of action, so as to accommodate, potentially, not only conventional utility maximisation but also procedural or expressive rationality.

In treating this matter I cannot conceal the obstacles that stand before any attempt at fruitfully extending economic reasoning to the domain of interpersonal relations – in particular, extreme complexity and difficulties of measurement. Still, I think that there is value in trying harder. The reason is that there remain real phenomena that risk not even being conceptualised in economic terms, and therefore are liable to be ignored in individual, corporate and governmental decision making based on economic reasoning; and when, confronting a situation, a significant element is ignored the search for efficiency is destined to damage that element seriously, in the attempt to obtain modest improvements in other objectives, with the result that inefficiency is actively promoted. The natural environment analogy is especially insightful in this regard. In recent decades we have developed a much greater awareness than before of the need to include ecological consequences among the costs and benefits of individual or collective actions. The time has now come that we also learn to account for those hidden costs and benefits of our choices that are associated with their impact on the social environment – which is no less important, both instrumentally and intrinsically, than the natural environment.

No doubt, interpersonal relations are particularly hard ground for economic policy. First of all, spontaneity is a crucial condition for high-quality relational interaction, while the outcomes of public intervention are, almost by definition, artificial (see Ng, 1975). A second reason for caution is that it is not the government's duty to shape the forms of interaction in the business sphere, much less in families, friendships or associations. Were it to interfere in so delicate a matter, it would either waste money or unduly restrict the sphere of action of civil society. Still, there remains ample room for indirect public intervention: promoting actions that favour the accumulation of relational capital goods, and discouraging other actions that lead to their depletion. For instance, social services (e.g. day care for children) can be so designed as to promote the creation of cooperative relationships among families (see Normann, 1984, sect. 3.3.2). Moreover, the design of retail trade can strengthen local connections (e.g. keeping commercial sites close to where people live, so they have the opportunity of regularly visiting non-anonymous meeting places); similarly, pedestrian areas and other meeting places favour repeated personal interaction and so counter alienation. Job and residential mobility – which on the one hand contribute to a better allocation of skills or dwellings and to the diffusion of ideas – on the other hand may lead to inefficient depletion of relational capital goods. Indeed, only when mobility does not exceed a certain threshold can networks of lively social relationships integrate returning movers and newcomers. Of course, responsibility for these matters is not primarily public, but there are a host of public decisions that have a bearing on this terrain.

The second channel by which greater awareness of relational goods can make a difference is cultural. Were the prevailing mental representation of the economic domain to be updated, so as to include relational goods among the concerns of household or company decision makers, many choices would be affected: from housing, time schedules, the design of services, the organisation of work, up to interpersonal attitudes for business effectiveness. The appreciation of relational goods is also inevitably subject to social influences, if for no other reason than that confirmation by others reinforces personal convictions (see Hargreaves Heap, chapter 9). However, some encouraging changes are already occurring in management culture, as is witnessed by recent approaches that stress the impact of interpersonal relations on company performance (see, for instance, Cohen and Prusak, 2001).

Taking interpersonal relations seriously is going to entail not only practical implications that we can only partially envisage at present but also new challenges for economic theorising. On the one hand, as we have discussed at length, new entities that previously we felt authorised to neglect must be accounted for. On the other, as the conceptualisation of economic interaction is modified, the received view of what constitutes appropriate economic behaviour also needs to be updated: as Robert Solow (1999, p. 7) remarks, in these matters '[t]he simple combination of rationality and individual greed that provides the behavioural foundation for most of economics will go only that far'.

3   Fellow-feeling

Robert Sugden

1.   Introduction

Vilfredo Pareto was one of the first economists to use indifference curves as an analytical tool. Explaining their usefulness, he described a person's indifference map as a 'photograph' of his tastes. 'Provided he has left us this photograph, the individual may disappear' (1909, ch. 3, sect. 57). In other words: once we know a person's indifference map, we have everything we need to analyse his economic behaviour. The idea that, for the purposes of economics, a human being is just an indifference map has become something of a folk saying among economists. The point of this saying is that economic theory models human beings as abstract rational agents; their identities *as particular people* are represented only in the preferences that they have as individuals. This approach commits economics to a modelling strategy in which relations between people are impersonal and instrumental.

Over the last twenty years, however, it has become increasingly common for economists to consider the possibility that economic behaviour is *not* always instrumental in its motivation. (Of course, economics has never been committed to the position that *all* relations between people are instrumental. Economists have been able to claim that there are areas of human life, such as the family, in which relations are non-instrumental – and then to say that these areas lie outside the domain of economic explanation.) This more recent re-thinking seems to reflect a growing sense that non-instrumental motivations affect behaviour in relations that are indisputably economic – for example, contracting between firms, employer–employee relationships, and the supply of public goods through voluntary contributions – and that economics needs to recognise sociality as a characteristic of human life. The result has been an outpouring of theoretical and experimental work by economists on such topics as trust, social capital, social norms, reciprocity and fairness. The chapter you are now reading belongs to this genre, but its line of approach to the problem of understanding sociality is more direct.

In trying to model sociality, economists have generally worked within a paradigm of rational choice. One broad strategy has been to represent individuals' social orientations as properties of their preferences – for example, as tastes for altruism, fairness or equality – and then to use standard theories of instrumental rational choice to explain the inter-actions of individuals with those preferences. An alternative strategy, which I have sometimes used, is to represent sociality by developing new concepts of rational choice that are not instrumental in the standard sense – for example, by invoking principles of reciprocity or team think-ing.[1] In this chapter, in contrast, I go outside the paradigm of rational choice – indeed, outside the paradigm of *choice*. My concern is with the processes by which the *affections* of different individuals interact with one another. I develop this idea by using a concept of *fellow-feeling* that derives from Adam Smith's *Theory of Moral Sentiments* (1976/1759).

My approach is influenced by Gui's (1996, 2000a) work on *relational goods*. Gui is concerned with what he calls 'face-to-face interactions' or *interpersonal relations*. Following Gui, I shall use this latter expression to refer to interactions between actors who are conscious of one another as *particular* human beings, and who, by virtue of the ways in which they relate together, give their interactions an affective 'tone'. The affective and communicative components of interpersonal relations are relational goods (or bads). I propose a theoretical strategy for analysing the affect-ive component of interpersonal relations. The aim is to understand some of the mechanisms by which interpersonal relations generate affective states that are valued or disvalued by participants, and by which they induce sentiments that sustain norms of cooperation.

2.   Is this economics?

Some readers may ask whether what I am proposing to do is economics at all. Economics is often understood as the study of choice. Usually, the only mental states that enter into economic models are preferences and beliefs. Preferences are defined over the entities among which economic actors can choose; beliefs are defined over states of the world; and choices are explained in terms of preferences and beliefs. In contrast, I am proposing an analysis of affective states.[2]

---

[1] Bardsley, chapter 4 in this book, surveys this literature in relation to the problem of explaining voluntary contributions to public goods.

[2] David Sally (2000) makes a similar Smithian proposal for the analysis of affective states and sympathy in economics, in the context of the prisoner's dilemma. More generally, there are scattered signs that economists are beginning to introduce affective states into their analysis: see, for example, Frank (1988), Loewenstein (2000) and Oswald (1997).

Affective states, such as happiness, conviviality and distaste, are not preferences. They have positive or negative *valence* – that is, we perceive them as forces of attraction or repulsion – but they are not directly revealed in our choices. They are not, as preferences are, comparative relations among objectively described options. Rather, they are our subjective experiences of the world. Because our preferences tend to adapt to these experiences – because we tend to prefer actions that have previously led to pleasurable outcomes – affective states are important in the process of preference formation. But that process is not normally represented in economic models, in which preferences are usually taken as given.

If the physical characteristics of goods are clearly defined, and if preferences between goods can be held constant in economic modelling, it is perhaps unnecessary to enquire into the affective states that lie behind preferences. But the physical characteristics of a relational good (a friendly smile, a hostile remark) are often more difficult to define than the affective state that it expresses (friendship, hostility). And one person's preferences for an 'objective' relational good (say, conversation with a particular other person) often depend on his perception of another person's affective state, as directed towards him. I cannot see how we can hope to understand preferences for relational goods without investigating affective states directly. Indeed, one might well think that the economic analysis of conventional goods would benefit from taking explicit account of consumers' affective states, as the early neoclassical economists did. As William Stanley Jevons (1879, chapter 3) said in justification of a scientific study of 'the laws of human want': 'Every manufacturer knows and feels how closely he must anticipate the tastes and needs of his customers: his whole success depends on it; and, in like manner, the theory of economics must begin with a correct theory of consumption'. The idea of *anticipating* tastes hints at a model in which people's affective states, and hence their preferences, evolve over time, and in which an entrepreneur is successful by virtue of imaginative empathy with her customers, enabling her to predict the directions in which that evolutionary process will move.

Some readers may accept all this and still be surprised that I go back to Smith's *Theory of Moral Sentiments* to find a theoretical framework. Even if *economics* has not given much attention to the affective states induced by interpersonal relations, surely psychology has? Am I not revealing the familiar prejudices of economists against other disciplines? Perhaps so: I am an economist, after all, and I am predisposed to look to my own discipline for the resources I need for my theoretical models. But I think there are more substantial reasons for using Smith's theory of moral sentiments as a template.

Although Smith's theory starts from assumptions about human nature (in modern language, from assumptions about human psychology), it is presented as a contribution to social theory rather than as an investigation of individual psychology. Smith's aim is to explain certain complex social phenomena – specifically, the social practices of morality. His psychological assumptions are used to define the principles of motion for the individual actors in a model of social organisation. Social phenomena are then explained as emergent properties of interaction among those individuals. Not surprisingly, given Smith's role as a founder of economics, this way of understanding moral sentiments has strong affinities with much theorising in economics. We should not expect psychologists to have produced the kinds of theories of social organisation that we need to understand the economic significance of relational goods. Of course, if we are to take Smith's work seriously as a starting point for present-day modelling, we need to be convinced that his psychological assumptions are compatible with current knowledge. I shall argue that they do indeed satisfy this test.

3.   Fellow-feeling[3]

Smith's *Theory of Moral Sentiments* opens with the famous sentence: 'How selfish soever man may be supposed, there are evidently some principles in his nature, which interest him in the fortune of others, and render their happiness necessary to him, though he derives nothing from it except the pleasure of seeing it' (1976/1759, p. 9). Smith immediately goes on to claim that, when we become vividly conscious that another person is in a situation that would cause us extreme pain, we feel pain too (pp. 9–10):

By the imagination we place ourselves in his situation, we conceive ourselves enduring all the same torments, we enter as it were into his body, and become in some measure the same person with him, and thence form some idea of his sensations, and even feel something which, though weaker in degree, is not altogether unlike them ...

When we see a stroke aimed and just ready to fall upon the leg or arm of another person, we naturally shrink and draw back our own leg or our own arm; and when it does fall, we feel it in some measure, and are hurt by it as well as the sufferer.

---

[3] This and the following two sections draw on my discussion of Smith's theory in Sugden (2002).

On Smith's account, the affective state of the sufferer, as imagined by the observer, produces a state *of the same kind* in the observer. To avoid confusion with other definitions of 'sympathy', I shall use Smith's term *fellow-feeling* to represent this kind of interdependence of feeling. That is: one person B's fellow-feeling for another person A is to be understood as B's lively consciousness of some affective state of A's, such that B's consciousness has similar affective qualities to A's state.

Smith's hypothesis is that there is a general tendency for fellow-feeling among human beings with respect to all affective states, whether pleasurable or painful. However, the strength of fellow-feeling is greater the more closely related the individuals are (for example, there tends to be more fellow-feeling between friends than between acquaintances, and more between close relatives than between distant ones) and the more vividly the circumstances of the person directly affected are represented to the observer (thus, strong fellow-feeling can sometimes be induced by theatrical and literary representations of affective states). Further, some kinds of affective states are more effective in inducing fellow-feeling than others. In particular, Smith proposes that emotional pains are more conducive to fellow-feeling than physical pains are, because 'our imaginations can more readily mould themselves upon [another person's] imagination, than our bodies can mould themselves upon his body' (p. 29). As I shall explain later, Smith's concept of 'imagination' involves some degree of *perspective taking* – that is, the ability to recognise that other people's orientations to the world can differ from one's own. Thus, imagination has cognitive elements as well as affective ones. Crucially, however, the fundamental mechanism of fellow-feeling is represented as involuntary.

Sympathy and empathy have been the subjects of a huge amount of theoretical and empirical work in biology, psychology and neuroscience.[4] The findings of these research programmes confirm many of Smith's insights about fellow-feeling. There is strong evidence of processes of 'emotional contagion' – that is, the transfer of emotional states between individuals – working below the level of conscious control, and present not only in humans but also in many other social mammals. Emotional contagion seems to be particularly robust in relation to the emotions of fear and distress. Its effect is generally stronger the greater the familiarity of the 'object' (the individual with the directly induced affective state) to the 'subject' (the individual in whom a corresponding

---

[4] The following discussion draws on Stephanie Preston and Frans de Waal's (2002) comprehensive survey of research on empathy. The discussion of mirror systems draws on Rizzolatti, Fogassi and Gallese (2001) and Chaminade and Decety (2003).

affective state is induced by emotional contagion), the greater the similarity between object and subject, the more experience the subject has of the state experienced by the object and the greater the salience of the cues that direct the subject's attention to the object. It seems likely that this kind of unconscious transfer of affective states is the basic ingredient of the more cognitive forms of empathy of which human beings and great apes are known to be capable.

Given what we now know (but Smith did not) about the way our brains are organised, the prevalence of emotional contagion should not be surprising. In a system made up of a dense network of interconnections, we should expect that perceptions that have significant common features will be processed in overlapping ways, and thus have some tendency to activate similar affective states. For example, it is now known that, in both monkey and human subjects, seeing the hand of another monkey or human grasping an object with apparent purposefulness does not merely activate in the subject's brain a *visual* representation of that act, as seen from outside. It also activates a *motor* representation of the performance of the act, *as performed by the subject*. In other words, the subject's consciousness of another individual's act of grasping has much of the neural content of *actually grasping*. There is some evidence that affective states are subject to similar mirroring. For example, when sad stories are read to human subjects, neural structures that are known to be involved in emotional processing are activated.

Writing, I have to say, from ignorance, I am impressed by the explanatory power of the *perception–action model* of the ultimate evolutionary base of empathy, as presented by Stephanie Preston and Frans de Waal (2002). A perception–action organisation of the nervous system works by means of direct connections between perceptions (the presence of a predator, the approach of a projectile) and appropriate actions (running away, ducking). Among animals that live in groups, one individual's reproductive success is often served by matching the actions of other members of the group (running away when another member of the group becomes aware of the presence of a predator, ducking when a nearby member of the group becomes aware of the approach of a projectile). Thus the direct perception of some phenomenon and the indirect perception that another individual has perceived it call for the same response; it is natural to expect that corresponding direct and indirect perceptions will activate similar representations in the nervous system. If this combination of perception and action is also linked to an emotional response such as fear, we have a rudimentary mechanism of fellow-feeling.

4.   The correspondence of sentiments

Smith's theory of moral sentiments requires an additional psychological mechanism, which he calls 'the pleasure of mutual sympathy'. This is the hypothesis that human beings *derive pleasure from* all forms of fellow-feeling. Smith introduces this hypothesis by considering the implications of a model in which fellow-feeling is the only mechanism, and feelings are simply 'reflected' from person to person. Consider a case in which one person A is in pain. Another person B experiences fellow-feeling for A's pain. By the nature of fellow-feeling, this is painful for B. But then what if A becomes conscious of B's fellow-feeling for him? The same analysis would seem to imply that this consciousness is *painful* for A, since A is conscious of a painful affective state in B. This makes perfectly good theoretical sense, but Smith thinks it is inconsistent with what we know about human psychology (p. 14):

> The sympathy, which my friends express with my joy, might, indeed, give me pleasure by enlivening that joy: but that which they express with my grief could give me none, if it served only to enliven that grief. Sympathy, however, enlivens joy and alleviates grief. It enlivens joy by presenting another source of satisfaction; and it alleviates grief by insinuating into the heart almost the only agreeable sensation which it is at that time capable of receiving.

Smith's claim, then, is that A's consciousness of B's fellow-feeling for his pain is *pleasurable*.

Notice that, for Smith, this pleasurable consciousness is 'another source of satisfaction': it is the product of a mechanism that is *additional to* fellow-feeling. The source of the satisfaction is the *correspondence of sentiments* between the two people: '[T]his correspondence of the sentiments of others with our own appears to be a cause of pleasure, and the want of it a cause of pain, which cannot be accounted for [by a theory of reflected feelings]' (p. 14). It seems that Smith is proposing a very general mechanism. Whenever one person A is conscious of a correspondence between his own affective response to some state of affairs and the response of another person B, that consciousness in itself has a positive affective quality for A. Conversely, if A is conscious of dissonance between his response and B's, that consciousness has a negative affective quality for A.

Smith thinks that the pleasure derived from the correspondence of sentiments (and the pain induced by dissonance) is sufficiently strong that we are *pleased* when we are able to feel sympathy for the painful feelings of others, and feel *hurt* when we are unable to do so (a hurt that is often expressed as contempt for the other person). Sometimes

Smith suggests that the overall experience of sympathising with another person's distress is pleasurable, so that we are naturally inclined to 'run ... to condole with the afflicted' (pp. 15–16). But other elements of his theory imply that this is not always the case. The act of offering sympathy to someone in distress does not automatically generate the correspondence of sentiments necessary for the production of positive feelings. One obvious obstacle is that the sympathetic pain felt by the sympathiser (B) is naturally less than the actual pain felt by the person sympathised with (A), particularly when A and B are not closely related and when the pain is physical rather than emotional. Smith recognises this as a source of dissonance of sentiment, and hence of distress to B. In Smith's ethical system, a sense of stoic virtue requires A to 'lower his passion' to the 'pitch' at which B can sympathise (pp. 21–2); but, if A is in extreme pain, or suffering depression or dementia, this kind of self-awareness and self-control may be beyond him. So Smith need not be read as asserting that being sympathetic is a form of enjoyment.

Still, it is crucial that, for Smith, all correspondences of sentiment are pleasurable in themselves. The pleasures of mutual fellow-feeling can be enjoyed in any joint activity between people whose sentiments are suitably aligned. Smith gives an example of one person reading aloud to another, which will strike a chord with many parents (p. 14):

When we have read a book or poem so often that we can no longer find any amusement in reading it by ourselves, we can still take pleasure in reading it to a companion. To him it has all the graces of novelty; we enter into the surprise and admiration which it naturally excites in him, but which it is no longer capable of exciting in us; we consider all the ideas which it presents rather in the light in which they appear to him, than in that in which they appear to ourselves, and we are amused by sympathy with his amusement which thus enlivens our own. On the contrary, we should be vexed if he did not seem to be entertained with it, and we could no longer take any pleasure in reading it to him.

Pursuing this example, suppose that the listener is a child, the reader is a parent, the book is written for children, and the parent enjoyed the book himself when he was a child. We might think of the book's being read aloud as a stimulus that acts directly on parent and child. This stimulus impacts on the parent directly, just as it would if he were reading to himself, inducing a *direct* affective response – say, mild pleasure. In addition, the parent imaginatively attributes an affective response to the child, by imagining himself in the child's position. This *imaginative* response – say, excitement – may be different from his own direct response: this is perspective taking. By virtue of Smith's mechanism of fellow-feeling, the parent experiences this child's-eye excitement in a weakened form. But the reading of the book also induces a direct affective response in the child, which may be more or less similar to the one the parent has imagined. Interpreting the child's gestures, words and facial expressions, the parent becomes conscious of (what he takes to be) the child's actual response: this is the *perceived* response.

Smith's hypothesis about the affective qualities of correspondences of sentiment seems to apply to correspondences between any two of these three responses and, *a fortiori*, to correspondences between all three. Smith is particularly concerned with correspondences between imaginative and perceived responses because (for reasons I shall explain in section 5) he sees this type of correspondence as fundamental to the development of moral sentiments. But many of his examples suggest that there may also be positive affective qualities to correspondences between a person's direct responses to a stimulus and his perception of another person's responses to the same stimulus.

For example, Smith discusses the rule of etiquette that forbids visits by strangers and casual acquaintances to people who are suffering great family distress – say, as a result of a death. Smith's gloss on this rule is that it is difficult to achieve a correspondence of sentiments between a stranger and a bereaved person, and that this lack of correspondence would be a source of embarrassment and constraint to both (p. 146). Smith emphasises the dissonance that arises from the lack of intensity in the stranger's imaginative response, as a result of the weakness of the relations between the two. But suppose the would-be visitor, while completely unknown to the bereaved person, was a close friend of the person who has died. Then, I think, etiquette *would* permit the visit: the correspondence between the two people's direct responses to the death makes up for the initial weakness of their fellow-feeling.

As far as I know, the correspondence of sentiments mechanism postulated by Smith is not central to modern psychological theories of empathy. Of the psychological evidence bearing on Smith's hypothesis that I know of, the most significant concerns *comforting* behaviour. To explain this evidence, I must first take a step back.

One area of controversy in the literature on empathy focuses on the connection between sympathy in the sense of emotional contagion and sympathy as a motivation for apparently non-selfish behaviour. There is evidence, not only for human adults but also for human infants and for some non-human social mammals (including apes, monkeys and rats), that individuals not only are distressed by the distress of another individual of the same species but also will sometimes perform acts that, at some cost to themselves, relieve the other's distress. It is disputed whether the motivation for such acts is 'genuine' empathy, or merely aversion to the state of distress generated in the actor by emotional contagion.[5]

What I find most interesting in this controversy is the fact that acts of comforting are treated as paradigm cases of 'helping'. For example, one of the main forms of evidence of helping behaviour in human infants concerns cases in which the infant subject comforts an object (a child, an adult, a pet or a toy that is treated as a living thing) that is in apparent distress. Such comforting often involves simple gestures (hugging, stroking hurt places) that express sympathy. Another characteristic form is for the subject to offer one of his own possessions to the object. Often this possession is one that the subject uses to comfort himself (a favourite doll, a comfort blanket) and that, to him, has the character of a sympathetic living thing.[6]

One experiment that investigated comforting behaviour among infants accidentally revealed an additional phenomenon. When parents feigned distress in controlled tests of their children's capacity for empathy, family dogs often responded with canine equivalents of the infants' comforting behaviour.[7] Comforting behaviour is certainly not restricted to human beings. In chimpanzee societies, comforting is one of the most universal forms of interaction, taking forms that are remarkably similar to comforting among humans. For example, if one chimpanzee has been injured in a fight, other chimpanzees hug, pat and groom it. Another parallel between the two species is that, when a chimpanzee is distressed, it *demands* comforting from others – by pouting, whimpering or, if all else fails, throwing a temper tantrum.[8] Similar behaviour patterns are well known in young children; any self-aware adult will recognise that the urge to solicit comforting in distress does not disappear with age, even if we learn to suppress its most blatant expressions.

This evidence suggests that for human beings, and for at least some other social mammals, there is a deep-rooted desire to receive comfort when distressed, and an equally deep-rooted motivation to engage in comforting behaviour in response to other individuals' distress. This suggests that both sides of the comforting activity have positive affective qualities. (By this, I do not mean that comforting behaviour is an instrumentally rational response to psychological incentives. I mean that the positive affective qualities are the manifestation of the hard-wired

---

[5] This debate is reviewed by Elliott Sober and David Wilson (1998). Whether the question is meaningful is itself a matter of dispute. Sober and Wilson treat it as meaningful and consider how it might be resolved; Preston and de Waal (2002) argue that it is 'mistaken'.
[6] See Zahn-Waxler et al. (1992).
[7] See Zahn-Waxler, Hollenbeck and Radke-Yarrow (1984).
[8] See de Waal (1996, pp. 53–62).

motivation, just as the pleasures of sex are manifestations of a hard-wired motivation that is directed towards reproduction.)

But what *is* comforting behaviour? In many of its characteristic forms, the benefit to the object seems to be entirely *affective*: there is no 'objective' help. If there is a problem in explaining why individuals comfort others who are in distress, there is just as much a problem in explaining why those who are in distress want to be comforted.

Comforting behaviour, I suggest, typically has two affective components. Most obviously, it is a means by which the subject expresses an affective state of his own that in some way reflects the distress of the object: that is, it is a vehicle for the expression of fellow-feeling. At the same time, this expression calms the object's more direct and intense emotions by exhibiting an affective response to the object's distress that is less painful than the object's own, but that the object can take on through emotional contagion. (Think of the role of reassurance in comforting fear.) In each case, the core ingredient of comforting behaviour is a correspondence of sentiments between subject and object. The fact that humans and chimpanzees spontaneously engage in and solicit such behaviour is strongly suggestive of a fundamental desire for the correspondence of sentiments.

It is natural to ask what biological function is served by a desire for the correspondence of sentiments. De Waal (1996) suggests that correspondence between individuals' affective states is important for the stability of social organisation when – as is the case for social mammals – social life is a fragile combination of cooperation and competition. If individuals can be expelled from groups, an inability to align one's emotions with those of the rest of one's group is individually as well as socially disadvantageous. Thus, there is selection pressure in favour of traits that work to bring affective states into correspondence.

5.   Propriety and the mutual adaptation of sentiments

Although Smith, writing in the eighteenth century, could not use the language of natural selection, he explains the mechanisms of fellow-feeling and correspondence of sentiments in functional terms that are not far removed from those used by de Waal. Smith starts from the presupposition that the natural world is a work of design. Sometimes he invokes the idea of a benevolent deity who has given the world its laws of motion but who does not intervene in their operation; sometimes he speaks of 'Nature', and attributes to it (or to 'her') the 'two great purposes' of 'the support of the individual, and the propagation of the species'. He takes it as self-evident that the human species is social. This gives us reason to expect that, as human beings, we are naturally endowed with psychological dispositions that equip us to live in social groups. The human capacities for fellow-feeling and for taking pleasure in the correspondence of sentiments are interpreted as just such dispositions (Smith, 1976/1759, pp. 85–91).

For Smith, these dispositions are the natural building blocks from which morality is constructed. Morality is represented as a complex order that is an emergent property of the interactions of individuals who act on simpler motivations. Crucially, this is an order *of corresponding affective states.*

In Smith's analysis, the psychology of fellow-feeling and the correspondence of sentiments is tightly linked with that of approval and disapproval. His first formulation of the link between fellow-feeling and approval is that we approve of other people's sentiments just to the extent that we 'go along with' them (p. 16):

When the original passions of the person principally concerned are in perfect concord with the sympathetic emotions of the spectator, they necessarily appear to this last just and proper, and suitable to their objects... To approve of the passions of another, therefore, as suitable to their objects, is the same thing as to observe that we entirely sympathise with them.

In terms of the analysis I offered in section 4, Smith's concept of approval is correspondence between the affective response that a subject attributes to an object by virtue of imaginative fellow-feeling and the object's actual response, as perceived by the subject. He goes on to qualify this formulation by allowing that we can approve or disapprove of another person's sentiments by recognising that we are *capable of* going along with them, even if, because of the particular circumstances of the case, we do not actually do so; this is *conditional sympathy* (pp. 17–18).

Smith uses the term 'propriety' to refer to judgements of approval of sentiments based on fellow-feeling or conditional sympathy. In Smith's theory, moral sentiments are nothing more than norms of propriety: 'the general rules of morality ... are ultimately founded upon experience of what, in particular instances, our moral faculties, our natural sense of merit and propriety, approve, or disapprove of' (p. 159).[9]

---

[9] The reader may ask what Smith means by 'merit' here. For Smith, an action has propriety to the extent that the motivating sentiment of the actor is in proportion to the cause that has excited it. It has merit or demerit to the extent that it is deserving of reward or punishment (p. 18). But our sense of the merit of an action depends on our sympathy with the gratitude of those who are benefited by it; and our sense of its demerit depends on our sympathy with the resentment of those who are harmed by it (pp. 67–9). In effect, judgements of merit and demerit are judgements of propriety with respect to gratitude and resentment.

Propriety, as defined by Smith, clearly involves cognition and perspective taking. These elements receive greater emphasis in Smith's construction of the *impartial spectator*, which he uses to represent the concept of conscience. The viewpoint of the impartial spectator is the ideal standard of propriety. To take this viewpoint is to bring one's own sentiments into correspondence with what others can go along with (p. 83). Thus the impartial spectator is construed as feeling the whole range of natural sentiments, in just those proportions that people in general have fellow-feeling for. This takes us some distance away from *actual* fellow-feeling. But the basic ingredients from which we construct judgements of propriety are still affective states.

It is crucial for Smith's account of propriety that fellow-feeling, even in its idealised form, does not necessarily involve a subject's imaginatively taking on the perceived affective state of the object. Smith is not proposing, as some modern theorists have done,[10] a standard of ideal empathy in which the subject imaginatively takes on the actual preferences of the object, irrespective of their content. It is only because there can be dissonance between the subject's fellow-feeling for the object and his perception of the object's actual sentiments that disapproval is possible; and, without the possibility of disapproval, the concept of approval would be empty. This form of dissonance lies behind the laws of motion that, on Smith's account, operate in the domain of morality.

Smith represents the formation of morality as a *social* process in which the sentiments of different individuals are brought into alignment. Through interpersonal interaction, each person becomes conscious of correspondences and dissonances between his own sentiments and those of others. Because of the tendency for correspondences of sentiments to induce pleasure and for dissonances to induce pain, we receive pleasure from the consciousness of approval and pain from the consciousness of disapproval.

The psychological mechanisms of approval and disapproval tend to induce norms of propriety of sentiment within any group of interacting people. Because we desire approval, we earn subjective rewards for changing our sentimental repertoires in ways that bring them into line with prevailing norms, and we incur subjective penalties for changes that deviate from those norms. These inducements lead us, consciously or unconsciously, to adapt our sentiments so as to align them with whatever norms of propriety are approved of by others. This social process – Smith

---

[10] I am thinking of the conceptions of empathy proposed by Harsanyi (1955) and Binmore (1994, 1998). In Sugden (2002) I contrast these conceptions with Smith's account of fellow-feeling.

calls it 'the great school of self-command' (p. 145) – imparts a tendency for people who live together in a society to develop similar affective responses to similar stimuli, and to subscribe to norms that give approval to those common responses.

It is an implication of this analysis that social interaction is essential for the development of the senses of propriety and of morality. People who live mostly in solitude, or who interact only with others who are predisposed to sympathise with them, do not have enough opportunities to learn to align their sentiments with those of others (p. 153):

In solitude, we are apt to feel too strongly whatever relates to ourselves: we are apt to over-rate the good offices we may have done, and the injuries we may have suffered: we are apt to be too much elated by our own good, and too much dejected by our own bad fortune. The conversation of a friend brings us to a better, that of a stranger to still better temper.

Similarly, the mechanisms of approval and disapproval depend on social interaction. It is by constantly coming into contact with people who can express their approval or disapproval of our sentiments that we come to internalise norms of propriety (p. 127):

Very few men can be satisfied with their own private consciousness that they have attained those qualities, or performed those actions, which they admire and think praiseworthy in other people; unless it is, at the same time, generally acknowledged that they have actually obtained that praise which they think due both to the one and to the other.

There is undoubtedly some tension between Smith in the role of moralist, committed to the value of specific virtues (particularly benevolence, justice and self-command), and Smith in the role of social theorist, explaining the structural similarities we observe in moral norms across societies. Revealingly, one of the most opaque passages in *The Theory of Moral Sentiments* is a much-revised attempt to reconcile two apparently conflicting thoughts: the idea that a firm-minded moral agent, by taking the viewpoint of the impartial spectator, can withstand the unjustified censure of the society in which he lives, and the idea that each person's conception of the impartial spectator is constructed out of his own experience of approval and disapproval within his own society (pp. 128–30). If we are to treat Smith's theory as a starting point for understanding social order as it really is, we may have to recognise that interaction within a social group can generate and sustain norms that outsiders find morally repugnant. But, if Smith's fundamental analysis is correct, the ability of human beings to develop and maintain normative standards of any kind depends on their exposure to interpersonal relations.

6.   The intrinsic value of interpersonal relations

Smith's analysis of the correspondence of sentiments helps to explain how interpersonal relations can create value, independently of their contribution to the satisfaction of preferences in the standard sense of economics.

An example borrowed from Gui (2000a) provides a simple model. Gui uses the friendly atmosphere of a hairdresser's shop as an example of a relational good. In order to get a haircut, you have to spend some time at the hairdresser's shop, waiting to be served and then having the haircut itself. In terms of instrumental rationality, as conventionally construed, this time is merely a cost you incur to gain the benefit of tidy hair. But if you patronise the right kind of hairdresser, you spend that time in conversation with the hairdresser and with the other customers. At a traditional men's hairdresser's shop, conversation might range, apparently inconsequentially, over sport, current news items, television shows, local affairs, and so on. In contrast, imagine that robotics develops far enough to provide a substitute for human hairdressers. Instead of going to a hairdresser's shop, you sit alone in a booth, enter your credit card number and choose from a menu of haircuts. Would something be lost in the transition to this automated technology? Gui suggests the answer is 'yes'. Merely through interacting together, the hairdresser and the customers create some intangible good. In Gui's analysis, such relational goods are *produced* by the joint actions of individuals. But this prompts the question: what is the technology of production?

Smith's hypothesis implies that relational goods of the kind exemplified by the hairdresser's shop arise from a perceived correspondence of sentiments. Sociality creates added value when social interactions allow people to become conscious of fellow-feeling. On this account, the technology for producing relational goods must involve the identification, the expression and (in the longer term) the cultivation of corresponding sentiments. I suggest that this is exactly what we observe in situations such as at the hairdresser's shop, where transitory relations of friendship are formed between strangers or casual acquaintances.

Take the case of a conversation between two people. One of them begins by expressing commonplace sentiments of a kind that he is confident are shared by the other – perhaps comments on the weather. (Notice how much easier it is to begin a conversation when both people can be confident that they have some more significant sentiment in common. Think of strangers on a station platform who together hear the announcement that the train they are to travel on is to be delayed by several hours.) Different topics are gradually introduced into the conversation, exploiting connections with what has already been said, with the general aim of finding a topic on which the two partners have common opinions or beliefs. If a topic begins to provoke disagreement, it is dropped. Issues on which people are liable to have strong and opposed private feelings are avoided as conversational minefields: recall the familiar saying that religion, sex and politics (some people say religion, sex and money) should never be introduced into a conversation.

Similar tendencies can be seen in more substantial forms of sociality. One of the characteristic features of friendship is that friends engage in activities together. These are often activities that, on the face of it, might equally well be pursued individually – eating meals, watching films, taking walks, and so on. How is added value created by doing such things *together*? What I take to be Smith's answer, that this value arises from the consciousness of fellow-feeling, strikes me as convincing. For example, two hikers may gain pleasure from walking together – experiencing the same challenges, enjoying the same views, enduring the same discomforts – even though their apparent interaction is minimal. Friendships and family relationships are cultivated by finding activities that the partners in those relationships can enjoy together.

In fact, it is not necessary that the activities that are pursued together are *enjoyed*. Domestic chores, repetitive workplace tasks and coping with unforeseen problems are all activities that, although not intrinsically pleasant, seem to be made less burdensome by being done together by people who are conscious of their fellow-feeling. Notice that this fellow-feeling may be specific to the particular activity being pursued, or to the particular event being experienced: it does not depend on each participant's having a *general* altruistic concern for the others. For example, two motorists may have nothing in common except the fact that their cars have become stuck in the same snowdrift; but, if they work together to dig their cars out, they are likely to experience a pleasant sense of camaraderie.

On the much larger scale of war, it seems that this kind of fellow-feeling can maintain morale in many fearsome situations. Most reports from veterans of the trench warfare of the First World War express horror at the carnage but also an intensely positive feeling of comradeship with their fellow soldiers. In the Second World War, neither the Allied nor the German military commands made sufficient allowance for this factor, wrongly assuming that saturation bombing of enemy cities would induce a collapse in civilian morale. From the perspective of Smith's theory, there is no surprise in all this: wartime situations tend to generate the correspondence of strong emotions – fear, exhaustion, boredom, sympathy, aggression, hatred, hope, relief – among groups of people who are forced into close interpersonal relations.

This account of the technology by which relational goods are produced also explains one sense in which capital can be embedded in *networks* of recurrent interpersonal relations. If value is created through the expression of corresponding sentiments, then, within a group of interacting individuals, a shared knowledge of attitudes, beliefs and emotional repertoires is a valuable asset. So too is a shared stock of cues for affective responses, such as are common to people who live in the same locality, work in the same occupation, watch the same television soap or support the same football team. As these examples illustrate, this kind of relational capital can be distributed within a large population and accessed by individual members of that population when they engage in interpersonal relations with one another.

So far, I have discussed ways in which interpersonal relations can create value. However, there are relational bads as well as relational goods. According to Smith's theory, relational bads come about when interpersonal relations involve the expression of *dissonances* of sentiment. A disturbing example was recently reported in the British press. A young female paintshop worker at a car plant in north-east England won a legal claim against her former employers for unfair dismissal. She had been one of only two women in a workforce of 300. Her case was that her male workmates had spent their lunch breaks watching pornographic videos in the common rest area, and that she had felt forced to eat her lunches in a lavatory. Her complaint to her supervisors had been ignored; she alleged that this complaint was the reason for her dismissal.[11] As far as one can tell from the newspaper report, the male workers did not engage in any overt harassment; their offence, I take it, was their very public display of a correspondence of sentiments among themselves that they knew their female workmates could not enter into.

One general feature that emerges from the foregoing analysis is that the market is not necessarily antithetical to the supply of relational goods. The essential ingredients for the production of relational goods, I have argued, are fellow-feeling and the correspondence of sentiments. Altruism, in the sense of acting contrary to one's own interests for the good of others, need not be required. Gui's hairdresser's shop illustrates how interpersonal economic relations between the supplier of a good or service and his customers can generate relational goods. As Nancy Folbre and Julie Nelson (2000) have pointed out, reliance on the market for the supply of personal care services does not necessarily exclude the

---

[11] This case was reported in the *Independent* (2002).

affective component of *caring*. On my Smithian analysis, this component depends on correspondences of sentiment between the provider and the consumer of care; such correspondence is not made impossible by the existence of a payment mechanism. Similarly, interpersonal relations between paid employees in a work team are particularly conducive to correspondences of sentiment, because the tasks given to such workers require them to face common problems in pursuit of common goals.

In these examples, the value created by interpersonal relations is internal to a set of economic transactions, and so behaviour that tends to reproduce the institutional structures in which that value is generated is rewarded. If customers value friendly relations with those who supply them with personal services, suppliers of those services are rewarded for using delivery mechanisms that foster friendliness. If workers value the affective qualities of working in teams, employers are rewarded for using team structures in the workplace. Thus, relational goods are not necessarily exceptions to the general hypothesis that the market tends to supply us with the private goods and services that we want, provided we are willing and able to bear the costs of their being supplied to us.

However, relational goods might not be capable of being produced through the market if people consciously construe economic relations in a wholly instrumental way. For example, as Folbre and Nelson suggest, it may be important for the market in personal care services that care workers have a conception of their work as something that is linked to their sense of identity; perhaps they have to conceptualise their wages as an *acknowledgement* of the value of their work rather than as a payment in exchange for giving up control over their labour power.[12] Thus, excessively instrumental understandings of interpersonal relations may frustrate the production of relational goods. We need to be alert to the danger that some institutional frameworks – perhaps ones that are favoured by market competition – may promote such understandings as by-products.

7.   Interpersonal relations, norms and morality

An essential feature of Smith's analysis of the correspondence of sentiments is that, through recurrent interaction, the members of any given social group tend to converge on common affective responses to given stimuli and that, within the group, such responses – *any* such responses – come to be perceived as having normative status. The normative significance of correspondences of sentiment may help to

---

[12] This distinction is explored by Bruno Frey (1998).

explain why interpersonal relations are important for our sense of well-being.

On most plausible accounts of well-being, we derive subjective well-being from the sense that our lives are going well for us – that we are being reasonably successful in our pursuit of what we take to be worthwhile goals. But what gives us our sense that our goals *are* worthwhile? If, as Smith maintains, morality is founded on the correspondence of sentiments, then the answer must be: our perception of other people's approval. To the extent that interpersonal relations involve the expression of corresponding sentiments, they can act as homeostatic mechanisms, maintaining each person's sense of self-worth. Thus, for example, recurrent interactions among ambitious academics help to sustain each person's sense that the pursuit of academic ambition is worthwhile; recurrent interactions among parents of small children help to sustain the same sense about the sacrifices of parenthood.

Because recurrent interpersonal interactions tend to endow corresponding sentiments with normative status, such interactions can be important in maintaining practices of trust and reciprocity. Of course, we should not assume that face-to-face relations necessarily support just the kinds of norms that would be endorsed by liberal advocates of civic society. What Smith's analysis tells us is that interpersonal relations play an essential part in the emergence and reproduction of *norms in general*. The history of the last hundred years reveals all too many examples of illiberal norms that have proved capable of reproducing themselves through interpersonal interactions. These facts are consistent with the main structural properties of Smith's model, even if Smith was too optimistic to foresee them. But, without offering the delusion that spontaneous norms are always as we would wish them to be, I shall consider the role of interpersonal relations in reproducing norms of trust and reciprocity.

In a philosophical investigation of trust, Martin Hollis (1998) tries to explain social practices that, when widely followed within a population, work to everyone's overall benefit, but that in specific cases involve one person's bearing a cost (or choosing not to take a benefit) for the benefit of others. I shall call these *cooperative practices*. The supply of public goods through voluntary contributions is one class of such practices. Hollis considers the case of blood donation. In the United Kingdom, the blood needed for transfusions is supplied entirely through unpaid donations; all blood collected is treated as a national stock to be allocated according to medical need. Given this institutional structure, the stock of blood held nationally is a public good, supplied through voluntary contributions. We might also consider another large class of cooperative practices: *courtesies*. For example, consider the practice by which individuals who have lost their way in a city ask for, and are given, directions from passers-by. Or consider the practice by which, when traffic is heavy, drivers on main roads waive their right of priority to allow other drivers to enter the flow of traffic from minor roads. These courtesies are regularities of behaviour in situations that directly involve only a few individuals; these situations recur frequently within the population as a whole, but the particular combination of individuals involved in any one interaction may recur only rarely.

From the viewpoint of a theory of rational choice, cooperative practices have a puzzling combination of features. First, in each interaction an individual who is called on to incur a cost seems to have an immediate incentive to take a free ride on other people's compliance with the practice. Second, there is very little scope for reputation building or for reciprocity in the sense of far-sighted self-interest. In the case of the blood donors, even if there is a general tendency for potential donors to take account of one another's behaviour, the number of donors is so large that the action of any one individual has a negligible impact on the total amount of blood donated by others, and hence on the availability of blood in the event that the first person needs it. In the case of courtesies, even if one person's courtesy induces the beneficiary of that courtesy to be more courteous in subsequent interactions, almost all the benefits of this change in behaviour will accrue to third parties. Third, when an individual complies with a cooperative practice, the immediate benefits of his action often accrue to people with whom his personal contact is minimal or non-existent. This environment does not seem conducive to the development of imaginative sympathy between the person who complies and the people who benefit. Fourth, compliance with cooperative practices is far from universal. Only a minority of British people are blood donors; many people avoid eye contact and move on when they sense that someone is about to speak to them in a city street. Given the obviousness of the fact that so many people already free-ride, it seems implausible to suppose that an individual who complies with a cooperative practice imagines that his own free-riding will endanger the practice as a whole. To make matters worse, it is clear that, in following the practice, one is sometimes giving benefits to free-riders.

Hollis suggests that, when people follow a cooperative practice, they are motivated by reciprocity: in order for any one individual to be motivated to follow the practice, he has to have the confidence that enough others follow it too. In terms of human psychology, this surely rings true. Reciprocity is *generalised* in the sense that, if person A follows the practice in an interaction with person B, incurring a cost to provide a benefit for B, A does not need to know that B has provided a corresponding service for A in the past, or to have assurance that B will provide a corresponding service for A in the future. By the nature of these practices, such knowledge about the past and assurance about the future is unattainable. (If a stranger asks me for directions in central London, how can I tell whether he is the sort of person who would help me if our positions were reversed?) On Hollis's account, the confidence that A needs is confidence that A and B are fellow members of some social group, identified by some feature that has meaning for its members, and that, within this group, *enough* members follow the practice to warrant A's joining in. What is enough? Using the example of blood donors, Hollis says (1998, p. 147):

There is a logic of 'enough', I submit, which can overcome the dominance of defection, provided that a sense of membership is in play. Donors cooperate if confident that enough blood is being provided by enough members. Thus, public goods which depend on creative altruism are a matter both of a large enough total to secure the good and of enough contributors for mutual reassurance that contributing is a worthy activity. Enough is then enough.

This account of motivation involves a mixture of rational and affective elements. The rationality is that of 'team thinking', of acting as a member of a team. Each participant construes the practice as a *combination* of actions by different individuals, in which he performs *his part* alongside other participants who perform theirs. The rationality of the practice is to be understood in terms of the collective interests of the social group. In order for this kind of motivation to come into play, the individual needs to be able to conceptualise his own action as part of a collection of actions that, taken together, achieves something worthwhile. That, I take it, is the point of Hollis's clause about 'a large enough total to secure the good'. There is a developing literature in economics and philosophy that explores the logic of this form of rationality.[13]

In relation to the theme of this chapter, however, the affective components of Hollis's account of motivation are of more interest. There are two such components. First, there is what he calls the 'sense of membership' – the sense that individuals have of *identifying with* the collective as a unit of agency. A theory of team thinking as a form of rational choice may be able to represent the reasoning of individuals who already conceive of themselves as members of a team; but I do not see how the perception of *being* part of a team can be construed in terms of

---

[13] See, for example, Gilbert (1989), Bacharach (1993, 1999), Sugden (1993, 2000a) and Tuomela (1995).

rational choice.[14] Smith's theory of the correspondence of sentiments seems to offer a way of understanding how we can come to *feel* part of a collective.

The second affective component is what Hollis calls 'mutual reassurance'. In sustaining a motivation to act contrary to your own interest for the benefit of others, it is surely important to have the consciousness that other people share that motivation, and that they approve it in you. On Smith's analysis, mutual reassurance is a form of correspondence of sentiments. At British blood donor sessions, this correspondence is enhanced by the mutual presence of donors: donors have the consciousness of shared motivation and of incurring the minor discomforts of blood donation together. In the case of courtesies, the consciousness that being courteous is a worthwhile activity – that you are not just being taken advantage of – is sustained by observing other people performing similar courtesies, by receiving similar courtesies from others and by receiving what you perceive to be gratitude from the people you benefit. Notice that gratitude, like comforting, is essentially affective. Through conventional signals of gratitude and the acknowledgement of gratitude (the exchange of forms of words such as 'thank you' and 'that's all right', or the eye contact and hand waves used by road users), a brief correspondence of sentiments is induced; the positive quality of this correspondence is surely important in reproducing the motivation to be courteous. Conversely, it is significant that, when we choose *not* to follow a practice of courtesy, we try to avoid eye contact with the would-be beneficiary: we try to screen out the unease that would be induced by dissonances of sentiment.

I have been appealing to what I take to be common experience of what it feels like to engage in (and to refuse to engage in) cooperative practices; but there is solid evidence too. Controlled experiments in natural situations have shown that a person is more likely to participate in cooperative practices if he has recently seen someone else participate, and if, the last time he participated, he was thanked.[15] Studies of the characteristics of people who volunteer for organised cooperative and charitable activities show that *being asked* is one of the most robust determinants of volunteering. Although hardly surprising, this points to the role of correspondence of sentiments. When you have been asked to volunteer to take part in a cooperative practice – particularly when, as

---

[14] I defend this claim in Sugden (1993, 2000a).

[15] See the classic experiments of James Bryan and Mary Test (1967) and M. K. Moss and R. A. Page (1972), carried out in public places on subjects who did not know they were being studied.

is typically the case in social interactions among equals, the person who asks is already a participant – saying 'yes' induces an immediately pleasurable correspondence of sentiments and saying 'no' an uneasy dissonance. Interestingly, too, volunteering is positively correlated with many other forms of interpersonal interaction, including employment, membership of secular and religious organisations and entertaining friends at home. The direction of causation here is not clear, but one interpretation is that through interpersonal interaction we become more exposed to the forms of mutual reassurance that sustain cooperative practices.[16] There is also some evidence from laboratory experiments that people are more likely to engage in cooperative behaviour in situations that have been manipulated to induce a sense of common group membership among the potential cooperators. One such manipulation (known in social psychology as *common fate*) is to make the potential cooperators participants in a common lottery, so that their payoffs depend on the same random process. This manipulation can be interpreted as an attempt artificially to induce a correspondence of sentiments (compare my example of the passengers whose train has been delayed).[17]

The implication of all this is that cooperative practices depend on the prevalence of motivations of generalised reciprocity; and these motivations are at least partly sustained by correspondences of sentiment that are most effectively induced by interpersonal interaction. This conclusion points to another way in which capital can be embedded in networks of recurrent interpersonal relations. In this case, the affective value of interpersonal relations is not internal to specific transactions. For example, I have suggested that person A's help to person B, if observed by C, may strengthen C's motivation to help D. If this is so, the relational capital embedded in recurrent cooperative practices is, in part, a public good.

8.   Conclusions

I have proposed a way of thinking about the affective qualities of interpersonal relations. Viewed in relation to what is now the conventional methodology of economics, the approach I have proposed is unusual, in that it explicitly sets out to model people's affective states, and the ways

---

[16] See the research summarised by Robert Putnam (2000, pp. 118–22).

[17] A series of such experiments has been carried out by Marilyn Brewer and Roderick Kramer; see, for example, Brewer and Kramer (1986). It should be said that the experimentally observed effects of group identity on cooperation are relatively weak: see the discussion of these results by Kramer and Lisa Goldman (1995).

in which one person's affective state impacts on another's. Nevertheless, I have argued that this approach can help to explain how interpersonal relations can be sources of value – directly, through inducing correspondences of sentiment that are intrinsically pleasurable and that help to maintain people's sense of self-worth, and indirectly, by helping to sustain motivations of trust and reciprocity. How far these sources of value are tapped can depend on economic factors; these values can be important parts of employment contracts and of packages of services that are bought and sold on markets; and practices of trust and reciprocity may be preconditions for many economic transactions. On any plausible definition of the subject matter of economics, the value created in interpersonal relations is a matter of economic significance.

ACKNOWLEDGEMENTS

The ideas presented in this chapter have developed in discussions with many people, but I particularly acknowledge the contributions from Michael Bacharach, Nick Bardsley, Luigino Bruni, Jean Decety, Robert Gordon, Benedetto Gui, Shaun Hargreaves Heap, Paul Harris, Norbert Kerr, Shepley Orr, Stephanie Preston, Giacomo Rizzolatti, David Sally, Paul Seabright and Jung-Sic Yang. My work has been supported by the Leverhulme Trust.

4 Interpersonal interaction and economic theory: the case of public goods

Nicholas Bardsley

1. Introduction

Many important phenomena of interpersonal interaction are opaque to standard economic analysis. This is particularly clear regarding the decentralised provision of public goods.[1] I start with the standard model, discuss relevant evidence, then critically review the main alternatives. These all posit some form of non-selfish behaviour. Also, the accounts often propose some form of interrelatedness between individual agents in order to attenuate the crowding out prediction of the standard model. I argue that, to accommodate experimental data, models should be capable of predicting crowding *in*.[2] Consideration of non-economic approaches to explaining contributions indicates that progress might require investigating the importance of social context and/or a departure from methodological individualism. Attention ought also to be paid to distinguishing between the effects of moral motivation and conformism.

Real examples of the explanandum include donations by individuals to organisations that produce goods and services but either do not, or cannot, practise exclusion. This comprises cases such as the Royal National Lifeboat Institute (RNLI) in the United Kingdom, large-scale international voluntary organisations such as Friends of the Earth, the World Wide Fund for Nature (WWF) and Greenpeace, and cancer research organisations. Non-financial voluntary contributions comprise, *inter alia*, the voluntary recycling of household waste, voting and blood donation[3] where it is not remunerated.

---

[1] A good is termed 'public' if it is non-rival and non-excludable. Goods are non-rival if many people can consume them simultaneously and non-excludable if it is either impossible or impractical to prevent consumption (if someone does not pay). Examples are national defence and environmental cleaning.

[2] Crowding out is a negative correlation between each agent's contribution to the public good and contributions from other sources (other individuals, the government or whatever). Crowding in is a positive correlation.

[3] See Titmuss (1970) for a classic study of voluntary donations of blood.

These cases are of great practical, not just theoretical, importance. Though individuals typically give a tiny fraction of their income, in aggregate this generates significant economic activity. The Charities Aid Foundation (Saxon-Harrold and Kendall, 1995) reports the following statistics. In the United Kingdom in 1993 individuals donated around £1.6 billion to the 500 largest UK charities, around 50 per cent of the charities' total income, with around 80 per cent of the population contributing. In addition, some 1.4 to 2.4 million hours of labour were volunteered. The sector as a whole constituted between 1 and 5 per cent of GDP on available estimates.

2.   The theory of the voluntary provision of pure public goods

For a formal treatment of the theory, see Theodore Bergstrom, Lawerence Blume and Hal Varian (1986) or Richard Cornes and Todd Sandler (1986). The theory is based on three central assumptions: one about individuals' decision problems, one about their motivation and one about how individuals interact. These assumptions are that income is spent either on private consumption or on a pure public good, that individuals are utility maximisers and that they take the actions of others as given, respectively. The first two assumptions mean that agents maximise a utility function of the form $U_i(x_i, z)$ where x_i is a private consumption good and z a public good.[4]

From these assumptions, which do not seem particularly strong, striking but false conclusions follow. First, there is the equilibrium prediction of the theory, which says that the quantity provided voluntarily will fall far short of the efficient level. Roughly, the amount provided should be what is in one person's self-interest to buy, namely the person most disposed to purchase the public good, if others did not contribute. If this amount is provided, no individual has an incentive to increase provision.[5]

The equilibrium prediction has long been seen as a key case for government intervention in the economy. It has become something of a stock proposition, explaining failures of voluntary collective action whilst raising a puzzle about successes – see, for example, any standard text on public economics (such as Stiglitz, 1988, ch. 5). Any *large-scale*

---

[4] Consumed equally by i and everyone else (because it is non-rival and non-excludable), hence the absence of a subscript for z.

[5] This is the equilibrium prediction in the absence of income effects. The more general theoretical prediction incorporates income effects, but these do not increase provision substantially.

voluntary provision, as in the examples already cited, is ruled out. In these cases the income of the organisation providing the good is huge in comparison to that of a typical contributor (see Sugden, 1982). This makes the actions of the latter impossible to rationalise according to the theory. For example, someone donating a small sum to a cancer research organisation, with an independent income several hundred times that of his own, would have to believe that spending the same sum on a private health product was less personally beneficial.[6]

The theory also has strikingly false comparative static predictions, which are instructive about the asociality of the standard microeconomic agent. Because others' behaviour matters to that agent only as a determinant of the opportunity set, individuals' contributions come to be related as perfect substitutes. Each agent would be so acutely sensitive to others' behaviour that contributions crowd each other out virtually penny for penny.[7] This implies that it makes no difference to the equilibrium quantity of the public good how many agents make a contribution. So it ought to make no difference to that quantity if ten, one hundred or even ten thousand people make contributions (see Sugden, 1982, or Andreoni, 1988a). This implies, further, that government provision will be ineffective until individuals' donations are completely crowded out. Combining the equilibrium and crowding out predictions, there is no scope in theory for voluntary cooperation between the government and private sector in the provision of public goods. If individuals contribute, efficiency has not been achieved.

Unsurprisingly, empirical studies of donation reject the extreme crowding out prediction. Studies typically focus on the correlation between individuals' contributions and government grants, and usually find a negative correlation, but of a far weaker magnitude than the theory implies. The theory predicts a value of the correlation coefficient of approximately -1,[8] whilst studies by Richard Steinberg (1985), Burton Abrams and Mark Schmitz (1984) and Karl Heinz Paquè (1982) found

---

[6] It is possible to show within the theory that, with heterogeneous tastes and incomes, almost no one ought to contribute (Andreoni, 1988a).

[7] Imagine you are about to give £5 to a certain cause. As a rational agent, this means you rank the consequent state of affairs above any other you can bring about. Now, suppose another individual surprises you by giving £5 before you arrive (case 1). In terms of the states of affairs that then obtain, it is exactly as if you had given your donation and the other person had given £5 to you (case 2). If you would not donate all the extra income in case 2, you could not, consistently with this, give your £5 in case 1. The example is borrowed from Margolis (1982).

[8] For example, econometric analysis of charitable giving presented by David Collard (1978) and Robert Sugden (1982) implies within the model minimum values of the extent of crowding out of 96.8 per cent and 99.2 per cent, in the United States and United Kingdom, respectively.

coefficients of -0.005, -0.3 and between -0.06 and -0.35 respectively, for examples.[9]

The empirical picture regarding crowding out is complicated by some studies reporting a crowding *in* effect. A study by Jyoti Khanna, John Posnett and Todd Sandler (1995) finds such an effect between large donations, such as government grants and bequests, and individuals' donations, whilst Laura Connolly (1997) finds a dynamic crowding in effect in the case of internal and external funding of academic research, for instance.[10] At least one stylised fact from the field supports crowding in: fund-raisers typically see themselves as reliant on 'seed money' to set campaigns in motion, the possession of which is publicly announced beforehand. (Andreoni, 1998, cites references from fund-raising literature to the effect that seed money of between 20 per cent and 40 per cent of the target is regarded as a practical necessity.) There is also evidence of crowding in from field experiments in social psychology (Bryan and Test, 1967; Cialdini, Kallgren and Reno, 1991).[11]

One conclusion to be drawn is that it is not the case that individuals' behaviour is interrelated in public goods contexts as pictured in the standard theory. This conclusion is the external negation of this picture. It seems that agents are interrelated in some other way. Supportive experimental evidence is presented below.[12]

3. Evidence from public goods experiments

In laboratory public goods experiments, subjects are given a cash endowment, to be allocated between a public and a private account, as each individual chooses. The contributions to the public account generate a monetary public good. This environment is called the 'voluntary contribution mechanism' (VCM). In one extensively used version, the total contributed to the public account is multiplied up by some factor and the resulting sum distributed equally. This ensures cash payoffs (C) of the form

$$C_i = e - w_i + \frac{a \sum_{h=1}^{n} w_h}{n} \qquad (1)$$

---

[9] See also Clotfelter (1985).

[10] Steinberg (1991) considers some sources of discrepancies in empirical studies.

[11] Consider also that street musicians and waiters tend to 'salt' their collections to make it look as though many others have already contributed.

[12] The evidence covered in section 3 is also reviewed in Davis and Holt (1993) and Ledyard (1995).

where a is the multiplication factor, e a player's endowment, w_h his contribution and n is the number of players, with $n > a > 1$.[13] This determines a unique Nash equilibrium vector of zero contributions, both for a one-shot game and a finitely repeated game played with prior knowledge of the number of repetitions, but implies a Pareto optimal vector of maximum contributions to the public account. (This assumes that individuals care only about their personal cash payoff – that is, for all i, $U_i = U_i(C_i)$.)

The equilibrium prediction differs from that of section 2, in that non-contribution is now a dominant strategy – whereas earlier the prediction was *under*-provision. This is because there is only one commodity, money, in the experimental games. Consequently, these often induce straight indifference curves (as equation (1) does), enabling a much stronger prediction to be made. The dominant strategy equilibrium prediction implies there should be *no* relationship between one individual's behaviour and another's, or, indeed, between that behaviour and *any* parameter of the environment.

Robust results from VCM designs include the finding that the equilibrium prediction is false: subjects tend to make non-zero contributions, of 40 per cent to 60 per cent of the Pareto efficient level, both in one-shot VCM games and the early stages of finitely repeated games, though there is substantial free-riding (Dawes and Thaler, 1988). In repeated games, contributions usually diminish over time (Isaac, Walker and Thomas, 1984; Andreoni, 1988b; and Burlando and Hey, 1997, are some examples). Contributions are generally found to be sensitive to the ratio of benefits from the public account to the private account (the 'marginal per capita return' (MPCR)), which happens to be simply a/n in equation (1).

Some economists have interpreted contributions as errors. The point is that, if individuals have a dominant strategy of zero contribution, any errors necessarily result in over-contribution. Some recent experiments therefore investigate the effects of moving the Nash equilibrium, allowing errors to fall either side of the prediction. Some researchers find either aggregate contributions close to Nash when the equilibrium lies in the interior of [0, 100]% (Walker, Gardner and Ostrom, 1990; Ortmann, Hansberry and Fitzgerald, 1997), or significant *under*-contribution relative to a dominant strategy prediction when MPCR > 1, so that the

[13] In other, 'threshold', versions, a certain amount must be contributed to the public account for a public good to be provided. In threshold environments contribution is rationalisable – since one could believe that one's contribution will secure the threshold. I concentrate on the non-threshold designs because of the unambiguous free-riding prediction.

Nash equilibrium is a vector of 100 per cent contributions (Saijo and Nakamura, 1995; Palfrey and Prisbey, 1996). It is therefore tempting to suggest that the bulk of the data may be accounted for by errors plus selfishness on these grounds (Ledyard, 1995, is inclined to this view).

There is now a large amount of evidence from interior equilibrium VCMs. Recent papers by Martin Sefton and Richard Steinberg (1996) and Claudia Keser (1996) find significant 'over-contribution' (relative to the non-cooperative equilibrium) in the interior solution case, against the errors plus selfishness view. Jordi Brandts and Arthur Schram (2001) provide further evidence against it, finding different patterns of divergence from the Nash equilibrium for different values of MPCR. Mark Isaac and James Walker (1998) find that with low equilibria (relative to the choice space) contributions are systematically above the Nash equilibrium, whilst with high equilibria they are systematically biased below it. Moreover, in the high equilibria conditions no convergence to equilibrium was observed.

Perhaps these results taken together indicate a *centre of the scale bias*;[14] with two options available for token use, subjects are reluctant to use one option exclusively. This strikes me as a more elegant explanation than the alternative, that under-contribution when MPCR >1 shows 'spite' and over-contribution with MPCR <1 shows altruism, as posited by Tatsuyoshi Saijo and Hideki Nakamura (1995). Further, with contributions still sensitive to the MPCR and other factors, this kind of 'error' is clearly not the whole story and is consistent with an element of non-selfish behaviour.

That contributions decay with repetition has also been taken by many to indicate that subjects learn to be selfishly rational, and that many contributions are errors. It is crucial to notice, though, that inter-subject responsiveness is also capable of explaining decay. It may be that people are prepared to match others' donations, but reluctant to reward free-riding, and that there is not enough cooperation present to keep the system going. That contributions typically diminish over time is not necessarily, therefore, evidence of convergence to the Nash equilibrium. Two strands of results support this interpretation: evidence of crowding in, and eagerness to punish.

Regarding crowding in, Rachel Croson (1996) elicits beliefs about others' contributions using a system whereby subjects are paid for correct guesses, finding substantial positive correlation between a subject's contributions and both actual and expected contributions from others. Her study does not address the question of the direction of causation; it

---

[14] I owe this suggestion to Sugden.

may be behaviour that causes expectations, and not vice versa. Evidence that does bear on the direction of causation comes from experimenters who have deceived subjects to make 'others' behaviour' a controlled variable. Wim Liebrand, R. W. T. L. Jansen and V. M. Rijken (1986) and Liebrand, Henk Wilke, Rob Vogel and Fred Wolters (1986) use n-person prisoner's dilemma games, which have a similar incentive structure to public goods games. Reporting a high degree of cooperation from others reduced free-riding in games with rounds both before and after feedback. Joachim Weimann (1994) examines responsiveness to others' behaviour within rounds of a repeated-play VCM. In a sequential public goods game based on equation (1), it was found that contributions are lowered dramatically when subjects are shown very low levels of contribution from the other members, compared to a baseline condition with real (higher) contributions. However, showing very high contributions had, curiously, no effect relative to this baseline.[15] There is also a surfeit of evidence of direct reciprocity-like responsiveness in simpler experimental games with a sequential structure, such as the ultimatum and gift exchange games.[16]

Regarding punishment, there are now several repeated game studies allowing sanctions against free-riders. In experiments carried out by Ernst Fehr and Simon Gächter (2000) subjects could punish non-contributors at a cost to themselves. Free-riders were zealously punished and the outcome was near efficiency. Samuel Bowles, Jeffrey Carpenter and Herbert Gintis (2001) report similar results. Subsequent experiments by Olivier Bochet, Talbot Page and Louis Putterman (2002) and Martin Sefton, Robert Shupp and James Walker (2002) indicate that the dramatic efficiency-enhancing effect of punishment is not robust to changes in its cost. They do support, however, the findings that individuals like to punish free-riders even when this is costly. That is interesting since inflicting punishment is then itself a contribution to a public good. However, for the same reason, the result is not very informative about motivations for contribution (see below), and one should note that in many contexts, both laboratory and real, contributions are forthcoming without any punishment scheme. One can explain decay, though, without recourse to initial errors.

---

[15] Deception is generally proscribed by experimental economists, since it may pollute the subject pool. Bardsley (2000) has developed a method of controlling 'others' behaviour' that avoids deception, and finds results similar to Weimann's.

[16] See below. In a gift exchange game, a player has the choice of making a monetary gift to his partner, who then has the option of reciprocating. The experimenter usually multiplies the gifts up by some factor, ensuring that the Pareto optimum occurs through exchange, whilst the subgame perfect equilibrium involves no exchange. Substantial gifts are observed (Fehr and Gächter, 1998b).

A further suggestion of pro-social motivation is the 'restart effect' – a tendency noted by James Andreoni (1988b) and Robert Burlando and John Hey (1997) for subjects to give more following a restart of a multi-period VCM than they had done in the previous ('final') round. A restart effect was found in both 'partners' and 'strangers' settings – the former consisting of a group the composition of which remains constant during a repeated game, the latter a session in which the composition of the group changes between stages, so eliminating any possible strategic rationale for it. If contributions diminish as the game progresses because of learning, there should be no restart effect in a 'strangers' condition. At an intuitive level, the restart effect would appear to point towards theories of cooperation or reciprocity (discussed below) since it can be interpreted as giving people another chance or as attempts (collectively) to restart cooperation.

There is some evidence that manipulating 'group identity' affects contributions (see Brewer and Kramer, 1984, 1986, and, using binary choice 'social dilemma' games, Wit and Wilke, 1992).[17] The techniques employed include creating group identity, by grouping subjects into different VCM games on the basis of some prior, personality-engaging task, and using one that already exists, by grouping, say, arts students and science students in different games. Alternatively, games can be framed as involving intergroup rivalry, as with Gary Bornstein and Meyrav Ben-Yossef (1994) or Arthur Schram and Joep Sonnemans (1996). The results on the whole support the thesis that inducing a group identity improves cooperation.[18]

Finally, the datum that within-group, pre-play discussion substantially increases cooperation provides perhaps the most direct evidence from public goods experiments of the potential for social relationships, even of a transient and artificial nature, to guide behaviour (examples are Dawes, McTavish and Shaklee, 1977; Orbell, Dawes and Van de Kragt, 1988; and Isaac and Walker, 1988). The last even provides some evidence that discussion can reverse the usual decay effect. It is not clear how it works; the most pronounced effects are with unstructured, face-to-face communication, but in these conditions many factors may be at work simultaneously (Ledyard, 1995, p. 129). The two leading hypotheses are that discussion creates group identity and that it enables the exchange of promises (an irrelevance in standard game theory). The impact of informal intra-group discussion, however, would appear to

---

[17] Richard Lalonde and Randy Silverman (1994) provide qualitative evidence to the same effect.
[18] For a supportive field study, see Tyler and DeGoey (1995).

be confined to public goods settings involving a small number of agents, and seems therefore of little relevance to the examples already cited from the field, though it may, of course, be important in a great many other real contexts. The potential importance of communication more generally is considered further on page 99.

Other results include a wide range of individual behaviour, with extreme degrees of cooperation and free-riding at the limits, and contributors tending to split their endowment between its two uses. A range of factors has been found to aid and inhibit contributions: subjects' experience has a negative effect, as does the heterogeneity of endowments and payoffs. The number of subjects also seems to increase contributions. It is often claimed that there are gender effects and subject pool effects, but the overall picture is rather unclear (see Ledyard, 1995).

To conclude, there are numerous factors at work in these experiments. Among them appears to be an element that is neither error nor selfishness. There is a set of effects indicative of pro-social behaviour, the significance of which would seem by no means confined to the laboratory, since they involve factors present in many real contexts. These include the MPCR effect,[19] the restart effect, *positive* correlation between contributions, and the responsiveness of cooperation to discussion and manipulations of group identity.

4.   Alternative accounts of contributor behaviour

There are many responses to the challenges raised by the data. No discussion is offered below, however, of 'reciprocal altruism', in the sense of Robert Axelrod (1984),[20] or other accounts of cooperation based on the repetition of a stage game (such as Kreps et al., 1982) in which, effectively, agents build a reputation for being cooperative. Such explanations of pro-social action seem unsuited to an n-player public good game. *In principle*, generalised versions of 'tit for tat' can work for any value of n. This just follows from the 'folk theorem' of the theory of repeated games. However, these notions are more at home *in practice* in the context of two-player interactions in which an uncooperative agent can be, first, identified and, second, punished by the other. In an n-player public good game, such as the real contexts or typical experimental games discussed above, neither of these conditions holds. There, it is not known who has or has not contributed. Even if this were known, it would not be possible to single out individual agents to be punished

[19] Indicating a trading off of pro-social against selfish behaviour.
[20] That is, cooperation that emerges because of the successfulness of a strategy that rewards cooperation and punishes defection.

through non-contribution because *that* punishment affects all agents equally. Starting from non-universal cooperation, one would therefore expect the punishing of free-riders to trigger punishment generally, leading to an almost immediate collapse of cooperation.[21]

Of the theories I consider below, some have been worked out as utility theories of public goods provision, and some are utility theories of non-selfish behaviour that should apply to public goods environments (these might both be classed as 'economic theories' and are set out in the first four subsections below). The others are suggestions from other disciplines, such as social psychology and philosophy, that have not been worked up into testable theories at all (the next three subsections). There is reason to believe the latter to be inconsistent with utility theory, for reasons given below, and so no attempt is made to 'formalise' them, in the sense of turning them into utility theories. The subsections are organised according to the motivation represented, though there is some overlap, particularly with altruism and selective incentives models.

Rational choice altruism

In the model of section 2, individuals do not care about others' enjoyment of the public good. An obvious ploy, then, is to modify the maximand by having individuals derive utility not merely from their own consumption but also from others' consumption of the public good. Since, for a set of altruists, a welfare improvement for one individual also augments everyone else's utility, there is a potential problem of altruism generating more public goods problems. It is possible to curtail this by defining welfare in terms of utility from the consumption of goods only, which I notate as u functions below, rather than 'inclusive' utility functions that represent altruists' concern for others' consumption (notated 'U'). An account that does this explicitly is proposed by John Elster (1989).[22]

Elster proposes that altruists' utility is a weighted average of public and private consumption (this is put forward as but one ingredient of a cocktail of public goods motivations). This can be represented as

$$U_i = u_i(x_i, z) + \sum_{j \neq i}^{n} \omega_{ij} u_j(x_j, z)$$

---

[21] For a fuller statement of these doubts, see Sugden (1986, chs. 6 and 7).

[22] The choice of Elster is rather arbitrary, in the sense that there are several models of this form in the literature. Ley (1997, p. 24) discusses the alternative way of representing altruism, with interdependent inclusive utility functions, concluding that acceptable formulations should reduce to a set of equations of the form in the text.

where $\omega_{ij} > 0$ for all j. The special case where the weights are unitary is a kind of utilitarianism.[23]

Selective incentives

Another class of economic models can be seen as extending the argument of Mancur Olson's (1965) treatise *The Logic of Collective Action*. Olson proposes that adequate voluntary provision is possible only in the presence of jointly supplied private goods ('selective incentives'). Such cases comprise state provision, where the incentive is the punishment of non-contributors, provision within small groups, where social sanctions can be effective, and cases such as trade unions, which allegedly secure support by providing members private consumption goods (such as cheap insurance and legal advice) in joint supply with their other activities. This account, then, attaches a private benefit to an act of contribution to the public good; assumption 1 of the standard model is modified.

Cornes and Sandler (1984, 1986) effectively provide a modern formalisation of Olson's reasoning about selective incentives, in which individuals allocate their income between two uses (first, expenditure on a pure private good (x), and, second, expenditure on a commodity (q)), which jointly provides a public characteristic (z) and a private characteristic (c). (A good example would appear to be national lottery tickets, a percentage of the revenue from which is given to charities and other bodies serving the public interest.) Utility then is a function of x, βq, γq and v, where β and γ determine how much of the private and public characteristics, respectively, the purchase of a unit of q generates, and v denotes others' provision of the public characteristic.

The individual's utility function is given by $U_i(x_i, c_i, z)$, a standard, well-behaved utility function exhibiting diminishing (positive) marginal utility in all three arguments. Given the source of x and the public characteristic, this can be written as

$$U_i = U_i(x_i, \beta_i q_i, \gamma_i q_i + v_i)$$

The novel point is that, since $\partial MRS_{i_{cx}}/\partial z$ may be positive,[24] $\partial q_i/\partial v_i$ may be positive because of a positive substitution effect. This would mean that there is complementarity between c and z. Defence would appear to offer an example: if a neighbouring country had a higher military

---

[23] The thinking of Howard Margolis (1982) shares some features of rational choice altruism but falls into the class of warm glow theories, discussed in the next subsection. This is, effectively, conceded by Margolis (1982, appendix B).

[24] $MRS_{i_{cx}}$ denotes i's marginal rate of substitution between c and x.

capability, the threats from common enemies might be less, but the threat from one's neighbour could easily be worse, so the need for national defence could be greater overall.

The model can therefore generate upward-sloping reaction functions (q purchases of each individual that are best responses to the q purchase of the others) – that is, crowding in. It can be shown that the extent of free-riding diminishes as n increases, and, given eventual satiation in the public characteristic, voluntary provision need not be sub-optimal.

Andreoni (1990) provides a model that is a special case of the Cornes and Sandler framework, in which the private characteristic produced by a contribution is the 'warm glow' or pleasant sensation that results from it, and the public characteristic is the fractional increase in supply of the public good. The utility function takes the form (using our initial notation): $U_i(x_i, w_i, z)$ (p. 465). This is a special case of the Cornes and Sandler model where contributing jointly produces warm glow and z. The model therefore postulates benefits from the act of giving itself. This is therefore not a utility maximisation model in a standard sense, since the utility function is not defined over an ordering of consequences. Andreoni's model predicts crowding out, but less than the standard model.

Distributional theories

Another pair of models attempts to capture egalitarianism. The exponents are Gary Bolton and Axel Ockenfels (1998, 2000) and Ernst Fehr and Klaus Schmidt (1999). These accounts have been formulated primarily with experimental evidence in mind, both from public goods games and other games such as ultimatum and dictator games, which seem to provide evidence of concern for the distribution of benefits between experimental subjects.

In a dictator game, a subject has to decide how to divide a sum of money between self and another subject; for a cash maximiser there is a dominant strategy to keep everything, whilst subjects often leave something to their partner. In the ultimatum game, after an initial division is proposed (in the same manner as for the dictator game), the second player has the option to accept the division (in which case the money is divided accordingly) or reject it (in which case neither player receives anything). Here, the responder has a dominant strategy of accepting *any* offer, whilst significant positive rejection rates are recorded for offers of substantially less than half the sum. Both these decisions can be rationalised as means of avoiding very unequal outcomes.

In Bolton and Ockenfels's formulation,[25]

$$U_i = U_i \left[u_i, \frac{u_i}{\dfrac{1}{n} \displaystyle\sum_{j=1}^{n} u_j} \right]$$

That is, an individual cares about his own welfare and the ratio of this to mean welfare (his 'reference share'). For a given u_i, U_i is maximised when this constitutes a mean share – that is, when the reference share has a value of 1.

In Fehr and Schmidt's version,

$$U_i = u_i + \frac{\psi_i \displaystyle\sum_{j \neq i}^{n} \max(u_i - u_j, 0)}{n} + \frac{\zeta_i \displaystyle\sum_{j \neq i}^{n} \max(u_j - u_i, 0)}{n}$$

with $\zeta_i < \psi_i < 0$. Since the third term on the right-hand side of this equation represents disadvantageous inequality, this amounts to the proposition that agents care about their own welfare but dislike inequality between themselves and others, with disadvantageous inequality being worse than advantageous.

These models are capable of predicting reciprocity-like inter-contributor responsiveness without any actual concern for reciprocity – all agents care about is the distribution of payoffs; whereas, with reciprocity as defined below, it matters intrinsically how others' behaviour affects oneself.

Reciprocity theories

Reciprocity essentially involves doing as one is done by; a reciprocator benefits those who are helpful (positive reciprocity) and hurts those whose actions are harmful (negative reciprocity). There are two main approaches to modelling reciprocity: one offered by Sugden (1984) that models positive reciprocity (returning benefits), and one by Matthew Rabin (1993) (followed by Martin Dufwenberg and Georg Kirchsteiger, 1998). The latter approach models a concern for the beliefs behind others' actions, in the sense that it matters to an agent whether or not others believe they are conferring benefits. It also covers both positive and negative reciprocity (returning harms).

[25] The Fehr and Schmidt, and Bolton and Ockenfels, models are all actually stated as functions of cash payoffs, because of the experimental data they are primarily addressing.

In Sugden's theory, a model of positive reciprocity is proposed abandoning the utility maximisation postulate. Instead, people honour obligations to each other, conditional on other people honouring theirs, with obligations being defined relative to ideal levels of contribution. For any agent i, i's obligations are as follows: for any set of people G including i, the ideal level of contribution is what i would prefer everyone in G to make, himself included. If the other people contribute at least this amount, i is obliged to do so too, otherwise he is obliged only to reciprocate the minimum contribution in the set, with the proviso that i may be under an obligation to another set of agents, such as a subset of G. The ideal level for a set to contribute is located using i's (standard) utility function.

In equilibrium, everyone makes the smallest contribution compatible with their obligations to all groups. For example, in a typical public goods experiment, because of the induced preferences the level of contribution any agent would prefer all to make is maximum contribution. However, if one expects everyone to give half the endowment, one is obliged to do likewise, since this is the minimum contribution in the set. Now suppose instead you expect there to be one free-rider, whilst everyone else gives half their tokens. One can still be under an obligation to the other contributors, since, whilst one would prefer the set consisting of the contributors plus oneself to give maximally, if the public good is productive enough, the outcome is better when that set give half rather than nothing.

It is shown that the theory predicts under-supply of the public good, positive comparative static relationships between individuals' contributions and also that individuals will contribute to those public goods that benefit them personally (Sugden, 1984, pp. 781–4 and appendix). Sugden's model combines elements of expressive and collective rationality (see below). For individuals are acting on a moral belief that free-riding is wrong, whilst available actions are judged by the consequences of *everyone's* adopting them.

Rabin's (1993) approach to modelling reciprocity is a utility maximisation model with the proviso that beliefs may alter payoffs. It uses the framework of the *psychological game theory* of John Geanakoplos, David Pearce and Ennio Stacchetti (1989) and is extended to sequential games by Dufwenberg and Kirchsteiger (1998). In the simpler formalism of the latter,

$$U_i = u_i + R_i \sum_{j \neq i}^{n} (K_{ij} . K_{ji})$$

where R_i represents an individual's concern for reciprocity and K_{ij} and K_{ji} are i's kindness to j and j's kindness to i respectively. K_{ij} is defined as

$$K_{ij} = u_j - u_e$$

where u_e is a reference payoff used to judge the kindness of another's act. The most general form of Rabin's theory leaves the reference payoff unspecified. However, to use it one needs to impose a specific standard. Rabin (1993) proposes that

$$u_e = \frac{u_{max} + u_{min}}{2}$$

where u_{max} and u_{min} are the maximum and minimum material payoffs that the other player is capable of inflicting, and the components of the K functions are relative to players' beliefs about the strategies being played, and players' beliefs about each other's beliefs about those strategies. K_{ij} is thus defined relative to the strategy that i believes other agents (including j) are following. K_{ji} is defined similarly but depends on i's beliefs about what strategies j believes the other agents, including i, are playing. In equilibrium, the agents maximise utility, acting on 'consistent' first- and second-order beliefs: beliefs about (the others' beliefs about) the strategies played must be correct.

Rabin's model supports cooperation as an equilibrium in prisoner's dilemma games, and Dufwenberg and Kirchsteiger extend the analysis to sequential prisoner's dilemma games and ultimatum games. The basic prediction is, again, one of responsiveness in kind to others' behaviour.[26] It should be apparent that Rabin's is a very different model of reciprocity from Sugden's; intentions play an explicit role and behaviour can exhibit either positive or negative reciprocity. Other contrasts are that individuals are allowed to differ over the degree to which they care about reciprocity, and trade off this concern against material incentives.

Expressive rationality

'Expressive' rationality is usually contrasted with *instrumental* rationality – that is, action that is rational as a means to some end. This distinction was articulated originally by Max Weber (1956/1922), whose concept 'Wertrational' transliterates from German to 'value-rational'. A clear statement of what it amounts to is offered by Stanley Benn (1978a, p. 3): 'An action may be rational for a person regardless of its payoff if

---

[26] Armin Falk and Urs Fischbacher (1998) offer a further extension of the Rabin approach.

it expresses attitudes or principles that it would be inconsistent of him not to express under appropriate conditions, given the character which he is generally content to acknowledge as his own. This is what is known as being true to oneself.'

This is frequently coupled (as in Benn, 1978a, 1978b, or Hargreaves Heap, 1997) with a thesis of the social determination of appropriate expressive actions.[27] The significance of an action, or its connotation(s), does not on this view arise between the agent and it, but instead depends on the existence of a shared rule (standard or 'norm'). This is supposedly what makes *voting* an appropriate expression of political opinion, rather than singing political songs in the bath, for example, or heckling others as they turn out to vote. An influential source of argument for this social determination of meaning thesis is Ludwig Wittgenstein's celebrated 'private language argument' (Wittgenstein, 1953).

One reason for seeing expressive rationality as inconsistent with utility maximisation (*pace* Geoffrey Brennan and Loren Lomasky, 1985) is that it involves agents trying to realise an ideal self, or 'identity', thus placing themselves at a distance from some of their internal states (preferences or values) so as to affirm them or modify them (Hargreaves Heap et al., 1992, pp. 22–3). This requires a theory with more structure than standard rational choice theory (RCT) (Frankfurt, 1971; Sen, 1977).

Another reason for this incompatibility is simply that the agents are concerned with the meanings of their acts, not the consequences. This involves a different picture of interaction from the one that obtains in game theory, because, given the social determination thesis, there are *communal* constraints on actions. That is, there are constraints and opportunities imposed not through interaction with specific others but by the attitudes prevalent within a community. In standard game theory, in contrast, because of its consequentialism, the relevant attitudes are those of the specific people an agent is to interact with.

The relevance of expressive rationality to the public goods context is that contribution to a public good may be a statement of values – through contributing, an agent affirms pro-social attitudes, so contribution is rational independently of its consequences. The standard theory fails, its advocates would say, because it posits the wrong kind of connection between the internal states of the agent and the reasons for action.

---

[27] Francesca Cancian (1975) offers a view of social norms as rules mapping actions to character attributes, which is very amenable to the social determination of meaning thesis.

Collective rationality

Another approach to the issue involves a stark rejection of methodological individualism. In the model of section 2 the agents are atomistic, in the sense that their collective behaviour is an unintended by-product of individuals' maximising behaviour; in reality, there is no collective behaviour at all. The individuals behave essentially as they would in isolation, with the presence of other agents merely providing a different opportunity set. There is therefore no genuine sense of *participation*, of *joining in*. The alternative thesis is that a set of agents can somehow unite to become a group agent, in which the individuals act as parts of the whole.

The intended contrast between standard economic agents acting severally and collectively acting agents is nicely captured by Martin Hollis (1998, p. 68): 'When [someone] is trying to thread a needle, success does not depend on separate strategic choices by his right and left hands each deciding where best to position itself, after considering what the other will do, since all choices are [his own].' Agents acting collectively, then, are like members (or parts) of a single body, behaving as if moved by a common mind.

The relevance of this to the public goods scenario should be obvious. The socially desirable outcome occurs with widespread contribution, but when individuals act severally, not jointly, the predicted outcome is that of the equilibrium prediction. If this is a false prediction, perhaps the explanation is that people are acting jointly, not severally; the standard theory fails because it specifies the wrong unit of agency.

Conformism

An alternative reason why contributions do not crowd out may be conformism. If agents imitate each other's behaviour, this would lead to the kind of matching observed in experiments, supposedly indicative of either reciprocity or inequality aversion. Conformism is a central topic of social psychology, where the relevant literature is vast (Moscovici, 1985, is a useful review).[28] One recent social psychological approach that is interestingly close to a bounded-rationality account of conformism is offered by Robert Cialdini (1993, p. 95): 'We view a behaviour as correct in a given situation to the degree that we see others performing it.' The 'principle' is supposedly more powerful the more similar are the

---

[28] Stephen Jones (1984) offers a full-rationality economic model of conformism.

others performing the action to ourselves, and 'when we are unsure of ourselves, when the situation is unclear or ambiguous, when uncertainty reigns' (p. 106). With regard to its rationality, it is claimed that '[t]he evidence it offers about the way we should act is usually valid and valuable. With it we can cruise confidently through countless decisions without having to investigate the pros and cons of each' (p. 127).

This version of conformism shares with economists' 'information cascade' models[29] the feature that people treat the frequency of an action's performance as providing evidence of its rationality. It differs, however, in that the interpretation of 'correct', or rational, behaviour is left open, whereas in the former it is defined through utility theory. In cascade models, agents behave fully rationally by using others' actions to make inferences about the information dispersed within the population, about, typically, the quality of some good, using Bayesian updating of prior probabilities. This can lead to 'herd' behaviour in sequential contexts, since after a few agents have made a choice an individual's private information is outweighed by the information value of the preceding decisions. However, in a public good context it is difficult to find a suitable candidate for the dispersed information. So long as the agents are informed that the good is indeed public, information about quality is irrelevant, for, no matter how good it is, the free-rider problem ought to apply. Leaving the interpretation of rationality open might allow social proof, in contrast, to be relevant even here.

5.   Critique of the alternatives

Altruism

Some philosophers have been drawn to accounts of cooperation based on altruism, because it can rationalise contribution in consequentialist terms, despite the fact that donation has no apparent effects. Derek Parfit (1984, pp. 83–6), for example, espouses a version of rational choice altruism, arguing that, although an individual's contribution may have an imperceptible effect on the level of a public good, an imperceptible benefit multiplied across a large number of recipients can easily be quantitatively significant. Parfit is right: this move can resolve the theoretical problem of producing *enough* of the public good because now any incremental increase in the supply of the public good gives rise to benefits the multiplication of which across recipients is a concern of potential contributors.

---

[29] See Hirschleifer (1995) or Bikhchandani, Hirschleifer and Welch (1998) for examples.

However, altruism is of no help with the false comparative static predictions, since all that has happened in comparison to the model in section 2 is that the public good has become more productive. Individuals' contributions are still related as perfect substitutes implying full crowding out. This is, from the field data, false in itself and implies a false pattern of contributions.[30] Moreover, altruism is impossible to reconcile with the experimental data because it is an *unconditional* behaviour, whilst the positive correlation between the contributions and expected contributions of others signals *conditional* cooperation.

Selective incentives

One question to raise about Cornes and Sandler's model is whether any tangible selective incentive is in fact provided by the public-good-producing organisations. Insistence on this amounts to an assertion that there are *no* pure public goods voluntarily supplied. At least some of the organisations of interest, for instance the WWF and Friends of the Earth, clearly *do* provide goods such as information and magazines to paid-up members.

On the one hand, though, where there *is* joint supply, one should ask why production of the selective incentive is not separable – for an organisation producing the same information as the WWF, for example, could produce it at lower cost, being unburdened by any public good production, and so be in a position to undercut them. On the other hand, there are many real-world cases, such as the RNLI and blood donation, for which there seems to be *no* material good jointly supplied with contribution. Moreover, impersonal collection methods are generally used, such as newspaper appeals and collection boxes which operate without any material quid pro quo. Other clear examples where a tangible selective incentive is absent are *all* the public goods experiments outlined above. For these reasons, the fundamental selective incentive, if there is one, would have to be that specified by Andreoni.

Warm glow theory circumvents the problem by postulating *psychological* income arising from the act of giving. Andreoni says the following about the nature of warm glow (1990, p. 1): '[S]ocial pressure, guilt, sympathy, or simply a desire for a "warm glow" may play important roles in the decisions of agents.' Social pressure, if instrumental in securing public good provision, is itself a public good, and in any case is unlikely to be effective where agents can refrain from giving

[30] See footnote 7.

undetected. Sympathy would presumably count as sympathetic consumption and so enter into an Elster-type model. Guilt avoidance and warm glow seeking may be seen as equivalents, and it is clear from one of the title quotations (an American Red Cross advert announcing 'Feel good about yourself – give blood!') and Andreoni's own title ('A theory of warm glow giving') that these are the principal concerns of the model.

Recall that in this model $U_i = U_i(x_i, w_i, z)$. The contribution motive, then, is a mixture of outcome orientation and warm glow. Andreoni posits that there should still be a *negative* relationship between individuals' contributions, but one could posit a Cornes-and-Sandler-type complementarity. There are interpretational problems, though, with the whole approach. Most damningly, there are grounds for arguing that warm glow *presupposes* the rationality of contribution. Benn (1978a, p. 8), in a discussion of the rationality of voting, states the basic case:

The point of a wertrational act, if not immediately evident, can be explained only by exhibiting it as an instance of some principle or ideal of conduct. In that sense, it is true, something done for its own sake may be done for the sake of something else: but it would be a caricature to say that it is done for the sake of the satisfaction of having done it. For there would often be no satisfaction either in doing it or having done it if the agent had no prior belief that it was worth doing apart from the satisfaction.

The standard public good model supplies Benn's 'no satisfaction without prior belief' premise. Without an account of why it is that warm glow adheres to contribution and not free-riding, it should be equally admissible to have as a premise that one can obtain warm glow only from free-riding. Moreover, we can give a reason why this might be so: the standard theory says that for most potential contributors only free-riding is rational. A free-rider might then derive self-satisfaction (feeling good about oneself) from reflecting on the fact that he has acted rationally, but as contributing is irrational no such satisfaction is available from donation. (Notice that Benn's point would still stand for the non-contributors; the warm glow would add nothing to our understanding of free-riding.)

If, as Andreoni's text indicates, warm glow arises from contribution because of people's moral beliefs that donation is either dutiful or good, this implies Benn's 'prior belief'. To deny this implication one would have to hold that the belief that donation is virtuous does not provide a reason for action. If this were the case one should have to ask why a (rational) agent should feel good about doing something he has no reason to do. In sum, if warm glow arises from reflecting on an act well done, then it must fall into the class of states that Elster (1983) calls 'essentially by-products'. The notion of an act well done implies that there were reasons for which it was done, so warm glow in this sense presupposes the rationality of making a contribution; it cannot found it.

This critique leaves open a non-hedonistic interpretation of Andreoni's model. One might say that people *just want to give*. However, this 'explanation' just amounts to a redescription of the facts the theory was designed to explain; we already know that in some sense people 'want' to contribute from the fact that they voluntarily and intentionally do so. The puzzle is *why* they want to, given the apparently compelling logic of the free-rider problem.

Distributional theories

The distributional theories and reciprocity theories have the advantage of some degree of experimental support. A concern for equity would explain giving in dictator games *and* the conditionality of one person's contribution on others' laboratory public good games. These theories are likely to attract those with strong attachments to orthodox utility theory since the only departure from the standard theory lies in the content of the utility functions.

Though capable of predicting positive correlations between contributions, they have the disadvantage in field contexts that they imply that it will be relatively well-off agents who contribute. This is because the only motive to contribute, in either version, is that one's own payoff is otherwise disproportionally large. Consider a person with less than average income, and consider income to be a proxy for consumption or utility. The agent has, effectively, to choose a value of u_i to maximise U_i. For a person with less than mean income, $\partial U_i/\partial u_i > 0$ in Bolton and Ockenfels's theory, since by increasing u_i one increases both one's own welfare and the reference share. And one free-rides to maximise u_i. Under Fehr and Schmidt's theory, such a person is experiencing disadvantageous inequality since, by hypothesis, there is greater disadvantageous inequality in total than advantageous, so again, $\partial U_i/\partial u_i > 0$. Perhaps these implications could be parried by reformulating inequality aversion so that the agents care only about inequalities within their own reference group (for example, social class).

As stated at present, though, this consideration should count heavily against them. It should be remembered, however, that these theories arose from a laboratory context. If they survive laboratory testing, questions may arise about the realism of the experimental public goods environment.

Reciprocity

Both reciprocity theories are consistent with crowding in. Also, they allow endowment splitting[31] and a degree of inter-subject variation in contributions. Rabin's reciprocity theory, formulated with laboratory data in mind, has an unfortunate implication though. Consider one agent, i. Suppose that i expects each other agent to contribute the amount that constitutes the reference standard, *whatever* level we choose for this, such that no one is being either kind or unkind to i. Then although every agent might be making a contribution and the public good might therefore be a worthwhile scheme for everyone, i would have no reason to make a contribution and would be happy to contribute nothing. This holds *regardless* of the value of his reciprocity parameter. Also, note that Rabin's theory is compatible only with the funding of a public good through small individual contributions if we set the reference standard at a very low level.

Sugden's reciprocity theory does better here. It attempts to model a contribution norm appropriate to a public good context starting from an intuition about what might be seen as morally defensible, whereas Rabin's model takes an exogenous norm for granted. As a result, Sugden's model is consistent with the funding of public goods by small contributions from a multitude without an arbitrary assumption about what is regarded as an acceptable contribution.

One problem for Sugden's approach is raised by Bardsley (2000) and Urs Fischbacher, Simon Gächter and Ernst Fehr (2001), who seem to find a self-serving bias in reciprocity. When contributions from others are *all* high, subjects who do reciprocate often return substantially less than the average contribution from others. Other shortcomings of the model include the fact, arguably, that it does not model *negative* reciprocity effects, whereas the Rabin approach does. The Rabin model therefore appears more general in scope; it can explain rejections of unequal splits in the ultimatum game, for example, that cannot be attributed to positive reciprocity. It *is* possible to rationalise punishment behaviour in public good experiments using either approach, however, though Rabin's is more direct for this. A Rabin reciprocator would punish a free-rider because he has been unkindly treated whilst a Sugden reciprocator would do it out of obligation to other punishers, provided punishment worked in securing public good provision and enough others were punishing.

---

[31] In Rabin's theory this requires a concave utility function – not the simple linear one assumed in the text.

Note, finally, that Rabin's model relies on a notion of kindness specified independently of social or moral norms. Failing to make a transfer is
an unkind action in the model, harming others regardless of property
rights. However, it is only in special settings where something of that
kind can be maintained. One such context is the typical laboratory
experiment, where endowments are handed out as 'manna from heaven'.
Property rights over such endowments might not be as keenly felt as
when the endowments are earned. In a real public good context, however, it would be a departure from the normal use of the word 'harm' to
say that a small contribution harms anyone. The model actually seems to
be describing behaviour specific to a narrow domain where a particular
set of norms apply. The same point can be made about the inequality
aversion theories. It indicates the existence of social factors that determine the domains of these theories. To understand the relevance of these
factors, and to identify the relevant domain, we need some insight into
these contextual factors. This may point to the need for a more social
model of agency.

Expressive rationality

Turning to expressive and collective rationality, these have the status of
radical suggestions, generally offered in reaction to RCT, rather than
either developed theories of behaviour or notions that readily yield
quantitative predictions in the style of the economic theories. Take the
former. The notion is especially useful for the voting case, since, presumably, a collective rationality theory could not justify the decision to
vote for a minor or 'crank' party that has no realistic chance of being
elected. It could also provide us with a better account of altruism than
that obtained by slotting other-regarding preferences into rational choice
theory, since it is a non-consequentialist notion and so likely to escape
the crowding out prediction of rational choice altruism. Hargreaves
Heap (1997) provides an argument for the proposition that one might
expect to find expressive behaviour in public goods contexts, drawing on
the social determination thesis outlined above. Social norms, it is
claimed, depend on 'instances of instantiation'; it is only if an action
cannot be rationalised in terms of personal preference satisfaction that it
can acquire a public meaning. Contributing to a public good cannot be
so rationalised.

It is also worth mentioning that, in the various accounts of public good
provision considered above, it is taken for granted that the technology
for the provision of the good exists. It is just there, in abstraction from

any human interactions that may have given rise to it. Typically, the technology is not context-free in this way – for example, fund-raisers *communicate* to potential donors; they *request* contributions. Not to contribute under these conditions is to *refuse a request*. This is so, perhaps, even if the technology is just a collection box with a message on it.

Refusing a request to do something is, arguably, an act with different connotations from merely not doing it. To take an example from a different context, not to help someone find their dropped contact lens if they do not ask for help may be construed as minding one's own business. One is not merely minding one's own business, though, if one is asked to help and does nothing, despite the fact that the 'consequences' may be the same in both cases. The importance of communication is a common observation from laboratory public goods experiments, but may extend beyond simply the example of *promising* – and, after all, the practical significance of promising for many real public goods is likely to be negligible because of the numbers of people involved. Discussion of this point seems to fall under expressive rationality; it has to do with the significance of an act.

However, as things stand, the notion of expressive rationality is likely to strike economists as predictively opaque since it has not been worked into a theory with distinctive behavioural implications. The theory could perhaps be developed operationally, via a theory of what it is that people generally wish to express.

Collective rationality

The notion of collective rationality as an explanation is likely to be anathema to many economists. If all it amounts to is the suggestion that people perform socially beneficial actions in response to the collective need for them, then it is tantamount to ignoring the existence of the free-rider problem. The Marxist theory of class mobilisation is often criticised on precisely these grounds (see Olson, 1965, or Scott, 1990, for example). However, there is more to the notion than that, because it is capable of yielding a different substantive picture of agency from that set out in rational choice theory; one that has implications for other game theoretic puzzles such as coordination games, and one that carries with it a distinct notion of common good. Sugden (1993) offers an account of 'team thinking' along these lines: agents acting as parts of teams take the existence of a team-optimal plan as a reason for action, with expectations about others' behaviour derived from their team membership rather than from strategic reasoning.

The basic idea is that agents adopt a distinctive 'we' mode of thinking; if subjects asked: 'What should *we* do?' in a VCM public goods experiment, a plausible answer is: 'We should invest our endowments in the public good.' Individuals who are 'thinking as a team' take this as a reason for action. In this crude form, then, the theory predicts that anyone thinking collectively will contribute maximally to the public good – a prediction violated by the fact that individuals tend to split their endowments between the private and public accounts. A more sophisticated version might incorporate partial compliance and punishment considerations, say, as part of the team-optimal plan. The strength of the notion is that it rationalises the successful play of 'impure' coordination games, which is difficult to rationalise fully in any other way.[32] Moreover, with regard to maximal contribution, it has been found that, after pre-play communication, the VCM is capable of producing outcomes close to efficiency (see section 3), and one explanation is that this communication gives rise to group identity.[33] Also, we noted that standard social psychological techniques for manipulating 'group identity' appear to influence behaviour in public goods experiments.

A more serious objection is that it involves a commitment to a strong notion of a group mind. A thorough investigation of this issue is beyond the scope of this chapter, but I submit that the real problems lie elsewhere, since it can be argued that all that would really be involved is a set of individuals acting in a fundamentally different way from how they do in game theory. Philosophers have proposed analyses of a distinctively collective type of behaviour, consistent with individualism concerning minds (Gilbert, 1989; Hurley, 1989; Searle, 1995).

Consider also that, without a notion of collective rationality on which individual people are capable of acting, it is hard to see why certain topics in rational choice theory have generated the interest that they have. I have in mind principally the one-shot, two-person prisoner's dilemma, originally attributed to A. W. Tucker, about which there is a large literature. Ken Binmore (1992, p. 310) speaks for many when he writes: 'Tucker could have had no notion of the enormous literature his invention of this simple "toy game" would spawn. However, for those

---

[32] An impure coordination game is one in which one equilibrium Pareto-dominates the other(s). Note that the hypothesis that agents perform pro-social actions is not capable of this feat, for it is only once the coordination game has been solved that a pro-social action can be identified.

[33] The other explanation is that agents are keeping promises. Margaret Gilbert's (1989) analysis, though, merges the two theses, because mutual exchanges of promises supposedly give rise to plural-subject agency.

who understand game theory, there is little that needs to be said.' In a sense this is correct, for if rationality consists in individual utility maximisation there is no *di*lemma at all; each player has *one* lemma to solve, which because of the symmetry of the game is exactly the same as the other player's. Moreover, because each has a dominant strategy, it is an extremely easy lemma to solve.

Binmore's comment should perhaps be rephrased, though, to begin 'for those who *believe* game theory'. If we wish to understand why the one-shot prisoner's dilemma has been seen as a dilemma by intelligent people, and a puzzling one at that, without an uncharitable dismissal of this as mere confusion, the notion of collective rationality is very helpful. For then both actions can be rationalised, one as individually, and the other as collectively rational, and between them there is a genuine conflict. The problem with the collective rationality account of cooperation, from the point of view of a rationalistic social science, is the point of view (group or individual) from which the conflict is to be resolved. That is, if there are two points of view and related modes of practical reasoning available to an agent, we need to know which one will (rationally) be adopted. Marilyn Brewer (1989) discusses the issue of the determination of the unit of agency from a non-rationalistic, social psychological perspective.

Conformism

One criticism of a conformism interpretation of contribution is that uninfluenced contribution is logically prior; conformism cannot be true of everyone since followers presuppose leaders. Granting this, however, conformism could still be an important effect in reality. From an empirical point of view, the problem is how to distinguish conformism from the motivations that predict crowding in.

Personally, I find it plausible that there is an element of conformism amongst the phenomena underlying contribution. The public good environment is just the type of setting where you might expect conformism, since it involves a large number of agents making a similar decision. The potential power of conformism is well known from the data on Solomon Asch's experiments (1951).[34] It would provide an alternative way of

---

[34] In the original experiment, subjects were asked to judge the relative length of two lines after hearing other subjects (stooges) pronounce judgement. Some one-third of the subjects conformed to erroneous stooge opinions despite the obviousness of the error, compared to universal correct judgement in free controls.

explaining the importance of 'seed money' in fund-raising, and the enthusiasm of telethons in constantly broadcasting the total raised, which would also apply in contexts where a reciprocity interpretation might not fit. One such context is the case in which one community provides a good for another – as in the case of famine relief. In such cases, it stretches the meaning of 'benefit' to say that contributors are reciprocating benefits to other donors, because in normal speech one would say that the people who benefit from the provision of the good are the recipients, not the donors.[35]

One way to deal with the empirical problem is to consider specific accounts of conformism. Take Cialdini's theory, according to which an action is perceived as appropriate to the extent that similar others perform it. This is conceptually distinct from theories based on moral motivations, because, in the latter, inter-subject similarity is simply not a relevant factor. This is a feature preserved in the economic models of moral motivation considered above. To operationalise this distinction one then needs a subsidiary hypothesis of inter-subject difference. A field experiment supportive of Cialdini's hypothesis was carried out by James Bryan and Mary Test (1967), which found that stooge contributions to Red Cross collectors were more effective in influencing others when the stooge was white than black, in a predominantly white area.

6.   Conclusions

I have argued that the least satisfactory approaches to understanding contribution are rational choice altruism and warm glow, the former because it does not escape the false predictions of the standard theory, the latter because it presupposes an unspecified motive for contribution and therefore predicts nothing new. Other alternatives tend to postulate some form of moral agency, and involve different ways in which behaviour is interrelated to that in the standard theory. The experimental data suggest that some form of pro-social motivation is indeed at work. The positive correlation between contributions counts further against an altruism interpretation but may favour a theory of reciprocity, inequality aversion or collective rationality. It could also conceivably point to a less rational conformism. One way forward would be to explore different accounts of inter-contributor responsiveness in public goods experiments – to see if, for example, it should really be read as morally motivated or

---

[35] Such cases raise problems for welfare economics. See Schwartz (1982).

conformist, and, if the former, reciprocal or inequality-averse. I have also urged that the theories proposed with laboratory data in mind are too crude; this is an argument for refining them.

Perhaps greater use could also be made of qualitative data such as questionnaires, in a direct attempt to unearth motivation. John Ledyard (1995) expresses the scepticism of many in his comment that in casual, post-experimental quizzing, subjects generally cannot account for their own behaviour (note 104, p. 179), but the argument is really a case for the more sophisticated use of questionnaire techniques. It should be remembered that much of the information that economists treat as hard data originates from incentiveless surveys. This includes data on consumer expenditure, for example, which is a key element of national income accounting.

To conclude, interpersonal interaction in public goods contexts is not easy to capture using a simple, tractable motivational assumption in the style of conventional economics. The suggestive behavioural regularities unearthed by experimentalists, though, should continue to tempt theorists to more sophisticated departures from standard theory. Personally, I find the ideas of expressive and collective rationality intuitively appealing, since they both concern procedural (rule-governed) aspects to behaviour whilst traditional modelling deals with consequentialist motivation. I finish with some observations that back this intuition.

First, consider again the emerging experimental literature on the punishment of free-riders. David Masclet, Charles Noussair, Steven Tucker and Marie-Claire Villeval (2003) report an experiment in which punishment does not lower the payoffs of free-riders; punishers merely allocate costless and ineffective 'disapproval points'. These were directed by subjects against free-riders, and, more surprisingly, appeared to have a positive impact on contributions despite their material ineffectiveness. If robust, the impact of harmless disapproval is highly consonant with the view that the expressive pitch of an action (here, free-riding) is socially determined. Next, consider that what evidence there is of crowding out tends to show the substitution of individuals' contributions by government grants, whilst crowding in has been observed (experimentally, at least) between individuals. Steinberg (1991) reports evidence of crowding in between central and local government. Could it be that the crowding out/in relationship breaks along social structural lines? In any case, the challenge for economists who find such ideas appealing is how to model them without resorting to ad hoc devices such as a taste for giving. Sugden (1984) is an inventive example, incorporating aspects of collective and expressive rationality, but modification is required to accommodate better the diversity of individual behaviour and perhaps an element of negative reciprocity.

ACKNOWLEDGEMENTS

I wish to acknowledge the helpful criticism from Robert Sugden, Chris Starmer and Robin Cubitt in connection with drafts of this material, which formed the opening chapter of my Ph.D. thesis submitted to the University of East Anglia.

5 Under trusting eyes: the responsive nature of trust

Vittorio Pelligra

> (Razumov) Have I by a single word, look, or gesture given him reason to suppose that I accepted his trust in me?
>
> Joseph Conrad (1998/1909, p. 45)

1. Introduction

In his *Under Western Eyes*, first published in 1909, Joseph Conrad tells the story of Razumov, a solitary but well-respected young student, and of his charismatic colleague Victor Victorovitch Haldin. While Razumov is considered by his fellow students as reserved but reliable, Haldin has been classified as restless and unstable even by the local authorities. Razumov has a good reputation: a man who is always willing to help others, even at personal cost. Knowing this, one day Haldin knocks desperately on his door. Razumov lets him in. Haldin looks distraught; he immediately confesses his secret to Razumov: it was he who was responsible, that morning, for the act of terrorism against the carriage of Mr de P., the feared and brutal president of the notorious 'repressive commission'. Razumov is horrified, first for the gravity of what has happened, but also because, knowing Haldin's secret, he too now is part of that tragic and dangerous conspiracy. Still shocked, he replies to Haldin's confession: 'But pardon me, Victor Victorovitch. We know each other so little... I don't see why you...' 'Trust,' replies Haldin. 'This word' – Conrad tells us – 'sealed Razumov's lips as if a hand had been clapped on his mouth. His brain seethed with arguments' (p. 5). These are brief excerpts from the novel's prologue; the rest of the story narrates the details of Razumov's reaction to having been so heavily trusted, his inner struggle and, finally, the consequences of his behaviour.

This story also introduces us to the so-called 'problem of trust', the main topic of this chapter. We develop a theoretical framework to reveal the reasons and feelings that such an episode probably elicited in Razumov, taking this episode as emblematic of a generic trusting relationship. How can we describe and analyse such a strategic interaction between a trustor (Haldin) and a trustee (Razumov)? What motivational process does Haldin's trust activate in Razumov? If we consider, together with John Stuart Mill, how trust 'penetrates into every crevice and cranny of human life' (1848, p. 131), it is not difficult to appreciate the relevance of these questions. And, in fact, the problem of trust has recently gained importance and centrality in many areas of the social sciences: economics (Dasgupta, 1988; Fehr and Gächter, 1998a; Harvey, 2002), sociology (Coleman, 1990; Misztal, 1996; Szompka, 1999), political science (Hardin, 2001; Braithwaite and Levi, 2002) and organisational sciences (Kramer and Tyler, 1995; Lane and Bachmann, 1998).

In the economic domain, trust is perceived as playing a crucial role in inter- and intra-organisational relationships, contract theory, labour economics, in the area of socio-economic development and in the huge literature focused on social capital, to quote only a few relevant fields.

Several explanations have been proposed to account for the 'trust phenomenon'. Here, in particular, I focus on game theoretical explanations. Many strategies have been developed, some more conservative, others more heterodox (see Pelligra, 2002), to account for trusting behaviours. Which of these strategies best explain the wider class of fiduciary relationships is eminently an empirical matter. Experimental data have recently been produced to test alternative theories. Evidence seems to support the principle of trust responsiveness as the most pristine explanation of trustful and trustworthy behaviour (Dufwenberg and Gneezy, 2000; Bacharach, Guerra and Zizzo, 2001; Pelligra, 2003, 2004). This chapter focuses in particular on the understanding of the hypothesis of trust responsiveness, its functioning, historical roots and philosophical foundations.

2.   'Telling a secret' formalised

Let us now describe in formal terms the interaction between Haldin and Razumov, by means of the game in extensive form, as depicted in figure 5.1a. Haldin first has the choice between telling Razumov his secret or keeping it to himself. If he decides to tell his secret, then Razumov will have the choice between remaining silent about it or telling the truth by reporting Haldin to the police, and eventually receiving a reward. The numbers represent, ordinally, the preferences of the two subjects. If Haldin says nothing to Razumov, we have a status quo (0,0). If he decides to share his secret and Razumov keeps it to himself, Haldin will be relieved by not bearing the weight of his act alone, and therefore better off with respect to the status quo, whereas Razumov will be in the status quo (1,0). But, if Razumov decides to opt for the reward,

(a) 'The telling-a-secret game'

(b) 'The basic trust game'

Figure 5.1. Two games.

then Haldin will be sent to prison and Razumov will end up richer (−100,10).

This interaction has three basic elements:

(i) *potential gain*: if the trustee fulfils the trustor's trust, the latter will end up better off;

(ii) *potential loss*: if the trustee is trusted and does not fulfil the trustor's trust, the latter will be worse off;

(iii) *temptation*: if the trustee is trusted, he will be materially better off by letting the trustor down.

In more general terms, the situation can be formalised as a 'basic trust game' (figure 5.1b), in which the first element is described by imposing $c > a$, the second $b < a$ and the third $e > f$. It must be noted, however, that the 'telling-a-secret game' represents a particular instance of the basic trust game, since it is characterised by the additional condition $d = f$. This condition, together with the others, describes what may be defined as a 'gratuitous trust game' (Pelligra, 2003), which formalises a situation in which the trustee's payoff from not having been trusted and the payoff from having repaid the trustor's trust are equal. The relationship between Razumov and Haldin is one in which the latter's trust is 'gratuitous' in the sense that the former's trustworthiness does not yield mutual gains.

The central question now is: how would a rational Razumov and a rational Haldin behave in such a situation? Game theory provides an answer through the so-called Zermelo's algorithm, which suggests to a rational Haldin to reason backwards before deciding: he should imagine what a rational Razumov would do if called upon to play, and then the consequences of their joint actions. Haldin's reasoning goes backwards as follows: 'If I tell him my secret, he will choose the reward (10) and I will be sent to prison, which is, from my viewpoint, the worst of all possible outcomes (−100). Therefore,' continues Haldin, 'in keeping my secret, if not 1, at least I can get 0, which is better than −100.' Thus, classical game theory suggests that player A should not play R (right), and at the same time that player B should play L (left).

But, if − contrary to this normative advice − we observe a pair of strategies such as (R,R) (i.e. share the secret, keep the secret), then common sense would say that A trusted B and B repaid his trust by behaving trustworthily.

Observationally, we define trustful and trustworthy behaviour as follows.

A strategy is *trustful* when:
(1) in a situation that can be modelled as a trust game;
(2) player A plays R.

Correspondingly, B's behaviour is *trustworthy* when:
(1) and (2) apply; and
(3) player B plays R.

Was, then, Haldin irrational by playing R? He himself explains his reasons to Razumov: it is not a matter of irrationality, but of *trust*.

On the empirical side, the prediction that emerges from the backward induction argument is often falsified by robust experimental findings (Camerer, 2003, ch. 2; Ostrom, 2003) that show that people are more trustful and trustworthy than theory would suggest. How can we theoretically account for these anomalous behaviours? Let us find some good reasons for Haldin to behave as he actually did.

3.   Tautologism

The most radical response to the divergence between theoretical prediction and observed behaviour implies the interpretation of the payoffs in the game as *ex post* indexes of players' preferences − that is, as utility in the theory of revealed preferences: we attach the highest index to the chosen action (Binmore, 1998). According to this view, having observed actual behaviour that seems to disconfirm the theory's predictions only means that we are considering an ill-specified game and that, consequently, it should be re-described to fit the data correctly. As already mentioned, this is a radical position that tends to 'throw the baby out with the bath water', in the sense that, while, on the one hand, it saves the empirical validity of the theory, on the other it dramatically impairs its practical applicability.

4.   Enlightened self-interest

A second, less radical though still conservative, reaction is based on the idea of *repetition of the interaction*. If the players know that there is a positive though small probability that there will be another round after that actually being played, they may be motivated to forgo an immediate gain in order to foster a long-standing and more remunerative relation. The main limitation of this theory is that most of the experimental evidence we have on trust has been produced using one-shot games, where long-term considerations do not apply.

Another explanatory strategy aims at developing models in which the players' utility functions contain some additional element to account for behavioural principles other than self-interest. In some models, these additional factors are introduced into an extended utility function that the players aim at maximising in the usual way. These models may be defined as 'forward-looking', since, in fact, players' actions are motivated only by their consequences. Other models develop new solution concepts based on an idea that an agent is actuated not only by the outcomes of his choices but also by the way such consequences are attained. These models may thus be defined as 'procedural'.

5.   Altruism

The first model I present was proposed to formalise the idea of altruism, which implies that the *ego*'s own welfare is directly affected by the *alter*'s welfare. In game theoretical terms, an altruist is defined as a subject whose utility increases (decreases) as the other's payoff increases (decreases). Since this assumption is still self-centred, the variations are weighted in a way that *ego* attributes more importance to his own payoff than to *alter*'s (Margolis, 1982). It is immediately clear that a subject who is sufficiently motivated by altruism would behave trustworthily in the trust game.

Was Haldin assuming that Razumov was an altruist?

6.   Inequity aversion

A second principle that has recently been incorporated in game theoretical models to explain non-selfish behaviour is that of inequity aversion (Fehr and Schmidt, 1999; Bolton and Ockenfels, 2000). An agent is considered inequity-averse when he aims both at maximising his payoff and minimising the difference between his own payoff and those of other agents. The basic idea is twofold: first, people dislike being part of an unequal distribution of wealth; second, in such unequal distributions they dislike being in the disadvantageous position even more than in the advantageous one. In a trust game, trustworthiness is consistent with player B being motivated by distributional concerns. Should we now ask: was Halding counting on Razumov's taste for equity when he decided to tell him his secret?

It is worth noting that the two previous models are based on a purely forward-looking logic, since player B is motivated exclusively by the consequences that his actions would produce and not at all by A's choice. A's trustful action, in fact, does not affect B's motivations. In this respect, all the other theories described from now on are basically different.

7.   Team thinking

The strategy underlying the two above theories was focused on a modification of the subject's preference orderings by means of some additional behavioural principle – although, in the end, agents continue to be *individually* instrumental as they aim at reaching their most *individually* preferred outcome. On the contrary, theories of team thinking (Sugden, 1993, 2000a; Bacharach, 1999) postulate a connection between preferences and action that is not only different from that usually assumed by the standard framework but also is by no means reducible to it. When an agent comes to perceive himself as a member of a team, his reasoning style switches to a mode that no longer responds to the question 'What should I do optimally to attain my goal?' but to 'What should I do to play my part in accomplishing the team's plan?' From this perspective, a team thinker is considered to be rational when he chooses actions that are part of the team's plan, whether they lead to optimal outcomes or not. For a team thinker, good outcomes are reasons for action by the team, but not reasons for action by individual agents; for individual agents, they are contingent consequences of good plans. Individual optimality is no longer a criterion by which to judge the rationality of a certain course of action.

While altruism and other theories affect the preference formation process, team thinking postulates a different way of satisfying the team's preferences.

Given this criterion of rationality, we can expect that, if in the trust game the two players A and B perceive themselves as belonging to the same group, and if we assume the team's goal to be to gain as much as possible, joint strategy R,R will be preferred to R,L or L. Should we, then, be induced to think that Haldin was considering Razumov as a member of his own team?

8.   The motivating power of expectations

Another strategy that may be followed to account for the trust phenomenon is based on the hypothesis that *alter*'s expectation of *ego*'s behaviour, in given circumstances, may have a motivating power that makes *ego* act in ways different from those suggested by mere material self-interest. Sugden (1998, 2000b) has developed a theoretical framework to analyse situations in which a norm determines the formation of subjects' expectations. Subjects' extended utility is broken down into two different parts: material and psychological. To fulfil or to frustrate *alter*'s expectations about *ego*'s choices causes an increase or a decrease in *ego*'s psychological utility. In Sugden's model, *alter*'s expectations come from the existence of a norm that generally applies to that given situation, and that gives rise to generalities of behaviour. Which norm has to be applied to any given situation is not established a priori, but it is inductively inferred by the agents from their past experiences.

The crucial assumption in this theory is the so-called 'resentment hypothesis'. 'Resentment' is a feeling 'which compounds disappointment at the frustration of one's expectations with anger and hostility directed at the person who is frustrating (or has frustrated) them'. Similarly, 'aversion' stands for an emotion that is the negative of desire, triggered by a sense of fear or unease about being the focus of another person's resentment (Sugden, 2000b, p. 113). It would not be difficult to show that the pair of trustful and trustworthy strategies constitutes an example of such an equilibrium. Did Haldin suspect that?

9.   Reciprocity

Theories of reciprocity incorporate the idea that an agent would be willing to sacrifice part of his material wealth in order to be kind to someone who has been kind, or is expected to be, kind to him and to punish anyone who has been, or is expected to be, unkind to him. This principle has been formalised in various ways. Here I focus on the well-known model of reciprocating fairness, proposed by Matthew Rabin (1993). In his model, payoffs depend not only on players' actions, as in the traditional theory, but also on players' intentions. Intentions can be formalised by considering not only what the players do but also what they could have chosen to do and did not. As a benchmark to assess the degree of kindness or unkindness incorporated in a given action, Rabin introduces the so-called equitable payoff: if player A expects player B to choose a strategy that leads A to a payoff larger than the equitable one, then B's expected choice is kind; otherwise it is unkind. If B expects A to choose a similarly kind action and A knows B's expectation and B knows A's expectation, both psychological utilities increase, and if, in this way, each player's overall utility (material and non-material) is maximised then there exists a *fairness equilibrium*, which allows two rational players to coordinate their action to reach, for example, the Pareto superior cooperative outcome in a prisoner's dilemma. The player's psychological utility crucially depends on the degree of perceived kindness in the way that A's being kind (unkind) to B when he expects A to be kind (unkind) positively contributes to both A's and B's utility; while mixed situations are a source of disutility. This type of reasoning implies that players form expectations not only about each other's actions but also about each other's expectations; these are called 'second-order expectations'.

Let us now consider a trust game[1] and presume that A expects B to play R, to be trustworthy. To be trustful is the only Pareto optimal strategy for A, so this choice conveys neither kindness nor unkindness to B. Let us now presume that B expects A to be trustful by playing R. Logically, replying trustworthily by playing R would be considered as kind, while playing the opportunistic strategy L would be considered as unkind. But, in Rabin's *fairness equilibrium*, we cannot have one player being kind and the other not. Therefore, although outcome R,R seems coherent with the *logic* of reciprocating fairness, it is not a *formal implication* of the model; it is not, in fact, a fairness equilibrium.

To apply Rabin's model to a trust game, the model must be amended in various respects. Some of these emendations have recently been suggested by Daniel Hausman (1998). In particular, he substitutes the value of the payoff deriving from the predicted Nash equilibrium to the equitable payoff.[2] The intuition behind this substitution is: 'If you

---

[1] Rabin's model applies only to normal-form games, so we should re-describe the trust game in normal form and consider the players playing simultaneously. This can be done without substantially modifying the underlying argument.

[2] Assuming that the game has a single equilibrium.

provide a benefit to me in playing your materially self-interested equilibrium strategy, then you are not being kind to me, and there is nothing unfair if I pursue my own material self-interest' (p. 10). Genuine kindness needs intentionality. In this way, the expectation of reciprocal behaviour may well be considered as the rationale for trustful and trustworthy behaviour in the trust game. Would Haldin agree?

10.   Trust responsiveness

While trust tends to appear at first glance as a candidly clear concept, its essential nature turns out to be rather elusive. One consequence is the proliferation of theoretical characterisations that the concept has received in past years. Trust has been defined as a *personality trait* (Baker, 1987; Jones, 1996), an eminently *probabilistic phenomenon* (Baier, 1986, 1994; Gambetta, 1988) or as a matter of *encapsulated interest* (Hardin, 1993, 2001). Among all these conceptions, however, the characterisation that best seems to account for the primary quality, the essential feature of the trust phenomenon, is the idea of trust as *responsive* behaviour (Horsburgh, 1960; Jussim, 1986; Pettit, 1995; Pelligra 2003).

The main idea of the responsive conception of trust is that trust is basically a matter of interpersonal relationships and that the relational factor should play a central part in its understanding. An act of trust takes place within an (often personalised) relationship between two subjects. It is extremely unlikely that a theory that considers the reasons to behave trustfully and trustworthily as external to that relationship will be able to give a satisfactory account of what trust is. Nevertheless, at least theories based on (enlightened) self-interest, altruism, inequity aversion and team thinking consider the reasons to be trustworthy as exogenous. This means that, at a given node of the interaction, whether or not *alter* decides to behave trustworthily does not depend on *ego*'s particular behaviour in previous nodes. A more satisfactory theory of trust should be able to account for the influences that *alter*'s observed choices exert on *ego*'s preferences and choices. In the trust responsiveness hypothesis, a trusting move induces trustworthiness through an endogenous modification of *ego*'s preference structure. A single act of genuine trust may provide *additional* reasons to behave trustworthily. The remainder of this chapter is devoted to exploring the main features of this hypothesis.

Assume two subjects, A and B: when A behaves trustfully, he overtly manifests his expectations about B's behaviour. The idea of trust responsiveness assumes that this manifestation induces in B a tendency to fulfil A's expectations, even at some material cost. In this respect, trust is said to be self-fulfilling. A similar process of inducement, defined as *therapeutic trust*, was first described by H. J. N. Horsburgh (1960), who claims that, in a situation similar to the trust game, '[O]ne of the reasons for [A's] willingness to risk the loss of his money is a belief that this may induce [B] to act more honourably than he originally intended' (p. 345). Therapeutic trust is also defined as 'reliance which aims at increasing the trustworthiness of the person in whom it is placed' (p. 346). A peculiar aspect of 'therapeutic trust' is its purposiveness, namely that it 'requires that the person trusted should be aware of the reasons for the trust which is placed in him' (p. 346) and that the trustful action explicitly aims at increasing the trustee's trustworthiness.

Other forms of 'responsive trust', less extreme or purposive, have been described in the philosophical literature. Philip Pettit (1995), for an explanation of the self-fulfilling nature of trust, has suggested the idea of *interactive reliance*. We observe interactive reliance when, relying on B, A thinks that his manifest reliance 'will strengthen or reinforce [B's] existing reasons to do that which [A] relies on him to do' (p. 206). This is because A believes that, once his reliance has been manifested, 'the utility [B] gets [from fulfilling A's] increases with the recognition that [doing so] will serve [A's] purposes' (p. 206).

The rationale of this process is to be found, according to Pettit, both in exogenous traits displayed by the trustee and in an endogenous process of belief formation. The first element is related to broadly conceived self-interested factors (i.e. individual taste for loyalty, virtue and prudence). The second element is more interesting, as it is based on an original desire for the good opinion of the others. However, in Pettit's interpretation this desire is not 'a trait that many will be proud to acknowledge in themselves... [I]t counts by most peoples' lights, not as a desirable feature for which they need to strive, but rather a disposition – a neutral or even shameful disposition – that it is hard to shed' (p. 203). The existence of this desire implies that, by manifesting his reliance, A implicitly manifests his belief that B is trustworthy; that belief represents for B a precious good that, however, can be enjoyed only by actually behaving trustworthily. The enjoyment derived from that good is nothing but the satisfaction deriving from having confirmed A's good opinion.

Despite the centrality of such an interactive process to the understanding of trust and of many other relational phenomena, as far as I know, apart from Pettit's proposal, it has received very little formal exploration.

At an intuitive level, many scholars emphasise the importance of something similar to trust responsiveness. Psychologist Jonathan Baron, for instance, suggests that '[f]ollowing the norm of trust has an effect

on both the beliefs and the norms of others. It creates a virtuous circle
. . . if we act as if we expect the best from the others, they will often
behave better as a result' (1998, p. 411). From the same psychological
perspective, Lee Jussim (1986) describes and analyses 'situations in
which one person's expectations about a second person lead the second
person to act in ways that confirm the first person's original expectation'
(p. 265).

Among economists, Partha Dasgupta (1988) notes how 'the mere fact
that someone has placed his trust in us makes us feel obligated, and this
makes it harder to betray that trust' (p. 54). Rabin himself suggests an
integration of his model to take account of the fact that, in a sequential
non-repeated game, if the first mover trusts the second, the latter may
feel motivated to behave fairly even if he has the last move. 'If player 1
plays "trust", rather than "split", he is showing he trusts player 2. If
player 2 feels kindly towards player 1 as a result of this trust, then he
might not grab all the profits' (1993, p. 1297). A similar hypothesis was
also advanced by David Good (1988), who claims: 'There are probably
many reasons why these relationships between trusting, being trustworthy, and psychological well-being exist, but the fact that trust at a
basic personal level is psychologically rewarding is unsurprising' (p. 33).

Surprisingly enough, despite having noted the phenomenon, most
social scientists and, notably, economists remain silent about its origin
and functioning. In the following sections I shall try to fill this gap.

11.   Relational motivation: the evolution of an idea

As we have seen, one of the most complete accounts of trustworthiness,
that provided by Pettit, is grounded on the agent's desire to be well
regarded by his peers. However, Pettit attaches to this desire, which he
calls a 'shameful disposition' (1995, p. 202), a negative moral status. My
position on this maintains, firstly, that – although crucial – this motive
should not be considered the ultimate source of motivation and, secondly, that having a desire for the good opinion of others should not
always be considered 'shameful'. This is because there is a wide range of
motives, going from vanity to the genuine desire of being praiseworthy,
and all these motives are, to different degrees, related to others' opinion.
We cannot fully understand trust responsiveness without exploring these
varieties.

In the following, I briefly explore the development of the idea of 'self-
love', broadly conceived as 'desire for the good opinion of others'. This
is necessary to create a context and to isolate the historical roots of
some of the elements that are crucial in explaining the mechanism of

trust responsiveness: in particular, that self-love is 'relational' and that self-love motivates us to be praiseworthy, not just eager for praise.

On the one hand, there is the position developed mainly by philosophers such as Thomas Hobbes and Bernard Mandeville, according to which the mere pursuit of self-love is necessarily a source of conflict; on the other hand, there are the champions of the idea of self-love as a source of love of others. There is also a third position, personified mainly by David Hume and Adam Smith, that aims at the reduction of this dichotomy through a purification of self-love's moral status. Here, I focus mainly on the latter. Aristotle's (see Aristotle, 1980) theory of sociality constitutes the starting point of Hume's and Smith's systems. Its pivotal element is the concept of *philautia* (literally, 'self-love'). *Philautia* is the source of *philia*, or friendship, which, in Aristotle's system, is the source of self-knowledge and self-consciousness. And it is by virtue of this mirroring process that, in a friendly relation, one has the opportunity to develop all one's virtues. According to Aristotle, therefore, self-love represents the bedrock of one's moral development and flourishing.

Hume's position (1978/1739, 2001/1751) goes explicitly against both cold cynicism (Hobbes) and candid optimism (Francis Hutcheson, 1971/1725), as he maintains that behaviour should be explained through a mix of coexisting self-interest and benevolence. His crucial assumption is that of an innate sense of sympathy that generates the basic human propensity to sociality. It is through sympathy that we assess whether our actions are 'useful' or 'pernicious' for others. This assessment is, in turn, the basis for establishing a sense of justice and honesty. This is why virtue is considered 'desirable on its own account, without fee and reward, merely for the immediate satisfaction which it conveys' (appendix 1, sect. 5). Man is generally moved by the desire for fame and reputation, a kind of desire that is not radically different from vanity. Here, Hume introduces a distinction, which was further clarified by Smith, between aiming at being praised and approved and aiming at being worthy of praise and approval. This shift is based on what Hume defines as the 'reverberating' or 'reflective' nature of sympathy (*Treatise*, book 2, part 2, sect. 5), a quality that implies that we aim at gaining our own approval at least as much as we desire to obtain others'. The reverberating nature of sympathy leads us to internalise other people's moral judgements and induces us to see ourselves as we appear to others, being pleased with our virtues and disliking our own vices, although they may be of great material benefit.

Smith builds his *Theory of Moral Sentiments* (1976/1759) around two main empirical assumptions. The first is that the most basic motive for social action is the desire to be loved and approved: 'There is a satisfaction in the consciousness of being beloved, which, to a person of delicacy and sensibility, is of more importance to happiness, than all the advantage which he can expect to derive from it' (part 3, chap. 2, sect. 1).

But vanity and self-love alone are not enough to explain the genesis of social sentiments; Smith needs a second assumption that refers to individuals' 'separateness'. We do not have direct experience of what others feel, but we have the natural ability of 'feeling with others' – that is, of imagining ourselves as the subject of others' experiences. To sympathise with others implies not to imagine what *I* would feel in a given situation but what the *subject* I am sympathising with would feel in that situation. This imaginative ability is the basis for our self-consciousness, produced by our natural inclination to view ourselves as others see us. Therefore, the ultimate consequence of reciprocal sympathy is that the subject becomes capable of self-reflection. The logic of self-evaluation develops through our imaginative process, which, fuelled by sympathy, leads us to imagine others' reactions and sentiments in a given situation. Through such exercise we first imagine what they feel and then decide whether or not we would conform to them, in that particular situation. Conformity of sentiment suggests 'approbation', the contrary 'disapprobation'. Once established, this ability for self-approbation and self-disapprobation is supplemented with a morally objective reference point that is provided by the 'man within', a 'cool and impartial spectator', who, according to the logic of sympathy, does not feel the agent's emotion and sentiments to the same degree as the agent does, so that a certain degree of detachment between the agent and the spectator is reached, to guarantee the required degree of objectivity.

At this point we have an agent who, because of his innate sociality and sentiment of sympathy, is naturally inclined to self-evaluation. The impartiality, although not the absolute objectivity, of his judgement is guaranteed by the action of the impartial spectator. Therefore, our actions turn out to be motivated by the desire for others' approbation, which we may represent to ourselves even in the physical absence of others. But what, at this stage, is the difference between the desire for praise and mere vanity? According to Smith's original view, we are moved by something more than vanity as we aspire not only to be praised but also, and more fundamentally, to be praiseworthy. 'Man naturally desires, not only to be loved, but to be lovely; or to be that thing which is the natural and proper object of love... He desires, not only praise, but praiseworthiness' (part 3, chap. 2, sect. 1).

What emerges from the previous discussion is the centrality of the desire for being loved and approved, as a primary, if not the only, source of motivation. We observe that at the end of this itinerary, from Aristotle's *philautia* to Smith's praiseworthiness, this concept emerges as morally purified from any residue of selfishness. According to Smith, this desire cannot be considered either selfish or self-centred, as it is based on the imaginative act of leaving one's self in order to enter others' contingencies. I think that it is precisely this imaginative leap that may be considered as the rationale for trustworthiness, as it is depicted in the trust responsiveness mechanism.

12.   Self-reflection and trustworthiness

A subject's ability with regard to self-reflection turns out to be the pivotal element in the functioning of the mechanism of trust responsiveness. This ability cannot be entirely generated internally, since it arises within the relationship in its mirroring function. The trust responsiveness hypothesis suggests that some of the reasons for being trustworthy derive from the mere fact of having been made an object of trust. In my interpretation, Smith's idea of self-reflection constitutes the starting point for providing a potential justification for that proposition.[3]

Consider two subjects, A and B; let them interact in a situation like the trust game. Subject A moves first and, according to game theory, he should end the game there by being prudently distrustful. Presume, instead, that he decides to opt for the trustful strategy. Now game theory tells us that B, with certainty, will behave opportunistically. Presume further that, contrary to such a prediction, he decides to play trustworthily. We would observe a pair of trustful and trustworthy strategies. How can we rationalise the reasoning process that motivates B to resist the temptation of an opportunistic move?

First, assume that B is interested in the material payoff and, second, that he is also interested in A's opinion. We know that subjects have an innate desire for the good opinion of others, and that they also have the ability, through imagination, of changing their point of view to that of others. Having observed A's move, although he may not know the real reason, B conjectures that A has an expectation of a trustworthy response. In other words, he knows that, because he played trustfully, A must think B is trustworthy. Now, B knows that A believes him to be

---

[3] It must be noted that Smith's argument is only the starting point for my tentative rationalisation of trustworthy behaviour. With respect to his original construction, I go somewhat further by assuming that the desire for being praised and the desire for being worthy of praise are two distinct, albeit related, sources of motivation, and although this is a philologically sound interpretation of Smith it is still disputed. Elsewhere (Pelligra, 2003), I have provided a more detailed justification for this interpretation.

trustworthy. B, then, has two options: to confirm that expectation by behaving trustworthily, or to let A down by being opportunistic. In thinking about such options, B considers two different orders of judgements: first, he tries to imagine A's reaction to both responses. Given his prior expectation, A will be satisfied with the former choice and frustrated by the latter. B knows that such reactions will have, respectively, a positive or a negative impact on A's opinion of him and consequently on his 'vanity'. That first order of judgements affects what we may understand as B's desire for praise. But there is also a second order of judgements, that of our own self-appraisal. Nature has, in fact, made us desire not only to be praised but to *deserve* praise. This is what makes us concerned about what an impartial and well-informed spectator may think and feel about what we are doing, irrespective of the reactions of the actual spectators. I suggest that this second-order judgement affects B's desire for praiseworthiness – that is, his self-esteem, and not his vanity, as in the previous case. At this point, then, B must balance the effect of the material gains and psychological losses attached to his available options: the material gain and the psychological loss from having been (materially) self-interested, or the material loss and psychological gain from having been trustworthy. What is important to note at this point is that the psychological impact has two distinct sources: it derives not only from the idea that A would form of B, following his actions, but also, and I think principally, from the idea that B himself would form of his own actions, as seen from the external standpoint of the *impartial spectator*.

The mechanism of self-evaluation works in two stages. In the first, the impartial spectator *determines* the balance between the actor's (B) interest as agent and that of the trustor (A). In the second, the impartial spectator *determines* B's conscience towards the action, according to what was determined in the first stage. This mechanism provides what may be termed *internal psychological reasons* for the action. At the same time, B perceives or imagines the kind of reaction that A may express towards B's action. These are the *external psychological reasons* for B's action. Thus, B is in relation with two subjects: the external spectator, trustor A, and the 'man within', Smith's impartial spectator, and he is influenced by the reactions of both.[4]

In this sense, B's action is determined by three orders of motives: first, his direct material interest; second, A's approbation or disapprobation; third, his own self-approbation or disapprobation as derived from the perspective of the impartial spectator.

[4] The former is real, the latter is only metaphorical.

This motivational structure is neither narrowly self-interested, because it takes into account A's interests, nor narrowly self-centred, because it is partially determined by B's expected reaction. That is, it is relational, because alongside the two self-centred and other-regarding motives there is also a third source of motivation – i.e. what derives from the internalised judgement of others, as described in the metaphor of the impartial spectator. According to this mechanism, our actions are assessed and determined by the consequences that they produce on us, both internally and externally. The *internal reasons* are those related to our sense of worth, the *external reasons* are those related to our vanity. These two sources of motivation account for the difference that exists between having a desire for conformity to others' expectations because of the fear of others' reactions and having the same desire because of intrinsic reasons related to one's own sense of worth. Trust responsiveness is based on both. And this composite nature is able to explain why, for instance, we often observe trustworthiness even in anonymous interactions – that is, when A's reaction cannot be observed directly. Consider, for instance, what happens when someone finds a lost wallet in a street and takes it to the nearest police station. Although this behaviour cannot be aimed at gaining praise from the owner of the wallet, it may be driven by a desire for praiseworthiness. In such a situation there is no room for vanity, but there is still room for the working of the *internal reasons*, which may, in fact, counterbalance the subject's material interest – that is, his desire to keep the wallet. In such a situation, B does not directly perceive A's reaction, but he may still be able to imagine it. By the same means, B may imagine A's reaction even before materially having done a certain action.

Thus, the actual choice is the compound effect of material self-interest, others' approbation or disapprobation and a personal sense of self-worthiness. Self-worthiness is a second-order construct, deriving from the good opinion of one's self, which the self, in turn, derives from the impartial spectator's approval.

13.   How trust responsiveness is different

Having considered in the previous sections several alternative theories of trust and trustworthiness and having described the basic elements of the trust responsiveness hypothesis, it is now natural to ask where the peculiarities of the latter theory lie, and how they render it different from the others.

As far as the theories of altruism and inequity aversion are concerned, the main divergence can be found in their being eminently forward-looking. In these theories, subjects aim at achieving their most preferred, although not narrowly self-interested, outcome. It is as if they were maximising a social welfare function. Agents are by no means responsive to others' behaviour, and their actions or preference orderings are unaffected by interactions with others.

If we consider theories of team thinking, we realise that they differ radically from trust responsiveness in the kind of rationality they imply. For a team thinker, a rational action finds its explanation in the fact that it is functional to the plan of the team. Thus, to play trustworthily in a trust game is rational only if we first assume that the outcome R,R is beneficial for the team, which is not always the case.[5] Within the framework designed by trust responsiveness, being trustworthy may be rational even though the agent, from a purely material perspective, would prefer the outcome to be achieved by opportunistic play L,L. Team thinkers are rational but, because of their team preferences, the two types of rationality cannot be compared.

Yet the idea of normative expectations differs from that of trust responsiveness in the sense that, while the trustee actually responds to the trustor's expectations, those expectations are grounded on a convention shared by the population as a whole. The trustee's behaviour does not depend on the character of the relationship in which he is interacting.

Lastly, the idea of reciprocity, as embodied in Rabin's model, is the most similar to that of trust responsiveness. Both reciprocity and trust responsiveness are principles of norm-guided behaviour. These norms, because of their effect on subjects' psychological utility, may, in certain conditions, offset the effect of the material payoff. Although both principles may lead subjects to act in ways that appear to be contrary to their material self-interest, they differ regarding the mechanism that elicits individuals' psychological utility. In Rabin's theory, the trustee's motivation is a response to the trustor's intentions, but in the sense that the trustee assumes the position of a judge, evaluating the trustor's action and deciding whether to reward or punish it. The trustee considers the trustor as forward-looking, infers his degree of altruism or selfishness from his intentions and then decides to react consequently. It is noteworthy that the degree of altruism or selfishness is inferred by comparing the outcome that the expected action will lead to with the equitable payoff. In this sense, therefore, the perceived kindness (unkindness) is

---

[5] The outcome R,R may well be mutually beneficial for subjects, but that is not a strict implication of the conditions defining a trust game. The 'gratuitous trust game', for example, is an instance of a trust game in which the cooperative outcome is beneficial for the trustor but not for the trustee.

a measure of material gain (loss). The idea of reciprocity is ultimately based on the *joint* effects of material and psychological incentives. The perceived kindness that elicits reciprocal behaviour is a measure of the material benefit that one agent's choice attributes to another. Instead, in trust responsiveness the potential material benefit plays no role in motivating the trustee.

Relative to Pettit's (1995) account, one of the differences between his trust mechanism and the idea of trust responsiveness is that Pettit grounds trustworthiness ultimately on 'a shameful disposition', self-love or vanity. Trust responsiveness, as I have described it, has two main sources of motivation. The first is the desire for the good opinion of others, or 'vanity', which maintains the negative moral flavour Pettit assigns to it, but there is also a second source of motivation, which derives from our sense of self-worth. Following Smith's *Theory of Moral Sentiments* in this, I think that the latter, 'the tribunal of [our] own consciences', must be considered as the ultimate 'judge and arbiter of [our] conduct'. It is perfectly understandable that we follow our own desire for praiseworthiness even when there is no possibility of being praised; it would be more problematic, at best pathological, if we were merely to follow others' praise with no respect for our own sense of worth.

14.   Trustworthiness as relational good

From the above, it emerges that the nature of trustworthiness is neither self-centred, because it is based on others' imagined reactions, nor completely other-regarding, because it is not based exclusively on others' opinion. I think the best way of describing the nature of trustworthiness is by using the term 'relational'. Trustworthiness comes about as a product of the action of self-reflection, which, in turn, arises from the *relation* with others – *others as a mirror of the self*. There then arises the similarity between such a conception of trustworthiness and the idea of 'relational good'.

A 'relational good' is, essentially, a kind of good that is produced and consumed within a specific relation. On the production side, this good emerges thanks to a technology that is embedded in 'encounters' (Gui, 2000a, chapter 2 in this book), in which the motivations of the inter-actors are considered the essential, although not unique, inputs in the production process. If we consider trust as a three-way relation – A trusts B to do C – trustworthiness can be manifested only within a relation. I cannot *reveal* that I am trustworthy if I am not trusted. Furthermore, trustworthiness, as the trust responsiveness hypothesis considers it, *emerges* because I have been trusted. While one may have a certain a priori degree of trustworthiness, it is in the trusting relation that trustworthiness is elicited. In this sense, trustworthiness is a genuine product of the trusting relation. Because it is grounded in our desire for self-approval, which in turn is based on our sense of sociality, trustworthiness can be neither produced nor enjoyed alone, in isolation from a trusting relation.[6] Trustworthiness, ontologically, needs to be externally recognised.

15.   Concluding remarks: what happened to Haldin?

This chapter has discussed the phenomenon of trust and some of the theories that have been developed to explain trustful and trustworthy behaviour. In particular, a novel explanatory principle is proposed, grounded on the relational nature of any trusting interaction. The hypothesis of trust responsiveness is unravelled in its philosophical and historical roots, functioning, and underlying psychological structure.

Our discussion began, however, with the story of Haldin and Razumov, to the point at which Razumov's trustworthiness was being tested. What happened next? Did Razumov turn out to be trustworthy, or did he betray Haldin? After having explored the cunning of trust, it would be interesting now to reread that story *under trusting eyes* and ask ourselves what we would have done in Razumov's place. Although it is impossible to provide a generally valid answer to the question, we may say that a genuine and somehow desperate act of trust such as Haldin's necessarily produces a sense of obligation to maintain the secret. Razumov's actual behaviour, however, emerges as the result of a balance between the material gain from having helped the notorious oppressive regime and the psychological losses due to his betrayal of a desperate friend. In Conrad's book, Razumov cannot foresee that cost and decides to report Haldin to the police. The rest of the novel tells us how Razumov spends the rest of his life repenting his untrustworthy behaviour. Through literary fiction, what emerges clearly is the nature of the psychological cost that most of us wish to avoid by being trustworthy when someone trusts us. The very essence of that cost derives from our

---

[6] We know that trustworthiness may arise from a process of self-valuation that is triggered by the relationship with others. At the centre of this process there is a desire for being praiseworthy and, therefore, for being pleased with oneself. It is interesting to note that the Italian word for 'to be pleased', *compiacere*, comes from the Latin *cum placere*, which may be translated as 'to be pleased *together*'. This provides etymological support for the idea that our own sense of worth emerges, at least partially, as a reflex of others' judgement.

own social nature, our own need for mutual recognition. Our identity is shaped in a social environment and we acquire a good amount of self-knowledge through the mirroring effect of others. I am not completely sure that '[a] man's real life' – as Conrad suggests – 'is that accorded to him in the thoughts of other men by reason of respect or natural love' (p. 21). However, what I hope I have shown is that, if economics aims at providing a descriptively adequate picture of economic interactions, we cannot avoid understanding concepts such as trust, and that trust cannot be fully understood if the role of our relational egos continues to be underestimated.

ACKNOWLEDGEMENTS

The ideas expressed here owe a great deal to constant and fruitful exchanges with Michael Bacharach, Luigino Bruni, Benedetto Gui, and especially Shaun Hargreaves Heap and Robert Sugden. This chapter would not have been as it is without their stimulating and attentive support. Philip Pettit provided useful comments on a previous version of the work. The usual attribution of responsibility applies.

6 Interpersonal relations and job satisfaction: some empirical results in social and community care services

Carlo Borzaga and Sara Depedri

1. Introduction

Involvement in a labour relation, like most things in economic life, can be viewed as a series of encounters (Gui, chapter 2 of this book) between entrepreneur and worker, worker and client, and among workers themselves. The relational environment resulting from these encounters is likely to influence workers' effort and their willingness to collaborate and exchange information useful for better performance. Hence, it can influence both the quantity and the quality of output. At the same time, the patterns and quality of relations affect the creation of relational goods, thus influencing the utility of the actors involved.

The obviousness of these statements notwithstanding, the economic analysis of labour relations largely overlooks the interpersonal side. This is true first of all for those theories that interpret the interaction between worker and firm exclusively in terms of market exchange and consider the wage to be the most powerful device for increasing the intensity of labour supply. The influence exerted by aspects of work activity other than wages, among which are included relational ones, is deemed to be of limited importance and unpredictable, owing to workers' heterogeneity.

The importance of interpersonal aspects in labour relations is underlined even by scholars who stress the importance of motivations to work and of other non-monetary factors. Instead of depicting the connection between wages and labour supply (in terms of hours or effort) as the result of individual utility maximisation, they focus on specific norms regulating group behaviour (Helper, Bendoly and Levine, 1999), on the emergence of trust between worker and firm (Akerlof, 1982) or else on the hypothesis that workers have altruistic feelings towards fellow employees (Rotemberg, 1994b). Relational aspects play some role in these models, but they are never considered to be important explanatory factors.

Nor do managerial studies take specific account of relational aspects. It is asserted that employee satisfaction and performance depend on the so-called 'organisational climate', which is only partially influenced by monetary compensation, and more so by social and symbolic elements such as recognition and intrinsic rewards (Herzberg, 1966). However, despite awareness that relations with and within firms help create the organisational climate, these are not made a specific object of study.

This is also the case for managerial approaches that investigate the dynamic nature of the relation between employees and organisations – for instance, psychological contract theory (Rousseau, 1995) or the theory of distributive and procedural justice. The same applies to the human resources management approach (O'Reilly and Pfeffer, 2000; Hammer, 1995), in that the relations between employees and organisations are viewed as instrumental.

Moreover, when relational aspects are taken into account, attention concentrates on the effects of the relational context on output and productivity, rather than on workers' well-being. In other words, relations within the firm are not considered valuable per se but only as a way to increase intrinsic motivations, and hence workers' effort and organisational performance (Frey, 1997). In these circumstances it is not surprising if empirical tests of the influence of relational aspects on workers' behaviour and satisfaction are rarely found in the literature (an exception being Sousa-Poza and Sousa-Poza, 2000).

For a better understanding of what happens between firms and workers we believe it necessary to analyse the role of relational goods from the workers' point of view, enquiring if and how they may represent a sort of remuneration. To this end it is useful to isolate the role of relations on the job from that of other kinds of non-monetary rewards.

In what follows we draw on a survey that offers information on relational contexts in organisations engaged in the provision of social services, doing so to study the impact of relations on two aspects of worker well-being: satisfaction and loyalty to the firm.

We start by presenting our hypotheses (section 2) and by describing the data set (section 3). We then look at the demand that workers express for relational goods (section 4), and enquire whether satisfaction is influenced by the relational aspects of the job (section 5). Then we highlight the existence of a trade-off between relational and other kinds of rewards (section 6). Finally, we test whether the enjoyment of relational goods influences workers' intentions to quit (section 7) and present our conclusions (section 8).

The analysis carried out is exploratory in character. Indeed, the data refer to a sample of workers operating in an industry where interpersonal relations and workers' commitment to the social mission of the firm are particularly strong. This characteristic of the data set, on the one hand, makes it easier to identify effects that otherwise might escape measurement; on the other hand, it demands that caution be exercised in interpreting the results as valid for the entire universe of the working population.

2.   On-the-job consumption of relational goods

As suggested by Gui (chapter 2), the relational environment can be seen as a source of the goods that workers consume in the workplace, where they spend a part of their lives (Demsetz, 1988). The benefits that workers derive from such goods can be seen either as an addition to the utility derived from other goods consumed on the job and off the job, or as a reduction in the disutility of work (Almond and Kendall, 2000). Whatever the case may be, the quality of the relational environment is one of the incentives that a firm can use to motivate workers. For simplicity, we next discuss the choice of the mix of just two incentives: the wage, as a proxy for off-the-job consumption; and relational goods, as a proxy for on-the-job consumption.

In general, for a worker, the two can be substituted for each other. However, it is reasonable to maintain that there is a threshold wage level below which a wage reduction cannot be compensated by an increase in relational goods, however large; and vice versa if the amount of relational goods is below its own threshold. Furthermore, it can be assumed that, if either component of the compensation package is below the threshold, a worker's utility is less than his reservation utility level, below which he is not willing to fill a job.

A graphical representation of such preferences is provided in figure 6.1. In areas A and B the level of one of the two goods is below the threshold. Above both thresholds (area C) the two goods become substitutable – so indifference curves are well behaved.[1]

Among the combinations of the two goods that ensure a worker a given level of utility, the firm that employs him is interested in offering the combination that minimises the cost of attaining this level. Firms having lower costs of providing relational goods will offer combinations with greater amount of these, and lower wages.

---

[1] These kinds of preferences can be represented analytically by a Stone–Geary utility function (Stone, 1954; Geary, 1950).

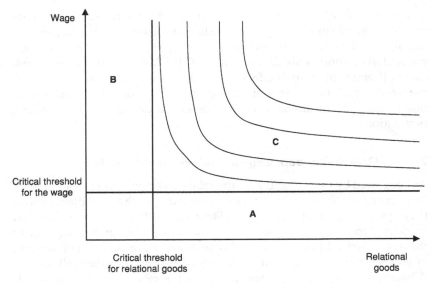

Figure 6.1. Preference for wages and relational goods.

If workers are also heterogeneous, those who give more weight to relational goods in their utility function will prefer to work just in such firms.

In the following sections we elaborate on the available data to determine whether these hypotheses are supported by empirical evidence. The data presented allow verification of how workers evaluate relational goods with respect to the wage and to other extrinsic aspects of their jobs. We test: (a) the existence of heterogeneity in worker preferences with respect to the consumption of relational goods; (b) the impact of the consumption of relational goods on workers' satisfaction; and (c) the hypothesis that substitution between wages and relational goods occurs only above thresholds.

3.   The data

The data derive from a survey conducted in Italy in 1998 on a sample of organisations delivering social services. Questionnaires were administered to 228 organisations, 266 managers, 2,066 paid workers and 724 volunteers (Borzaga, 2000).

The questions addressed to the workers were intended to gather information on, amongst other things, their attitudes, motivation and job satisfaction. Although acquiring data on relational aspects was not among the aims of the survey, the answers to some questions gave an insight into workers' relations with the organisation, their colleagues, their superiors and the users of services.

Fifty-four of the organisations surveyed were public, seventeen were for-profit and one hundred and fifty-seven were non-profit, further subdivided into social cooperatives, secular non-profit and religious non-profit (table 6.1). Most of them were of small size, and had both employees and volunteers.

Most of the 2,066 employees (table 6.2) were women, and belonged to the middle age group (more than two-thirds were aged between 30 and 49). More than one-third of the workers had upper secondary school leaving certificates, and 16.5 per cent were graduates. Length of service in the organisation was generally rather short (however, note that one-third of organisations had been in existence for less than ten years).

The great majority of the employees interviewed received hourly wages net of taxes amounting to less than 7.5 euros, and 34 per cent received less than 5 euros. On a monthly basis, most of them (54 per cent) earned between 700 and 900 euros. However, the data show the existence of significant wage differentials among workers. From further investigation into the wage structure (Mosca, Musella and Pastore, 2003) it emerged that fewer than two in five of these wage gaps were explained by differences in socio-demographic and other characteristics

Table 6.1. *Main characteristics of organisations (percentage values)*

Variable	Category	Percentage
Type of organisation	Public	23.7
	For-profit	7.5
	Social cooperative	32.5
	Secular non-profit	22.4
	Religious non-profit	14.0
Number of employees	Fewer than 10	39.6
	Between 10 and 19	21.2
	Between 20 and 50	19.3
	More than 50	15.7
Presence of volunteers	None	40.2
	Fewer than 10	26.3
	Between 10 and 20	15.4
	More than 20	18.1

Table 6.2. *Main characteristics of employees (percentage values)*

Variable	Category	Percentage
Gender	Male	22.9
	Female	77.1
Age	Under 25	6.1
	25–29	18.3
	30–39	39.7
	40–50	25.3
	Over 50	10.6
Education	Elementary school	5.4
	Lower secondary school	21.3
	Vocational qualification	19.0
	Upper secondary school	37.7
	University degree	16.5
Tenure	Less than 1 year	20.6
	1–2 years	12.2
	3–5 years	21.8
	6–10 years	23.6
	More than 10 years	21.9
Employment contract	Permanent	75.2
	Fixed-term	11.5
	Temporary/freelance	13.3
Monthly net wage	Less than 500 euros	13.8
	500–699 euros	15.3
	700–799 euros	24.9
	800–900 euros	29.1
	More than 900 euros	16.9
Hourly net wage	Less than 5 euros	34.1
	5–7.4 euros	58.1
	7.5–10 euros	5.6
	More than 10 euros	2.2

of the workers (including education and length of service). Also accounting for the wage gap were the field of activity and the type of organisation in which workers were employed. In general, pay levels were lower in private organisations, especially non-profit, confirming the findings of other studies.[2]

[2] Wage differentials among different types of organisation, and especially between public and non-profit organisations, have also been reported by Philip Mirvis and Edward Hackett (1983), Richard Disney, Alissa Goodman, Amanda Gosling and Chris Trinder (1998), Burton Weisbrod (1983) and Stephen Almond and Jeremy Kendall (2000).

4.   Relational attitudes to work

The data make it possible to distinguish three groups of attitudes to work: extrinsic, intrinsic and relational (table 6.3). Workers gave high scores to items describing both extrinsic and intrinsic aspects of their work. They regarded work as a necessity, a way to make a living and support their families. However, they also regarded work as an opportunity for professional and personal fulfilment, as well as for developing new relationships. This last item, which indicates the existence of a demand for relational goods, received an average score of 4.85 out of a maximum of 7.

Greater average scores to relational attitudes were given by workers: of feminine gender; with medium to low educational qualifications; with low pay; who were previously unemployed or inactive (e.g. housewives); and who were employed either in non-profit organisations other than social cooperatives or in for-profit firms (table 6.4). One can conclude that workers are actually heterogeneous with respect to demand for relational goods, and that most workers interested in the on-the-job consumption of relational goods are those with fewer opportunities to consume such goods in non-work settings: housewives and previously unemployed workers with low human capital. Now we turn to determining whether this demand is satisfied, and whether the on-the-job consumption of relational goods influences workers' utility.

Table 6.3. *Attitudes to work (average scores)*

	Score
Extrinsic aspects	
A necessity	5.64
To earn a living	5.71
To support the family	5.38
A hobby	2.13
To earn as much as possible	2.97
Intrinsic aspects	
An experience for realising oneself	5.57
A contribution to society	4.34
A way to gain recognition	2.65
Relational aspects	
The possibility of opening new relationships	4.85

Note: Workers could choose between a minimum of 1 and a maximum of 7.

Table 6.4. *The importance of working activity in commencing new relationships (average scores)*

Variable	Category	Score	F-test/*t*-test[a]	Significance[b]
Gender	Male	4.52	−4.402	★★★
	Female	4.95		
Age	Under 25	5.10	1.164	
	25–29	4.85		
	30–39	4.88		
	40–50	4.77		
	Over 50	4.81		
Level of education	Lower secondary school certificate	4.95	5.000	★★★
	Vocational qualification	5.10		
	Upper secondary school certificate	4.70		
	University diploma, degree/MA	4.72		
Tenure	Less than 1 year	5.00	0.338	
	1–2 years	4.97		
	3–5 years	4.63		
	6–10 years	4.76		
	More than 10 years	4.97		
Monthly net wage	Less than 500 euros	5.02	2.712	★★★
	500–699 euros	4.86		
	700–799 euros	4.96		
	800–900 euros	4.73		
	More than 900 euros	4.65		
Hourly net wage	Less than 5 euros	4.90	0.484	
	5–7.4 euros	4.85		
	7.5–10 euros	4.80		
	More than 10 Euros	4.36		
Previous condition	Employed	4.86	2.251	★★★
	Unemployed	4.98		
	Student	4.78		
	Housewife	4.92		
	Other	4.85		
Previous employer (if any)	For-profit	4.92	2.373	★★★
	Social cooperative	4.74		
	Other non-profit	5.14		
	Public organisation	4.75		

[a] These tests are statistical applications to verify if each class inside the considered variable is significantly different from the average or not. In particular, a *t*-test is applied to the 'gender' variable, given the dual nature of the variable (male vs. female). On the other variables the F-test is applied in order to have a multi-comparison. In particular, simple Pearson's correlation coefficients between the importance of working activities in commencing new relationships and workers' personal and job characteristics are tested on the basis of the *t* statistic, distributed as a random variable 'student' with $g = n - 2$ degrees of freedom.
[b] Significance levels of simple correlation coefficients on the basis of the *t* statistic: ★ = less than 10%, ★★ = less than 5%, ★★★ = less than 1%.

5.   Job satisfaction and relational goods

The questionnaire contained questions on employee satisfaction, with regard not only to their job as a whole but also to some of its aspects, which we can group into intrinsic, extrinsic and relational.

Analysis of the results shows that the workers interviewed are rather satisfied with both the job as a whole (average score 5.27) and its intrinsic aspects – the social usefulness of work, the recognition of one's work and decision-making autonomy (table 6.5). Opinions on extrinsic aspects are more diversified: positive for some (working hours and professional development), and negative for others (wages, career advancement). Satisfaction with relational aspects is the highest overall: the interviewees gave high average satisfaction scores (above 5) to relations with colleagues, volunteers and superiors.

Thus, the organisations surveyed seem to adopt a mix of incentives that satisfies their workers. If we look at the matter in more detail, this mix seems to satisfy workers' demand for relational goods, and their expectations regarding the intrinsic value of their job, but much less their expectations as to the off-the-job consumption of goods in either the

Table 6.5. *Areas of satisfaction (average scores)*

Area of satisfaction	Score
The job as a whole	5.27
Extrinsic aspects	4.45
The working environment	4.48
Professional development	4.50
Variety and creativity of the job	4.63
The salary	4.07
Working hours	4.81
Previous career advancements	3.10
Future career advancements	2.93
Job security	4.70
Intrinsic aspects	4.71
Decision-making autonomy	4.36
Recognition of one's contribution	4.54
The social usefulness of the job	5.31
Relational aspects	5.48
Relations with superiors	5.17
Relations with colleagues	5.51
Relations with volunteers	5.47

short or the long run, as evidenced by dissatisfaction with both the wage and career prospects.[3]

Satisfaction with the job as a whole is not correlated with gender (see table 6.6), but significantly depends on age (workers under 25 and over 50 are the most satisfied) and education (the least educated workers are the most satisfied). The type of contract does not show a significant relation with workers' satisfaction. Instead, the organisation's characteristics matter for worker satisfaction: workers in public bodies are significantly less satisfied than workers in private (for-profit and non-profit) organisations; workers in small organisations are more satisfied than workers in larger ones (however, the relation is not completely monotonic); finally, the presence of volunteers, and their number, positively affects worker satisfaction.

In order to identify the determinants of satisfaction with the job as a whole, and in particular to verify the influence exerted by the on-the-job consumption of relational goods, we estimated an ordered probit in which the dependent variable is satisfaction with the job as a whole.[4] The independent variables are worker, organisational and job characteristics, including the direct and indirect provision of relational goods (table 6.7).

The estimation shows that less educated, older and more tenured workers are more satisfied with their jobs,[5] while satisfaction is correlated with neither age nor sex.[6] Moreover, the wage level does not significantly influence job satisfaction, whereas a younger organisation is better at satisfying workers' aspirations since workers tend to share its mission

---

[3] Binomial estimation of correlation coefficients between general satisfaction with one's job and the other, more specific items of satisfaction shows that all correlations (using both Spearman's rho and Kendall's tau-b, which deliver the same results) are significant at the 1 per cent level. Coefficients are all positive and high. Only in the case of previous and future career advancements do we notice coefficients equal to or less than 0.3. Satisfaction with the job as a whole is most strongly correlated with satisfaction with some intrinsic aspects of the job (decision-making autonomy, recognition of one's contribution) and some extrinsic aspects (training and professional development, variety and creativity, job security). Coefficients for satisfaction with relations (with superiors and colleagues) are positive and high, though they are not among the highest.

[4] Since the answers are concentrated in the values 2–6, the level of satisfaction was reclassified *ex ante* into 'low' (scores 1–3), 'average' (4–5) and 'high' (6–7). Proceeding in this manner, the ordered probit estimation gives better results and higher total significance. The three classes were chosen *ex ante* on the basis of the relative frequencies of answers in each class.

[5] This is in accordance with the findings of Naci Mocan and Deborah Viola (1997).

[6] This is in contrast to the findings of Mirvis and Hackett (1983). For the United States, they found higher female than male satisfaction over the 1970s. Their main conclusion is that women's satisfaction is boosted by weaker working position and lower expectations about professional role and pay.

Table 6.6. *Workers' satisfaction, by individual and organisational characteristics*

Variable	Category	Percentage	Average score	F-test/ t-test[a]	Significance[b]
Gender	Male	22.9	5.26	−0.119	
	Female	77.1	5.27		
Age	Under 25	6.1	5.48	4.460	**
	25–29	18.3	5.35		
	30–39	39.7	5.20		
	40–50	25.3	5.14		
	Over 50	10.6	5.62		
Education	Elementary school	5.4	5.91	3.567	*
	Lower secondary school	21.3	5.26		
	Vocational qualification	19.0	5.21		
	Upper secondary school	37.7	5.26		
	University degree	16.5	5.34		
Vocational qualification	Yes	41.5	5.24	−1.161	
	No	58.5	5.32		
Employment contract	Permanent	75.2	5.22	2.219	
	Fixed-term	11.5	5.36		
	Temporary/freelance	13.3	5.49		
Hourly net wage	Less than 5 euros	34.1	5.27	1.275	
	5–7.4 euros	58.1	5.22		
	7.5–10 euros	5.6	5.61		
	More than 10 euros	2.2	5.12		
Type of organisation	Public	23.7	4.99	8.805	**
	For-profit	7.5	5.39		
	Social cooperative	32.5	5.39		
	Secular non-profit	22.4	5.25		
	Religious non-profit	14.0	5.53		
Number of employees	Fewer than 10	38.0	5.42	4.879	**
	Between 10 and 19	10.6	5.59		
	Between 20 and 50	28.0	5.32		
	More than 50	23.4	5.29		
Presence of volunteers	None	40.2	5.09	4.632	**
	Fewer than 10	26.3	5.57		
	Between 10 and 20	15.4	5.39		
	More than 20	18.1	5.32		

[a] These tests are statistical applications to verify if each class inside the considered variable is significantly different from the average or not. In particular, a t-test is applied to the 'gender' variable, given the dual nature of the variable (male vs. female). On the other variables the F-test is applied in order to have a multi-comparison. In particular, simple Pearson's correlation coefficients between the importance of working activities in commencing new relationships and workers' personal and job characteristics are tested on the basis of the t statistic, distributed as a random variable 'student' with $g = n - 2$ degrees of freedom.
[b] Significance levels of simple correlation coefficients on the basis of the t statistic: * = less than 10%, ** = less than 5%, *** = less than 1%.

Table 6.7. *Satisfaction with the job as a whole (ordered probit)*

Variable	Coefficient	P[|Z| > z]^a	Significance^b
Constant	−2.3624	0.0002	***
Year of birth	−0.0016	0.6481	
Gender (0 = male, 1 = female)	−0.1104	0.1126	
Level of education (incremental variable from lower secondary school certificate to degree or MA)	−0.1059	0.0001	***
Activity in direct contact with clients (0 = activity in direct contact with clients, 1 = other activities)	−0.2428	0.0013	***
Time spent with clients	0.0735	0.0005	***
Hourly wage	0.0000	0.5212	
Tenure in the organisation (years)	0.0085	0.0427	**
Year of foundation of the organisation	0.0006	0.0381	**
Quality of organisation–client relations^c	0.0655	0.0218	**
Nature of the organisation (0 = public organisation, 1 = private organisation)	0.0874	0.0844	*
Collaboration between workers and managers^c	0.1303	0.0000	***
Interest in clients' involvement^c	0.2321	0.0000	***
Intrinsic attitudes^c	0.1577	0.0000	***
Economic attitudes (interest in the wage)^c	−0.0548	0.0242	**
Other extrinsic attitudes^c	−0.0194	0.5122	
Relational attitudes^c	0.0468	0.0059	***

^{a} The P value is the probability that the corresponding variable is not significantly different from 0, run by means of the Z statistic.
^{b} Significance: *** = less than 1%, ** = less than 5%, * = less than 10%. Maximum likelihood estimates: observations 1,847; iterations completed 23; log likelihood function −1,599.978; restricted log likelihood −1,730.467; chi-squared 326.9778; degrees of freedom 16; significance level .0000.
^{c} Discrete variable, ranging from 1 (minimum) to 7 (maximum). All other variables are continuous.

more deeply. Job satisfaction is also correlated with the type of ownership: workers are less satisfied in public organisations.

As for relational aspects, the ordered probit enables analysis of two different features: (i) the correlation between satisfaction and relational variables identifiable as relational goods consumed on the job; (ii) the presence of a correlation between satisfaction and attitudes towards work.

With reference to relational goods, several of the variables of a relational nature exert a positive influence on job satisfaction. Workers in direct contact with clients and spending more time with them are more satisfied. Job satisfaction is also correlated with the quality of the relations between organisation and clients and with the importance assigned by workers to clients' involvement (both in their job and in the organisation).[7]

As for workers' extrinsic attitudes, in this and the following estimations we differentiate between economic and other extrinsic attitudes. The former refer to workers' attitudes to the wage; the latter refer to attitudes to all other extrinsic aspects of the work.[8]

The estimation shows that workers with high intrinsic and relational attitudes have greater job satisfaction, extrinsic attitudes are not correlated with job satisfaction, while workers who are more interested in the economic aspects of the job (wage level) are systematically less satisfied. In other words, workers giving greater importance to the intrinsic and relational aspects of work are significantly more satisfied than the others.

In conclusion, the estimation confirms first and foremost the importance of relational aspects in determining job satisfaction. Secondly, it shows that workers' satisfaction is positively related with relational and intrinsic attitudes; this suggests that satisfaction can be increased by selecting workers who view their job as an opportunity to achieve social and relational goals. Moreover, it demonstrates that private organisations, in particular non-profit ones, are better than public ones at satisfying their workers.

6.   The trade-off between wage and relational goods

Having ascertained the positive influence exerted by the intensity and quality of relations on job satisfaction, we turned to verifying the presence of a trade-off between wages and the on-the-job consumption of relational goods. This analysis was carried out by testing the correlation between satisfaction with relational goods and the economic aspects of the job (primarily the wage).[9]

The analysis of the degree of satisfaction with relational aspects by wage level (table 6.8) seems to confirm that satisfaction with relational

[7] The variable 'interest in clients' involvement' is the average of the scores given by workers to the following statements: 'the contribution made by the user and his/her involvement are vital in my work', 'the user is effectively involved in the work of the organisation' and 'I believe it to be of primary importance that the client should derive the maximum benefit from the service provided'.
[8] This is the average score assigned to the extrinsic aspects presented in table 6.5, except for the wage.
[9] Remember that satisfaction with relations is directly and strictly correlated with satisfaction with work in general.

Table 6.8. *Satisfaction with relational aspects of the job, by wage level (average scores)*

	Satisfaction with relationship		
	With superiors	With colleagues	With volunteers
Monthly wage			
Less than 500 euros	5.62	5.73	5.96
500 to 699 euros	5.25	5.64	5.32
700 to 799 euros	5.11	5.53	5.13
800 to 900 euros	5.22	5.50	5.65
More than 900 euros	4.59	5.20	5.17

aspects diminishes as one moves from the lowest to the highest monthly pay levels. It is, above all, satisfaction with relations with superiors that diminishes, followed by relations with colleagues. Though the relation is not completely monotonic, it seems to show that organisations granting fewer relational goods try to compensate with higher salaries.[10]

In order to investigate whether this relation between satisfaction and wages is mediated by other workers' characteristics, we conducted an ordered probit estimation in which the dependent variable is satisfaction with relational aspects – the average of satisfaction scores assigned by workers to relations with colleagues and with superiors (table 6.9).[11] As in the case of satisfaction with the job as a whole, satisfaction with relational aspects is positively correlated with workers' age and tenure, while it is negatively correlated with their educational level.

Moreover, workers engaged in the direct delivery of services (and therefore in direct contact with users), as well as workers more interested in the involvement of clients, are systematically more satisfied with relational aspects than are workers in administrative roles. As in the previous

[10] The monotonic descending relation between satisfaction with relational aspects and the wage is broken at the 800–900 euro level for relations with superiors and volunteers. Here it is possible to hypothesise that a strong monotonic relation would hold if workers were sorted into skilled and unskilled; 800 euros is likely to be the lower bound of the pay for the skilled workforce. However, if we take educational attainment as a proxy for workers' ability, exploration of the data reveals a monotonic negative relation between relational satisfaction and pay only in the case of graduate workers. For the other classes of educational attainment the results are not univocal, though the negative trend remains pronounced. In absolute terms, the least satisfied are workers with a secondary school diploma, while graduate workers and workers with low educational attainments exhibit similar levels of satisfaction.

[11] The dependent variable includes only satisfaction with relations with colleagues and superiors, because a significant number of workers belong to organisations without volunteers.

Table 6.9. *Satisfaction with relational aspects of the job (ordered probit)*

Variable	Coefficient	$P[|Z| > z]^a$	Significance[b]
Constant	−2.9238	0.0000	***
Year of birth	−0.0098	0.0015	***
Gender (0 = male, 1 = female)	0.0138	0.8280	
Level of education (incremental variable from lower secondary school certificate to degree or MA)	−0.0607	0.0067	***
Activity in direct contact with clients (0 = activity in direct contact with clients, 1 = other activities)	−0.1502	0.0326	**
Time spent with clients	−0.0104	0.6187	
Hourly wage	−0.0056	0.0802	*
Tenure in the organisation (years)	0.0142	0.0000	***
Year of foundation of the organisation	0.0005	0.0766	*
Quality of organisation–client relations[c]	0.0681	0.0137	**
Nature of the organisation (0 = public organisation, 1 = private organisation)	0.2596	0.0000	***
Interest in clients' involvement[c]	0.1993	0.0000	***
Intrinsic attitudes[c]	0.0796	0.0000	***
Economic attitudes (interest in the wage)[c]	0.0508	0.0570	*
Other extrinsic attitudes[c]	−0.0191	0.4619	
Relational attitudes[c]	0.0524	0.0005	***

[a] The P value is the probability that the corresponding variable is not significantly different from 0, run by means of the Z statistic.
[b] Significance: *** = less than 1%, ** = less than 5%, * = less than 10%. Maximum likelihood estimates: observations 1,885; iterations completed 23; log likelihood function −2,445.788; restricted log likelihood −2,580.731; chi-squared 269.8862; degrees of freedom 15; significance level .0000.
[c] Discrete variable, ranging from 1 (minimum) to 7 (maximum). All other variables are continuous.

estimation, workers in public organisations are systematically less satisfied with relational aspects than their colleagues in private organisations, especially non-profit ones. Once again, workers who give more importance to the intrinsic and relational aspects of work prove also to be more satisfied with relations with their colleagues and superiors.

Finally, the estimation shows the presence of a trade-off between relational goods and wage level: satisfaction with relational aspects and the hourly wage are, in fact, negatively correlated.[12] This confirms that

[12] Albeit with a significance equal to the 8 per cent level.

Table 6.10. *Satisfaction with relational aspects, by type of organisation (average scores)*

Area of satisfaction	Public ownership	For-profit	Social cooperative	Other non-religious non-profit	Religious non-profit	Total
Relations with superiors	4.72	5.34	5.40	5.18	5.61	5.17
Relations with colleagues	5.22	5.65	5.69	5.59	5.56	5.51
Relations with volunteers	5.17	4.91	5.45	5.66	5.79	5.47
General satisfaction for relations	4.98	5.48	5.55	5.38	5.59	5.45

lower wage levels are at least partly compensated for by opportunities to enjoy good-quality relations.[13]

A more in-depth analysis of the relation between satisfaction with relational aspects and the type of organisation (table 6.10) confirms that workers in non-profit organisations (especially in religious non-profit ones or social cooperatives) appear to be much more satisfied with relations (with superiors, with colleagues and with volunteers) than are those employed by public organisations. Instead, there are no significant differences in satisfaction with relational aspects among workers employed in private organisations. Moreover, with regard to public organisations, it emerges that relations with colleagues are significantly better than relations with superiors. But this is not the case in for-profit and non-profit organisations (especially social cooperatives and religious non-profit organisations, where the average scores of both type of satisfaction are quite similar).

To sum up this section, the results of the analysis show that relational aspects and attitudes towards work seem especially important with regard to job satisfaction. Furthermore, non-profit organisations (and private organisations in general) seem better able than public ones to supply relational goods. Data confirm that there is a trade-off between monetary remuneration and the supply of relational goods: satisfaction with relational aspects is negatively correlated with the hourly wage in the ordered probit estimation, decreasing as pay increases. Workers are

[13] The cross-sectional nature of data at our disposal does not permit the investigation of causality, for which longitudinal data would be needed.

likely to trade off different kinds of incentives. Given the costs of production, each organisational form seems characterised by a different incentive mix. For example, public organisations seem to generate less satisfaction with relational goods and less overall work satisfaction.

If we recall that workers' overall utility does not increase with the wage (table 6.7), we can draw the conclusion that other, non-monetary goods take the place of monetary remuneration above the reservation wage by way of a process of substitution. In other words, workers do not seem to maximise their wages, but instead maximise their utility.

7.   Loyalty to the organisation

The hypothesis that wages enter workers' utility functions mainly as a threshold, an acceptance level below which they are dissatisfied (independently of other elements, at least), can be tested using other information contained in the data set: data on workers' loyalty to the organisation proxied by their stated willingness to stay. About 35 per cent of the interviewees intended to leave the organisation – 1.5 per cent in any case and 33.2 per cent in pursuit of a better job (table 6.11). The majority (65 per cent) intended to stay, 52 per cent as long as possible and 13 per cent for some years at least. These figures indicate a low incidence of extreme dissatisfaction, thereby confirming the results obtained in analysing satisfaction.

In order to determine the factors influencing workers' willingness to stay, two types of logit estimations were used. Workers were sorted, in the first, according to whether they intended to stay as long as possible (long-period loyalty) or had other intentions; in the second, according to whether they intended to stay at least for some years or intended to leave. For both estimations, two specifications were calculated: the first

Table 6.11. *Future intentions of workers*

	Total	Percentage
Intend to stay as long as possible	1,049	51.9
Intend to stay for some years at least	271	13.4
Will leave for a better opportunity in the same field	327	16.2
Will leave for a better opportunity in another field	345	17.1
Will leave in any case	31	1.5
Total	2,023	100.0

Table 6.12. Loyalty to the organisation with regard to attitudes (logit estimation)[a]

Variable	Intention to stay with the organisation as long as possible			Intention to stay with the organisation at least for some years		
	Coefficient	Pr[|Z| > z][b]	Significance[c]	Coefficient	Pr[|Z| > z][b]	Significance[c]
Constant	-0.9981	0.0821	*	-1.8937	0.0013	***
Year of birth	0.0418	0.0000	***	0.0425	0.0000	***
Gender (0 = male, 1 = female)	0.2450	0.0558	*	0.3956	0.0031	***
Level of education (incremental variable from lower secondary school certificate to degree or MA)	0.1933	0.0000	***	0.1581	0.0011	***
Specific vocational qualification (0 = no, 1 = yes)	0.3297	0.0049	***	0.3294	0.0054	***
Labour contract (0 = open-ended contract, 1 = other type of contract)	0.5429	0.0000	***	0.6649	0.0000	***
Hourly wage	0.0000	0.4392		0.0000	0.9361	
Tenure in the organisation (years)	0.0448	0.0485	**	0.0521	0.0683	*
Total number of volunteers in the organisation	-0.0010	0.9825		-0.0788	0.0819	*
Quality of organisation–client relations[d]	-0.1378	0.0189	**	-0.0796	0.1767	
Nature of the organisation (0 = public organisation, 1 = private organisation)	-0.4594	0.0002	***	-0.3933	0.0016	***
Centrality of managers in defining strategies[d]	-0.1022	0.0594	*	-0.1183	0.0313	**
Collaboration between workers and managers[d]	-0.0018	0.9726		-0.1029	0.0525	*
Interest in clients' involvement[d]	-0.1497	0.0011	***	-0.1369	0.0032	***
Intrinsic attitudes[d]	-0.1125	0.0048	***	-0.1110	0.0061	***
Economic attitudes (interest in the wage)[d]	0.0234	0.6141		0.0998	0.0353	**
Other extrinsic attitudes[d]	0.1014	0.0752	*	0.0716	0.2162	
Relational attitudes[d]	-0.0604	0.0639	*	-0.0220	0.5087	

[a] The values of the dependent variable are: 0 = stay; 1 = leave.

included among regressors workers' attitudes towards work; the second included instead the areas of satisfaction.[14]

In the former (table 6.12), long-period loyalty is significantly correlated with various characteristics of both the worker and the job. Older men and women, with lower educational qualifications and without a specific qualification for employment in the field, are the most loyal. In contrast, younger workers show a greater desire to leave, probably because they have not acquired a stable working position, or they have not yet found their preferred job or organisation. Those who have been hired on open-ended contracts and workers who have stayed longer with the organisation want to stay as long as possible. Loyalty is not significantly correlated with pay, nor with economic attitudes.

Moreover, as with satisfaction, it is also the case that a desire to stay with the organisation as long as possible is significantly correlated with the type of organisation: workers are less loyal in public than in private organisations, especially non-profit ones.[15] With regard to relational aspects, the estimation shows that the interviewees who declare an intention to stay as long as possible work for organisations with relations with users that are very good and in which users are more involved in the organisation. They also consider their job to be important because it provides opportunities to develop new relationships.

---

[14] In the following estimations the dependent variable is defined as $0 =$ stay, $1 =$ leave. As a consequence, the positive sign of the coefficient means positive correlation with the intention to leave.

[15] If in the estimation of the intentions to stay the dichotomous variable public body/ private organisation is replaced by the variable non-profit organisations/other organisations, this is negatively correlated with the intention to stay as long as possible. This means that workers in non-profit organisations are willing to stay longer than those in other organisations. Similarly, if we exclude workers in for-profit enterprises, being employed in public organisations (rather than in non-profit ones) reduces the likelihood that they intend to stay as long as possible.

Notes to table 6.12. (*cont.*)

[b] The P value is the probability that the corresponding variable is not significantly different from 0, run by means of the Z statistic.

[c] Significance: *** = less than 1%, ** = less than 5%, * = less than 10%. Intention to stay as long as possible: observations 1,713; iterations completed 5; log likelihood function $-1,073.088$; restricted log likelihood $-1,183.621$; chi-squared 221.0871; degrees of freedom 20; significance level .0000. Intention to stay for at least some years: observations 1,713; iterations completed 5; log likelihood function $-1,034.396$; restricted log likelihood $-1,153.995$; chi-squared 239.1978; degrees of freedom 20; significance level .0000.

[d] Discrete variable ranging from 1 (minimum) to 7 (maximum). All other variables are continuous.

Table 6.13. *Loyalty to the organisation with regard to satisfaction (logit estimation)[a]*

Variable	Intention to stay with the organisation as long as possible			Intention to stay with the organisation at least for some years		
	Coefficient	P[|Z| > z][b]	Significance[c]	Coefficient	P[|Z| > z][b]	Significance[c]
Constant	-0.2200	0.7043		-0.9725	0.1028	
Year of birth	0.0447	0.0000	***	0.0471	0.0000	***
Gender (0 = male, 1 = female)	0.1627	0.2153		0.3435	0.0126	**
Level of education (incremental variable from lower secondary school certificate to university degree or MA)	0.1393	0.0039	***	0.0947	0.0558	*
Specific vocational qualification (0 = no, 1 = yes)	0.3175	0.0091	***	0.2960	0.0168	**
Labour contract (0 = open-ended contract, 1 = other type of contract)	0.4981	0.0001	***	0.6357	0.0000	***
Hourly wage	-0.0001	0.8920		0.0000	0.4053	
Tenure in the organisation (years)	0.0085	0.0848	*	0.0125	0.1256	
Presence of volunteers (number of volunteers)	0.0045	0.9208		-0.0840	0.0737	**
Quality of organisation–client relations[c]	-0.0999	0.0968	*	-0.0382	0.5345	
Public organisation versus private (0 = public organisation, 1 = private organisation)	-0.2994	0.0205	**	-0.2161	0.0968	*
Centrality of managers in defining strategies[d]	-0.0949	0.0900	*	-0.1122	0.0483	**
Collaboration between workers and managers[d]	0.0664	0.2207		-0.0276	0.6211	
Interest in clients' involvement[d]	-0.0848	0.0784	*	-0.0692	0.1607	
Intrinsic satisfaction[d]	-0.0839	0.1650		-0.0791	0.1942	
Economic satisfaction (interest in the wage)[d]	-0.0875	0.0851	*	-0.0605	0.2313	
Satisfaction with other extrinsic goods[d]	-0.2308	0.0004	***	-0.2014	0.0019	***
Relational satisfaction[d]	-0.1955	0.0000	***	-0.3010	0.0000	***

[a] The values of the dependent variable are: 0 = stay; 1 = leave.

In the second estimation, where loyalty is defined as a desire to stay with the organisation at least for some years, the importance of some relational variables increases. Workers who are employed in organisations making significant use of volunteers, who have collaborative relations with the manager and who see the manager as occupying a key role in defining the organisation's strategies declare the greatest loyalty. The quality of the relations between organisation and clients becomes insignificant. Relational attitudes are less significant, while the least loyal are workers attracted by economic incentives.

Summarising, we can state that workers intending to stay with their organisations belong to two groups: on the one hand, those with few alternatives (because they are insufficiently qualified or rather old); on the other hand, workers – mainly male, young and well-educated – who would not change jobs even if they could. Both the relational attitudes to work and the relational aspects of the job have limited impact on loyalty; they are weakly significant only for workers who intend to stay as long as possible.

When the variables representing the four aspects of satisfaction[16] are inserted in the estimations in place of attitudes to work, they are found to impact heavily on workers' willingness to stay (table 6.13). The greatest influence is exerted by satisfaction with extrinsic and relational aspects; but satisfaction with intrinsic aspects also affects loyalty. In contrast, satisfaction with the wage level influences only the intention to stay with the organisation as long as possible, and not in a very significant way. Furthermore, the hourly wage does not exert a significant influence on loyalty in any of the four estimations. These last results support the idea that workers take the wage into account only as an acceptance level, while relational goods weigh more in the definition of workers' utility.

[16] Each of these variables is an average of several items (see above).

Notes to table 6.13. (*cont.*)

[b] The P value is the probability that the corresponding variable is not significantly different from 0, run by means of the Z statistic.

[c] Significance: *** = less than 1%, ** = less than 5%, * = less than 10%. Intention to stay as long as possible: observations 1,713; iterations completed 5; log likelihood function −1,019.666; restricted log likelihood −1,183.631; chi-squared 327.9309; degrees of freedom 24; significance level .0000. Intention to stay at least for some years: observations 1,713; iterations completed 6; log likelihood function −966.3121; restricted log likelihood −1,153.995; chi-squared 375.3893; degrees of freedom 24; significance level .0000.

[d] Discrete variable, ranging from 1 (minimum) to 7 (maximum). All other variables are continuous.

This seems to confirm that the opportunity to consume relational goods on the job is a form of remuneration that attracts workers. Furthermore, note that intrinsic aspects are important for loyalty only in the form of attitudes (table 6.12), not in the form of satisfaction (table 6.13). It is quite clear that workers driven by intrinsic attitudes towards their job (a quite common phenomenon in the field of social services) are more loyal, while workers driven by relational attitudes are more loyal, but only weakly so in the case of long-run loyalty. When it comes to the influence exerted by satisfaction, relational and intrinsic aspects count more, while satisfaction for intrinsic aspects becomes insignificant.

Closer scrutiny of the data yields a more precise identification of the relation between the level of satisfaction with monetary variables and relational goods, and workers' willingness to quit the firm. Table 6.14 shows the percentage of workers willing to quit within each level of satisfaction with wage and relational goods.[17]

The percentage of workers willing to quit[18] shows a clear tendency to decrease when satisfaction increases. When satisfaction is very low at least half of the workers are willing to accept better opportunities or intend to quit anyway.[19]

The percentage of workers willing to quit is higher, for each level of satisfaction, in the column concerning relations, while the standard deviation is the same. The strength of the impact of dissatisfaction with relations seems to be no less than that of dissatisfaction with wages. Table 6.14 does not highlight the interaction between the two variables in determining the intention to quit or stay. Table 6.15 displays useful information in this regard. In order to keep it simple, we redefine satisfaction variables as dichotomous: satisfied or dissatisfied, the latter with scores from 1 to 4. The finding is that nearly two-thirds of workers who are satisfied with both relations and wages intend to stay as long as possible; this figure reduces to values in the 41–45 per cent range when workers are satisfied with only one of the two characteristics. For each of

---

[17] In table 6.14 we do not consider the other items of satisfaction in order not to complicate the analysis. Correlation with the desire to leave the organisation is negative and statistically significant at the 1 per cent level for all the areas of satisfaction. However, in the case of wages and relational goods it is the strongest (and completely monotonic). Finally, the willingness to stay with the organisation is completely uncorrelated with the *level* of the wage: what counts seems to be the level of satisfaction it generates, not its value. Observe that we cannot make the same check in the case of relational goods, since we do not have at our disposal a measure of their amount.

[18] This category includes workers who answered that they would 'quit the firm if a better job in the same sector is found', 'quit the firm if a better job in a different sector is found' and 'quit anyway, as soon as possible'.

[19] Equivalently, for very low levels of satisfaction (equal to 1 or 2) the median worker is willing to quit.

Table 6.14. *Willingness to quit, by the level of satisfaction with wages and relations (percentage values)*

Level of satisfaction	Area of satisfaction	
	Wages	Relationship with superiors and colleagues[a]
1	0.60	0.67
2	0.55	0.58
3	0.35	0.49
4	0.35	0.45
5	0.32	0.38
6	0.27	0.36
7	0.16	0.21
Mean	0.37	0.45
Standard deviation	0.15	0.15

[a] Relations with volunteers were not taken into consideration since volunteers are absent in many organisations.

Table 6.15. *Intentions to stay with the organisation and satisfaction with wages and relations (percentage values)*

	Intention to stay with the organisation as long as possible	Intention to stay with the organisation at least for some years	Intention to leave for another job in the same field	Intention to leave for another job in a different field
Satisfied with both relations and wages	62.3	12.5	10.2	15.0
Satisfied with wages but not with relations	44.7	6.4	29.8	19.1
Satisfied with relations but not with wages	41.2	15.5	20.4	22.9
Dissatisfied with both relations and wages	33.3	18.7	27.4	22.6

Note: Workers on fixed-term contracts and workers intending to leave as soon as possible (the latter a negligible number) are not included.

these a lower bound for satisfaction seems to exist for a large number of workers, below which they would rather quit the organisation, despite being satisfied with the other characteristic. In the case of relational goods this level is about 50 per cent, while in the case of wages it is about 43 per cent.[20] Here too, the data suggest that the impacts of these are roughly symmetric.

Note that, among workers satisfied with pay but not with relations, a relatively high percentage intend to leave their organisations to take up other opportunities in the same field. This indicates that there is a sizable group of workers who are satisfied with pay levels in the field but who are looking for organisations providing better relations. In contrast, workers who are satisfied with relations but not with wages intend more often to look for jobs in a different field (they may consider wages too low in the entire social service sector).[21]

To sum up the section, the results add to the negative correlation between satisfaction with relational goods and the hourly wage (see sections 5 and 6) in confirming the hypothesis that extrinsic and monetary rewards are substitutable with relational goods. Moreover, when satisfaction with one aspect falls below a critical threshold, satisfaction with the other aspect often no longer suffices. We take these findings as corroborating the hypothesis on worker preferences put forward in section 2 and represented in figure 6.1.

8.   Conclusions

The main aim of this study has been to test the importance given by workers to the relational aspects of their jobs and, furthermore, to test the ability of relational goods consumed on the job to act as an incentive sufficiently strong to attract workers and secure their loyalty to the organisation.

The results, though provisional, confirm these hypotheses. First, the opportunity to create new relations appears to be an important motivation to take or keep the job, especially for persons from a poor external relational context. Second, worker satisfaction does not depend predominantly on the wage level; non-monetary rewards, among which are included the relational features of the workplace, also seem to be

---

[20] These figures are the sum of the percentage of workers willing to leave for the same sector or for another sector if a better job opportunity is found.

[21] The fact that not all workers intend to quit even when their satisfaction with both wages and relations is low may be due to satisfaction with other characteristics of the job – for example, other extrinsic goods and intrinsic motivations (see tables 6.12 and 6.13) – or to the perception of having no alternatives.

important. At least in the social service sector, workers set high value on the relational goods consumed on the job, and apparently give no less importance to these than to wages. In particular, when interpersonal relations are poor, satisfaction is low, regardless of the wage level. The analysis conducted above also shows that wage and relational goods are substitutes, so the latter can legitimately be viewed as a peculiar sort of remuneration. However, substitution seems to occur only in a certain range, since, when either job characteristic falls below a threshold, workers often decide to quit the organisation, irrespective of the other. Furthermore, it seems that different organisations adopt different mixes of intrinsic, relational and extrinsic (monetary and non-monetary) incentives. Relational goods are scarce in public organisations, where wages are systematically higher, while the reverse is true in non-profit organisations. Since both worker loyalty and satisfaction with the job as a whole are higher in non-profit than in public organisations, one can deduce that – at least for social service workers – the incentive mix implemented by non-profit organisations makes them more efficient at securing adequate labour resources.

ACKNOWLEDGEMENTS

The authors wish to thank Luigi Bonatti, Bruno Frey and Benedetto Gui for their valuable comments and suggestions. Special thanks go to Ermanno Tortia for his work in perfecting the chapter. As always, all errors and omissions are the authors' responsibility alone.

7   On the possible conflict between economic growth and social development

Angelo Antoci, Pier Luigi Sacco and Paolo Vanin

1.   Introduction

In the long run, individual and aggregate well-being depend on both material growth and social and cultural development. Although this has, perhaps, always been true, systematic and sustained material growth has been absent for most of human history, with some positive and negative exceptions (see, for example, Goodfriend and McDermott, 1995). Instead, since the Industrial Revolution a significant fraction of the world has kept growing at a positive rate, accumulating physical capital, developing better and better technologies and accumulating human capital. Indeed, these processes have captured most economists' attention, whereas social and cultural dynamics have remained at the margin of economic analysis. In recent years, however, an increasing number of economists have begun to take into consideration the interplay between material growth and social development.

When material needs have been satisfied to a substantial degree, as is the case in advanced economies, well-being depends to an increasing extent upon social factors, such as the social environment, individual relative position and social status, and the ability to construct and enjoy meaningful and satisfactory relations with other people.[1] Social status has already received a great deal of attention by economists. Here, instead, we focus on the social environment and the enjoyment of social relations, building on the notions of 'social capital' and 'relational goods'.

This chapter proposes a simple growth model with private and social capital accumulation. We investigate whether these two processes move in the same direction or whether they conflict with each other, and show that both outcomes are possible, depending on the parameters and initial conditions of the economy. Taking into account the effects of these

---

[1] Pier Luigi Sacco, Paolo Vanin and Stefano Zamagni (2005) provide an extensive discussion of these issues.

dynamics on the consumption of both private and relational goods, we draw conclusions about well-being that apply to advanced economies. Section 2 clarifies the concepts and motivates our set-up. Sections 3 and 4 introduce the static and dynamic versions of our model. Section 5 concludes.

2.   Motivation

Social capital is the collection of those productive assets that are incorporated in the social structure of a group (rather than in physical goods and individual human beings, as physical and human capital) and that allow cooperation among its members to reach common goals. If we bear in mind that the group considered may range from being very small to including the whole of society, this definition of social capital encompasses most of the definitions to be found in the literature. At one extreme, some scholars even define social capital as an individual asset, but we prefer to consider it as a collective asset, in order to emphasise its interpersonal nature.[2] Examples of social capital range from trust to effective civic norms and to the networks of voluntary associations typical of civil society. A peculiar feature of social capital is that it is not accumulated through a standard mechanism of individual investment, since most of its benefits are not privately appropriable.[3] Rather, or at least to a much greater extent, it is accumulated through social participation in group activities. This participation may only partially be regarded as an investment, since it is, perhaps mainly, an activity that entails the simultaneous production and consumption of a particular category of goods: relational goods.

Relational goods display two peculiar features. They cannot be enjoyed alone, but exist only inasmuch as they are shared; and their production and consumption very often cannot be separated: relational goods are produced and consumed at the same time through participation in

---

[2] Edward Glaeser, David Laibson and Bruce Sacerdote (2002) call social capital the 'social' component of human capital. Since we distinguish social capital from human capital, we do not follow their approach. Denise DiPasquale and Glaeser (1999) define individual social capital as an individual's connections to others, and argue that it is important for the private provision of local amenities and of local public goods. This is in line with our focus, although we emphasise more the role of aggregate social participation.

[3] Glaeser, Laibson and Sacerdote (2002) make the opposite point, namely that social capital accumulation responds to incentives to investment in exactly the same way as human capital. Indeed, this result is natural if one defines social capital as a component of human capital, but it does not hold if one considers social capital a group asset rather than an individual asset.

some social activity with other people.[4] Examples range from going out with friends to participating in a choir, a football club, a voluntary organisation, and so on.

We focus on two aspects of the relationship between relational goods and social capital. On the one hand, a higher social capital increases the return on the time spent in social participation. For instance, it is easier and more rewarding to participate in an association with people whom we trust and who share our values and norms, and in a social context characterised by a rich network of associative opportunities; similarly, it is more rewarding to go out with friends with whom we share a higher capital of confidence, long-lasting relations and common norms, and in a context that offers many options for socially enjoyed leisure. In other words, social capital may be seen as an input in the production of relational goods.[5] On the other hand, higher social participation brings about social capital accumulation as a by-product. For instance, trust (or empathy) may be reinforced and generalised through social interactions (if individuals do not behave opportunistically). Likewise, high social participation may lead to the formation of new associations, while continuing to feed the existing ones.

Social participation is an activity intrinsically characterised by external effects (generally speaking, there is no market in which other people's participation may be bought, and even less is there a market for social capital). If other people's participation is low, or if the level of social capital is low, the time spent in participating is not very productive, and it becomes worthwhile to shift to private activities – that is, to ones that yield private goods. For instance, if my friends do not have time to go out with me, or if they do go out with me but the environment does not offer any interesting social opportunities, I may decide that I could better spend my time watching television or reading a book. Indeed, Corneo (2001) presents striking empirical evidence that the time devoted to watching television and working are positively correlated across countries, and proposes an explanation based on the substitution between privately enjoyed and socially enjoyed leisure (i.e. between some private

---

[4] The concept of relational goods is due to Carole Uhlaner (1989). Giacomo Corneo and Olivier Jeanne (1999b) refer to them as to socially provided private goods and study their interplay with social status and growth. Gui (2000c) provides a number of interesting contributions on the interpersonal dimension of economic interaction.

[5] Much of the literature on social capital also stresses its positive impact on the productivity of traditional private goods. We do not examine this effect here, thus making our point sharper; as, in our framework, a problem of under-accumulation of social capital exists, this problem will become even worse if we also consider the effect of social capital on private production. We discuss this point in more detail in the concluding section.

goods and relational goods). While our work is quite close in spirit to Corneo's paper, the main difference is that we analyse the dynamics of private and social capital accumulation, whereas he displays a simple static model with multiple equilibria.

Specifically, we propose here a model in which a reduction in social participation implies at the same time an increase in labour supply and a substitution of private for relational goods. On the one hand, such a shift stimulates the economy;[6] on the other, it generates a negative externality on the productivity (in terms of relational goods) of social participation. Dynamically, this change has a negative effect on social capital accumulation, whereas the sign of its effect on private capital accumulation depends on whether total savings increase (together with private production) or decrease (due to a more than proportional increase in private consumption).[7] Theoretically, private and social capital may be either positively or negatively correlated.[8]

Both ideas – that private growth brings about social development, and that it generates social disruption – are supported by long-standing traditions of thinking. We do not attempt to reconstruct this fascinating intellectual debate here, but limit ourselves to referring to Fred Hirsch (1976) as a representative of the view that private growth may entail negative social externalities. In particular, Hirsch argues that growth makes individual time constraints increasingly binding, thereby inducing a shift from time-intensive activities (among which there is indeed social participation) to time-saving ones (among which there are many forms of private consumption – e.g. fast food).[9] We emphasise here that this kind of shift may even reinforce private growth.

The idea that negative externalities, either on the natural or the social environment, may foster growth was first studied within an evolutionary framework by Angelo Antoci (1996) and Antoci and Stefano Bartolini (1997). The environmental economics literature on this subject has subsequently been rapidly expanding. For instance, Bartolini and Luigi Bonatti (1997) and several other contributions have further explored the basic idea within a neoclassical framework.[10] While our work is closely related to theirs, the main departure consists in our focus on social

---

[6] While most private goods enter GDP, most relational goods do not.
[7] While this is consistent with an interpretation of private capital in terms of physical capital, an extension of the concept to include human capital would not alter the picture significantly.
[8] See also Robert Putnam's (1995, 2000) empirical findings about the rise and decline of social capital in the United States.
[9] See Becker (1965) for a pioneering economic analysis of time allocation.
[10] Among recent contributions, see Antoci and Bartolini (2004) for an evolutionary one and Bartolini and Bonatti (2004) for a neoclassical one.

capital accumulation, which depends on social participation, whereas the above literature, although it mentions the possibility of a sociological interpretation, is more focused on natural resources, which are typically subject to a spontaneous flow of renewal.

In two companion papers (Antoci, Sacco and Vanin, 2002, 2005) we explore a similar framework, respectively with the tools of evolutionary game theory and of neoclassical economics. In both studies we find that growing economies may fall into social poverty traps, defined as situations in which, although material wealth is high, social poverty forces down overall well-being. For the sake of simplicity, in those models we consider the dynamics of only one asset, social capital. Here, we extend the analysis to include the accumulation of private capital. One might expect that, once the latter is taken into account, possibly together with the positive externalities it causes, material growth may be strong enough – from the point of view of well-being – to more than compensate for its negative social externalities. Indeed, we show that this may – but need not – be the case, and that whether it happens or not depends on the parameters of preferences and technology. An interesting result is that impatience may increase steady-state well-being, since it reduces the inefficient over-accumulation of private capital.[11]

3.   Static model

We now present a simple growth model with private and social capital accumulation. Since some of the basic insights may be appreciated even in a static framework, we first introduce a static version, in which private and social capital are considered as exogenously given in some strictly positive amount, and then introduce their dynamics (in continuous time).

Preferences and technology

We model an economy populated by a continuum of identical, infinitely lived individuals, of size normalised to 1, whose utility depends on three goods: a private consumption good C, used to satisfy basic needs (e.g. food and clothes); a relational good B (e.g. enjoying time with friends); and a private consumption good C_s that serves as a substitute for the relational good (e.g. a luxury good). Instantaneous preferences are described by the utility function $u(C, B, C_s) = \ln C + a \ln (B + bC_s)$, where $a > 0$ is the elasticity of substitution between basic needs satisfied by

---

[11] A similar result is also found in the above-mentioned environmental economics literature, since in that case too growth is the result of a failure of coordination.

C on the one hand and needs satisfied by either B or C_s on the other, and $b > 0$ is the marginal rate of substitution between B and C_s.[12]

The key point is how individuals decide to allocate their time (they are endowed with one unit) between social participation, labour and private consumption, besides the allocation of the latter between the two private goods. Since it is not in our focus, we disregard the allocation of time to C and C_s, simply assuming that both require income but not time; on the contrary, B may be enjoyed only if an individual spends time in social participation. Time must therefore be allocated between social participation (fraction s) and labour (fraction $1 - s$). A single individual considers average social participation $\bar{s} = \int_0^1 s(i)\mathrm{d}i$ in the economy as exogenously given.

We assume a backyard technology,[13] by which identical individuals produce private goods for their own consumption using labour and private capital K, according to production function $Y = (1 - s)^\epsilon K^{1-\epsilon} A$, where $\epsilon \in (0, 1)$ is a parameter. Term $A \equiv (1 - \bar{s})^\sigma \bar{K}^\vartheta$ captures a positive externality in production, which can be due to either the observability of other people's production or the availability of help when needed. Average private capital $\bar{K} = \int_0^1 K(i)\mathrm{d}i$ is considered as exogenously given by each individual and, consequently, the same is true for the whole term A (σ and ϑ are strictly positive parameters).

Besides private capital, our economy is characterised by the presence of social capital K_s. Social capital is not the private property of any individual but is, rather, an endowment of the entire economy, which each single individual considers as exogenous.

The quantity of relational good B enjoyed by the representative individual is a function of his own social participation, average social participation and social capital, all of which are indispensable factors: $B = s^\alpha \bar{s}^\beta K_s^\gamma$, where $\alpha, \beta, \gamma > 0$.

The maximisation problem of the representative individual, and symmetric Nash equilibria

The problem solved by the representative individual is

$$\max_{s,C,C_s} u(C, B, C_s) = \ln C + a \ln \left(s^\alpha \bar{s}^\beta K_s^\gamma + bC_s\right) \quad \text{s.t.} \qquad (1)$$

[12] The assumption of perfect substitutability between B and C_s greatly simplifies the mathematics. Relaxing this assumption may have non-obvious economic consequences and make closed-form solutions hard to obtain. We simulated a version of this model with the hypothesis of imperfect substitution, but did not gain any interesting insight.
[13] This simplifying assumption allows us to rule out any concern about market structure.

$$C + C_s = Y = (1 - s)^\epsilon K^{1-\epsilon}(1 - \bar{s})^\sigma \bar{K}^\vartheta, \quad C, C_s \geq 0, \quad s \in [0, 1] \quad (2)$$

A symmetric Nash equilibrium (SNE) is a triplet (s^*, C^*, C_s^*) that solves problem (1) under constraint (2), given that every other individual in the economy chooses s^*, so that, in particular, $\bar{s} = s^*$.

It is easy to show that there is always an SNE with no social participation. To see this, let $\bar{s} \equiv 0$, $\tilde{C} \equiv 1/(1 + a)K^{1+\vartheta-\epsilon}$ and $\tilde{C}_s \equiv [a/(1 + a)]K^{1+\vartheta-\epsilon}$.

Proposition 1 *The triplet $(\bar{s}, \tilde{C}, \tilde{C}_s)$ is always an SNE; that is, for any parameter constellation, there exists an SNE with no social participation.*[14]

In this equilibrium, no time is devoted to social interaction, since each individual believes that every other one will spend his entire amount of time working, thus rendering social participation not worthwhile.

To be able to investigate analytically the existence of an SNE in which $s > 0$, we make the following simplifying assumption.

Assumption 1 $\alpha + \beta = \epsilon + \sigma = \varphi < 1$: *this implies that, at an SNE, the elasticity of relational goods with respect to social participation equals the elasticity of private production with respect to labour; we call this elasticity φ, and assume that the two functions are concave ($\varphi < 1$).*[15]

Proposition 2 *Under assumption 1, there exists a unique SNE with strictly positive social participation, namely the triplet $(\hat{s}, \hat{C}, \hat{C}_s)$, defined as follows:*

case (a): $K_s < h(K)$: $\begin{cases} \hat{s} \equiv \dfrac{1}{1 + \left(\dfrac{b\epsilon K^{1+\vartheta-\epsilon}}{\alpha K_s^\gamma}\right)^{\frac{1}{1-\varphi}}} \\[30pt] \hat{C} \equiv \dfrac{1}{b(1 + a)}\hat{s}^\varphi K_s^\gamma + \dfrac{1}{(1 + a)}(1 - \hat{s})^\varphi K^{1+\vartheta-\epsilon} \\[20pt] \hat{C}_s \equiv \dfrac{a}{(1 + a)}(1 - \hat{s})^\varphi K^{1+\vartheta-\epsilon} - \dfrac{1}{b(1 + a)}\hat{s}^\varphi K_s^\gamma \end{cases}$

$$(3)$$

---

[14] All proofs are given in the appendix.
[15] The equality plays no other role than to enable us to derive an analytic solution, whereas the assumption that $\varphi < 1$ allows a strictly positive equilibrium social participation, even for a low ratio of social over private capital.

$$\text{case (b): } K_s \geq h(K): \begin{cases} \hat{s} \equiv \dfrac{a\alpha}{a\alpha + \epsilon} \\[2mm] \hat{C} \equiv (1 - \hat{s})^{\varphi} K^{1+\vartheta-\epsilon} \\[2mm] \hat{C}_s \equiv 0 \end{cases} \tag{4}$$

where $h(K) \equiv [(\epsilon b/\alpha)^{\varphi}(ab)^{1-\varphi}K^{1+\vartheta-\epsilon}]^{1/\gamma}$.

Note that $\hat{s}$ is an increasing function of K_s and α and a decreasing function of K. We will come back to the interpretation of these findings in the context of the dynamic specification of the model. Observe also that cases (a) and (b) of proposition 2, defined as $K_s < h(K)$ and $K_s \geq h(K)$ respectively identify an economy in which social capital is, firstly, scarce and, secondly, abundant relative to private capital. Whatever the economy's (exogenous) endowment of the two forms of capital, proposition 2 gives us the SNE with participation $(\hat{s}, \hat{C}, \hat{C}_s)$ as a function of them and of the parameters.

Proposition 3 *Let assumption 1 hold.*

In case (a), there are both parameter constellations for which the SNE with positive social participation $(\hat{s}, \hat{C}, \hat{C}_s)$ Pareto-dominates the SNE with no participation $(\tilde{s}, \tilde{C}, \tilde{C}_s)$, and other ones for which the reverse is true.

In case (b), let $g(K) \equiv \{[(a\alpha + \epsilon)^{(1+a)/a}/(1 + a)^{(1+a)/(a\varphi)}]^{\varphi}(ab)^{1-\varphi} K^{1+\vartheta-\epsilon}\}^{1/\gamma}$. For any parameter constellation, the SNE with participation $(\hat{s}, \hat{C}, \hat{C}_s)$ Pareto-dominates the one with no participation $(\tilde{s}, \tilde{C}, \tilde{C}_s)$ if, and only if, $K_s > g(K)$, the reverse being true when $K_s < g(K)$.

Proposition 3 tells us that, in economies relatively poor in social capital and rich in private capital (meaning $K_s < h(K)$), which of the two equilibria Pareto-dominates the other depends on the parameters of preferences and technology; but, when social capital is abundant enough relative to private capital $(K_s \geq h(K))$, it eventually (that is, for $K_s > g(K)$) becomes more efficient to devote a positive fraction of time to social participation, thereby forgoing some (or all) luxury consumption but enjoying relational goods. Since, for any parameter constellation and for any strictly positive endowment of both forms of capital, both equilibria are present, it is possible that, due to coordination failure, an economy becomes stuck in the Pareto inferior equilibrium. The limitation of proposition 3 is that it does not tell us anything about the sources of the relative abundance of private versus social capital. To investigate this aspect, we have to turn to the dynamic specification of our model.

However, before doing this, a further comment may be made on the externalities that drive the story of this static model. Since both average social participation and average labour time are supposed to exert positive external effects (on the production of the relational good and of the private goods, respectively), it is not a priori clear whether, overall, social participation displays positive or negative spillovers.[16] In general, in this game there tend to be positive spillovers from social participation when social capital is high relative to private capital, whereas they are, overall, negative when the reverse is true.[17]

Remark 1 *Under assumption 1, since, generically, in the SNE with positive participation* $(\hat{s}, \hat{C}, \hat{C}_s)$ *spillovers are present, this equilibrium is inefficient even when it Pareto-dominates the SNE with no participation* $(\bar{s}, \bar{C}, \bar{C}_s)$.[18]

Remark 1 tells us that the common result that, in the presence of non-internalised externalities, even the best SNE is generally inefficient also applies to our case.

4.   Dynamic model

In the dynamic specification of the model, preferences and technology are the same as above, with the only difference that now private and social capital are endogenously determined. The dynamics of the representative individual's private capital is given by $\dot{K} = Y - C - C_s - \eta K$, where $\eta \geq 0$ is the private capital depreciation rate.[19]

Social capital is not accumulated through a process of investment; rather, its stock increases when a high average social participation brings about a high average enjoyment of the relational good (denoted $\bar{B} = \int_0^1 B(i)\mathrm{d}i$. Since relations deteriorate over time if individuals do not actively take care of them, we also assume that K_s depreciates at a rate $\delta > 0$. We can thus summarise the dynamics of social capital as $\dot{K}_s = f(\bar{B}) - \delta K_s$, where f is a strictly increasing function.[20] The more rewarding social participation is in terms of relational goods, the more it contributes to social capital accumulation.[21]

---

[16] According to Russel Cooper and Andrew John's (1988) terminology, social participation has positive (negative) spillovers if an increase in average social participation raises (decreases) individual utility – i.e. if $\partial u(C, B, Y - C)/\partial \bar{s}$ is positive (negative).

[17] Formally, under the reasonable assumption that $\beta, \sigma < 1$, which is even weaker than assumption 1, $(\partial u(C, B, Y - C)/\partial \bar{s}) > 0 \Leftrightarrow \beta s^\alpha \bar{s}^{\beta-1} K_s^\gamma > b\sigma(1-s)^\epsilon(1-\bar{s})^{\sigma-1} K^{1+\vartheta-\epsilon}$; i.e. when K_s is high relative to K, s is high and $\bar{s}$ is low.

[18] Precisely, in the SNE $(\hat{s}, \hat{C}, \hat{C}_s)$ there are positive spillovers when $\alpha < (\beta\epsilon)/\sigma$ and negative ones when the reverse is true. There are no spillovers only in the non-generic case in which $\alpha = (\beta\epsilon)/\sigma$. Remark 1 then follows from proposition 2 of Cooper and John (1988).

[19] For notational simplicity, we omit the time index $t \in \Re_+$.

[20] The idea that non-material forms of capital may be accumulated through a 'consumption' activity rather than through investment, although unconventional in economics, is neither new (it goes back to Aristotle's analysis of ethical virtues, the influence of which is to be found in Martha Nussbaum's (1986) discussion of relational goods) nor surprising (e.g. knowledge, which is accumulated through the use of knowledge itself).

[21] This specification seems a good first approximation for both main forms of social capital (namely trust and social norms, on the one hand, and association networks, on the other), since the ability of both of them to prosper and expand depends crucially on

For the sake of simplicity, we make the following assumptions.

Assumption 2 $\eta = 0$: *we ignore private capital depreciation.*

Assumption 3 $f(x) \equiv x$: *this means that* $\dot{K}_s = \bar{B} - \delta K_s$.

Assumption 4 $\epsilon > \vartheta$ *and* $\gamma < 1$: *this means that we do not allow either K or K_s to grow steadily at a strictly positive rate.*

Assumption 2 is an innocent one. Assumption 3 is made only for the sake of analytical simplicity.[22] Assumption 4 means that, in our model, there is no engine for endogenous growth.

The representative individual's maximisation problem

Let $r > 0$ be the intertemporal discount rate. The representative individual chooses at time $t = 0$ how to allocate, at present and at any point in the future, his own time to participation and labour, and his private production to subsistence and luxury consumption, on the one hand, and investment in new private capital, on the other, in order to maximise lifetime utility. At any given point in time, his control variables are therefore s, C and C_s (which must respect $C, C_s \geq 0$ and $s \in [0, 1]$). A strategy is a time path of controls. Initial stocks of social capital (K_s^0) and private capital (K^0, assumed to be the same for every individual: $K^0 = \bar{K}^0$) are exogenously given. When choosing his strategy, the representative individual regards as exogenously given the strategies of the rest of the population. Since the time path of social capital and population averages are independent of any single individual's strategy, this amounts to taking the entire future path of $K_s, \bar{K}$ and $\bar{s}$ as given. The set of variables that the representative individual considers as predetermined at any point in time therefore includes these three variables and the state variable that is under his own direct control – namely his own private capital K.[23] In short, taking for granted the constraints imposed by technology and by the set of admissible controls, the representative individual's problem may be written as follows:[24]

---

the reward they yield to the people involved, and this reward consists to a high degree of relational goods. The reason it is a first approximation is that material rewards may also play a role; we discuss this point in the concluding section.

[22] In principle, there is no reason for the 'gross investment' in social capital to be exactly equal to the average benefit from social participation, although it is an increasing function of the latter; however, this specification is by far the easiest one. For instance, all our results would still hold if we assumed $f(x) \equiv \psi x, \psi \in (0, 1)$.

[23] Notice that, in the absence of uncertainty and in the impossibility for the representative individual to affect population averages (which eliminates any incentive to behave strategically to influence other people's future choices), in the present model considering open-loop as opposed to closed-loop strategies makes no difference.

[24] Recall that all the variables here (both the controls s, C, C_s and the predetermined variables $K_s, K, \bar{K}, \bar{s}$, as well as the rates of change $\dot{K}_s$ and $\dot{K}$) should appear with a time

$$\max_{s,C,C_s} \int_0^\infty u(C, B, C_s) e^{-rt} dt = \int_0^\infty [\ln C + a \ln (s^\alpha \bar{s}^\beta K_s^\gamma + bC_s)] e^{-rt} dt \quad \text{s.t.}$$

$$\tag{5}$$

$$\dot{K}_s = \bar{s}^{\alpha+\beta} K_s^\gamma - \delta K_s \tag{6}$$

$$\dot{K} = (1-s)^\epsilon K^{1-\epsilon} A - C - C_s, \quad A \equiv (1-\bar{s})^\sigma \bar{K}^\vartheta \tag{7}$$

Symmetric Nash equilibrium

An SNE of this economy is a strategy (that is, a time path of the controls s^*, C^* and C_s^*) that solves problem (5) under constraints (6) and (7), given that every other individual in the economy chooses the same strategy.

We now study the SNE of our economy and its dynamic properties.[25] In order to maintain the analytical tractability of the static version also in the dynamic version of the model, we modify assumption 1 into the following one.

Assumption 5 $\alpha - \beta = \epsilon + \sigma = \varphi = 1$: *this implies that, at any SNE, the relational good is obtained as a linear function of social participation, and private production as a linear function of labour.*

Proposition 4 *Let assumptions 2 to 5 hold, and consider an SNE of the economy. At any point in time the curve*

$$K_s = \left(\frac{\epsilon b}{\alpha} K^{1+\vartheta-\epsilon} \right)^{\frac{1}{\gamma}} \tag{8}$$

separates in the (K, K_s) plane the region in which $s > 0$ and $C_s = 0$ from that in which $s = 0$ and $C_s > 0$ (see figure 7.1).[26]

---

index t, omitted for notational simplicity. The maximisation is taken over the time path of the three controls, with a slight abuse of notation.

[25] Notice that, although the representative individual *ex ante* (i.e. when deciding) considers the future time path of $\bar{s}$ and $\bar{K}$ as exogenous, *ex post* (i.e. at an SNE) it turns out to be equal to that of his own values s^* and K.

[26] The difference between $\varphi < 1$ and $\varphi = 1$ is that the latter assumption rules out the possibility of a strictly positive equilibrium choice of social participation for low values of social capital relative to private capital (i.e. in the lower region of figure 7.1). For high values, the choice of $s = 0$ is still an SNE, but not an interesting one, since the resulting dynamics are trivial. Therefore, we examine only the case in which individuals coordinate on the equilibrium with $s > 0$ in the upper region of figure 7.1.

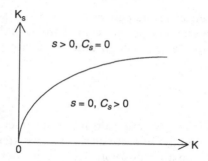

Figure 7.1. A graphic representation of cases (a) and (b) of proposition 4.

Precisely, in the two regions, s and C_s are chosen as follows:[27]

$$\text{case (a): } K_s < \left(\frac{\epsilon b}{\alpha} K^{1+\vartheta-\epsilon}\right)^{\frac{1}{\gamma}} : \quad \begin{cases} s = 0 \\ C_s = \dfrac{a}{\lambda} \end{cases} \tag{9}$$

$$\text{case (b): } K_s > \left(\frac{\epsilon b}{\alpha} K^{1+\vartheta-\epsilon}\right)^{\frac{1}{\gamma}} : \quad \begin{cases} s = \min\left\{1, \dfrac{a\alpha}{\epsilon\lambda K^{1+\vartheta-\epsilon}}\right\} \\ C_s = 0 \end{cases} \tag{10}$$

Case (a) identifies a situation in which, at a given point in time, social capital is scarce relative to private capital, so that, rather than spending time in social participation, the returns on which are low, in equilibrium it is better to choose a high labour supply, which has a high return, and to substitute a high consumption of private goods for the relational good.

On the contrary, case (b) captures a situation of relative scarcity of private capital as compared to social capital. In equilibrium, social interaction (besides subsistence consumption) is the basic source of individual well-being. On the one hand, labour productivity is too low to make it worthwhile to work more in order to substitute some private consumption for the relational good; on the other hand, the social environment is rich in opportunities and makes returns on social participation high. The difference between cases (a) and (b) shows why we

---

[27] λ is the shadow price of K. All variables are considered at time $t \in \Re_+$. Observe that the conditions spelled out in this proposition do not just hold at steady states but, rather, at any point in time.

observe large differences in the patterns of time allocation across countries of comparable size and private capital stock; indeed, these differences may be due to the presence of different relative stocks of private and social capital.

Fixed points

Exploiting proposition 4, we are now able to characterise the dynamic properties of our economy. In particular, we focus attention on the fixed points by stating the next proposition,[28] where we define

$$K^* \equiv \left(\frac{1-\epsilon}{r}\right)^{\frac{1}{\epsilon-\vartheta}} \tag{11}$$

$$K_s^* \equiv 0 \tag{12}$$

$$K^{**} \equiv \left[\frac{\epsilon(1-\epsilon)}{r(\epsilon+a\alpha)}\right]^{\frac{1}{\epsilon-\vartheta}} \tag{13}$$

$$K_s^{**} \equiv \left[\frac{a\alpha}{\delta(\epsilon+a\alpha)}\right]^{\frac{1}{1-\gamma}} \tag{14}$$

Proposition 5 *In the plane* (K, K_s), *point* (K^*, K_s^*) *is always a fixed point of the economy. Such a point is locally saddle-path stable.*

There exists at most one more fixed point, namely (K^{**}, K_s^{**}). *It is a fixed point if, and only if,*

$$\frac{a\alpha}{\delta(\epsilon+a\alpha)} > \left(\frac{\epsilon b}{\alpha}\right)^{\frac{1-\gamma}{\gamma}}\left[\frac{\epsilon(1-\epsilon)}{r(\epsilon+a\alpha)}\right]^{\frac{(1-\gamma)(1+\vartheta-\epsilon)}{\gamma(\epsilon-\vartheta)}} \tag{15}$$

If this condition is met, (K^{**}, K_s^{**}) *is locally saddle-path stable.*

Remark 2 *Straightforward calculations show that* $K^{**} < K^*$.

Remark 2 emphasises the fact that, when both fixed points are present, private capital is lower in the fixed point in which social capital is higher.

Remark 3 *For given values of the other parameters, condition (15) holds if* δ *and* b *are low enough and* r, α *and* a *are high enough.*

Remark 3 tells us that the fixed point at which social capital is positive exists when:

---

[28] For expositional purposes, we do not mention here the steady-state values of λ, which are in any case uniquely determined.

δ *is low*: social capital does not depreciate too fast (an intuitive condition);

r is high: individuals are not too patient; while impatience clearly reduces private accumulation, it may foster social capital accumulation, to the extent that this reflects the external effects of relational consumption;

α *is high*: the relational good is sufficiently a private and not too much of a public good – i.e. its enjoyment is sufficiently sensitive to one's own contribution;

a is high: enough weight is attributed to the needs satisfied by either the relational good or its private substitute (again, an intuitive condition); and

b is low: the balance between the relational good and its private substitute as a means of satisfying preferences for non-subsistence goods is not excessively in favour of the private substitute.[29]

It is interesting to speculate on the meaning of such parameters in terms of real-world examples. One might argue, for instance, that a high degree of individual mobility is associated with a high δ, the social capital depreciation rate.[30] It is true that mobility gives rise to many 'weak' ties, which are indeed a form of social capital;[31] but they are also a form that depreciates quickly. More generally, individual mobility may make many forms of previously accumulated social capital unproductive (in relational terms). From this point of view, we might speculate that a steady state with high social capital is more likely to exist in Europe than in the United States, precisely because individual mobility is lower in the former than in the latter.

Another interesting discussion concerns parameter α, which captures the relative degree to which the relational good is a private rather than a public good.[32] We may associate a high and a low α, respectively, with

---

[29] To have a numerical intuition, let us parameterise the model in a simple way, so that $a = b = 1$, $\alpha = \epsilon = 0.5$, $\vartheta = 0.1$ and $\gamma = 0.8$. In this case, if the social capital depreciation rate δ is, for instance, 10%, then condition (15) is met even at a discount rate r of 1%. If we lower γ to 0.5, then, with the same $\delta = 10\%$, condition (15) fails to be met up to a discount rate r of 8%, whereas it is met for $r \geq 9\%$.

[30] Maurice Schiff (1999, 2002) analyses the clear-cut difference between the two traditional forms of factor mobility, namely migration and trade, which becomes apparent once we consider their different impacts on social capital.

[31] Mark Granovetter (1973) makes the point that weak ties may be economically very important, since they are often the vehicle of new information.

[32] Note that B is a pure public good if $\alpha = 0$, in which case any private incentive to social participation is absent. On the other hand, B is a pure private good if $\beta = 0$ – that is, under assumption 5, if $\alpha = 1$. In general terms, relational goods are an intermediate case between private and public goods.

more active forms of social participation, in which my return depends crucially on my contribution (say, organising an event and enjoying its success), and to more passive ones, in which my benefit depends mostly on other people's contribution (say, attending the same event as a member of the audience). Another interpretation is that a high α reflects an open context, where integration is easy and my benefits from participation (suppose I am a newcomer or an immigrant) depend to a high degree upon my own choice, whereas a low α reflects closed contexts, where integration is difficult and I may be excluded anyway, despite my efforts to participate.

Therefore, while individual mobility (both geographical and social) may increase the depreciation rate of social capital, it may also render relational goods more private and less public. This second effect would then probably favour the United States over Europe as regards the existence of a steady state with high social capital. However, as we show in the next subsection, the crucial point is not just whether this steady state exists (e.g., to follow our illustrative speculation, that it exists both in the United States and in Europe) but, rather, whether it is more or less desirable than the other one.

Analysis of well-being

Let us now consider, when both fixed points exist (i.e. under condition (15)), which one is Pareto superior. Let u^* and u^{**} be the representative individual's utility in fixed points (K^*, K_s^*) and (K^{**}, K_s^{**}), respectively.

Proposition 6 *Assume that condition (15) is satisfied. Then fixed point* (K^{**}, K_s^{**}) *Pareto-dominates* (K^*, K_s^*) *– i.e.* $u^{**} > u^*$ *– if, ceteris paribus, δ is low enough and r and γ are high enough. The reverse is true if δ is high enough and r and γ are low enough.*

Proposition 6 tells us that the same two forces, impatience and a low social capital depreciation rate, that let (K^{**}, K_s^{**}) be a fixed point also make it Pareto superior. Moreover, as it is natural to expect, high elasticity γ of the relational good to social capital contributes to the comparative efficiency of the fixed point with positive social capital.[33]

When fixed point (K^{**}, K_s^{**}) Pareto-dominates (K^*, K_s^*) and the economy becomes stuck in the latter, it may be described as a social poverty

---

[33] Let us consider again the simple parameterisation $a = b = 1$, $\alpha = \epsilon = 0.5$, $\vartheta = 0.1$ and $\gamma = 0.8$. In this case, $u^{**} - u^* = \frac{3}{2} \ln r - 4 \ln \delta - 4 \ln 2$, which, for instance, is positive for $\delta = 10\%$ and $r = 3\%$, as well as for any lower social capital depreciation rate and higher discount rate. If $\delta = 5\%$, then $u^{**} > u^*$, even at a discount rate of 1%. If we lower γ to 0.5, then $u^* > u^{**}$ for any reasonable value of δ and r.

trap.[34] The convergence to such a trap may have two basic causes: it may be due to a low initial endowment of social relative to private capital (for instance, Russia);[35] or it may be because of the general problem posed by externalities, the presence of which may lead to inefficient private choices. If the outcome is an over-accumulation of private capital, at the expense of social capital and individual and social well-being, we may say that private growth and social development come into conflict with each other, and that it would be efficient to increase social participation and decrease the labour supply, sacrificing some accumulation of private capital but gaining in terms of an improved social environment. Of course, this remains true only if fixed point (K^{**}, K_s^{**}) Pareto-dominates (K^*, K_s^*) and the economy becomes stuck in the latter; since the former fixed point is also locally stable, the economy will converge to it if its initial endowment of social capital is high enough.[36] When convergence to fixed point (K^{**}, K_s^{**}) takes place from below along both dimensions, social development and economic growth move together.[37]

Instead, we have seen that (K^*, K_s^*) may Pareto-dominate fixed point (K^{**}, K_s^{**}) if the 'social technology' is 'bad' (high δ and low γ), and if individuals are very patient (low r). Moreover, we have shown that, in the same conditions, (K^{**}, K_s^{**}) may even fail to be a fixed point. In the first case, (K^{**}, K_s^{**}) should be regarded as a situation in which individuals devote too much time to socially enjoyed leisure, while working and saving too little to reach a more efficient steady state. In the second case, since there is no alternative, there is no comparative discussion.

5.   Conclusions

This chapter sheds light on the interplay between the private and social components of well-being in a scenario in which both private and social capital are present, relational goods play a role and their substitutability with some private goods is taken into account.

[34] The use of an infinitely lived agent model may lead to underestimating the consequences of social impoverishment. If, as stressed by James Coleman (1988, 1990), social capital is relevant for children's identity formation and for the creation of human capital, the consequences are likely to be more serious than pointed out here.

[35] Richard Rose (1998) considers in detail how the centralisation of the Soviet Union may have eroded many forms of social capital, inducing individuals to rely on a narrow circle of family ties, which represents at the same time a response to the state of affairs and a social trap that inhibits the mechanism of social development.

[36] More precisely, if initial endowment (K^0, K_s^0) is close enough to (K^{**}, K_s^{**}). Note that even this case, although more favourable, does not solve the problem of externalities.

[37] However, recall that, because of assumption 4, neither private growth nor social development may be endogenously sustained for ever.

We first present a static model, in which social and private capital are constant at some exogenously given stock. This model displays two equilibria: a privately oriented one, in which labour time and private production are high and relational goods are substituted by private goods, and a socially oriented one, in which labour supply is low and social participation high, so that, besides private consumption, relational goods become a key determinant of well-being. If social capital is low relative to private capital, the privately oriented equilibrium tends to be Pareto superior; if the reverse is true, the socially oriented equilibrium definitely becomes more efficient. Since equilibrium selection is a matter of coordination, it is possible for the economy to become stuck in the Pareto inferior equilibrium.

The static model does not explain the determinants of the relative endowment of social and private capital. We confront this issue in the dynamic extension of the model, in which we assume that private capital is accumulated, as usual, through savings, while the accumulation of social capital is a by-product of the generation of relational goods. The most interesting case is when parameters are such that the dynamics of the system admit two fixed points: one in which there is only private capital, and another in which both forms of capital are present. We further discuss the conditions in which the latter steady state Pareto-dominates the former, and show that, in this case, both equilibria are saddle-path stable, so the system can converge to the Pareto inferior one. In this case, we witness a conflict between economic growth and social development, since growth drives the economy into a social poverty trap. If, instead, the economy converges to the Pareto superior fixed point, we may have economic growth and social development moving in the same direction. The distinction between these two cases once again depends upon the initial relative endowment of private and social capital, but also upon the technology of social interaction and the degree of impatience.

Some of the assumptions under which we derive our results warrant a short discussion. First, we assume, for simplicity, that social capital does not matter for the production of private goods, nor private capital for relational goods. An interesting future extension could include these cross-influences.[38] Second, while we consider positive learning-by-doing externalities in private production, we do not allow them to be strong enough to generate endogenous growth. This is another possible extension of the model. Third, we assume that private consumption does not require time, so that all leisure time is devoted to social participation. Although unrealistic, we make this modelling choice because, generally

---

[38] See, along similar lines, Bartolini and Bonatti (2004).

speaking, social participation is a more time-intensive activity than private consumption.[39] Fourth, the assumption that the 'gross investment' in social capital is exactly equal to the average production of the relational good could easily be generalised (for instance, by assuming that only a fraction of the relational good produced accumulates as social capital) without changing any of the results of the model: it has simply been dictated by notational economising. Last, perfect substitutability and assumptions 1 and 5 are crucial to obtain simple analytical solutions.[40] Relaxing assumption 1 to some extent would not alter the results of the static model, although it would preclude the possibility of expressing them in closed form.[41] As regards assumption 5, a comparison with Antoci, Sacco and Vanin (2002) allows us to conjecture that its main effect is to rule out a repulsive fixed point that separates the two stable ones. Since our mathematical findings are supported by a clear economic intuition, we are quite confident in their general validity.

The model and its results may aid the better understanding of a number of concrete situations. For instance, it is widely recognised that, besides more traditional economic fundamentals, social factors played important roles in the crises of both Russia and Argentina. In these cases, past political history was responsible for the widespread disruption of the essential structures of civil society. In terms of our model, this amounts to a sharp reduction in the stock of social capital. Indeed, both countries faced a very low ratio of social to private capital, a situation to which individuals reacted by shifting to privately oriented strategies, thus worsening the problem. While the present version of our model allows us clearly to understand these dynamics and their socially disruptive consequences, the above extension to include the effects of social capital on private productivity may help in explaining the relatively low success of the private sectors of these economies.

Another quite different situation that may be explained by our model is the case of successful professionals who devote much of their time to working, earning high incomes and consuming great quantities of luxury goods but who have poor social lives and are, overall, dissatisfied. Casual observation tells us that this is quite a common case in advanced

---

[39] Clearly, the consumption of some private substitutes of the relational good (e.g. watching television) is also time-intensive, so an interesting extension would be to take this into account, along the lines set by Corneo (2001).

[40] Recall that assumption 1, made for the static model, implies the equality in equilibrium of the degree of concavity of the relational good and of private production as functions, respectively, of social participation and labour; assumption 5, made for the dynamic model, implies a linear specification for both functions in equilibrium.

[41] More precisely, this would be the case if one just assumed that $\alpha + \beta < 1$ and $\epsilon + \sigma < 1$ without requiring them to be equal.

societies. In terms of our model, this is precisely what one would observe along the convergence path towards a social poverty trap. Moreover, when this situation is widespread, individual reactions tend to be to invest even more time in private activities, thus exacerbating the problem. Again, pursuing this application rigorously would probably require an extension of the model towards a non-homogeneous society or an asymmetric equilibrium. Our hope is that our contribution may serve as a starting point for future research.

Appendix

Proof of proposition 1

Using the production function and the budget constraint to substitute for C_s, and calling $v(s, C) = u(C, B, Y - C)$, we can rewrite problem (1)–(2) as

$$\max_{s,C} v(s, C) =$$
$$\ln C + a \ln \{s^\alpha \bar{s}^\beta K_s^\gamma + b[(1 - s)^\epsilon (1 - \bar{s})^\sigma K^{1+\vartheta-\epsilon} - C]\} \quad \text{s.t.} \tag{16}$$

$$C \geq 0, \quad (1 - s)^\epsilon (1 - \bar{s})^\sigma K^{1+\vartheta-\epsilon} - C \geq 0, \quad s \in [0, 1] \tag{17}$$

If $0 < C < Y$, the first-order conditions of this problem are

$$\frac{\partial v}{\partial C} = 0 \tag{18}$$

$$\frac{\partial v}{\partial s} \leq 0, \quad s\frac{\partial v}{\partial s} = 0, \quad 0 \leq s \leq 1 \tag{19}$$

Equation (18) immediately yields

$$C = \frac{1}{b(1 + a)} [s^\alpha \bar{s}^\beta K_s^\gamma + b(1 - s)^\epsilon (1 - \bar{s})^\sigma K^{1+\vartheta-\epsilon}] \tag{20}$$

which, substituted into inequality (19), after rearranging, yields

$$\frac{(1 - s)^{1-\epsilon}}{s^{1-\alpha}} \leq \frac{b\epsilon(1 - \bar{s})^\sigma K^{1+\vartheta-\epsilon}}{\alpha \bar{s}^\beta K_s^\gamma}, \text{with equality if } s > 0, \quad 0 \leq s \leq 1. \tag{21}$$

When $\bar{s} = 0$, we have $B = 0$ whatever the individual choice of s. Hence, the optimal individual response to $\bar{s} = 0$ is to choose $s = 0$. The rest of the proposition follows from equation (20) and from the production function, which also shows that, for $s = \bar{s} = 0$, constraint $0 \leq C \leq Y$ is not binding.

Proof of proposition 2

The value of $\hat{s}$ in case (a) follows from equation (21) after applying the SNE condition $\hat{s} = s$ and assumption 1. The values of $\hat{C}$ and of $\hat{C}_s$ then follow from equation (20) and from the budget constraint. The definition of function h, and therefore the distinction between case (a) and case (b), follows from equation (21) and the production function, setting $C = Y$. When this constraint is binding, i.e. in case (b), the representative individual sets $(\partial v/\partial s) = -(\partial v/\partial C)(\partial Y/\partial s)$. The values of $\hat{s}, \hat{C}, \hat{C}_s$ in case (b) follow from this equation, conditions $C = Y$ and $s = \hat{s}$, and the budget constraint.

Proof of proposition 3

Let $\tilde{u}$ and $\hat{u}$ be the representative individual's utility in the two SNE $(\bar{s}, \tilde{C}, \tilde{C}_s)$ and $(\hat{s}, \hat{C}, \hat{C}_s)$, respectively.

Consider first case (a). Using condition $K_s < h(K)$, it is easy to show that $\hat{u} - \tilde{u} > (1 + a)\varphi \ln (\alpha/(\alpha + ab^2\epsilon)) + (1 - a) \ln b$, and that this term is $\simeq 0.41$ for $a = 1/9$, $b = 3$, $\alpha = \epsilon = 0.5$ and $\beta = \sigma = 0.3$; therefore, for such parameters $\hat{u} > \tilde{u}$. Analogously, we show that $\hat{u} - \tilde{u} < (1 + a)$ $\ln [(\epsilon/(\alpha + ab^2\epsilon))^\varphi a^{1-\varphi} + 1] + (1 - a) \ln b$, where this term is $\simeq -0.21$ for $a = 0.5$, $b = 0.1$, $\alpha = \epsilon = 0.5$ and $\beta = \sigma = 0.3$; therefore, for such parameters $\tilde{u} > \hat{u}$.

Consider now case (b). The definition of function g comes from a straightforward substitution of the equilibrium values in the utility function. Note that g is strictly increasing. A comparison between functions h and g shows that a sufficient condition for $\hat{u} > \tilde{u}$ to hold is $(b\epsilon/\alpha) > [(a\alpha + \epsilon)^{(1+a)/a}]/[(1 + a)^{(1+a)/(a\varphi)}]$.

Proof of proposition 4

The current Hamiltonian value for problem (5) under constraints (6) and (7) is

$$H = \ln C + a \ln (s^\alpha \bar{s}^\beta K_s^\gamma + bC_s) + \lambda[(1 - s)^\epsilon K^{1-\epsilon}A - C - C_s] + \mu[\bar{s}^{\alpha+\beta}K_s^\gamma - \delta K_s] \tag{22}$$

By the maximum principle, we have

$$\dot{K} = \frac{\partial H}{\partial \lambda} = (1 - s)^\epsilon K^{1-\epsilon} A - C - C_s \qquad (23)$$

$$\dot{\lambda} = r\lambda - \frac{\partial H}{\partial K} = \lambda[r - (1 - \epsilon)(1 - s)^\epsilon K^{-\epsilon} A] \qquad (24)$$

$$\dot{K}_s = \frac{\partial H}{\partial \mu} = \bar{s}^{\alpha+\beta} K_s^\gamma - \delta K_s \qquad (25)$$

We omit the dynamics of μ, the 'shadow' price of social capital, since equations (23) to (25) are independent of it, due to the fact that the representative individual considers both $\bar{s}$ and K_s (and therefore $\dot{K}_s$) as exogenous.

The first-order conditions are

$$\frac{\partial H}{\partial C} = \frac{1}{C} - \lambda = 0, \quad C > 0 \qquad (26)$$

$$\frac{\partial H}{\partial C_s} = \frac{ab}{s^\alpha \bar{s}^\beta K_s^\gamma + bC_s} - \lambda \le 0, \quad C_s \frac{\partial H}{\partial C_s} = 0, \quad C_s \ge 0 \qquad (27)$$

$$\frac{\partial H}{\partial s} = \frac{a\alpha s^{\alpha-1} \bar{s}^\beta K_s^\gamma}{s^\alpha \bar{s}^\beta K_s^\gamma + bC_s} - \epsilon\lambda(1 - s)^{\epsilon-1} K^{1-\epsilon} A \le 0 \qquad (28)$$

$$s\frac{\partial H}{\partial s} = 0, \quad s \in [0, 1]$$

Note that s and C_s cannot both be set at zero. Thus, either condition (27) or condition (28) must hold with equality.

The transversality condition for private capital is

$$\lim_{t \to \infty} e^{-rt} \lambda(t) K(t) = 0 \qquad (29)$$

Substituting assumption 5 and equilibrium conditions $\bar{s} = s$ and $\bar{K} = K$ into equations (26) to (28), we obtain

$$C = \frac{1}{\lambda} \qquad (30)$$

$$\frac{\partial H}{\partial C_s} = \frac{ab}{sK_s^\gamma + bC_s} - \lambda \le 0, \quad C_s \frac{\partial H}{\partial C_s} = 0, \quad C_s \ge 0 \qquad (31)$$

$$\frac{\partial H}{\partial s} = \frac{a\alpha K_s^\gamma}{sK_s^\gamma + bC_s} - \epsilon\lambda K^{1+\vartheta-\epsilon} \le 0, \quad s\frac{\partial H}{\partial s} = 0, \quad s \in [0, 1] \qquad (32)$$

Inequality $(\partial H/\partial C_s) \leq 0$ may be rewritten in the form $[a/(sK_s^\gamma + bC_s)] - (\lambda/b) \leq 0$.

For $K_s > 0$, inequality $(\partial H/\partial s) \leq 0$ may be rewritten in the form $[a/(sK_s^\gamma + bC_s)] - [(\epsilon K^{1+\vartheta-\epsilon})/(\alpha K_s^\gamma)]\lambda \leq 0$.

Hence, if $(\epsilon K^{1+\vartheta-\epsilon}/\alpha K_s^\gamma) > (1/b)$, $(\partial H/\partial C_s) = 0$ and $(\partial H/\partial s) < 0$ hold, so that the representative individual's equilibrium choice is such that $C_s > 0$ and $s = 0$. If, on the contrary, $(\epsilon K^{1+\vartheta-\epsilon}/\alpha K_s^\gamma) < (1/b)$, then we have $C_s = 0$ and $s > 0$. If, lastly, $(\epsilon K^{1+\vartheta-\epsilon}/\alpha K_s^\gamma) = (1/b)$, we remain with one equation for two unknowns, and the choice of C_s and s is indeterminate. The remainder of proposition 4 follows from a straightforward substitution in equations (31) and (32).

Proof of proposition 5

For case (a), i.e. in condition (9), the equilibrium dynamics of our economy are described by

$$\dot{K} = K^{1+\vartheta-\epsilon} - \frac{1+a}{\lambda} \tag{33}$$

$$\dot{\lambda} = \lambda[r - (1-\epsilon)K^{\vartheta-\epsilon}] \tag{34}$$

$$\dot{K}_s = -\delta K_s \tag{35}$$

For case (b), i.e. in condition (10), if $(a\alpha/\epsilon\lambda K^{1+\vartheta-\epsilon}) \leq 1$,[42] the equilibrium dynamics are

$$\dot{K} = K^{1+\vartheta-\epsilon} - \left(1 + \frac{a\alpha}{\epsilon}\right)\frac{1}{\lambda} \tag{36}$$

$$\dot{\lambda} = \lambda\left[r - (1-\epsilon)\left(K^{\vartheta-\epsilon} - \frac{a\alpha}{\epsilon\lambda K}\right)\right] \tag{37}$$

$$\dot{K}_s = K_s^\gamma\left(\frac{a\alpha}{\epsilon\lambda K^{1+\vartheta-\epsilon}} - \delta K_s^{1-\gamma}\right) \tag{38}$$

---

[42] Since we are interested in the fixed points of these dynamics, we do not consider, in case (b), the possibility that $(a\alpha)/(\epsilon\lambda K^{1+\vartheta-\epsilon}) > 1$, since in this case $\dot{K} = -(1/\lambda)$ and there is no fixed point. Note, moreover, that this possibility is not a relevant one, since it means that individuals do not work at all, and derive their private consumption only from 'eating' their existing stock of private capital.

The analytical determination of (K^*, K_s^*) and (K^{**}, K_s^{**}) follows from a straightforward substitution in the systems (33) to (35) and (36) to (38), setting the left-hand side of each equation at zero. (K^*, K_s^*) satisfies the condition of case (a), $K_s^* < [(\epsilon b/\alpha)K^{*1+\vartheta-\epsilon}]^{(1/\gamma)}$, and is thus indeed a fixed point. (K^{**}, K_s^{**}) is a fixed point if, and only if, it satisfies the condition of case (b): $K_s^{**} > [(\epsilon b/\alpha)K^{**1+\vartheta-\epsilon}]^{(1/\gamma)}$. Equation (15) is simply a rewriting of this condition.

The stability properties are determined as follows. The Jacobian matrix of the systems (33) to (35), evaluated at (K^*, K_s^*), is

$$A = \begin{bmatrix} (1 + \vartheta - \epsilon)K^{\vartheta-\epsilon} & \dfrac{1+a}{\lambda^2} & 0 \\ (1 - \epsilon)(\epsilon - \vartheta)\lambda K^{\vartheta-\epsilon-1} & 0 & 0 \\ 0 & 0 & -\delta \end{bmatrix}$$

One eigenvalue is therefore $-\delta < 0$, and the other two have opposite signs, since the determinant of the sub-matrix obtained from A by deleting the third row and the third column is negative. Therefore, if (K, K_s) is initially close enough to (K^*, K_s^*), there exists a single initial value of λ that puts the representative agent on the stable arm (which, in turn, has dimension 2).

Observe now that the Jacobian matrix of the systems (36) to (38), evaluated at (K^{**}, K_s^{**}), is such that $(\partial \dot{K}/\partial K_s) = (\partial \dot{\lambda}/\partial K_s) = 0$ and $(\partial \dot{K}_s/\partial K_s) = -\delta(1 - \gamma) < 0$. Therefore, the latter value is one of the eigenvalues of the Jacobian matrix, and the other two have opposite signs, since the determinant of the sub-matrix is negative:

$$B = \begin{bmatrix} \dfrac{\partial \dot{K}}{\partial K} & \dfrac{\partial \dot{K}}{\partial \lambda} \\ \dfrac{\partial \dot{\lambda}}{\partial K} & \dfrac{\partial \dot{\lambda}}{\partial \lambda} \end{bmatrix}$$

To see this, observe that $(\partial \dot{K}/\partial K) = (1 + \vartheta - \epsilon)K^{\vartheta-\epsilon} > 0$, $(\partial \dot{K}/\partial \lambda) = [1 + (a\alpha/\epsilon)](1/\lambda^2) > 0$, $(\partial \dot{\lambda}/\partial K) = -(1 - \epsilon)\lambda[-(\epsilon - \vartheta)K^{\vartheta-\epsilon-1} + a\alpha/(\epsilon\lambda K^2)]$ and $(\partial \dot{\lambda}/\partial \lambda) = -a\alpha(1 - \epsilon)/(\epsilon K\lambda) < 0$.

It is then easy to obtain Det $B = -[(1 - \epsilon)(\epsilon - \vartheta)/(\lambda^2 K^2)][1 + (a\alpha/\epsilon)] < 0$.

Proof of proposition 6

In order to calculate u^*, observe first that, since we are in case (a), $s = 0$ and $u^* = \ln C + a \ln bC_s$. From equations (30) and (31), it follows immediately that $C = (1/\lambda)$ and $C_s = (a/\lambda)$, so that $C_s = aC$. Equations (33) and (11) then imply that $C = [1/(1 + a)]K^{*1+\vartheta-\epsilon} = [1/(1 + a)][(1 - \epsilon)/r]^{(1+\vartheta-\epsilon)/(\epsilon-\vartheta)}$ and $C_s = [a/(1 + a)][(1-\epsilon)/r]^{(1+\vartheta-\epsilon)/(\epsilon-\vartheta)}$. Therefore, $u^* = \ln [1/(1 + a)] + a \ln [ab/(1 + a)] + (1 + a)[(1 + \vartheta - \epsilon)/(\epsilon - \vartheta)] \ln [(1 - \epsilon)/r]$ is easily yielded.

Let us now calculate u^{**} in an analogous way. Since we are in case (b), $C_s = 0$ and $u^{**} = \ln C + a \ln (sK_s^\gamma)$. Remember that, in the fixed point $\lambda K^{1+\vartheta-\epsilon} = 1 + (a\alpha/\epsilon)$, equations (13) and (30) yield $C = (1/\lambda) = K^{**1+\vartheta-\epsilon}/[1 + (a\alpha/\epsilon)] = \{\epsilon(1 - \epsilon)/[r(\epsilon + a\alpha)]\}^{(1+\vartheta-\epsilon/\epsilon-\vartheta)}/[1 + (a\alpha/\epsilon)]$ and equation (32) yields $s = a\alpha/(\epsilon\lambda K^{1+\vartheta-\epsilon}) = a\alpha/(\epsilon + a\alpha)$. Since K_s is given by equation (14), we obtain $u^{**} = \ln [\epsilon/(\epsilon + a\alpha)] + [(1 + \vartheta - \epsilon)/(\epsilon - \vartheta)] \ln \{\epsilon(1 - \epsilon)/[r(\epsilon + a\alpha)]\} + a \ln [a\alpha/(\epsilon + a\alpha)] + a[\gamma/(1 - \gamma)] \ln \{a\alpha/[\delta(\epsilon + a\alpha)]\}$.

Proposition 6 follows from an analysis of the following expression:[43]

$$
\begin{aligned}
u^* - u^{**} = {} & \ln \frac{\epsilon + a\alpha}{\epsilon + a\alpha} + \frac{1 + \vartheta - \epsilon}{\epsilon - \vartheta} \left[a\ln(1 - \epsilon) - a\ln r + \ln \frac{\epsilon + a\alpha}{\epsilon} \right] \\
& + a\ln \frac{\epsilon + a\alpha}{\alpha + a\alpha} + a\ln b + a \frac{\gamma}{1 - \gamma} \left[\ln \delta + \ln \frac{\epsilon + a\alpha}{a\alpha} \right]
\end{aligned}
\tag{39}
$$

ACKNOWLEDGEMENTS

We would like to thank Benedetto Gui, Robert Sugden and an anonymous referee for some very useful comments, with the usual disclaimer.

---

[43] Note that the term in the last square brackets is negative if $\delta < [a\alpha/(\epsilon + a\alpha)]$, that $[\gamma/(1 - \gamma)]$ increases rapidly with γ, and that the absolute value of $\ln r$ is a decreasing function of r.

8   The logic of good social relations

Serge-Christophe Kolm

1.   Introduction

Good social relations are an essential aspect of a good society and of the quality of life, a crucial factor of people's happiness and intrinsic value, and an important cause of other achievements of society and of its members.[1] However, the explanation of the quality of social relations raises a number of puzzles.

The classical picture of human nature as being essentially motivated by individual egoism – which is the standard model of the 'dismal science' of economics – often seems all too real, and yet there are many instances of spontaneous pro-social behaviour of various types. People, however, commonly complain about the quality of social relations and attitudes and the paucity of good ones, even though these acts are in the end their own doing. And they cannot buy or sell most of this relational quality (even in exchange for similar behaviour), or have it imposed, because this quality basically rests on an aspect of the relationship in the category of gift giving, and it is in the very nature and definition of gift giving that it cannot be exchanged or imposed.

The existence and scope of these particular relational goods thus require a particular type of analysis, with a special concern for the possibilities of improvement within a realistic account of the capacities of human beings, who probably are 'neither angels nor beasts' (as Blaise Pascal puts it). The purpose of this chapter is to point out the crucial phenomenon underlying this question. This consists of an interaction between the structure of people's preferences concerning society and their own actions, on the one hand, and social interdependence, on the other.

---

[1] The analysis of social relations, emphasising their intrinsic value, notably in an economic framework, is the topic of a number of articles published by the author since the early 1970s and gathered in a book (Kolm, 1984). This chapter is closely related to some of this work.

In summary, good social relations consist of behaviours varied in form, intensity and scope, such as abstaining from harming others, respecting others, helping out and being honest, trustworthy, faithful and reliable, or relations of friendship and love. The relational and social value of these social behaviours depends greatly on the fact that, or the degree to which, they are voluntarily provided as gifts rather than being bought and sold or imposed. Both individuals and systems of morals value these relations and commonly complain that there is not enough of them. But gift giving in any form cannot, by nature, be bought, be part of an exchange in the strict sense, or be imposed: this would violate the essence and the definition of a gift. Instances of gift giving are, by their nature, 'market failures' and 'planning failures'. They can be promoted solely by changing people's motivations (besides issues of information).

However, the idea that people can become out-and-out altruists, substantially more than they are now, seems utopian and unrealistic. Yet, what is required is not that people give under any conditions, but only that they give when other people give too, in particular to themselves. This is reciprocity, a behaviour that is much less demanding than unconditional altruism from the point of view of motivation (and of the resulting material situation). Any agent will, individually, initiate giving (in the form of any behaviour favourable to others) if he knows that this will induce others to give, and, notably, to reciprocate, sufficiently. Gratitude – rather than self-sacrifice – or a sense of fairness are sufficient sentiments and behaviours for this situation. The promotion of such behaviour can be supported by the fact that everyone will be better off in the end, as a result of the corresponding social interaction. Moreover, this promotion by way of education, example and other means to influence people can rely on well-documented human propensities, such as genuine gratitude, helping if one has been helped (even by a third party), helping helpers, the voluntary provision of fair shares, imitation, following various social norms, and so on. Furthermore, reciprocity has a number of effects favourable to economic efficiency. In conclusion, the consideration of reciprocity should have a central place in any study or policy concerned with a good economy or a good society.

Section 2 briefly presents the nature of good social relations, including their gift giving aspect, their desirability, and the impossibility of obtaining them through exchange or coercion. Section 3 considers individuals' preferences about the various types of social relations, the corresponding behaviours, and the consequences for society. It turns out that selfishness often creates a prisoner's dilemma, with no possibility of improvement because gift giving can neither be agreed upon nor imposed, by nature and by definition. Unconditional altruism does not give rise to such an inefficiency but is very demanding from the point of view of motivation (it demands returning good for evil). However, an efficient outcome can also be obtained with conditional altruism, where people give if others do notably to themselves, but do not give otherwise. This can lead, notably, to reciprocity. Individual initiative can then generally secure the preferred equilibrium, where everyone gives. Section 4 then considers the possibility of comparing people's satisfaction when they have different preference structures, and concludes that people are likely to benefit, in the end, if reciprocitarian, altruistic or moral tendencies prevail in society. Section 5 notes that reciprocity also favours standard economic efficiency in many ways. The well-known psychological facts that favour the establishment of such reciprocitarian behaviour are briefly recalled in section 6. In section 7 it is concluded that reciprocity appears to be an essential behaviour, not solely for understanding societies and economies but also for normative concerns about them.

2.   Good relations, giving, and its reasons

Good social relations display innumerable types and intensities, such as: non-aggression (i.e. refraining from harming, killing, injuring, stealing, etc.); respect and consideration for others; politeness and civility; gift giving and generosity; help, aid, assistance and charity; compassion and pity; honesty, trustworthiness, faithfulness and reliability; love and friendship; and so on. Relations such as friendship or love, giving or aid resulting from altruism, compassion or generosity, spontaneous respect and consideration for others, spontaneous honesty and the resulting trustworthiness and faithfulness are not and cannot be imposed by force or threat, or bought and sold in exchange. Thus they are in the nature of gift giving, even when they come in addition to a relation of another type – that is, an exchange in the strict sense or a hierarchical relation. This aspect of social attitudes, behaviour and relations is praised by people who benefit from them and by the various morals (this excludes Nietzscheanism, Spencerism and the like). Indeed, the function of morals is to induce a range of actions and attitudes, among which those favourable to others are particularly important.[2]

---

[2] Indeed, this covers the whole domain of morals according to a widespread modern view, which withdraws acts that concern the actor alone from the field of moral considerations.

These relations, or aspects of relations, constitute our present topic. Their being in the nature of gift giving implies, first of all, that the acts that constitute the relation are free, not forced, not performed under coercion or threat of harm; and, secondly, that they are not provided in exchange for something, in the sense of a mutually conditional exchange of the market type (i.e. I do this if you do that). That is, the acts that are a part of these relations are not provided as a result of a threat either of being harmed or of being denied a good or a beneficial act. This does not preclude, of course, that they can – more or less – be induced by social pressure, social norms or a sense of duty, or by other people's behaviour when it is not a threat to do or withhold something, and that these actions themselves can influence or elicit others' behaviour. Moreover, such relations can accompany relations of exchange (in the strict sense) and hierarchical relations; but, then, the various aspects of such complex relations should not be confused. Because of the crucial gift-giving aspect of these positive relations towards others, their analysis in this respect will often use the vocabulary of gift giving for convenience in presentation, although this will generally cover a variety of relations. Note that the 'bad' gifts that everyone knows are not our topic here (they are gifts de facto imposed by oppressive norms or social pressure; gifts for manifesting a superiority or an inferiority; for creating a superiority; for binding the receiver with a moral debt – even for humiliating him; or solely for receiving a return gift; and so on).

One commonly hears complaints about the lack or scarcity of such positive social behaviour. This should not surprise economists, since one cannot buy gift giving, from the very nature and definition of a gift. One can sometimes buy the item that is given, but not the fact that it is given for free as a result of the corresponding specific favourable motivation. Gift giving elicits a 'market failure' for the intrinsic reason that it is not a market act, by nature and definition.[3] Hence, gift giving and good social relations are, a priori, bound to be in short supply from the benchmark of exchange and of the market (discarding income effects), in particular at their 'market price' of zero. Planning and public enforcement cannot cure this insufficiency, for the same reason: gift giving cannot be imposed.

One cannot even buy gifts with gifts, in the proper sense of 'buying': each act or transfer would not have the independent freedom that is

---

[3] Immanuel Kant (1991/1797) used to oppose things that have a price and things that have a dignity. With this terminology, the considered relations, attitudes and sentiments have a 'dignity'. In fact, they even imply that not having a 'price' can, per se, be a source of 'dignity'.

implied by the nature and definition of gift giving (and, correspondingly, each motivation would not be that of providing a gift but that of receiving one). One can, of course, more or less induce gift giving by various means; in particular, one can attract or induce gift giving with gifts if the other person is prone to return gifts or to imitate. However, this differs from exchange in the strict sense, and this kind of behaviour will turn out to be very important in our analysis.

Hence, complaints or regrets concerning disregard for others, insufficient helping or charity, and unsatisfactory social relations are about selfishness in various forms – that is, about people's motives and psychology. This seems natural, since proposing a gift is the decision of a single person, the giver. And there are various ways of more or less influencing people's propensities to give (or be honest etc.), such as providing reasons for such acts, persuasion, education, showing examples and various possible influences on the culture of society. Changes in preferences (including norms, habits, etc.) that underlie actions raises a problem for comparing efficiency (Pareto-wise), but there can be sufficient comparability to ensure improvement in this respect; this issue will be discussed further shortly. However, scepticism is often expressed about the possibility of people becoming much more altruistic than they already are. Christianity has been trying to make them so for two millennia now, with no evidence of progress.

Yet people's pro-social acts generally also depend on various conditions and not solely on motives or preferences. They depend, in particular, on such acts by others. Indeed, when people who complain about general selfishness are asked if they themselves give sufficiently, a common answer is 'I would if the others did'. This can mean 'I would give to them if they gave to me' (under similar circumstances). This is reciprocity proper (in the sense classically given to this term in the social sciences). However, this answer can also mean 'I would give if they also gave to the people to whom I give, or if they gave in general'. The reason can refer to efficiency: 'My own giving can solely be a small part of the needed giving, so it is ineffective unless the others also contribute.' But the reason can also be a demand for fairness: 'I would do my share of giving if the others did theirs.'[4] These reasonings can concern others' giving either to the same persons to whom the considered giver gives or in general, because it augments the general level of giving in society. But the answer can also

---

[4] This type of behaviour is well studied (see Kolm, 1983, 1984). It has sometimes been labelled 'reciprocity' (Sugden, 1984; Swaney, 1990), though this does not correspond to either the common or the scholarly use of the term, which describes giving and giving back. See also Kolm 1981a, 1981b.

just be a question of merit and reward: 'I would give to others if they themselves gave, because then they would deserve it.' In a dyad (two persons), the reason is essentially reduced to reciprocity proper, plus – possibly – some place for a general reward for the other's giving behaviour.

The foregoing applies to the various types of social relations, and reciprocity proper is the main reason for behaviour of the type 'giving if others give' in relations where the bilateral aspect dominates. Giving if others give, or acting morally if others do, and only in these cases, and the corresponding propensities or preferences can be called *conditional altruism*, or *conditional morality*. These cases contrast with unconditional cases, where the behaviour or preference holds whatever the others do. A conditional altruist is also, formally, a conditional egoist, but the benchmark retained here is pure egoism, and hence altruism is the attitude under scrutiny.

3.   Preferences and their consequences

The logic of the issue can be presented in the simplest way by considering individuals who can make two choices in acting towards others – described as 'giving' (a gift), denoted as g, and in contrast 'keeping', denoted as k – and who see others as globally either giving (G) or keeping (K). The latter alternatives will, notably, occur if all (or most) others respectively give (g) or keep (k). An individual's situation will be described by a pair of letters, the first denoting the individual's behaviour (g or k) and the second his perception of the others' behaviour (G or K). There are four possible situations: gG, gK, kG and kK. An individual will have preferences among his four possible situations, described by the (transitive antisymmetrical) binary relation '$\succ$' ('is preferred to'). As usual, an individual's choice of an act (g or k) given his perception of others' acts (G or K) is assumed to be consistent with his preferences.

Let us then add two other assumptions. First, given the individual's act (g or k), he prefers the others to give (G) rather than to keep (K); so $gG \succ gK$ and $kG \succ kK$. This can be both for the material advantage of receiving and for the intrinsic appreciation of being offered something or of living in a society with positive interpersonal relations.

Second, the individual prefers a society where everyone gives to a society where everyone keeps (including oneself); or $gG \succ kK$. The reason can be preference for good social relations – involving oneself or among others (with respect to material advantage, note that each individual both receives and gives in the giving case, that there can be reasons for either behaviour to be more productively efficient than the other – this will be discussed shortly – and that the relations discussed here will refer solely to a fraction of the whole of social relations). It will also be assumed that all (or most) individuals have the same considered preferences, which correspond to the general culture or ethos of society. Moreover, the relation $gG \succ kK$ will in fact be a consequence of the assumption $kG \succ kK$ when we introduce the condition of pure or unconditional altruism $gG \succ kG$.

Given the above assumptions, only four preference orderings are admissible.

The first ordering obtains when individuals prefer to keep whatever the (given) behaviour of others:

$$kG \succ gG \succ kK \succ gK. \qquad (1)$$

If agents act individually (non-cooperatively), each chooses k, which he prefers to g whatever the others' acts (a dominant strategy). Then kK prevails, a situation which each individual finds worse than the possible situation gG (a classic 'prisoner's dilemma'). Individuals cannot strike an agreement that all give to others given that others give back – which would achieve gG – even if they have the means to make such an agreement and to enforce it, because this would be opposed to g meaning gift giving, from the nature and the definition of a gift. Similarly, this 'exchange failure' cannot be corrected by the classical means of imposing the solution (gG), because gift giving cannot be imposed by force either, by nature and by definition. This constitutes the inherent inefficiency of egoism, and, more generally, of 'immoral' behaviour, sentiments and preferences, intrinsically entailed by the nature of gift giving and of good social relations.

By contrast, if people are unconditional altruists and prefer to give whatever the others' (given) behaviour, their preferences are

$$gG \succ kG \succ gK \succ kK \qquad (2)$$

or

$$gG \succ gK \succ kG \succ kK. \qquad (3)$$

In either case, each agent individually prefers to choose g, whatever the others' acts. Hence they all choose g, and therefore they achieve the situation gG, which they all prefer to all others, as if by immanent justice. These preferences, however, imply not only giving if the others give but also giving if they keep, and hence, with respect to others' behaviour towards oneself, not only returning good for good but also returning good for evil.[5] This is rather saintly behaviour, and one should probably

---

[5] The difference between preferences (2) and (3) is not relevant. The preference $kG \succ gK$ may be due to the resulting material situations for the individual (if G does not lead to a

expect that, in standard societies, it will be neither widespread nor easy to elicit on a sufficient scale by the means of influencing preferences and voluntary behaviour. Note, however, that since situation gG obtains, the problematic 'saintly' section of the preference structure, $gK \succ kK$, is in fact virtual.

If this problematic part of the preferences disappears, it will be replaced by $kK \succ gK$, which is 'an eye for an eye' with respect to reaction to others' behaviour towards oneself. The preference ordering then has to be

$$gG \succ kG \succ kK \succ gK. \tag{4}$$

This leads the individuals to give (g) if the others give (G) and to keep (k) if the others keep (K). This case is conditional altruism.

Doing as the others do because they do it, whatever the specific reason, can be called replicating behaviour, or *replication*. If the act of an agent affects another individual, who reacts with an act that has similar effects on the original actor, this is reciprocal behaviour or *reciprocation* (this 'similarity' implies, at least, that the acts are both either favourable or unfavourable to the other person). Reciprocation can be conceived as a particular case of replication (the acts are defined as concerning the other person considered). The reciprocation of acts favourable to the other is *reciprocity*. This corresponds to the classical concept of reciprocity in the social science, where this term denotes a set of gifts related by this kind of reaction. The reciprocation of unfavourable acts is, basically, revenge.[6]

These behaviours and their variants and specifications can rest on a number of reasons, motives or basic reactions. Notably, reciprocity can be motivated by gratitude. Giving to givers (who give to oneself or to others) can be motivated by the desire to reward their merit for a reason of retributive justice. The replication of giving to specific others or of giving in general can be elicited by the sense of fairness of doing one's share if the others do theirs. But it can also result from direct and basic imitation. Giving also elicits giving in the classical 'helping behaviour' in which someone who has been given to tends to give (even to persons other than the initial giver). This can be conceived as reciprocity between an individual and the group of others – 'general reciprocity'.

much less efficient economy than K). Hence, $gK \succ kG$ may describe a strong preference for one's giving behaviour, notably in contrast with others' behaviour – a preference that seems very 'altruistic'. However, a preference may be altruistic at a higher level, in the sense that the agent prefers others to behave altruistically rather than himself (this provides another reason for $kG \succ gK$).

[6] In all these cases, in their proper form, the motivation for the reaction should not solely be to influence future similar acts (e.g. retaliation solely for deterring future harm, or giving solely for receiving future gifts).

With preferences of type (4), however, if people act individually there are two possible stable (Cournot-Nash) equilibria: gG and kK. The former is unanimously preferred to the latter, and, indeed, it is unanimously preferred to all other situations. But it seems that society may be trapped into the inferior and inefficient situation kK. Indeed, if society is in kK it cannot move to gG by collective agreement, even if people could make an agreement and enforce it, because this would be contrary to the nature and to the definition of gift giving, as noted earlier. With such an agreement, there can be, in particular, no motivation of bilateral gift giving, reciprocity, gratitude, rewarding gift-giving behaviour, being influenced by receiving gifts and imitation of giving. However, two new phenomena have to be pointed out here.

First, the hypothesis of a simultaneous or timeless game is not realistic. It is, in particular, ill-suited for describing behaviour of replication, reciprocation or reciprocity. When an agent individually decides to give rather than keep, this may induce others to do the same, at least in proportion to the agent's act and importance in society. In particular, others may so behave towards this person in direct reciprocity to his choice. But the noted wider effects, such as 'helping behaviour', helping helpers, reward, doing one's share if others do, and so on, also lead to a situation of giving inducing further giving. All these are the reactions of conditional altruism. If they are sufficiently strong, the agent can in the end benefit from individually switching from k to g. Solution gG can thus be reached, and it is stable in the strong sense that each individual loses from deviating from it, whatever the others' behaviour when he does so.[7]

Moreover, giving (as a gift) is one way of yielding the corresponding item; this transfer can also result from coercion or from agreement or exchange in the strict sense.[8] A law cannot decide that people should (freely) give, but it can decide that they should yield the corresponding

---

[7] A detailed analysis and modelling of this dynamics can be the object of a long study. One parameter that can be of importance is the size of the population involved in an interrelated series of gifts (or other 'good' social relations). Large numbers of 'small' agents may hamper the diffusion of information about others' behaviour. However, the other phenomenon that makes large numbers an obstacle to cooperation in self-interested repeated games – the fact that punishment through non-cooperation cannot be focused towards past non-cooperators as it also affects former cooperators – does not exist with the motivations of (conditional) altruism under consideration at present.

[8] This 'transfer' can be an actual transfer for a gift in the strictest sense. It can also be any act favourable to the 'receiver' and more or less costly in some way and some degree for the actor. It can also sometimes be the external manifestations (in speech, gestures, and so on) of respect, compassion, pity, friendship, love, approval, praise, admiration, and so on, in the measure in which the manifestation without the sentiment helps or pleases the 'beneficiary'.

item. If the preference structure (4) implies that people choose to give (freely yield) if others yield (and do not solely give), then such a law induces them to (freely) give because it guarantees that the others will yield. But, then, this yielding behaviour is de facto voluntary, that is, the constraint is respected but it is not effective, and everyone (freely) gives. This solution fails, however, if preference structure (4) implies that the individual (freely) gives solely if the others also (freely) give and do not solely yield (even though, in the previous case, all people end up giving freely).

The main point is that, under normal assumptions, preference structure (4) can achieve the unanimously preferred – and probably morally most commendable – situation gG through individual choices. Now, these preferences are certainly more frequent than unconditional altruism (preferences of type (2) or (3)), and easier to elicit through influences on preferences. The aspects of balance in replication and, notably, in reciprocity and other reciprocation – doing as the others do, and possibly also incurring what they incur – can be justified by the particular rationality of equality.[9] Norms of reciprocity, balance or fairness can crystallise these reasons and motives into guidelines for behaviour.

In fact, (Pareto) efficiency, first-best optimality and, certainly, morality require that preference structures (2), (3) or (4) prevail. That is, only partial preference $gG \succ kG$ is required in addition to the basic assumption that agents always prefer others to give rather than to keep. This is not an innocuous demand, but nor does it justify deep pessimism.

The conclusion reached above as to the inefficiency of egoism (preference structure (1)) and the efficiency of either unconditional or conditional altruism (preference structures (2), (3) and (4)) strongly contrasts with the opposite famous message from Adam Smith's *Wealth of Nations* (if you need bread from your baker, do not rely on his altruism but on his selfish interest in an exchange relation).[10] However, Smith's previous *Theory of Moral Sentiments* emphasised sympathy, and this contradiction – German scholars' 'Das Adam Smith Problem' – may find an answer in the foregoing results.

---

[9] See Kolm (1998, foreword, sect. 5) and a number of previous works (among which in particular Kolm, 1996, ch. 2).

[10] This argument was, in fact, commonplace in Smith's time and place – the eve and locus of the Industrial Revolution, with merchants and capitalists seeking moral respectability. Smith read it in Bernard Mandeville and, more specifically, in the *Moral Essays* of the Jansenist Pierre Nicole (1675), translated into English by John Locke. The argument was, indeed, used as early as the fourth century by the fathers of the Church for justifying not excommunicating merchants whose business, selfish and uncharitable as it was, nevertheless served others in the end.

4.   Inter-preference comparisons

However, the noted intrinsic inefficiency of egoism and the efficiency of unconditional or conditional altruism do not imply that people are better off in the latter cases than in the former, because preferences are not the same in the various cases. Reaching conclusions of this type requires a hypothesis of 'inter-preference comparability', which is described by a second level of preference. These preferences have to be understood as meaning some ordinal level of enjoyment rather than directly and solely preference. That is to say, they do not directly describe the fact that someone prefers to be an altruist rather than an egoist, say. Such preferences would meet problems of meaning, logic and consistency. Rather, they simply admit the possibility of saying that, in given circumstances, someone would be happier (or more satisfied) if he were an altruist than if he were an egoist (the discussion of this issue has an analogue for interpersonal comparisons).[11]

The objects ranked by these new preferences will include a third parameter, which denotes which type of ordinary preference ordering the individual has. They will be triples xyz, where y is either g or k, z is either G or K and x can alternatively be e for *egoism* if the individual has type (1) preferences, u for *unconditional altruism* if he has preferences of type (2) or (3) or c for *conditional altruism* if he has type (4) preferences (there are twelve such alternative triples). For each given x, preferences about pairs yz are those implied by type x preferences.

One possible property is $ugG \succ egG$ or $cgG \succ egG$. This means that the individual enjoys more a society where everyone freely gives if he is an altruist than if he is an egoist. This can be explained by the fact that the egoist is less sensitive to the social and moral intrinsic value of the act of gift giving than the altruist who has a strong sensitivity in this respect and values such acts a great deal. It is again assumed that these preferences are shared by all individuals in society. Since $egG \succ ekK$ from relation (1), these assumptions respectively entail $ugG \succ ekK$ and $cgG \succ ekK$. But we have seen that kK is the outcome with type (1) preferences, and gG is the outcome in the other cases. Consequently, all individuals end up better off if they are altruists of some sort (u or c) than if they are purely selfish (e).

Morals judge actions and choices, including conditional ones, and the corresponding individual preferences. That is, they judge, here, the preference structures (1), (2), (3) and (4). In particular, they rank them; this ranking can be called the moral or ethical preference (an expression

---

[11] See the theory of 'fundamental preferences' in Kolm (1998, foreword).

not to be confused with the description of the morally best of these structures as being the moral ones). Very commonly, the selfish preferences (type(1)) are found to be the worst. Moreover, a number of morals praise returning good for evil, and hence they value unconditional altruism (preferences of types (2) or (3)) higher than conditional altruism (type (4) preferences). This is, for instance, the case with Christianity and with Buddhism. Christianity, in particular, sees unconditional altruism as Christian preferences; it could label conditional altruism as 'biblical' preferences, and it would probably describe the selfish case as 'pagan' preferences.[12] The foregoing results thus imply that the members of a more moral society end up being happier (with reasonable assumptions). Though this cannot be the direct aim of moral 'conversion' or *metanoia*, at least the members would not be indirectly 'discouraged' by the fact that it would lead to a situation considered to be worse. Moreover, an important result is that conditional altruism suffices, and this is less demanding from the point of view of motivation.

5.   Reciprocal and replicative behaviour, and efficiency

As we have noted, the foregoing holds for all types of pro-social behaviour, and not solely for giving in the strict sense. This holds, in particular, for all types of reciprocal, replicating and conditional behaviour (corresponding to 'conditional altruism'). This is, for instance, the case with people who contribute freely if the others contribute fairly, who respect norms if the others do, in particular who keep promises if the others do, or who 'act as if others acted similarly' (that is, popular Kantianism) if others follow the same principle (which actualises the assumption).

All such behaviours can have positive effects on economic and social efficiency, in addition to the noted intrinsic inefficiency of egoism and the efficiency of altruism or equivalent behaviour. These effects can also be indirectly favourable to the establishment of pro-social behaviour, with the sufficiency of conditional and reciprocal relations. The following list provides but a sample of these effects on efficiency.

The most classic type of inefficient interaction is that of the prisoner's dilemma. The structure is the one described above with preferences of type (1), while the available choices may represent very different things, such as helping or not, cooperating or not, contributing to a public good or not, and so on. The standard conclusion is that the inefficiency described above will be obtained. However, if one player

---

[12] However, Luke's 'Give and you will be given to' is just advice to exploit others' propensity to return gifts.

behaves reciprocally or replicatively and the other knows it, the latter's choice will be such that the inefficient outcome will be avoided, and so will the former's by reciprocity or replication; so the efficient outcome (which both players prefer to the inefficient equilibrium) will be reached without agreement between them. The game, of course, is transformed, since it becomes a sequence of non-simultaneous moves, with information about the first move for the reciprocating or replicating player (though all this can also be notional and simultaneous), and a new behaviour that can be described by one new payoff for this player. But this can describe many actual situations.

Similarly, if I need something from someone but can pay only later, and for some reason no binding agreement is possible, the other will not help me if he thinks I will not pay later, but he will if he knows that I react reciprocally. More generally, a common pattern is a sequence of alternate or simultaneous transfers (or other aid) between two agents, where each is motivated by the desire that the relation continues. But if this is the sole motivation, the last transfer – if known as such – will not take place, and so the whole relation may fail to materialise by 'backward induction'.[13] Then, an additional reciprocal motivation can secure the last transfer and, *ipso facto*, the whole relation.

All kinds of reciprocal and replicating behaviour can secure efficient relations through such effects. They can, more generally, replace contractual agreements and save the corresponding costs of transacting, contracting, monitoring, reporting, enforcing or collecting information, etc. They can also replace public coercion for respecting rights, financing public goods, implementing transfers, and so on, and, hence, again save the costs of information (or the lack of it), coercing, administration, etc. These behaviours can thus remedy standard 'market failures' and 'government failures'. In any social relation, they are bound to favour trust and loyalty, and to lower uncertainty about the other's behaviour. It is classical to note that the most efficient organisations (firms, bureaux, etc.) use fair amounts of voluntary, non-contractual but reciprocal support between members and between them and the organisation, in the form of goodwill, mutual help, loyalty, voluntary transmission of information, reciprocal relations between effort and productivity on the one hand and bonuses on the other, and so on.[14]

[13] See Hammond (1975) and Kurz (1978, 1979). Uncertainty, or bounded rationality that prevents backward induction, can permit this process with purely self-centred motivations.
[14] There is a vast literature on this topic in industrial sociology, the sociology of organisation and experimental sociopsychology; classical pioneering empirical work is found in

6. Psychological possibilities

Reciprocal and replicative behaviour thus suffices for avoiding the inefficiency of self-centredness in terms of the quality of social relations and of various other consequences of social interactions. It has been emphasised that one of the remarkable aspects of this result is that this behaviour seems to be less demanding from the point of view of motivation than pure and unconditional altruism or goodness. This proposition can be tested by introspection, casual observation and systematic investigation. Experimentation has been amply used by psychosociology to show the wide scope of reciprocitarian behaviour.[15] In particular, the propensity to act favourably towards others when one has benefited from different others' favours is one of the most documented results of the literature under the name of 'helping behaviour'.[16] Imitation can also play a role in this regard; in particular, being helped provides, in addition to a change for close observation, a telling experience. Moreover, the reverse effect – noted by René Descartes and Adam Smith[17] – also matters: one tends to give to people who give (and not necessarily to oneself). 'Helping behaviour' induces people to reciprocate towards others in general (or towards the 'generalised other', as George Herbert Mead puts it). Indeed, people tend to hypostasise these 'others' into 'society as a whole', and to give when they have been given to 'by society'. This is the very important social phenomenon of 'general reciprocity'. All this particularly applies to the crucial giving dimension of good social relations in general. Of course, education and the formation of the general cultural ethos of society play major roles in the establishment of these behaviours.

7. Reciprocity and the economy

A number of famous scholarly analyses of society claim that the paradigm of the market and of its type of exchange can or should be applied

Adam (1963, 1965) and Adam and Rosenbaum (1964). A noted recent sociological, historical and econometric study that strongly emphasises the productivity of reciprocity is Putnam (1993a).

[15] Economists have recently taken up this trend: see Güth, Ockenfels and Wendel (1997) and Fehr, Gächter and Kirchsteiger (1997).

[16] A sample is provided by the chapters of the contributory volume edited by J. Macaulay and L. Berkovitz, 1970 (this literature is fully referenced and analysed, and is used, in Kolm, 1984). See also Titmuss, 1970.

[17] Descartes, *Works*, Vol. IV, p.316, and Smith, *The Theory of Moral Sentiments*, part 6, sect. 2, ch. 1.

to all social relations, or have applied it beyond its field, for instance to the study of family life or politics. They have sometimes found a normative value in the free exchange that underlies this view. However, we have seen the paramount importance of social behaviours (or of aspects of social behaviours) that belong to the realms of gift giving and reciprocity, and that therefore cannot be bought, sold or marketed, and are opposed to both market exchange and coercion. Family life and family economics, in particular, consist primarily of relations of this type. From the normative point of view, good social relations, which are so important for the quality of society and good life, are based on behavioural traits that belong to this category (though the converse may not hold, because of the possible role of strong norms and social pressure in gift giving and in reciprocating). It has been stressed in this chapter that reciprocity and replication constitute basic ways of overcoming a number of 'failures' of exchange and other relations, and therefore of improving efficiency and economic productivity. But the normative aspect of the economy is also concerned with the intrinsic quality of social relations, since people spend so much of their lifetime engaged in economic activities, notably at the workplace. And the crucial giving aspect of these relations, which cannot be secured by exchange or command, can be induced and sustained by the interdependence among behaviours in reciprocities and replications with the corresponding plausible motivations.

Textbooks about economic systems are surprisingly different according to whether they lie on the economics or on the anthropology bookshelf. The former typically begin with 'There are two kinds of economic systems: market and planned', while the latter's usual opening is 'There are three kinds of economic systems: exchange, redistribution and reciprocity'. Exchange corresponds to market here, while redistribution is taking and giving by a central power, a process in the family of 'command' and 'planning' in the modern world. Hence, if one is not blind to the various possible shortcomings and 'failures' of hierarchies and markets on the grounds of human relations, morals, and also efficiency, one has to be curious about the third alternative, reciprocity. The various relational shortcomings referred to include reinforcing selfishness, rewarding cheating, nurturing hostile relations, alienation, exploitation, domination and considering others solely as means, as instruments – a violation of Immanuel Kant's 'imperative'. And although reciprocity – understood here as a set of gifts and return gifts – has its share of oppressive norms and social pressures for giving, and of gifts with poor motivations and effects, it happens that the pro-social behaviours that are almost universally praised and appreciated also belong to this category. Of course, reciprocity is the only mode of conducting economic transfers solely in a number of groups of limited size, but the degree to which it exists, associated with other modes in a variety of possible ways, is bound to be a crucial variable for society, how it performs and its intrinsic quality.[18]

ACKNOWLEDGEMENT

© CIRIEC 2000. First published in *Annals of Public and Cooperative Economics* 71(2): 171–188. Reprinted with permission from Blackwell Publishing.

[18] See Kolm (1984). The current state of the analysis of reciprocity, notably its economic aspect, is proposed in Kolm (2000, and particularly 2005).

9 The mutual validation of ends

Shaun Hargreaves Heap

1.   Introduction

Interpersonal relations do not arise simply because there is an opportunity for exchange between individuals. These relations help constitute the individual and form a backdrop against which exchange can occur. The purpose of this chapter is twofold. One is to give an account of why interpersonal relations might be constitutive in this sense. The other is to illustrate why this is a significant observation.

In the next section I address the first of these and begin to lay the foundations for the second. Adam Smith's argument in *The Theory of Moral Sentiments* (1976/1759) linking the interpersonal to the special pleasure that we gain from mutual sympathy is my starting point. I have chosen Smith in part because, unlike many contemporary economists, he offers a clear psychological account of this matter, which has been revived recently by Sugden (2002 and chapter 3 of this book). Smith is also interesting because he has the sketch of a more general argument that I shall develop, which is important as it brings out why the observation about the constitutive aspect of interpersonal relations might be significant.

The constitutive nature of interpersonal relations might matter in this sense for a variety of reasons. It could affect the explanations or prescriptions of economic theory and in doing this it might also mark a change in one of the key building blocks of that theory: the model of rational agency. It is not obvious that the latter is necessarily the case because, although the constitutive aspect of interpersonal relations is often associated with the heterodox tradition in economics (see Davis, 2003), it has a wider provenance. For example, George Akerlof and Rachel Kranton (2000) suggest that people gain 'identity' by belonging to and following the prescriptions of a particular group, and they represent this thought through an additional 'identity' argument in a person's utility function.

In this way, the rational choice model appears untroubled by the constitutive aspects of interpersonal relations; it is just that people have a preference for 'identity' that depends on social location. The strategy of appealing to a more nuanced account of people's preferences is, of course, commonplace among rational choice theorists when confronting some apparently anomalous behaviour (for example, see Becker, 1996), but I shall argue in section 3 that it needs careful handling in this instance. This is because a preference for 'identity' or 'self-respect' (or whatever vehicle is used for introducing the idea) is very different and needs to be distinguished from the usual preferences of rational choice theory. I bring out the importance of this distinction by considering how the recognition of the constitutive aspect of interpersonal relations affects conventional welfare economics in section 4.

2. Mutual sympathy or mutual validation of language concepts?

Why do interpersonal relations help constitute the individual? Or, to raise the point in the specific form of Akerlof and Kranton (2000), why do individuals value the sense of identity that comes from following the prescriptions of a group? Akerlof and Kranton take this as a given, but what is it about human psychology that explains why we value this kind of social embeddedness?

Adam Smith offers an answer to this question. He believed that people derived a sense of pleasure when their actions were approved of by others. He based this observation on what he treated as three facts about human psychology. The first was that people have a capacity to feel imaginatively the experiences of others and so share in their pleasures and pains. Second, this is the basis for judgements of approval and disapproval regarding their actions. That one can 'sympathise' with the feelings of others is the way that Smith describes it in *The Theory of Moral Sentiments*, and when one does one comes to approve of their actions. Third, the same process underpins a person's judgement with respect to the approval/disapproval of his *own* actions (pp. 109–10).

And, in the same manner, we either approve or disapprove of our own conduct, according as we feel that, when we place ourselves in the situation of another man, and view it, as it were, with his eyes and from his station, we either can or cannot entirely enter into and sympathise with the sentiments and motives which influenced it.

Such approval thus marks a form of *mutual* sympathy and is a source of particular pleasure. This is, in effect, a primitive in Smith's theory. It is a psychological observation about life that 'nothing pleases us more than to observe in men a fellow feeling with all the emotions of our own breast; nor are we so much shocked as by the appearance of the contrary' (p. 13); and this is, in effect, his answer to the question posed at the beginning of this section as to why interpersonal relations are constitutive. They just are.

This is not entirely satisfactory, since the special pleasure of 'mutual sympathy' may not be as clear to a contemporary individualist audience as it was to Smith. Smith, however, also had the sketch of an alternative argument as to why such a correspondence of sentiments is so special. It comes later in *The Theory of Moral Sentiments*, when Smith is considering how people form judgements with respect to whether their actions are likely to engage the sympathy of others. It is here that he acknowledges a problem of self-deception. Contemporary research has made this a familiar feature of human psychology, as people seem prone to adjust their beliefs or select evidence in ways that reflect well upon their actions (e.g. see Festinger, 1957). Of course, there is considerable debate in the philosophical literature over whether such self-deception is coherent (see, for example, Elster, 1983), but there is little doubt that it occurs. Smith expresses the problem this way (pp. 157–8):

When we are about to act, the eagerness of passion will seldom allow us to consider what we are doing, with the candour of an indifferent person... When the action is over, indeed, and the passions which prompted it have subsided, we can enter more cooly into the sentiments of the indifferent spectator. [...] It is seldom, however, that they are quite candid even in this case... It is so disagreeable to think ill of ourselves, that we often purposely turn away our view from those circumstances which might render that judgement unfavourable. He is a bold surgeon, they say, whose hand does not tremble when he performs an operation on his own person; and he is often equally bold who does not hesitate to pull off the mysterious veil of self-delusion, which covers from his view the deformities of his own conduct.

It is in this context, Smith argues, that we come to rely (in the manner assumed but not explained by Akerlof and Kranton) on norms or rules of moral conduct (p. 159):

Nature, however, has not left this weakness...altogether without remedy; nor has she abandoned us entirely to the delusions of self-love. Our continual observations upon the conduct of others, insensibly lead us to form to ourselves certain general rules concerning what is fit and proper either to be done or to be avoided.

It is thus that the general rules of morality are formed. They are ultimately founded upon the experiences of what, in particular instances, our moral faculties, our natural sense of merit and propriety, approve, or disapprove of. We do not originally approve or condemn particular actions; because upon examination, they appear to be agreeable or inconsistent with a certain general rule. The general rule, on the contrary, is formed by finding from experience, that all actions of a certain kind, or circumstanced in a certain manner, are approved or disapproved of.

What seems strange in this account is not the problem of self-deception or the reliance on social norms to guide our judgements regarding the worth of our actions, as these are frequent observations in psychology and sociology. Rather, it is the connection between them and Smith's psychological primitives of sympathy and mutual sympathy as the motives for action. If we do *just* have this capacity to experience the feelings of others, then it is not obvious where the scope for self-deception regarding others' feelings with respect to our own actions comes in.

An alternative primitive for a theory of action that avoids this problem has people being motivated by the sense of self-esteem that comes from reflecting upon their actions and finding them worthy. Or, to put this round the other way, people like to avoid the feelings of embarrassment, guilt or shame that are associated with actions judged unworthy. Introspection suggests that this is a more familiar contemporary starting point for a theory of action, as does the discipline of anthropology. More generally, it would not be surprising on evolutionary grounds, since the seeking of reasons for events is plausibly what has given our species an evolutionary advantage, and one kind of event in need of an explanation is our actions. Since they often involve conscious choices, an explanation of some of these events seems likely to turn on what justifies the choice. Of course, Smith also makes self-esteem important, but its importance derives from his primitives of sympathy and mutual sympathy. The suggestion, then, is that it is better, in the sense of being more plausible, to take a concern for self-esteem as a primitive rather than forms of fellow-feeling.

This choice of primitive has further advantages. The concern for self-worth also makes the problem of self-deception intelligible and so provides a bridge to the argument as to why interpersonal relations are constitutive. They are constitutive because we depend on the mutual validation of language concepts.

The point is this. If ideas regarding what is worthy play an important motivational role because they give content to a person's sense of self-worth, then people cannot have purely personal or private ideas of this sort. There are two connected difficulties with having a purely personal standard of what is worthy. The first is that a personal standard must, by definition, be chosen by the individual in question, and this is liable to create a problem since this means standards could change as actions do.

They would be as much matters of individual choice as are actions, and if this is the case then they potentially have no more authority than do the actions that one wishes to use the standard to judge. To give the kind of authority to the judgements regarding action that will generate the distinct feelings of self-worth, the standard must at least have some stability, and one way of insulating the standard from the instability of personal discretion is to make it external to the individual. Of course, it might be argued that this is also a matter of personal integrity and those individuals with integrity will be able to maintain a stable personal standard for judging actions. Indeed, one might suppose that a rational individual will understand that the pleasure of a sense of self-worth is, potentially, possible only if he maintains a stable standard. It is here, however, that the second difficulty surfaces.

Even if the individual maintains a stable standard in the sense that he applies the same rules, no standard or set of rules is exhaustive in its coverage. It is well known that no set of rules can contain rules for their implementation because every situation can be individuated to make that situation unique; and this is the problem here. How standards relate to particular situations requires interpretation, and the individual will always be able to individuate the circumstances to make the standard apply. Of course, it may be objected that, just as before, an individual with integrity will understand that a sense of self-worth is possible only when such manipulations are not self-serving. However, the problem here is deeper. The question is: when is manipulation self-serving? This would be easy to answer if *any* manipulation of the standard was self-serving, but this is not the case because some interpretation of the standard is always required. The individual has to decide what aspects of the situation need to be individuated in the application of the standard. There is no position that completely avoids the act of interpretation and so the suspicion of self-serving manipulation will always hover.

There is another way of expressing this problem. Any concept such as 'honour', 'good', 'just', etc. will be meaningless unless there are examples of action where the attribute does not apply. However, any set of rules associated with the application of such concepts will require interpretation, and there is a problem as to whether an action in a new situation represents an extension of the rules to a new setting or a transgression of the rules. Both interpretations will be possible, because any new situation can always be individuated to be different and so require an extension to the rules. However, there must be some way of circumscribing this possibility, otherwise the standard will be found to apply in all cases and so become meaningless. In short, it is a condition of holding meaningful concepts that this line be drawn. There is no option of not drawing the line, and when it is done by the individual the earlier problem arises: it ceases to be independent of that person's judgement and so will not have the authority that gives a sense of self-worth. The point here, to return to Adam Smith's argument, is not just that individual judgements are prone to self-deception; rather, it is that the situation of purely personal judgement means that the individual can never know whether he is engaging in acts of self-deception or not. To be able to make this distinction means being able to draw the line, and this is not something that can be decided on the basis of the rule itself. Instead, what gives authority to the judgement is the fact that the rule is interpreted externally by the actions of others. This is why ends have to be mutually validated: it is a condition of having ends that trade in concepts such as 'honour', 'just', 'good', etc. that they arise interpersonally.

As we have seen, Smith thinks (p. 159) that 'nature' saves us from the problem of self-deception because it supplies 'continual observations upon the conduct of others' that 'insensibly lead us to form to ourselves certain general rules concerning what is fit and proper either to be done or to be avoided'. If living in a society is a part of human nature then Smith's suggestion is consistent with the argument advanced here, because it is the fact that we live in society that enables us to use concepts that, in turn, allow us to judge our actions as worthy or otherwise.[1] Interestingly, Smith states this conclusion, albeit without the argument, quite baldly somewhat earlier in *The Theory of Moral Sentiments* (p. 110):

Were it possible that a human creature could grow up to manhood in some solitary place, without any communication with his own species, he could no more think of his own character, or the propriety or demerit of his own sentiments and conduct, than of the beauty or deformity of his own face. All these are objects which he cannot easily see, which naturally he does not look at, and with regard to which he is provided no mirror which can present them to his view. Bring him into society, and he is immediately provided with the mirror which he wanted before.

3.   Self-worth and the rational choice model

Can the rational choice model accommodate the idea that people are motivated in this way, by a sense of self-esteem that comes from reflecting on the worth of their actions?

---

[1] The argument here about concept formation may strike one as odd, since we all use concepts, apparently without effort, in our daily lives. But any strangeness here is equally understandable if we, as seems entirely natural, only ever think of our experience in society.

There are two possible strategies for making a concern with self-worth (or 'identity', to use Akerlof and Kranston's term) consistent with this conventional approach. One is to cast 'self-worth' (or the 'identity' that you get from this) as a preference. The other is to argue that it is through acting to satisfy best our preferences that we obtain a sense of self-worth (or 'identity').

The first strategy retains the language of preference satisfaction but admits a distinct category of preference – i.e. one for self-worth. This is unusual, in the sense that rational choice theory is typically quiet with regard to the content of preferences. Indeed, this is one of its strengths, as the theory appears, as a result, commendably general. Nevertheless, this in itself is not obviously troubling. 'Self-worth' is, however, more than a distinct preference; it is also a very special kind of preference. It is special because feelings for self-worth typically come from judging that actions are 'honourable', 'just', 'right', 'good', etc.; that is, they involve evaluative concepts.

There are two kinds of specialness here. One is the involvement of ideas concerning what is 'honourable', 'just', etc. The other is the need for a reference point regarding what would happen in the absence of these ideas. The point is that acting 'honourably' must be distinct from acting 'without honour', otherwise the concept of 'honour' is meaningless. The obvious reference point here is what people would do if they did not have a preference for self-worth associated with acting 'honourably'. In this way, the 'ordinary', non-self-worth, preferences for warmth, clothing, shelter and the like are actually used in the judgements regarding what would be honourable. So the preference for 'self-worth' can be understood only in relation to a transformation of the underlying 'ordinary' preferences. This creates, in effect, a two-tier structure for preferences.

This idea will be familiar from recent work in economics involving 'psychological payoffs' (see Rabin, 1993), where the symbolic properties of action explicitly motivate agents, and from the work on 'team reasoning' (see Bacharach, 1999; Sugden, 2000a), where team preferences are distinct from but related to the individual preferences of team members and they can motivate individuals to act when they feel that they belong to the team. This is, however, not always evident in rational choice formulations like those of Akerlof and Kranton (2000). They simply assume, for instance, that the norm tells the person how someone in his category (e.g. male or female) should act, and that following the norm gives the individual a sense of 'identity'. But how could the mere act of following a norm in this way create a sense of 'identity' for the individual? If this was all there was to the matter, then the individual would seem little more than a social dope and not a bit like the kind of agent that is hungry for an 'identity'. Of course, what is missing, and what grounds the assertion that identity might be at stake, is the constellation of beliefs about why, for example, 'acting like a man' is worthy. The famous injunction that 'a man has got to do what a man has got to do' was never simply a guide to what to do next; it was Hollywood shorthand for a version of why acting in some way was the 'honourable' thing to do.

There has to be a set of background beliefs and ideas of this sort; otherwise there would be no individual psychological charge at stake in following the prescriptions of a norm. And, again, once this is recognised it also becomes clear that there must be some reference point regarding what a 'man who is not a man' (so to speak) would have done; otherwise, 'being a man' in whatever are the circumstances would be quite unremarkable. In short, buried in the apparently simple rational choice formulations of this matter there has to be a similar two-tier structure of preferences if one is to make sense of the motivational power of a concern for something along the lines of 'identity'.

The second strategy makes acting on preferences and seeking self-worth one and the same thing. This appears to sidestep neatly any further discussion of the mechanics of self-worth, and will be tempting to those who naturalise the economic model of action, but having a preference for something does not supply a reason for acting upon it. Preferences are just that. In contrast, justifications deal in reasons; and what is required here are versions of these that explain why acting on preferences is warranted. In short, this approach also requires that agents have ideas that motivate – albeit rather special ones – regarding how actions are to be justified, and the same observation about the associated two-tier structure of preferences arises.

Thus, the rational choice model can 'accommodate' a preference for 'self-worth', but only by acknowledging that people have a two-tier structure of preferences. When this is allied to the earlier argument that the ideas that inform the evaluative tier of these preferences must be shared, we shall see that there is a new dimension to welfare economics.

4.   Welfare economics

In this section I consider how the aspect of interpersonal relations that flows from individuals having the special kind of preferences for self-worth might affect welfare economics. At first glance, it might appear to be negligible. Conventional theoretical welfare economics starts from people's preferences and is primarily concerned with whether there is scope, through institutional change, broadly understood, for Pareto improvements with respect to the satisfaction of these preferences. So, allowing that people have another kind of preference would not seem at first to be deeply troubling. However, the special character of the preference for self-worth and its relation to ordinary preferences suggest caution in drawing this inference.

The preference for self-worth is not all of a piece with other preferences. It is not implausible, particularly in liberal, individualistic societies, to take ordinary preferences for food, shelter, warmth and the like as givens – things that, as it were, belong to the individual. They may vary in intensity across individuals, but there is a universal character to these needs. The preference for self-worth, with its dependence on the mutual validation of ends, is rather different. It involves sharing ideas, and the substantive content regarding what is deemed worthy seems to vary quite considerably across groups over time and space. The two aspects are, of course, related, because the importance of sharing turns the selection of beliefs into a form of coordination game that is liable to have many solutions. The point, therefore, is that groups seem to face, in principle at least, choices concerning the character of the norms that they follow whereas people do not face choices over whether to seek food and other physical comforts. So, while it may be defensible to take ordinary preferences as given, the same cannot be said with respect to the norms that give content to people's preference for self-worth.

The natural question, then, is: where do norms come from? In Gui's (2000a) term, norms are an example of a relational good, and so the question is a particular version of a more general one: how do these goods get produced? This needs answering before one can tell whether welfare economics has to pay special attention to the way in which the 'preference for self-worth' is satisfied as compared with other preferences. So, how are ideas about what is worthy generated and acted upon?

For the purpose here, it is sufficient to note that norms have two broad requirements. First, there are the ideas themselves. In part they arise through processes of socialisation within institutions such as the family, and in part they are consciously considered and adopted through engagement and reflection. This happens explicitly in institutions such as churches, political parties and the myriad of voluntary organisations that are organised around the discussion and promotion of ideas. In addition, there is the implicit discussion of ideas that occurs in the movies, television drama, soaps, theatre and so on (i.e. there are also the institutions of the mass media). The second requirement is that ideas must be expressed in action (i.e. norms must be instantiated or, as Gui has suggested, 'interactions create relational goods'). So, norms have their broad origins in discursive institutions and in the opportunities that institutions more generally give for expressing ideas in individual actions.

Both conditions suggest a need for distinct institutions or aspects of institutions where the rational choice logic of individual (or 'ordinary') preference satisfaction is not all-determining. This is where the use of the term 'preference for self-worth' is infelicitous, because it suggests that self-worth is just another preference when actually the preference for self-worth is satisfied on occasion by acting in a manner that is distinct from what 'ordinary' preference satisfaction dictates. To recall the argument of the previous section, one often obtains a sense of self-worth by acting in a way that is 'honourable', 'just', 'good', etc., where what gives the action these qualities is that it is commanded by something other than the selfish interest that is associated with 'ordinary' (and individually based) preference satisfaction. This is the feature of the preference for self-worth that is picked out in the second condition, and the point is reinforced by a consideration of how ideas are formed for this purpose in the various discursive institutions. If these institutions (or all aspects of institutions) were themselves conceived and organised as if they were just another arena where people pursue the satisfaction of their own preferences, then the ideas that emerged would have no authority. They would not provide a reference point for judging action; they would simply be extensions of *one* way of acting: that is, of acting on ordinary preferences.

One has only to think of an institution, such as the judiciary, that is quite consciously organised with objectives *other* than advancing the satisfaction of preferences of those who participate in them to see the force of this argument. The judiciary decides on what happened in various settings relative to what the law requires, and if this was indistinct from the activity of the individuals involved pursuing their own self-interests then there would be no constraint on bribing jurors, witnesses and judges. Instead, what gives the judiciary authority is the fact that its judgements are insulated from these considerations. Alternatively, consider an institution that is organised around the objective of 'caring'; it is difficult to see how the activity of 'caring' can be a distinct activity if the people who engage in it do so *purely* for the selfish reason of satisfying ordinary preferences (see Folbre and Nelson, 2000). Thus, when 'caring' is purchased through the market, there must be some aspect of this institution that expresses the distinct unconditional character of 'caring', or the service will cease to be a 'caring' one.

In short, if people are to have feelings of self-worth, there is a need within a society's constellation of institutions for what I shall call 'public' aspects. That is, there have to be either distinct institutions (such as the judiciary) or distinct features within institutions that are otherwise organised around ordinary preference satisfaction that allow scope for the discussion and expression of ideas (e.g. as when 'caring' is marketed). In short, there has to be space in one form or another where ideas rather than interests reign. Three possible broad implications for the conduct of welfare economics follow.

First, if welfare economics remains narrowly concerned with how efficiently institutions promote preference satisfaction, then it must take care to confine the domain of its operation. Welfare economics, so construed, cannot apply to all institutions (or all aspects of the institutions) in society. In one sense, this conclusion will be obvious to any practitioner of applied welfare economics, where it is common practice not to recognise the force of all the ordinary preferences that might be held by individuals. For instance, few cost-benefit analyses would concede that a single person's refusal to put a price on some natural resource that would be lost through some development (i.e. an implicit price of infinity) should count in the calculation of whether the development is a potential Pareto improvement. Likewise, preferences for buying and selling body parts or people are ruled out; and so on. So we already implicitly accept that there are institutions that establish the domain for conventional welfare economics; and a moment's reflection will suggest that they must be governed by something other than the logic of preference satisfaction. Otherwise they would not be supplying a constraint to the operation of ordinary individual preference satisfaction; they would simply be extensions to the principle.

It may seem on the basis of this analogy with what already occurs in welfare economics that the domain of welfare economics is thereby nested, so to speak, in and relies upon institutions such as the legal system. But the implications reach further than this. Welfare economics must take care to understand the dynamics between the institutions of preference satisfaction and those of shared idea formation and expression; otherwise the institutional change recommended by conventional welfare economics solely on the basis of efficiency with respect to ordinary preference satisfaction may have further unexpected effects. Depending on the nature of the interaction between the 'public' aspects of institutions and those designed to advance ordinary preference satisfaction, a change in the latter may enhance or undermine the scope for interpersonal relations (i.e. may affect the processes that create or destroy relational goods).

To return to my starting point, Adam Smith supplies an illustration why such interactions might be a source of concern. In the less well-known

Book V of *The Wealth of Nations* (1976/1776), he is worried about the way that the transforming aspects of the market can undermine the capacity of people to form sympathetic judgements. The settled communities of rural areas, where there are shared codes of conduct, give way to an industrial society where ordinary people are largely anonymous and there are no codes of conduct.

While he remains in a country village his conduct may be attended to, and he may be obliged to attend to it himself. In this situation, and in this situation only, he may have what is called a character to lose. But as soon as he comes into a great city he is sunk in obscurity and darkness. His conduct is observed and attended to by nobody and he is therefore very likely to neglect it himself, and to abandon himself to every sort of low profligacy and vice. (p. 795)

In other words, the extension of the market may be efficient for the satisfaction of preferences but it could undermine or change the norms on which people depend for judgements of self-respect.

Smith is not alone in being worried in this way, and nor is the interaction between market and non-market institutions the only aspect of the problem. The worry can arise within a market institution when a part of the behaviour within that organisation is regulated by norms. For example, it is the scope for just this kind of interaction between the worlds of idea formation and expression and that of simple preference satisfaction within an institution that is used to explain why the introduction of systems of payments by results are sometimes surprisingly unsuccessful in commercial organisations (see Frey, 1997).

Frey's argument in this respect turns on a body of psychological theory that finds that people use two types of reason to explain their actions, the 'extrinsic' and the 'intrinsic', and the one can 'crowd out' the other. The connection with this chapter arises because these two types of reason map respectively onto simple rational choice calculation and the more complicated norm-guided action taken in support of self-worth. Doing something in response to a market incentive is a good example of an 'extrinsic' reason, because it is the terms of trade, which are external to the action, that explain why it is undertaken. In contrast, doing something because it is the 'right' or 'honourable' thing to do is a good example of an 'intrinsic' reason for action. The possibility of 'crowding out' an intrinsic reason or 'crowding it in' occurs in these theories because people adjust the 'intrinsic' reason to help rationalise or clarify the reason for an action. In particular, when the 'extrinsic' and 'intrinsic' reason both support the action taken, the actual reason for the action is unclear. It is over-determined, and a person typically adjusts his beliefs about the intrinsic worth of the action so that it is supported by an 'extrinsic' reason alone. The 'intrinsic' reason is 'crowded out'. Conversely, when neither the 'extrinsic' nor 'intrinsic' reason supports an action that has been undertaken, the person will tend to rationalise the action by adjusting his beliefs so that the 'intrinsic' value of the action can rise in such settings – i.e. 'crowding in' (or relational goods production).

Like Smith's observation with respect to the expansion of the market undermining norms, this kind of 'crowding out/in' is potentially important for prescriptive economics. Suppose, for example, it is ignored, as it would be from a pure rational choice perspective, and a principal–agent problem is perceived within an organisation when, in fact, this problem is mitigated because people are in some degree guided by 'intrinsic' reason. There are norms in the workplace that are a source of workers' judgements about their self-worth, and they happen to guide workers to behave non-opportunistically. The standard rational-choice-based prescription for overcoming the perceived principal–agent problem is to introduce a system of payments by results. But, in these circumstances, this is liable to create 'external' reasons for action that now overlap and that will, if these psychological theories are right, 'crowd out' the 'intrinsic' ones as people adjust their beliefs to remove the 'intrinsic' reason. The net effect of the new payment system, then, is not what was expected. Behaviour does not change significantly in the area of the new payment system, as one type of reason simply substitutes. Furthermore, performance may be undermined in other aspects of the job (those not covered by the new payment system) that had hitherto been regulated by the now weaker work norms.

The simple conclusion, then, is that welfare economics will have to understand better how the 'public' aspects of institutions form and function if it is to be in a position to take account of the possible interactions between them and the institutions (or the aspects of the institutions) that are guided by a concern with efficient preference satisfaction.

The second possible change to welfare economics would take matters further and would incorporate within welfare economics an evaluation of the performance of these distinct 'public' aspects of institutions. This, of course, is more ambitious. But it would be no more than to follow the lead that Smith also gave in this respect. He was not concerned simply with the case where some norm is better than none; he was also concerned with the character of the norms. For instance, he argues that ordinary people in cities would be drawn to religious sects (pp. 795-6): 'He never emerges so effectually from this obscurity...as by his becoming a member of a small religious sect.' This is some consolation for Smith, but not much, because he suggests that the 'morals of those little sects have...frequently been rather disagreeably rigorous and unsocial'.

Such ranking may or may not be possible across a significant set of possible norms. But it should not be excluded at the outset. Indeed, some version of the Pareto principle might be used – for instance, to exclude some versions of norms that involve relative comparisons because they can be counter-productive (as when everyone tries to stand up to get a better view at a sporting event). But, whichever is the case, a group of people needs these 'public' aspects to enable a decision over this so that the actual norms enjoy whatever degree of legitimacy is available; and there is a connection here to the first change in welfare economics: the recognition of the distinct domain of these 'public institutions'.

This again merely reiterates something that Smith hints at. His proposal to combat the disagreeable religious norms is twofold (p. 796):

The first of those remedies is the study of science and philosophy...science is the great antidote to the poison of enthusiasm and superstition... The second of those remedies is the frequency and gaiety of public diversions. The state by encouraging that is giving entire liberty to all those who for their own interest would attempt...to amuse and divert the people by painting, poetry, music, dancing; by all sorts of dramatic representations and exhibitions would easily dissipate...that melancholy and gloomy humour which is almost always the nurse of popular superstition and enthusiasm.

In short, we need 'public institutions'.

There is a third aspect of the change to welfare economics that follows from this and that is worth mentioning. Welfare economics will need to be concerned with how to regulate the behaviour of the people who work within the distinct 'public institutions'. Like all public institutions, they will have to be accountable, and it will be obvious from what has gone before that the traditional mechanisms of accountability in the public sector (e.g. the creation of internal markets or systems of payments by results) are liable to create a tension with the ostensive purpose of these institutions (i.e. to explore the world of ideas that extends beyond mere preference satisfaction). Or, to put this slightly differently, people who engage in activity where 'intrinsic' reason is important (to use Frey's terminology) will still need to be materially rewarded; and this creates a potential problem of 'crowding out'. For instance, if a 'carer' is paid, this could undermine the 'caring' aspect of his work. Does this mean 'caring' cannot be paid work? Or that 'public institutions' must depend on voluntarism?

In a sense, this merely amplifies the first observation. A welfare economics that is sensitive to interpersonal relations will have to understand better the relationship between the satisfaction of the two kinds of preference (or between 'extrinsic' and 'intrinsic' reason) when 'crowding out' is a possibility; and one aspect of this relation is the remuneration package of those who work in 'public institutions'. Geoffrey Brennan (1996) advances an interesting proposal in this context. He suggests, in effect, that there may be ways of negotiating the 'crowding out' problem that avoid the either/or of paid/voluntary work. He argues that one can devise a remuneration package that, while paying the person, will select someone who is motivated by 'intrinsic' reason for doing the job. His example refers to lecturers, but it will be obvious how the proposal could generalise. The problem here is a version of the 'crowding out' one: how to render lecturers accountable for what they do in their research time without destroying through a system of payment by results the quest for knowledge for its own sake that underpins creative research.

His solution depends on the existence of different types of people in the pool of potential lecturers: some are motivated to lecture (or do any job) by the material reward, and some value the activity of lecturing intrinsically because it gives them a sense of self-worth. In these circumstances, a relatively low pay package when combined with an in-kind benefit that connects symbolically with the intrinsic value of lecturing (e.g. a research fund) will do the trick. The low pay element will discourage those who are motivated by the money alone, while the in-kind benefit will compensate for this among those who are intrinsically attracted to lecturing. Thus, the accountability problem (of ensuring that lecturers actually do research) is overcome, as only those people who intrinsically want to do research are recruited and, although they are paid, this will not undermine the intrinsic value of the activity because the payment is relatively low.

The point of this example is not that it is decisive. Rather, it is that there is work to be done in understanding better the relation between ordinary preference satisfaction and the generation of self-worth (or the dynamic between 'extrinsic' and 'intrinsic' reason). This holds the key to the production or destruction of shared values, and is what welfare economics needs to attend to.

5.   Conclusions

Rational choice theory has enjoyed a remarkable period of ascendancy in the social sciences as it has been applied progressively to more and more aspects of human life – politics, the family, the law, and so on – apparently without bound. However, there are aspects of action that have to do with interpersonal relations that are difficult to fit within the model; and so, perhaps, there are limits to rational choice theory. This chapter has explored whether there are such limits and how they might be characterised. It has done this by focusing on one feature of interpersonal relations: the mutual validation of ends.

The mutual validation of ends exemplifies the way that interpersonal relations are affective and help constitute individual identity; it also illustrates the difficulty that the rational choice model has with this aspect of human agency. This not only marks a boundary; I have argued that it should produce a change in welfare economics. Welfare economics will have to consider the ecology of institutions. In particular, it will need to explore how the institutions (or the aspects of those institutions) concerned with ordinary preference satisfaction interact with those that deal in ideas. This is important, because there seems to be a potential dynamic whereby increasing the scope for ordinary preference satisfaction can undermine the ability to form, discuss and instantiate the ideas that help give people a sense of self-worth. This discovery is, in effect, one of the advantages for those concerned with interpersonal relations of connecting these relations to an individual psychology where self-worth (or 'intrinsic' reason) matters. There is, in short, a potential 'crowding out' problem that is exposed, and that may be better understood through drawing on psychological theory. As I have suggested at various points in the chapter, however, these conclusions are hardly novel. One need only read Adam Smith.

10   *Hic sunt leones*: interpersonal relations as unexplored territory in the tradition of economics

Luigino Bruni

Is there a place where relation is not merely exchange?

Massimo Cacciari

1.   Introduction

'Political Economy does not treat of the whole of man's nature as modified by the social state, nor of the whole conduct of man in society. It is concerned with him solely as a being who desires to possess wealth, and who is capable of judging that end...It makes entire abstraction of every other human passion or motive' (Mill, 1897/1836, pp. 132–3).

The present volume argues that 'relational goods' are actually part of that 'wealth' on which John Stuart Mill focuses, and which still occupies the greatest part of economists' minds. Indeed, interpersonal relations, both outside and inside the economic field, influence economic performance, personal well-being and 'public happiness'.[1] The aim of this chapter is to investigate what role the analysis of interpersonal relations has played in the various moments and traditions of the history of economics, and, in so doing, to bring to light the reasons behind the methodological choices made in this regard by some leading scholars.

I claim that economists – or, at least, the greatest – have recognised that the interpersonal dimension is important in economic life. Some have even acknowledged that friendship or good conversations are an important component of welfare, *generally understood*. Nevertheless, not even those who were most persuaded of this claim have thought of making interpersonal relations a *direct* object of economic investigation,

[1] In this chapter I use the expression 'interpersonal relations' (or, equivalently, 'sociality', 'relational dimension', etc.) in the sense specified by Gui and Sugden in chapter 1; that is, in order 'to refer to forms of human interaction in which the identity of the participants *as particular human beings* has affective or cognitive significance'.

on the basis of the consideration that these aspects have no great relevance for economics, that they are not 'wealth'. Some take into account interpersonal relations in their analyses (i.e. in the formations of wants), but nobody has thought that interpersonal relations may have an economic value in themselves, like shoes, bread, machines or education. So, implicitly or explicitly, they have left the task of studying them to other disciplines (sociology, psychology, anthropology, etc.), and concentrated their analyses on 'material goods' (wealth, or *economic* welfare). This was – they thought – their specific way of contributing to well-being or happiness in general, or even, although *indirectly*, to better interpersonal relations. This conviction was very clear in Alfred Marshall, but it also emerges in the works of classical economists such as Adam Smith, Mill, Thomas Malthus or Carl Menger. This chapter stresses the 'methodological trick' behind this position.

Among the greatest economists, Marshall was the one who drove the analysis of interpersonal relations furthest away within economics. However, it was not far enough to prevent his tiny construction from collapsing in the face of Vilfredo Pareto's 'new' economic science. And contemporary economic theory, *au fond*, with respect to the role assigned to interpersonal relationships, still follows the way paved by Pareto (and Philip Wicksteed).

The second section of this chapter contains a brief account of how two pioneers of classical economic thought, Adam Smith and Antonio Genovesi, conceived interpersonal relations. In section 3, Malthus's intellectual narrative helps us understand the reasons that brought economists, at the time when their science was consolidating, to 'sacrifice' interpersonal relations. The central sections of the chapter are devoted to an analysis of the neoclassical revolution and its definitive abandonment of the issue of interpersonal relations as part of economic analysis, with particular attention to Pareto (section 4), Marshall (section 5) and Wicksteed (section 6), by reason of their role in this methodological turn. Lastly, section 7 discusses how sociality is treated by contemporary rational choice theory.

2.   Classical political economy and interpersonal relations

In his *Grundrisse* Karl Marx writes that 'individuals producing in society is, of course, the point of departure. The individual and isolated hunter and fisherman, with whom Smith and David Ricardo begin, belongs among the unimaginative conceits of the XVIII century Robinsonades' (1994/1857–8, p. 119). In his *Capital* he restates: 'Robinson Crusoe's experiences are a favourite theme with political economists' (1906/1867,

p. 47). Marx saw in these *Robinsonades* an 'anticipation of 'civil society', in preparation since the sixteenth century. 'In this society of free competition, the individual appears detached from the natural bonds etc. which in earlier historical periods make him the accessory of a definite and limited human conglomerate... Not as a historical result but as history's point of departure' (1994/1857–8, pp. 119–20).

In acknowledging Marx's acute criticism directed towards classical economists, we must, however, recognise that the meaning of the recourse to the 'rude and primitive stage' by Ricardo, or Smith, is substantially different from the use of the metaphor of Robinson Crusoe that began to appear in economists' works in the prelude to the marginalist revolution. In fact, in Ricardo's or Smith's primitive economy, instead of the Robinsonian monad there were communities of hunters and fishers. In fact, until the mid-1800s English economists did not emphasise the psychology of the *individual agent* but, rather, the relationships among social groups or classes; their approach was holistic, as witnessed by Ricardo's political economy. Marx chose the wrong target; and yet he promptly noticed a tendency that was emerging in forerunners of marginalism such as Hermann Heinrich Gossen (1981/1854, p. 54) or Francesco Ferrara (1934/1849–51, Vol. I, pp. 49, 99), two authors who used the Robinson metaphor in an individualistic perspective. Nevertheless, in Ricardo's era classical political economy performed a methodological turn of great importance in shaping the epistemology of economics with respect to interpersonal relations.

The founders of classical political economy (Scottish or Italian) must be seen in continuation with the tradition of *civic humanism*.[2] They considered the individual as a social entity, so that the rights and freedom of *ego* were not seen in opposition to the existence, rights and value of others, or of the community.

Let us take the examples of the leaders of two important schools of classical political economy: the Neapolitan and the Scottish. Antonio Genovesi (1713–69) accepted the idea that three-quarters of human actions depend on sympathy; hence the criticism of Bernard Mandeville's and Thomas Hobbes's egoistic conceptions of man that we find in the entire work of Genovesi.[3] The most basic element of his vision of the person is *sociality*, one's desire for relationships with one's fellows. Sociality is 'an indelible feature of our nature', common to all social animals.

---

[2] The expression 'civic humanism' (Baron, 1955, 1988; Pocock, 1975) refers to a period of Italian history, Florentine especially, that was characterised by a re-evaluation of civic life.

[3] As is well known, sympathy is not altruism (that is, concern for the well-being of others): it is a matter of *relations* between people.

We are 'created in such a way as to be touched necessarily, by a musical sympathy, by pleasure and internal satisfaction, as soon as we meet another man'; no human being, not even the most cruel and hardened, can enjoy pleasures in which no one else participates (1973/1766, book 1, p. 42). Thus, to Genovesi's theory, even his economic theory, it is essential that social relations are not just means by which, or constraints within which, one satisfies individual self-interest. In his work, there is a strong sense that interpersonal relationships are valuable in their own right. For Genovesi, it seems, the chief advantage of society is not in cooperation for the production of material goods but in the enjoyment of social relationships, the basic ingredient of public happiness: '[E]very man acts looking for his happiness; otherwise he would be less of a man... The more one acts for interest, the more, if he is not mad, he must be virtuous. It is a universal law that it is impossible to make our happiness without making others' happiness' (1963, p. 449).

Contemporary historiography also agrees in reading Adam Smith in continuation with the tradition of *civic humanism*.[4] His *Theory of Moral Sentiments* is informed with a relational approach to the human person, seen as constitutionally in relation with others (Smith 1976/1759, pp. 9, 113–14). A person is fortunate if he receives consideration from others and unfortunate otherwise (pp. 89–91). The entire relationship between others and ourselves is mediated by how we are seen, considered, admired, imitated. Even riches and power, to Smith, are just means for attracting the attention of others, for being 'recognised'.

From this relational anthropology comes the idea that 'nothing pleases us more than to observe in other men a fellow-feeling with all the emotions of our own breast; nor are we ever so much shocked as by the appearance of the contrary' (p. 13). Fellow-feeling, an extraordinary anthropological intuition, may also be defined as 'mutual sympathy' or a 'correspondence of sentiments' (p. 14). Furthermore, wealth cannot automatically be transformed into happiness or well-being, but only in appropriate conditions (p. 212 et seq.). Wealth is only a means for being happy (p. 16 et seq.). However, according to Smith, it is not part of individuals' plans to be happy; human beings, in fact, want to be recognised and admired, also because of their wealth and fortune. As a philosopher, Smith knew that the expectation that wealth, social recognition and fortune would lead their beneficiaries to happiness was a *deception* (p. 182 et seq.). Social dynamics, however, are providentially based on this deception: individuals' desire to improve their material conditions (for their own happiness, they think) is guided by an *invisible*

---

[4] See Winch (1978) and Hont and Ignatief (1983).

hand to the promotion of public happiness, despite the 'natural selfishness and rapacity' of the deceived individuals (p. 185).

When a few years later Smith wrote *The Wealth of Nations*, the title itself defined the object of the newborn political economy: it deals with wealth, not happiness, although in his choice of the word 'wealth' – rather than 'riches' – one can rightly see the idea that wealth (weal, well-being) is something more than simply owning material goods.

Given the rich anthropology of Smith's *Theory*, his complex account of human agency and his theory of deception, the science he pioneered could have been very different; instead of the science of wealth, political economy could have become the study of how and in which conditions riches are transformed into happiness, *via* the mechanism of fellow-feeling.

If the wealth–happiness link is a deception that Smith the philosopher points out, why should Smith the economist devote himself to studying the ways of increasing wealth? His probable answer, as it emerges in particular from *The Theory of Moral Sentiments*, would have been that happiness is produced by an active life and *modest* wealth, not by idleness, luxury and *excessive* wealth. In general, the 'wealth of nations' is closely linked to the 'happiness of nations', because only a tiny minority of people are in the idle class. The pursuit of (excessive) wealth is a deception, but it provides the engine for an economic system that provides everyone with subsistence; and people's susceptibility to this deception is one of the mechanisms by means of which the 'invisible hand' mechanism works. The tradition of economics after Smith, apart from the few exceptions we will consider later on, neglected the subtle and slippery relation between wealth and happiness (or well-being), as the enthusiasm for the 'novelty' of the contemporary paradox of happiness clearly signals.

3.   Political economy in Ricardo's era: the sacrifice of relational goods

The first great economist who was aware of the existence of a complex 'technology of happiness' was Malthus. His intellectual evolution – from the *Essay on Population* (1966/1798) to the *Principles of Political Economy* (1986/1820) – is an icon of the approach to the interpersonal dimension that was followed by political economy.

In his *Essay*, published in 1798, he writes (pp. 303–4, my italics):

The professed object of Dr Adam Smith's inquiry is the nature and causes of the wealth of nations. There is another inquiry, however, perhaps still more interesting, which he occasionally mixes with it, I mean an inquiry into the causes which affect the *happiness* of nations... I am sufficiently aware of the near connection of these two subjects, and that the causes which tend to increase the wealth of a state tend also, generally speaking, to increase the *happiness*... But perhaps Dr Adam Smith has considered these two inquiries as still more nearly connected than they really are.

This sentence supplies us with the key elements for understanding Malthus's idea of happiness, and his evaluation of Smith's stand. Malthus also distinguished the two categories and, generally speaking, agreed that more wealth brings more happiness. In his view, however, Smith was not sufficiently aware that the relation between the two is complex and worthy of investigation in its own right.

Malthus belonged to that class of economists (such as Genovesi, Jean-Charles-Léonasa Simonde de Sismondi and many other nineteenth-century Italians) who thought that the 'happiness of nations' was 'another inquiry... perhaps still more interesting' than that into wealth – as the modern theorists of happiness also believe.

However, Malthus's intent of studying happiness directly as an object of political economy did not last long. Two decades later he wrote his *Principles of Political Economy*, with no further references to happiness; the object of his enquiries had become *wealth*, as for Smith and the classical mainstream tradition of economics. In particular, although he was fully aware that political economy, in focusing on the material and quantitative aspects of human interactions, was losing important elements of 'wealth', he coldly abandoned the interpersonal dimensions of wealth (1986/1820, pp. 31–2):

A man of fortune has the means of...collecting at his table persons from whom he is likely to hear the most agreeable and instructive conversation... It would not be denied, that these are some of the modes of employing wealth, which are always, and most justly, considered as much superior in respectability, to the purchase of fine clothes, spending on furniture, or costly jewels... But it is a wide step in advance of these concessions, at once to place in the category of wealth, leisure, agreeable conversation... The fact really is, that if we once desert matter in definition of wealth, there is no subsequent line of demarcation which has any tolerable degree of distinctness, or can be maintained with any tolerable consistency, till we have included such a mass of immaterial objects as utterly to confuse the meaning of the term, and render it impossible to speak with any approach towards precision, either of the wealth of different individuals, or different nations.

Here, the main reason that brought post-Smith economists to avoid dealing with interpersonal aspects of economic transactions is clearly stated. Malthus was convinced not only that 'enjoying conversations' with friends was an important and, indeed, 'superior' form of using wealth, but even that 'leisure and agreeable conversations' could rightly be considered as *components* of the wealth of a person. However, he considered these components to be too ill-defined to be included in the economic province, which instead needs data, objective measurement, 'matter'. Something had to be sacrificed to the altar of the new science, based on objective and scientific measurements: the interpersonal components of wealth were among the victims. A science seeking to encompass the first 'scientific' reflections on economic relations chose to concentrate its analyses upon objective elements such as labour value, the redistribution of income, or production, or – as neoclassical economists stated – on the 'supply side' of the economy. As a consequence, such a political economy did not find room for interpersonal relations, seen as a source of well-being, as a component of that 'wealth' of the nations to which so many intellectual efforts were devoted.

4.   Pareto's revolution in the theory of choice

The 'naked fact' of choice

In the process of expunging the interpersonal dimension from economics, a pivotal role was played by Pareto, an economist whose methodology has heavily influenced contemporary microeconomics and rational choice theory. His re-foundation of demand theory was a real revolution in economics, definitely with respect to Marshall; John Hicks, R. G. D. Allen and Paul Samuelson, the fathers of modern microeconomics, can all be seen as direct and aware followers of Pareto.

Between the end of 1899 and the first months of 1900 Pareto pursued two fundamental and distinct objectives, which can be considered his main legacy to contemporary economic science: (a) ordinalism, or the replacement of a cardinal by an ordinal utility function; and (b) the interpretation of ophelimity as an index of preferences. At that turning point he built up his economic theory on 'the naked fact of choice', without having to resort to cardinal measurement or even to the existence of utility (Pareto 1984, pp. 290–1). He intended to make as little recourse as possible to psychological and sociological data *within* economics. Even the analysis of *wants* (which he called '*tastes*', and considered as given)[5] was expelled from economics.

The distinction between utility (a concept similar to usefulness or well-being) and ophelimity (defined in the *Cours* (sect. 7) as 'the relation

---

[5] Several times Pareto stated that tastes, taken as given in economics but studied in sociology, are the *link* between these two disciplines.

of convenience, which satisfies a need or a desire, legitimate or not'), already made in the *Cours d'économie politique* (1896–7), was the first tool he used to bypass the issue of the interpersonal dimension. Ophelimity was in fact defined by him as 'a kind of subjective utility' (sect. 16), specifying that this 'characteristic of ophelimity as being subjective is fundamental. This must be kept in mind in everything that follows' (sect. 9). So, economics becomes 'the science of ophelimity' (sect. 16), on absolutely *subjective* bases (sect. 30). Pareto's mature economic theory is completely defined at the level of the individual. It deals only with the sensations inside the actor: all relationships, all the 'others', are present only in his demand curves; real individuals, and every *real* and personalised social interaction, can 'disappear'. This position, although founded on a somewhat different epistemology, recalls Wicksteed's 'non-tuism'.

Pareto, in fact, specified that *pure* economics deals with the 'choices that the individual makes considering solely the things that he prefers', omitting, or – better yet – making over to sociology, actions 'that the individual makes considering the effects that these choices will have on other individuals' (1900a, p. 223). Later, in his *Manual of Political Economy*, published in 1906, he was even clearer in stating that the object of economics is 'to compare the sensations of a man in different situations, and to determine which of these he would choose' (1971/ 1906, ch. 3, sect. 11).

At the same time, Pareto – like Francis Edgeworth, or Marshall – had no trouble in dealing with altruism, which easily finds a place in his still individualistic theory, based on preferences and choices.

[S]ince it is customary to assume that man will be guided in his choice exclusively by consideration of his own advantage, of his self-interest, we say that this class is made up of theories of egotism. But it could be made up of theories of *altruism* (if the meaning of that term could be defined rigorously), or, in general, of theories which rest on any rule which man follows in comparing his sensations. It is not an essential characteristic of this class of theories that a man choosing between two sensations choose the most agreeable; he could choose a different one, following a rule which could be fixed arbitrarily. (1971/1906, ch. 3, sect. 11)

In this way, no room is left for non-instrumental relations among human beings: economics becomes the science of the individual and is characterised by a system of preferences, rather than by an identity or personality. The impersonality of Pareto's theory reaches the point of stating: 'The individual can disappear, provided he leaves us this photo-graph of his tastes' (sect. 57). Economics becomes the science of rela-tions between 'things': 'Science proceeds by replacing the relationships between human concepts (which relationships are the first to occur to us) by relationships between things... Such a path is also the only one that can lead to the truth in political economy' (1900b, p. 162). This thesis echoes Marx's famous statement, that wealth 'is a relationship between persons expressed as a relation between things' (1906/1867, p. 45, fn. 1).[6] However, while Marx gave political economy the task of retrieving those social relations hidden behind commodities, Pareto went in the opposite direction, and saw progress in economic science in that replacement of persons by things.

At this point, the economic agent is completely impersonal, *a machine that maximises a function under constraints*. Because of this, Pareto asserted, his approach to choice can even be applied to animals, as long as their behaviour is uniform (1900a).

A 'material point' methodology

In order fully to understand Pareto's revolution in economics in all its implications with respect to human interactions, we must look at his methodology.

First of all, Pareto brought to extreme consequences the neoclassical dream of building a science on the paradigm of Newtonian physics. This was his chief objective. As a consequence, the economic agent is conceived as a 'material point'.[7] It is hard to imagine a material point enjoying conversations or developing friendships. A material point can be understood only through the law of minimum means aiming for the maximum result under constraints. Furthermore, a material point cannot have motivations for actions (let alone *intrinsic* ones), as it can only be passively driven by forces (*in primis*, self-interest).

Secondly, according to Pareto, a real action has two components:

(a) *logical*, based on *pure instrumental* reasoning, where the means are to be adequate to the end, subjectively and objectively; and
(b) *non-logical*, where *non*-logical does not mean *illogical* or irrational, but is simply based on a different type of logic (1916, sects. 150–2).

Economics deals with the logical part, so its task is simple. Sociology deals with the rest, so its task is very difficult.

---

[6] Marx in his turn borrowed from the eighteenth-century Neapolitan economist Ferdinando Galiani, the author of the treatise *Della Moneta*.
[7] See the famous synoptic table in a footnote of his *Cours* (Vol. II, sect. 592), *Manual* (Vol. I, sects. 7, 26) and *Treatise* (sect. 39).

Indeed, Pareto's analysis of human interaction can be understood only within his methodology, which was based – like Mill's – on the method of *analysis and synthesis* (see Bruni, 2002): the scholar must break down the action in question into its two parts (logical and non-logical), investigate each separately and then attempt a synthesis.[8]

For Pareto, economic laws explain only a small part of human behaviour: the kinds of logic behind economic and non-economic actions are substantially different; and to apply the theory of choice presupposes that agents perform logical actions. This is very clear in all his scientific work: 'What everybody surely knows, *since here we are dealing with logical action*, is that...' (Pareto, 1966/1898, p. 128, my italics). In fact, the theory of choice was introduced by Pareto in 1900, *after* he had developed his theory of logical and non-logical actions. His theory of economic action before 1900 was still based on *pleasure*, and full of *relational* elements.[9] A few years later he clearly specified that his whole economic theory was valid for 'many logical, repeated actions which men perform to procure the things which satisfy their tastes' (1971/1906, Vol. III, sect. 1). Therefore, it is not strange that we cannot find indifference curves in his *Sociology*.[10] Instead, we find an analysis of actions based on non-instrumental rationality. For example, the 'residues of the fourth class' (residues in relation to sociality; Pareto, 1916, sects. 113–26) are entirely devoted to 'the want for sociality'.

Pareto's methodological foundations of modern rational choice were re-proposed and publicised in 1934 by Hicks and Allen, the protagonists of the *final* 'ordinalist revolution', which replaced traditional utilitarianism in modern consumer theory. From the late 1930s onwards Samuelson took the ordinalist revolution to its extreme consequences with his 'revealed preferences' approach. The mathematical economists of the 1950s completed the task.

However, the theory of action that is found in Hicks and in contemporary rational choice theory is very distant from Pareto's, and this has an important bearing on how contemporary economists view personal interactions (Bruni and Guala, 2001).

In their 1934 paper, written under the influence of neo-positivistic philosophy, Hicks and Allen say: '[T]he methodological implications of [the new] conception of utility...are far-reaching indeed. By

---

[8] For Pareto, the last step is up to sociology (1971/1906, Vol. I, sects. 20, 26).

[9] See, for instance, the second volume of *Cours d'économie politique* (Pareto, 1896–7), or the analysis of social imitation and emulation in Pareto (1980/1897, p. 46 et seq.).

[10] Pareto devoted the second part of his life to the dream of writing a 'synthetic economics', a treatise able to explain the complexity of economic behaviour, but he never completed such a work.

transforming the subjective theory of value into a *general logic of choice, they extend its applicability over wide fields of human conduct*' (p. 45, my italics). The same concept is restated in *Value and Capital*: '[T]hat there are a great many such extensions appears at once when we consider how wide is the variety of human choices which can be fitted into the framework of the Paretian scale of preference' (Hicks, 1939, p. 24).[11] As mentioned above, Pareto had a completely different idea of action.

Thus Hicks and his followers took up Pareto's theory of choice, *separating* it from his theory of action; they extended a theory of choice, created to explain the small and 'simple' world of logical actions, to actions that are substantially different. The rational choice theory of the twentieth century has gone precisely in this direction.

5.   Another possible story: Marshall's *impure* economics

Sociality within economics: the social analysis of wants

Marshall, as is well known, left room for 'altruism' in his economics, denying that self-interest and hedonism were essential requisites of economic science. He wanted to study the 'man in flesh and blood', so that any human motive could, in principle, be taken into consideration (1946/1890, p. 27 et seq.). The only limitation on the economic domain was, for Marshall, the possibility of monetary measurement: economic goods were those that 'can be measurable by a money price' (p. 33).[12] This methodological stance is very close to that taken by Malthus in shaping the boundaries of economic *wealth*.

However, the 'right of citizenship' for altruism in economics is not an element of originality and departure in Marshall's theory with respect to the economists who preceded him. The first name that comes to mind is that of Edgeworth (1967/1881, p. 53) (see Collard, 1978). More generally, that self-interest represents the dominant motive in economic matters was indeed considered by classical and neoclassical economists (from Mill to William Jevons, and Pareto) as one of the most basic and universal economic laws, but it was more a common-sense thesis than an essential requirement of their theory. Even in Smith's *Wealth* – as Philippe Fontaine (1997) claims – one can find room for sympathy

---

[11] This methodological attitude is very close to that of Wicksteed, as the next section shows.

[12] The same thesis is present in Arthur Pigou (1920, ch. 1). For Marshall and his school, the domain of economics was determined by the *strength* of man's motives, 'not the motives themselves' – strength that 'can be approximately measured by the sum of money' (Marshall, 1946/1890, p. 15).

within standard market transactions.[13] The introduction of altruism did not, therefore, affect the hard core of the classical theoretical system. In fact, both Edgeworth and Marshall maintained full continuity with classical political economy.

What, instead, represented a real step forward with respect to English classical writers was Marshall's analysis of wants. Many leading neoclassical economists of the first generation, such as Menger (1871, ch. 1, sect. 1),[14] Jevons (1879, ch. 3) and Maffeo Pantaleoni (1889, ch. 3), in investigating the underlying subjective and psychological elements in economic life, in focusing on *people* rather than on *things*, brought back to the attention of economists the theme of *wants*, which at that time was languishing, forgotten, in the works of some thinkers of the classical tradition (from Scholastic philosophers to Genovesi). For these economists too, the psychology of wants was an essential part of economics. In this way, wants became (although only for a short while) the bridge between the interpersonal dimension and economic analysis. Menger based all his subjective theory of value on wants; the first line of his *Principles* states: '[T]he starting point of every economic inquiry are human wants.' In this sense, I agree with Joseph Schumpeter (1997/ 1952, p. 83) when he states that 'Menger belongs to those who have demolished the existing structure of a science and put it on entirely new foundations' – at least with respect to British political economy. In fact, in dealing with wants, economists must shift their attention from the isolated individual agent (such as Robinson Crusoe) to the agent immersed in a social environment, given the fact that most of our wants are generated by interactions with others.

'To know which sentiments of soul, which faculties of mind...push man to deliberately modify the forms of the world in which he lives' (Pantaleoni, 1925, Vol. I, p. 11) was an ordinary subject in the first marginalist synthesis. The early neoclassical economists hoped to develop an analysis of demand that could explain how human wants are formed and vary, calling for psychological and interpersonal explanations. Apart from very few exceptions (such as George Stigler and Gary Becker, 1977), contemporary economics has given up this ambition and taken wants as *given*, causing an already shaky bridge between the interpersonal dimension and economics to collapse.

Marshall was well aware of recent trends in Austria and Germany, and particularly of the great emphasis that economists there were putting on

---

[13] Fontaine's interpretation makes recourse to the Humean theory of 'spheres of intimacy', also present in *The Theory of Moral Sentiments* (Smith 1984/1759, pp. 223–4).
[14] In a footnote (sect. 1), Menger distinguishes between *egoistic* and *altruistic* wants.

wants and their social formation. These were given great importance in his *Principles*, in which *demand* and *consumption* are central. Marshall's theory of wants is centred on the thesis that economic activity is performed in society, so that the creation and modification of wants are interpersonal matters. 'Desire for distinction', 'emulation' and 'desire for excellence' (Marshall, 1946/1890, ch. 2, sects. 1–4) are considered among the most powerful determinants of wants, and therefore demand. At the same time, he includes among the tasks of economics only an 'elementary analysis' of the theory of consumption: '[T]hough it may have its beginning within the proper domain of economics, it cannot find its conclusions there, but must extend far beyond' (pp. 90–1). In a footnote (p. 91) he adds that a profound analysis of wants 'is a task not without interest', as it was conducted by Continental economists (he referred explicitly to Menger). Nevertheless, 'the rigid boundary which English writers have ascribed to their science has excluded such discussions'; the need to be in continuity with the English tradition was stronger.

Are interpersonal relationships wealth?

The last step in this analysis of the connection between Marshall's theory of wants and his account of the interpersonal dimension is to understand why, like Menger, he states that interpersonal relationships are not 'goods' for economic analysis.

Menger is very explicit in his *Manual*; despite his general statement that 'goods' are all things capable of satisfying humans' wants (1871, sect. 1), he then denies that 'happiness, well-being, love, friendship' are 'goods', and calls them instead 'free manifestations of personality' (fn. 1). The explanation of this methodological choice is related to the 'materiality' of goods: to him goods are 'things', commodities (fn. 1).

The same conclusion, although starting from a different epistemology and methodology, was reached by Marshall. In the *Principles* he writes: 'The affection of friends, for instance, is an important element of well-being, but it is not reckoned as wealth, except by a poetic licence' (1946/1890, p. 54). And, further on, defining individual wealth, he states: '[I]t excludes his personal friendships, in so far as they have no direct business value' (p. 57).

The explanation of this choice lies in Marshall's theory of human agency, which is in conformity with the classical philosophical tradition. In section 3 we saw the position of Malthus on happiness and wealth. This position of the founder of Cambridge's tradition was continued by Marshall and his school (Pigou in particular).

In the introduction to the *Principles* we find the theoretical key for understanding Marshall's view of the link between happiness and wealth, and his theory of interpersonal relations (p. 2):

It is true that in religion, in the family affections and in friendship, even the poor may find scope for many of those faculties which are the source of the highest happiness. But the conditions which surround extreme poverty, especially in densely crowded places, tend to deaden the higher faculties.

Therefore, to Marshall, the role of economists in society was very important: finding ways to increase wealth or reduce poverty, far from being in contrast with the general well-being or happiness,[15] was a means of augmenting them, partly by fostering the interpersonal dimensions of life.[16]

However, there is something missing in this position: analysis of the transformation of goods into well-being (happiness), subjectively and collectively. In fact, as both contemporary economies and economics show, economic goods do not always become welfare or well-being.

Yet, in the last chapter of the *Principles*, in the theory of the 'standard of life' there is an intuition of possible inverse (and perverse) effects – an intuition that was completely absent in both Pareto and Wicksteed. First of all, Marshall, in a thoroughly Aristotelian (and, today, we would say 'Senian') flavour, states that 'the true key-note of economic progress is the development of new activities rather than new wants', specifying that the question that 'is of special urgency in our generation' is 'the connection between changes in the manner of living and the rate of earning' (1946/1890, p. 688). In order to analyse this urgent question, he distinguishes between two concepts: the 'standard of life' and the 'standard of comfort'. The 'standard of life is here taken to mean the standard of activity adjusted to wants' (p. 688), and 'the standard of comfort [is] a term that may suggest a mere increase of artificial wants, among which perhaps the grosser wants may predominate' (p. 690). Then he repeats his thesis (p. 690).

It is true that every broad improvement in the standard of comfort is likely to bring with it a better manner of living, and to open the way to new and higher

---

[15] Those who know Amartya Sen's theory of the 'the standard of living' (1987) will find a strong assonance between the two economists. Marshall's line of thought was followed by his heir in Cambridge, Pigou, who moved the fulcrum of the issue towards the other magic word in economics: *welfare*. In his *Economics of Welfare* (1920, p. 16) Pigou states that he deals only with the economic aspects of total welfare; he calls it 'economic welfare' – i.e. that part of total welfare that 'can be expressed, directly or indirectly, by a money measure'.

[16] Underlining this view is the fact that Marshall was the first to use, in English, the word 'good' for 'commodity' in his *Principles*, following German writers.

activities; while people who have hitherto had neither the necessaries nor the decencies of life, can hardly fail to get some increase in vitality and energy from an increase of comfort, however gross and material the view which they may take of it. This rise in the standard of comfort will probably involve some rise in the standard of life.

But this is not always the case; the rest of the chapter is, in fact, an analysis of cases in which rises in the standard of comfort lead to a fall in the standard of life. He confronts the 'burning question of the limitation of the hours of labour' (Edgeworth 1970/1891, Vol. III, p. 14) and the related issues of the minimum wage and the redistribution of income. A first application of this analysis was Marshall's recommendation for a general reduction of the hours of labour, which was likely to cause a small material loss but much moral good: a case in which a reduction of income can lead to a higher standard of life (happiness). At the end of the chapter he explains why (1946/1890, p. 721):

Even if we took account only of the injury done to the young by living in a home in which the father and the mother lead joyless lives, it would be in the interest of society to afford some relief to them also. Able workers and good citizens are not likely to come from homes, from which the mother is absent during a great part of the day; nor from homes to which the father seldom returns till his children are asleep: and therefore society as a whole has a direct interest in the curtailment of extravagantly long hours of duty away from home.

Marshall's epistemology was potentially open to the analysis of some aspects of interpersonal dimensions *within* economics, but the main-stream has followed a completely different path: that of Pareto (and Wicksteed). However, it is not enough to report the success of Pareto's theory of action and epistemology. It is necessary to ask *why* it succeeded. In conclusion, I would point out two possible explanations.

The first is obvious. The cultural atmosphere of the 1930s, when modern microeconomics came to life, influenced as it was by neo-positivism and behaviourism, welcomed Pareto's anti-metaphysical and mathematical approach, and disregarded Marshall's social con-siderations, which appeared to be old-fashioned and somewhat imprecise.

Secondly, Marshall had his own responsibility. Of his sophisticated and anthropologically rich theory of sociality, his awareness of the complexity of the transformation of goods into well-being, only a small part affected the analytical part of his economics. The demand curve, Marshallian cross, representative firm, reservation price and rent of the consumer (i.e. his main legacies to twentieth-century economics) carry no stamp of that complexity and awareness. Marshall the economist did not fulfil the promise of Marshall the social scientist. Indeed, his anchorage to 'monetary measurement' was a methodological obstacle that also influenced his followers. Among these was Pigou; the category of 'externality' had the potential for being extended to relational or social effects, but was confined to standard economic ones.[17]

6.   Wicksteed's non-tuism

An escape from egoism (and interpersonal relations)

With Wicksteed's *Common Sense of Political Economy* (1933/1910) the process of the eradication of interpersonal relations from economic analysis, initiated by Pareto, moved ahead. Although he came from a different philosophical background (the Austrian tradition was very influential in his thinking), Wicksteed reached conclusions similar to Pareto's as to how to deal with the interpersonal dimension in economics.

First, Pareto's influence on Wicksteed's mature economics must be acknowledged.[18] When the latter reviewed Pareto's *Manual* in the *Economic Journal* he was very impressed by the book (Wicksteed, 1906): '[I]t is a work which is likely to modify and stimulate economic thought to an extent quite disproportionate to the numbers of its readers. It will probably be understood by few, but every one who understands it will be influenced by it.' Given the technical difficulties of the book, he looked forward 'to a long period of continued and intensified study, and probably to the exposition and comments of other students, before attempting to estimate its full significance' (p. 815). He actually did spend such a period of study: four years in writing his *Common Sense of Political Economy*, a work that 'bears witness everywhere to the extent to which Wicksteed himself had been affected' by Pareto's *Manual* (Robbins, 1933, p. xviii).

In fact, if we compare *The Common Sense of Political Economy* with his earlier *The Alphabet of Economic Science*, 'superficially, the two theories are the same... But a closer inspection will reveal important points of difference' (Robbins, 1933, p. xviii), in which it is easy to discern Pareto's influence: (a) *The Alphabet* starts from marginal utility, *The Common Sense* from the 'relative scale of preferences'; (b) in *The*

---

[17] However, a lateral stream of Marshallian economics has embodied some of his social exigencies: the theory of 'industrial districts' (Marshall, 1927/1919), based on concepts such as cooperation, trust and social culture (see Pyke, Becattini, and Sengenberger, 1990, and Raffaelli, 2002).

[18] In Bruni (2002, ch. 5) I discuss the differences between the two authors.

Alphabet utility is objective and measurable; in *The Common Sense* the idea of measurability gives way to that of the 'order of preferences'. In sum, 'there is no feature of the presentation which does not bear evidence of reformulation and improvement. In all this, the influence of Pareto is very strongly discernible' (p. xix).

The Common Sense of Political Economy is the most complete exposition of Wicksteed's thinking. In the introduction he immediately states that the vast shift impressed by neoclassical economists on economic science is the consequence of having based economics on the 'psychology of choice between alternatives' (Wicksteed, 1933/1910, p. 2). It follows 'that the general principles which regulate our conduct in business are identical with those that regulate our deliberations, our selection between alternatives, and our decisions, in all other branches of life' (p. 3). Thus, economics has nothing to say about wants and motives.

The Common Sense contains a methodology already present in Gossen (1981/1854, p. 54): Wicksteed starts his analysis from the behaviour of the isolated individual, Robinson Crusoe alone. Later (in ch. 4) he introduces Friday: 'Hitherto our examination of the administration of resources has been conducted purely from the personal or individual point of view... We must now turn, making the momentous transition from personal to communal economics' (Wicksteed, 1933/1910, p. 127).

The most interesting part of the story can be found in chapter 5, entitled 'Business and the economic nexus': here, with the praiseworthy intent of freeing economic science from egoism and hedonism, Wicksteed throws away *personalised* human interactions. In the introduction, after defining economics as the science of instrumental relations, he has already announced: '[T]he things and doings with which economic investigation is concerned will therefore be found to include...the things a man can give to or for another independently of any personal and individualised sympathy with him or with his motives or reasons' (pp. 4–5).

In the story of individualism in economics, Wicksteed has played a genuinely emblematic role. An expert in medieval and humanistic thought (his works on and English translations of Alighieri Dante and Thomas Aquinas are renowned), he aimed at infusing a moral outlook into neoclassical (Jevonian in particular) economics. His theory of distribution is witness to his genuine social concern, but nobody contributed more than Wicksteed to creating an economic theory with no space for interpersonal relations. The main theoretical tool he used was *non-tuism*.

Economic relations as a game of chess

Wicksteed defines the 'economic motive' as one of the worst confusions that prevented science from evolving (p. 163). The reason behind it was that many economists limited their studies to actions characterised by one particular motive, 'the desire to possess wealth' (p. 163). The methodology of the 'economic motive' excluded altruism from the economic field, a serious limitation for Wicksteed, given his humanitarian and Christian ethics. Viewing economics as *the science of human action* opened the economists' citadel to other motives: 'We are only concerned with the "what" and the "how", and not at all with the "why"' (p. 165). With this methodological goal in mind, he introduces the concept of *non-tuism*. The economic relation is a positive-sum game: *alter* cooperates with *ego* because the relation is advantageous to both (p. 166). All positive-sum types of relations, in which the other's interests are set in second place as an indirect way of reaching one's own, 'may be fitly called "economic"' (p. 166). Then, having defined relations and economic conditions (pp. 168–9), Wicksteed emphasises that the methodological pillars on which his economics is built are substantially different from those present 'in the current treatment of Political Economy' (p. 169).

The first pillar is 'that the economic relation is entered into at the prompting of the whole range of human purposes and impulses, and rests in no exclusive or specific way on an egoistic or self-regarding basis' (p. 169). So he can go back to the housewife he has mentioned earlier (p. 20) and state: 'It is often said or implied that the housewife, for example, is actuated by a different set of motives in her economic transactions in the market and her non-economic transactions at home; but this is obviously not so' (p. 170).

Similarly, St Paul could not have been inspired by altruistic motives when at Aquila and Priscilla's home in Corinth, and then by egoism when he made tents: '[T]he economic relation, then, or business nexus, is necessary alike for carrying on the life of the peasant and the prince, of the saint and the sinner' (p. 171). However, according to Wicksteed, a person cannot be altruistic towards *all people*, but only those 'at large' – that is, anonymous and faceless humans: 'In his attitude towards himself and "others" at large, a man may be either selfish or unselfish without affecting the economic nature of any given relation, such as that of Paul to his customers' (pp. 173–4).

The most interesting passage is the following: 'As soon as he is moved by a direct and disinterested desire to further the purposes or consult the interests of those particular "others" for whom he is working at the moment...*the transaction on his side ceases to be purely economic*' (p. 174, my italics).

In sum, for Wicksteed, economics is compatible with any motive, including altruism. What it cannot tolerate is that the other becomes a 'you' (in Latin, *tu*) – i.e. that the other whose interests the actor consults takes on the face of the person being dealt with: the butcher, the baker, or the candlestick-maker.[19] This is where his famous neologism comes from: 'It would be just as true, and just as false, to say that the business motive ignores egoistic as to say that it ignores altruistic impulses. The specific characteristic of an economic relation is not its "egoism" but its "non-tuism"' (p. 180).[20]

Economic relations are like a game: 'It would be absurd to call a man selfish for protecting his king in a game of chess... If you want to know whether he is selfish or unselfish you must consider the whole organisation of his life' (p. 181). He then repeats this idea in even clearer terms (p. 181, my italics):

Once more, then, if *ego* and *tu* are engaged in any transaction, whether egoism or altruism furnishes my inspiring motive, or whether my thoughts at the moment *are wholly impersonal*, the economic nature of the action on my side remains undisturbed. *It is only when tuism to some degree actuates my conduct that it ceases to be wholly economic. It is idle, therefore, to consider 'egoism' as a characteristic mark of the economic life.*

The last two phrases summarise Wicksteed's methodological project. The price paid for saving economics from the criticism of being founded on egoism, with no room for altruism, is by excluding *personalised face-to-face* economic relations.

It is interesting to note that Wicksteed's theory of action is exactly the opposite of Pareto's. In fact, in reviewing Pareto's *Manual* (1906) Wicksteed criticises the book for having restricted the domain of economics, which he says, for Pareto, makes up 'a very small part of the actual phenomena of the business' (p. 817). Pareto, according to Wicksteed, does not realise that his 'curves of indifference' can cover a much greater area of human behaviour.

---

[19] Wicksteed specifies that *tuistic* attitudes are often found in the market, but these are interferences from extra-economic spheres (p. 175).

[20] Wicksteed says of economists, however, if the 'tu' with which *economic man* is faced in his transactions were the only 'other' in his life, *non-tuism* would just be a new name for *egoism*; but for Robinson Crusoe there exist people, other than Friday, towards whom he can be, if he so wishes, an altruist.

Breaking away from non-instrumental rationality in economics

In Wicksteed's account, the only kind of interactions allowed within economics definitively have an *instrumental* nature, with no place left for intrinsic or 'expressive' motivations.[21] This is very clear in his essay 'The scope and method of political economy' (Wicksteed, 1914). There he writes (p. 773, my italics):

[I]f a peasant adorns his ox-yoke with carving because he likes doing it and likes it when done, or if he carves a stool for his friend because he loves him and likes doing it for him and believes he will like it when done, the action is not economic; but if he gets a reputation for carving and other peasants want his work, he may become a professional carver and may carve a yoke or a stool because other people want them and he finds that supplying their wants is the easiest way for him to get food and clothes and leisure for his own art, and all things else that he desires. His artistic work now puts him into an economic relation with his fellows; but this example serves to remind us that there may be an indefinite area of coincidence between the economic and non-economic aspects of a man's occupations and relations. That man is happy indeed who finds that in *expressing* some part of his nature he is providing for all his natural wants; or that in rendering services to friends in which he delights he is putting himself in command of all the services he himself needs for the accomplishment of his own purposes.

The most influential place in which this methodology crystallised is in Lionel Robbins's *An Essay on the Nature and Significance of Economic Science* (1932), which – together with the Pareto–Hicks–Samuelson approach – has most greatly influenced the epistemology of microeconomics in the twentieth century.

In the prologue to his *Essay*, Robbins explicitly recognises his indebtedness to the Austrians, Ludwig von Mises in particular, and to Wicksteed. Economics has become a matter of choices about scarce resources destined for alternative uses (p. 16), an entirely individualistic and instrumental operation. Therefore, it is not by chance that Robbins goes back to the Robinson Crusoe metaphor, as in Wicksteed, but without Friday. The example of Robinson Crusoe's economy is adopted to demonstrate how even an isolated man has an economic problem (p. 10). Thus, according to Robbins, starting from the isolated agent makes it possible to discover the nature of the economic problem, since Crusoe too 'has to choose. He has to economise... This example is typical of the whole field of Economic Studies' (p. 12).

---

[21] On intrinsic motivations in economic life, see Frey (1997); on 'expressive' or non-instrumental rationality, see Hargreaves Heap (1989).

Wicksteed's influence in this design is decisive, as Robbins himself recognises (1932, p. ix; 1933, p. xxii, fn. 2). Robbins considers the chapter 'Business and the economic nexus', in which non-tuism is introduced, as the most important and original part of *The Common Sense*. Certainly, it is the part that influenced his method – and contemporary neoclassical economics – to the greatest extent.

Instrumental rationality and non-tuism are therefore two sides of the same coin: within the framework of instrumental rationality, *ego* establishes a relation with *alter* only *when* and *if* the one needs the other, and the counterpart is seen only as a means in order to achieve some goal that is *external* to the relation itself.

7.   Rational choice theory: which sociality?

Far from providing a complete survey of contemporary economists' treatment of interpersonal relations (however, see sections 2 and 3), in this section I comment on just two noteworthy instances of the application of rational choice theory that are directly relevant for the historical reconstruction conducted thus far: Becker's approach to human behaviour, and conventional game theory.

The former extends the methodology of maximisation under constraints to intentional choices in all fields of life (Becker, 1996). As Nancy Cartwright points out, '[C]ontemporary economics provides models not just for the prices of the rights for off-shore oil drilling, where the market meets very nice conditions, but also for the effects of liberal abortion policies on teenage pregnancies, for whom we marry and when we divorce and for the rationale of political lobbies' (Cartwright, 1999, p. 1).

The extension of economic logic to a larger set of interactions – including those occurring within the family, in which agents' utility functions are interrelated – has *ipso facto* overcome the necessity of assuming non-tuism. Today's economists have no great difficulty in dealing with altruism.[22] Instead, they find intrinsic and relational elements hard to grasp, and repeatedly try to reduce them to forms of

---

[22] In discussing dilemmas of individual rationality such as the equilibrium of the 'centipede game', Martin Hollis points out that the main methodological assumption in contemporary game theory, its sine qua non condition, is not non-tuism but 'philosophical egoism', which he defines as follows: 'Provided that the adjusted pay-offs are as stated, it makes no difference whether Adam and Eve are selfish sods or ardent altruists. The sorry outcome depends solely on assuming that Adam is directly moved only by what Adam wants overall, and Eve directly moved only by what Eve wants overall' (Hollis, 1998, p. 17). Therefore, I do not agree with Ken Binmore, who claims that 'like arithmetic, game theory is not a manifesto for hedonism or egoism or any other *ism*' (1994, p. 103): game theory needs philosophical ego*ism*.

altruism. So, Becker is very close to Wicksteed when he analyses social interaction within a purely instrumental theoretical framework: in both approaches there is no room for what, in this volume, are called 'interpersonal relations'.

The same applies to the strategic logic of conventional game theory: no – or very little[23] – space is left for non-instrumental behaviour. Playing the game is not in itself a source of utility; what matters are payoffs that are defined before the game starts and are not affected by sentiments or fellow-feeling among players. *Alter* is not a 'tu' with whom *ego* can have a personal relation but merely a complex constraint of the latter's maximisation problem (the constraint is an 'alive' maximiser facing another 'alive' maximiser). As Hollis and Sugden observe, 'game theory provides an elegant, universal logic of practical reason, offering much to anyone whose notion of rationality is instrumental and whose view of social world is individualistic' (Hollis and Sugden, 1993, p. 32).

That interpersonal relations are not in the hard core of game theory's research programme was stated clearly by its founders, John von Neumann and Oskar Morgenstern. In the introduction to *Theory of Games and Economic Behaviour*, commenting on the so-called 'Robinson Crusoe economics', they write (1964/1944, pp. 10, 12):

The chief objection against using this very simplified model of an isolated individual for the theory of a social exchange economy is that it does not represent an individual exposed to manifold social influences. Hence, it is said to analyse an individual who might behave quite differently if his choice were made in a social world where he would be exposed to factors of imitation, advertising, custom and so on...Crusoe is given a number of data which are 'dead'; they are the unalterable physical background of the situation...Not a single datum with which he has to deal reflects another person's will or intention.

After this statement one might expect that interpersonal elements would eventually enter economic analysis, that adding 'alive' variables to the standard (or 'dead') economic variables would introduce emotions, identities and sentiments. But it is enough to look a few lines later in the same introduction to realise that von Neumann and Morgenstern were looking for something else (p. 12, my italics):

The study of the Crusoe economy and the use of the methods applicable to it, is of much more limited value to economic theory than has been assumed heretofore even by the most radical critics. The grounds for this limitation *lie not in the field of those social relationships which we have mentioned before* – although we do not

---

[23] Some very recent contributions present attempts at inserting non-instrumental elements within rationality: these include 'sympathy' (Sally, 2001), 'fairness' (Rabin, 1993) and 'fellow-feelings' (Sugden, 2002), among others.

question their significance – but rather they arise from the conceptual differences between the original (Crusoe's) maximum problem and the more complex problem.

In the end, all the 'alive' variables bring with them is greater complexity in calculating the maximum.[24]

8.   Exploring the whole continent?

In the story told in this chapter we have seen how economics' mainstream tradition – particularly neoclassical and post-Pareto economics – has become the science of instrumental interactions among individuals, under the methodological assumption that one can isolate the economic side, based on individualism, anonymity and instrumental rationality, from the wider social fact of economic life.

In this choice – that 'per se' is legitimate – there is an important *missing link*: ascertaining how and if economic goods bring about happiness, or well-being (not economic well-being). In fact, the recent debate on 'economics and happiness' suggests that the effort exerted in securing more and more material goods has systematic negative effects on other components of wealth, particularly interpersonal relations, so *more* income can lead to *less* well-being; this is Richard Easterlin's (2002) 'paradox of happiness'.

In the 'continent of social life', some areas have not been explored by economists: they are aware of the existence of these areas and of their non-negligible size, but knowing them is considered unimportant for shaping their theory of economic behaviour. They act like the ancient geographers who, ignorant of the topography of Africa's inner regions, drew their map of the continent and wrote on the unknown regions '*Hic sunt leones*'. To European scholars or merchants, these incomplete maps gave an idea of the shape of those distant regions, but they were of little help to explorers in penetrating the virgin forests of Africa. If economists now want to explore the territory of economic interactions in its entirety, they can no longer be content with a 'here are lions' methodology; they need to know more about its inner non-instrumental provinces.

ACKNOWLEDGEMENTS

I wish to thank Benedetto Gui, Shaun Hargreaves Heap, Robert Sugden and Stefano Zamagni for precious help in improving this chapter.

[24] After the 1950s this attitude of game theory towards interpersonal relations was reinforced by the spread of Nash methodology (Mirowski, 1999, pp. 304–5).

11 Authority and power in economic and sociological approaches to interpersonal relations: from interactions to embeddedness

Bernard Gazier and Isabelle This Saint-Jean

1. Introduction

We would like to explore some consequences of a very simple idea. If one analyses interpersonal relations in the economic domain, sooner or later one encounters power, authority, hierarchy and domination – i.e. what may be called the 'vertical' dimension of human relationships, as opposed to the 'horizontal' one. Violence, conflicts and relations of strength certainly exist in interpersonal relations, but too often economists tend to forget or bypass this aspect.

In fact, if we admit the existence of 'vertical relations', it is difficult to view interpersonal relations as always 'positive' for individuals – at least, for both parties in a 'face-to-face' relation – as too often happens in the economic analysis of this subject. This optimistic vision of interpersonal relations clearly appears, for example, in Gui's introduction to the recent special issue of *Annals of Public and Cooperative Economics* devoted to the topic,[1] although he does admit that 'the expression "relational"... does not necessarily mean nice, pleasant, or positive. Indeed, there also exists a "dark side" of relations... and "negative interpersonal exchanges" (Gui, 2000b, p. 143). If we are convinced of the relevance of vertical relations, beside or above horizontal ones, and of the importance of power, conflicts and relations of strength in vertical relations, it becomes difficult to neglect this 'dark side'.

In the same way, we could hypothesise that, alongside the indifference of the egoist depicted in standard economic models, and the

---

[1] We can find, for example, this optimistic vision in the little story that Gui presents in this text. Speaking about two identical residential buildings, he writes: 'The yard of the first was full of expensive flowers, but people never met there. [...] The yard of the second building had ordinary flowers, but people often met there, while their children played together. [...] Intangible phenomena make life gloomy in the first building... and fun in the second...' (Gui, 2000b, p. 133).

benevolence of the altruist in analyses of interpersonal relations (e.g. Zamagni, 1995; Gérard-Varet, Kolm and Mercier-Ythier, 2000), there also exist bad, wicked or even perverse people. Here again, 'vertical relations' and their strength relations seem a good way to illustrate this proposition.

It follows that interpersonal relations are not always desirable at a collective or social level, as too often presumed in economic analyses devoted to interpersonal relations, and especially to altruism.[2] Even peaceful relations may be undesirable and associated with inefficiency. Conversely, interactions in which conflicts and aggression exist may result in socially desirable situations. These ideas are not at all new in economics; we must just remember the alleged virtues of competition and emulation! The link between interpersonal relations and socially desirable situations is far from simple. It is especially far from simple in vertical relations.

We are not, of course, able to develop all the propositions implied by these 'dismal remarks'. We would just like to shed some light on the 'vertical' dimension of interpersonal relations, its forms and its importance. We have chosen to compare some important economic and sociological approaches about power and interpersonal relations. The borderline between the two disciplines has always been ill-defined and changeable. Currently some authors work explicitly in intermediate disciplines, such as economic sociology, socio-economics or what economists call 'social economics'. Power is a clear example of such a shared issue, and it may be interesting to undertake a methodological debate between these two independent but sometimes intertwined experiences.

Accordingly, the aim of this chapter is to illustrate some results and limitations of a few selected disciplinary and interdisciplinary developments with regard to the question of understanding, conceptualising and modelling authority and power in face-to-face economic relations. We start by clarifying a few issues about influence and power (section 2). Then we compare four economic and sociological analyses of power in the workplace, which illustrate two versions of authority: 'weak' and 'strong' (section 3). Lastly, we enlarge the perspective by introducing the economic–sociological concept of 'embeddedness', and evaluate its fruitfulness (section 4).

---

[2] Edmund Phelps writes in the introduction to his book on this topic: 'The price system would work less well and would be less widely applied, were it not that the economic agents... in fact display a decent regard for the interests of those with whom they exchange and for society as a whole' (Phelps, 1975, p. 3; cited by Zamagni, 1995).

2.   *Ego* influencing *alter*: a preliminary analysis

Influence in the domain of 'face-to-face relations'

We can define 'face-to-face relations' as deliberate interactions between people. These interactions are no longer anonymous, and no longer mediated by the institutions of the competitive market, as they are in the Walrasian world.

The domain of 'face-to-face' relations is enormous, and comprises most of everybody's daily experience. Here, we limit ourselves to inter-actions in the traditional economic field: the production, distribution and consumption of goods and services.

We focus on influence: an individual (A) may influence, consciously, directly and in a non-negligible way, another individual (B). This influ-ence bears on B's preferences, expectations and constraints, and there-fore on his level of satisfaction, choices or – more generally – actions. Of course, B reacts: the influence is never unilateral.

Seven modalities of influence

We can identify at least seven quite different modalities of influence.

(1) A's actions partially determine B's earnings, and/or the constraints he faces, and therefore, in both situations, his level of satisfaction. This is, for example, the case in interactions described by game theory.
(2) A introduces B's satisfaction into his utility function. Thus, his choices and behaviour aim at affecting B's satisfaction. A first example of such a situation, very important in economic theory today, is altruism. But other situations, unfortunately too seldom considered by economists, involve bad, wicked or perverse behav-iour on the part of people who want to hurt the people they face.
(3) B imitates A's behaviour (or expectations). Therefore, A influences the behaviour of mimetic agent B.[3] We may note here that, if some mimetic behaviours warrant no rational justification, others, on the contrary, are perfectly rational. The classical example here is the following: a fire breaks out in a theatre, and B sees two doors, but does not know which one leads outside. He decides to follow A, rightly; either A has the information, in which case it is in B's interest to follow A, or A does not have the information, in which case B loses nothing by following him.

---

[3] The assumption of mimetic behaviour or expectations is particularly important in the analysis of financial markets (see, for example Orléan, 1995, 1998).

(4) A follows a moral norm and treats B as a moral subject. He follows, for example, the maxim 'Do as you would be done by'. A's behaviour influences B's satisfaction. But this case differs from case (2). Now, if A wants to increase B's satisfaction, it is neither because B's well-being increases his own satisfaction nor because A takes pleasure in acting morally, but because he must do so, because he is a moral subject.[4]

(5) Social norms: A treats B according to the rules of the group in a given situation. For example, A gives way to B because he is older.

The last two cases cover situations in which B's behaviour is dictated by A: B obeys A. In other words, we could say that B is under the authority of A, if we define 'authority' as Claude Ménard does – i.e. the 'transfer of decision power from an agent or a class of agents to other agents' (1990, p. 28). As the same author explains, this definition in fact covers two rather different cases (1994, pp. 234–5), given below.

(6) Delegation: authority in a weak sense, without subordination or hierarchical principle. The example given by Ménard is the authority of the shop steward designated by his work colleagues to negotiate with their employer. This kind of authority has much to do with the traditional, symmetrical content of a contract: two free wills agree together on a set of reciprocal obligations.[5]

(7) Authority in a strong sense, with subordination and hierarchical principle. In his interesting thesis dedicated to hierarchy in economics, Bruno Tinel, following Max Weber (1956/1922), reserves the word 'authority' to this second meaning. For him, authority is 'the power to decide for the others the way they will act. According to this definition, if A possesses authority over B, B is subordinate to A. In other words, this definition implies a ranking, that is a hierarchical principle' (Tinel, 2000, p. 16).[6] Thus, although contracts may still exist here, this particular interaction depends on the asymmetrical positions of the actors.

Our purpose here is not to develop an exhaustive classification of influences, but to describe some important channels by which

---

[4] See the notion of 'commitment' developed by Amartya Sen (1977).

[5] Herbert Simon's well-known analysis of the employment relationship (1951) falls into this category, although some discretion is allowed to the employer. The worker lets the boss decide what to do, within an 'area of acceptance', because it is mutually advantageous to do so in some circumstances. Within this conceptualisation, the 'employment contract' is one possible outcome of the symmetrical bargain between workers and bosses, the other being a simple 'sales contract'.

[6] This definition is, in fact, very close to the meaning given by Weber in *Economy and Society* to the word 'Herrschaft'.

influence may arise, and to stress the importance of 'vertical' modalities in interpersonal relations, in which many other forms may coexist and interact.

3.   Power in the workplace: from sentiment to the labour/capital conflict, and vice versa

A group of workers is always engaged in at least two sets of relations: relations between peers, which are likely to be mainly 'horizontal', and relations with the employer, which are mainly 'vertical'. The first cannot be understood without reference to the second. In order to analyse and disentangle these relations, we have selected four conceptualisations of power in employer/employee relationships. The first was proposed by George Akerlof (1984), in his celebrated analysis of 'gift giving'. He borrows explicitly from the sociological and anthropological literature, and focuses on a 'weak' conception of authority. The second is due to the radical economists Stephen Marglin, Samuel Bowles and Herbert Gintis, and is grounded in a 'strong' conception of authority. The last two are found in two important sociological analyses of work relations inside organisations, and insist on a particular interactive game played between bosses and subordinates: a game not only in, but also around the interaction framework; a 'game on the rules'. Feelings and sentiment may be back, but, as we will see, not necessarily.

Akerlof and the 'sociological' economic analysis of gift exchange

The well-known article by Akerlof (1984, originally published in 1982) is centred on a case study written by a sociologist: George Homans's (1954) analysis of the behaviour of a group of young unskilled women working as 'cash posters'.

Their behaviour was puzzling from the point of view of traditional economic analysis. Some (but not all) of these workers systematically produced more than the minimum norm set by the firm, and the firm did not try to raise the norm or get rid of the less productive workers. If a worker failed to reach the minimum standard, she was only mildly rebuked. Akerlof interpreted this case as an example of 'partial gift exchange', in which the firm, as well as the workers, chose to engage in a relation of reciprocal gift, faced with a classical agency problem, and one of 'weak authority'.

Akerlof's first observation is that, in the workplace, workers engage in durable relations, and develop sentiments for each other and for the firm. This is reminiscent of our modality (2), where A influences B because A introduces B's utility into his utility function. But it is not exactly the case here: B's utility is not directly introduced into A's function; this would mean that A seeks to perceive B's welfare and to affect it. Instead, the sentiment takes the form of a more general feeling of solidarity with the workers and the firm, which translates into norms and collective gifts (1984, p. 152).[7]

The consequence of this solidarity feeling is a collective donation of goodwill and effort. Sentiments are the cement by means of which the group is composed, in which each worker has to help other less able or less efficient workers.

But how is the gift determined? As Akerlof puts it: 'Gift giving is almost always determined by norms of behaviour', not by the logic of maximisation. The group expects a 'fair wage' and sets the size of the effort proportionately. 'In most cases, the gift given is approximately in the range of what the recipient expects, and he reciprocates in kind' (pp. 152–3). So social and moral norms of reciprocity are at play here – modalities (4) and (5).

The satisfaction that each individual worker derives from this behaviour is made up of two elements: the positive utility stemming from the firm's potential leniency, and the excess remuneration paid by the firm, compared with the wage needed to attract equivalent workers. In this framework, satisfaction on the job leads to improved job performance. The firm gives 'a gift to the worker to increase his job satisfaction, so as, in turn, to increase his job performance' (pp. 156–7).

And the 'fair wage' is given by a reference group, 'most often' made up of similar workers (p. 158). We can identify here the influence of our modality (3), imitation, and again (4) and (5).

Where is power, here? It disappears under gifts; but they are only 'partial exchanges', and power appears more clearly when one considers the models spelled out at the end of the chapter. Two channels are used.

First, the firm is classically maximising profit, and must solve an incentive and agency problem: how to ensure that the workers give their optimal effort. The firm acts as the principal and makes the first move. It sets the rule of the gift-giving game, which is possible because it faces a group of, so to speak, 'sentimental' agents. Technically, it sets the 'wage

---

[7] Akerlof adds: 'Furthermore, if workers have an interest in the welfare of their co-workers, they gain utility if the firm relaxes pressure on the workers who are hard-pressed.' Here he reasons in terms of utility function, so solidarity reduces to an additional argument.

function' (i.e. the rules connecting wages to effort) and the level of the minimum effort required.

Second, the fall-back position of the workers, if they do not accept the rules of the game as set by the firm, is being unemployed. So the alternative considered here is 'take it or leave it', and unemployment is a classical disciplinary device.

But Akerlof presents a gift-giving system as a symmetric choice: the firm may choose to pay only the minimum wage required to attract workers, but then it suffers 'a slight loss of reputation' (1984, p. 163); similarly, workers may choose to work only the minimum standard, but then (in a gift-giving firm) they suffer from a slight loss of reputation.[8]

This model is particularly interesting, first because it suggests, from a quite particular starting point, a more general stable arrangement with empirical relevance. In this way, it may explain the segmentation of the labour market into 'primary' and 'secondary' markets. Another source of interest is the complex interaction between different modalities of influence. This particular agency relation relies on group behaviour, each worker taking into account the situation of his colleagues, as well as the situation of other reference groups in other firms.

The main limitation of this model appears when one questions the definition and stability of the reference group. How can such a group be defined? It is all the more important that the reference group should supply a yardstick of what is 'fair' treatment inside the firm and then avoid open conflict. Akerlof mentions that Homans's study alludes to some open conflicts with supervisors. In this case, the observed effort slackens. Here, again, he believes that it is a question of fairness, depending on the comparison groups.

But a reference group is indeed chosen and even built for action. As the sociologist Jean-Daniel Reynaud puts it (1997, pp. 154–5), workers may choose the nearby factory, a region or a group of people with the same level of education, etc. They probably do not choose the most favourable reference group, but one that may permit action. A 'good' reference group is one with which workers can make an alliance, even potentially, for common action. So the legitimacy of a reference stems from the opportunities for common action that it reveals. In the equilibrium framework presented by Akerlof, no collective or individual action is possible beyond participating in a gift exchange or exiting.

---

[8] One may find these arguments not fully convincing. What might be the manifestations/consequences of such a 'loss of reputation'? By introducing a weak sense of honour, Akerlof introduces a slight incentive to behave generously in a continuous manner, and enhances the stability of his model.

This subtle 'weak' vision of authority, grounded on a symmetric and fully contractual conception of labour relations, is not a general one, but remains quite specific. In order to enlarge our perspective, we can now consider analyses centred on explicitly 'strong' conceptions of power in the workplace.

'Contested exchange' and the radical vision of authority

'Strong' conceptions of power are developed by radical political economics, or the 'New Left', a current that appeared in the very particular political context of the 1970s in the United States. These works – 'translation at an academic level of social, cultural and political movements which cross through young North-American left in the middle of the 1960s' (Tinel, 2000, p. 44)[9] – share a number of common ideas. The most important for us is that they present a 'challenge' (this term appears explicitly in radical works; see Tinel, 2000, p. 54) to the community of economists: to take into account power in economics, and even to put it at the core of their analysis of a firm. In an article that, according to Tinel, is the 'manifesto' of the radical political economy (Edwards and MacEwan, 1970), the authors see 'conflict and power as the central notions needed for understanding American capitalism: because, according to them, its main institutions produce (and are the product of) a division of the society in classes which have antagonist interests' (Tinel, 2000, p. 51).

Stephen Marglin, in his famous article 'What do bosses do? The origins and functions of hierarchy in capitalist production' (1974), devoted to the transition from homework ('the putting out system') to the factory system, views power as a central concept for economists. He shows that, initially, capitalists had no function. They artificially created their own role, using in, particular, wage advances and manufacturing secrets. The hierarchical organisation of a capitalist firm is not the result of considerations of technological efficiency. It is the result of the fact that capitalists, as a class, succeeded in imposing their power.

More generally, a firm is a place of conflicts where capitalists exploit the labour force, during the time they hire it, in order to appropriate the largest possible amount of value added. For this purpose, capitalists use an old principle espoused by Niccolò Machiavelli: 'divide and rule'. They use racial, sexual or cultural differences in order to create artificial divisions between workers. They use this strategy both horizontally, in

---

[9] In this part we rely strongly on Tinel's analysis.

order to create a division of labour inside the firm, and vertically, in order to create a hierarchical division among workers. They also create division in the labour market, which is purposely 'segmented' (see, for example, Edwards, Gordon and Reich, 1982) to reduce the propensity of workers for collective action.[10]

So, differences in wages and hierarchy among workers result from the deliberate use of such strategies by capitalists. Contrary to the human capital theory, wage differences are not produced by differences in talents or previous investments. Two people with the same human capital and the same ability may have different kinds of jobs and different wages.

Radical authors also criticise the idea that the division of labour follows from considerations of technical efficiency. Technical choices are never neutral; there are always social reasons for them. Technology is a tool used by the various protagonists in conflict. The organisation of production and technological choices stem from criteria other than efficiency. Therefore, the capitalist organisation of production is not necessarily efficient.

The main problem of all these works, as Oliver Williamson (1993) has shown, is that radical authors use the notion of power without a precise definition.[11] At the end of the 1980s Samuel Bowles and Herbert Gintis (1988) tried to solve this problem, and developed their theory of 'contested exchange', using microeconomic theoretical tools.[12]

They start with the notion of exchange and state that, contrary to the tenets of the neoclassical theory, '[a] handshake is not always a handshake' (1993, p. 83). And there are no contractual relations without conflict, because complete contracts, enforceable without costs, do not exist. Some aspects of the goods exchanged cannot be specified. They write: 'Where some aspect of the good or service supplied is both valuable to the buyer and costly to provide, the absence of third-party enforcement of claims gives rise to endogenous enforcement strategies. We refer to this relationship as a "contested exchange", because unlike the transactions of Walrasian economics, the benefit the parties derive

---

[10] In this vein, Gintis (1976, pp. 36–54) insists on seeing the conflict between capitalists and labour about the rate of exploitation as a central item for understanding the capitalist organisation of production.

[11] For this reason, Williamson refuses to use this excessively hazy notion, like most 'mainstream' authors.

[12] These authors refer to earlier works (Gintis, 1976; Bowles, 1985), then develop this theory for the first time in Bowles and Gintis (1988) and take it further in Bowles and Gintis (1990) and (1993).

from the transaction depends on their own capacities to enforce competing claims' (p. 85).

Because of incomplete contracts, markets do not reach equilibrium. Thus, agents on the short side of the market have power over agents on the long side, because they can threaten them with stopping transactions if they refuse to obey. So agents located on the long side submit to the power of agents on the short side. These contested exchanges create a set of power relations, even in the absence of collusion or other obstacles to perfect competition. Bowles and Gintis define power as the 'ability of furthering one's interest by imposing (or credibly threatening to impose) sanctions on another agent when the converse is not also true' (1993, p. 88; see also 1990, p. 173). They go on to show that workers submit to the boss's authority by constraint, not by free choice. The power resulting from the 'contested exchange' of the labour force is based essentially on the contingent renewal of the labour contract. The threat of lay-off gives relational power to the boss because the non-clearing of the labour market makes the loss of a job costly for the worker. More generally, and for the same kind of reasons, power relations and hierarchy are always present in every economy.

Formalised or not, whether developed as an 'alternative' or incorporated in standard economics, the radical concept of interpersonal relations gives prominence to power and conflict. Radicals put them at the core of their analysis, not only of the firm but, more generally, of the economy. Inside the firm, not only vertical relations – between employer and employee – but even horizontal ones – among employees – are conflictual. It is impossible to understand the latter without taking account of the former. Every exchange gives rise to conflict and power. In other words, it stems from a macro and micro context-dominated vision of group interaction, in which the spontaneous tendencies of workers (sympathy, group solidarity) tend to be destroyed by the very organisation of production and the nature of social relations.

The 'game on the rules' in two sociological analyses of employment interactions

So far we have presented and discussed two different views of authority. In order to enrich this debate, we can again stress the interactive trait of authority, 'weak' or 'strong'. A assumes decisional power over B, but B reacts. This reaction is not only natural but also often functional. Many studies of Tayloristic work relations, a priori the most impersonal ones, showed that the system could not work if there was no active behaviour on the part of the workers. If they behaved like automatons, then not only could the workshop not function properly, it could not function at all. Even in the most automatised environments, the active and cooperative participation of workers is required. There are always initiatives needed, precisely in order to maintain the imposed routine.

This observation allows us to stress the importance of conceptualising active interaction and, at least, partial cooperation, even in the case of 'strong' authority. This point of view validates the interest given to the whole span of interpersonal influences in the workplace, in cases of both 'weak' and 'strong' authority.

Two complementary sociological concepts are of interest here. The first shows that the equilibrium is always unstable; the second that an 'asymmetrical exchange of behaviours' takes place within fuzzy and shifting frames.

Reynaud (1997) has coined the term *régulation conjointe* ('joint regulation') to explain how workers and their bosses/supervisors behave. He defines *régulation* as the way in which cooperation and exchange rules inside the firm are created, transformed or suppressed. Interactions between employees and management influence the rules and are always two-sided. The *régulation de contrôle* ('control regulation') is the hierarchical collective strategy of management, the conscious coordination of activities that define an organisation. The *régulation autonome* ('autonomous regulation') is the expression of the employees' strategy, who actively react to control and try to avoid it or master it. The underlying logic of this 'autonomous regulation' is social – i.e. dominated by the satisfaction of the sentiments of the group in question – and is connected to its internal relations. The aim is to preserve the group's internal equilibrium and to ensure that the situation will not be disturbed by external intervention. But an impressive number of studies have shown that this regulation also has strong rational and organisational aims: the group attempts to reach a satisfying distribution of work and competences, so that the motives of 'autonomous regulation' cannot be reduced to a few 'social feelings'. Each 'regulation' is necessary. The set of rules deriving from 'joint regulation' is unstable and heterogeneous, results from the past history of the interplay of the actors and is permanently subject to negotiation. Conflict is always possible.

So, complementarity and compromise exist between these two types of regulation. As Reynaud puts it: 'Each regulation has the ambition of gaining legitimacy from the aims of the organisation. It goes without saying that the controller and the controlled are, from this point of view, in a strongly unequal and very asymmetric position' (1997, p. 112).

Reynaud thus exploits an example opposite to that of Akerlof and Homans, given by the French sociologist Michel Liu (1981). He shows that systematic non-cooperative behaviour may constitute an integration strategy in the case of a strongly dominated group of workers. The example given is a workshop composed of unskilled women, who adopted individualistic, egalitarian and cold behaviour among their peers. Their working environment was characterised by high constraints and high pressure, with hard competition organised between workers. So the cold behaviour was a warning against the idea of looking for preferential treatment from the hierarchy. It was a collective attitude, ensuring that life at work remained possible without too many conflicts among workers. The unwelcome signal was an integration device.

We do not suggest that this example cannot be accommodated within another 'sociological economic model' in the spirit of Akerlof's work,[13] but our point is that the arrangement of cash posters may be not as stable or universal as Akerlof puts it. And a clear characteristic of today's labour market is that traditional 'internal market' arrangements are strongly criticised, often reformed and then abandoned: notably, this is the case with regard to the implicit cross-subsidising of workers. The 'reciprocal gift' model depends on dated political arrangements as well as on specific technical and organisational data.

This leads us to the idea of 'the game on the game' – the game of trying to change the rules. Here, the concepts of Erhard Friedberg (1993) add an interesting contribution.

Friedberg puts uncertainty and dependency at the roots of power. Power is not a political obsession: it means that everybody, faced with uncertainty and dependency, tends to accumulate resources that can be exchanged in social interaction. Power is defined here as the capacity to structure exchange processes to one's own advantage. Power is a negotiated exchange of behaviours (1993, p. 117): a generally, but not always, positive-sum game, where some gain much more than others.[14]

Two transactions occur at the same time in organisations, particularly in the workplace: one is economic, and is the immediate content, and one is political, and is an attempt at structuring the exchange. During the interaction, *ego* tries to increase the interchangeability of *alter*, in order to limit his power, and tries to limit his own interchangeability, in order to increase his power.

This is a mechanism by means of which some uncertainties are reduced and others are created. A good example is the behaviour of qualified technicians who prefer to cure breakdowns rather than to

---

[13] In his *Book of Tales*, Akerlof (1984) also presents models of 'rat races' and 'caste behaviour', where competition is either inefficient or constrained.

[14] When people voluntarily engage in an exchange, they do so only if a net gain is expected by both parties. In other cases, some may be affected negatively.

develop preventive action. The reason is that breakdowns are a good opportunity to show one's competences, and to learn. In some groups of workers, technicians speak of the 'beautiful breakdown' as a desirable event (1993, p. 278).

The conclusion is straightforward. 'The economic exchange is intrinsically unstable... The players will always seek to include into their exchanges bargains on the terms of the rule governing them' (p. 129).

Two consequences follow. The first is that the frame of the interaction is not defined once and for all, nor is it reduced to the formal identification of an organisation or a workshop. The frame may change over time, be reduced or be extended. This explains why feelings may develop, or be repealed by actors, and do not simply depend on benevolent 'goodwill' from one of them.

The second consequence is that we have enlarged the perspective to consider the asymmetric 'pre-existing' resources controlled by the actors. When they engage in workshop interactions (as well, incidentally, as in other personal interactions), these do not come from nowhere, nor from a social vacuum.

4.   From social to political embeddedness

Here is another enormous domain of social relations: the various kinds of resources that are accumulated, possessed and used by actors. Quite different concepts have been developed. One of these, the most familiar to economists, is based on the notion of 'social capital' developed by James Coleman (1990) and Robert Putnam (1993b).[15] Social capital is the whole set of social relations (personal acquaintances, goodwill, etc.) that can be used by people in their personal lives and in economic interactions. It is also one of the characteristics of social organisations, such as networks, norms and trust, that ease collaboration for mutual gain.

We cannot engage here in a detailed assessment of this concept. Our preceding arguments lead to the idea that these 'pre-existing resources' cannot simply be characterised as separable 'social capital', as Coleman puts it. Social interactions engage actors in repeated contacts. The resources depend themselves on previous interactions, and the actors act in a nexus of more or less structured, more or less durable interactions. Thus, 'social capital' (as well as other kinds of intangible capital: cultural, symbolic, etc.) depends on the structure of the social fields in which actors are situated. One can develop this idea by using the

---

[15] Pierre Bourdieu used this notion of 'social capital' in the 1960s, as he has recently recalled (Bourdieu, 2000). See below.

notion of 'embeddedness'. More generally, social position, in an intentional as well as unintentional manner, affects every interpersonal relation.

We will show that this is true, first for 'weak' concepts of authority. If we introduce 'strong' ones, then we have to turn to political, not only social, 'embeddedness'.

Networks of relations in Granovetter's economic sociology

Mark Granovetter is known as one of the prominent figures in the renewal of economic sociology since the end of the 1970s and, more precisely, as one of the founders of the 'new economic sociology', which developed in the United States from the 1980s onwards.[16] His works include three main theses that are of interest for economists concerned with interpersonal relations.

The first proposition is that every economic action is a social action, oriented by motivations that belong not only to the economic order. Granovetter believes that the assumption of a purely selfish individual, typical of conventional economic theory, is not satisfactory; it is too restrictive. It is necessary to take into account social considerations, such as the search for recognition, status, sociality and power. The social dimension of economic action is not simple 'friction' that impedes maximising rationality; it is, in a much more fundamental way, an essential component of every economic action.

An important consequence of this viewpoint is that the preferences of the economic agent are not given once and for all. His preferences and even his identity may evolve, particularly as a result of the interactions in which he is engaged. In a well-known article, Granovetter (1978) has studied a kind of model, the so-called 'threshold models', in which individual choice (to take part in a riot or not, for example) is directly determined by the number of others already engaged in it – a number that, of course, evolves over time. According to Granovetter, this kind of model may be used to explain a very large set of economic and social phenomena (from the diffusion of innovations to strikes, the propagation of rumours, votes, etc.).

Granovetter's second central proposition – the well-known 'embeddedness' argument – states that individuals are not 'monads' but are 'embedded in concrete, ongoing systems of social relations' (1985, p. 487), using a term coined earlier by Karl Polanyi (1944). 'The

---

[16] In general, economic sociology is defined as a 'sociological perspective applied to economic phenomena' (Smelser and Swedberg, 1994, p.3). Swedberg (1997, p. 239) believes that the new economic sociology was born with Granovetter's article of 1985.

embeddedness argument', Granovetter writes, 'stresses... the role of concrete personal relations and structures (or "networks") of such relations' (1985, p. 490). So economic action is 'embedded' in networks of personal relations, in which individuals are continuously in contact with each other. Networks are defined here in a wide sense, as regular sets of contacts and social relations among individuals or groups of individuals. Every action taken by one member of the network generates an interaction with other individuals; the choices of this individual depend on others' choices, behaviours and personal links.

In various works, Granovetter shows that, in modern societies, the economy is embedded in networks of social relations that are necessary to its functioning, 'generating trust and discouraging malfeasance' (1985, p. 490).[17] In his famous analysis of the labour market, in particular, he develops the well-known idea that people obtain their jobs partly by means of their personal relations (1974, 1988). He shows that the efficiency of the network is not proportional to the intensity of the personal ties between the job-seeker and the other persons; rather, the reverse. The reason is simple: when someone recommends a candidate for a job, he has to show his impartiality by indicating that he is not too close a friend nor a member of the same family. Here, the influence works best at some distance, because the network aims at generating and diffusing credible information. This is the thesis of 'the strength of weak ties' (Granovetter, 1973).

In a recent presentation of his work to French readers, Granovetter has claimed that, if methodological individualism must be adopted and individual motivations must be considered, one cannot think 'that all social action could be understood by looking at incentives and reinforcements driving the behaviours of individuals. The analysis of social networks was very centrally a sociological rather than a psychological analysis. *The relationship rather than the individual was the main element of study, and the overall structure of social networks was important in a way that could never be captured by understanding the motives of individuals*' (2000, p. 34, our italics). Granovetter criticises in particular what he calls the 'atomised' and 'undersocialised' concept of individual action in conventional economics. In his view, the main criticism is not the lack of realism of its view of rationality but the fact that it identifies economic actors with 'independent atoms' making their decisions in isolation, without considering their social relations (1985, p. 482). In neglecting the interactions and structures of interactions (networks) in which actors are engaged, one misses the social structure, which plays a crucial role.

---

[17] This functional role does not exclude conflicts and collusion.

And this criticism concerns not secondary phenomena of the economy but its very heart – namely markets, production, the determination of price levels, distribution and consumption. As analysis of interpersonal relations is essential in order to understand any economic action, one is obliged to leave the level of simple face-to-face relations. Every interpersonal relation must be understood within the overall structure of social networks.

The third proposition extends the argument to economic institutions. 'Economic institutions are social constructions' and must be analysed as such (Granovetter, 1990, 1992). This analysis is based on the sociology of knowledge developed by Peter Berger and Thomas Luckmann in *The Social Construction of Reality* (1966) in order to show that, in spite of their apparently objective existence, institutions are in fact the result of a long social process of creation. This is why an institution cannot be understood without studying the historical process from which it derives. Before an institution is created there exist many possibilities, and the resulting institution is the product of the 'crystallisation' of some peculiar personal relations.[18]

He develops the case of the creation of the American electricity industry, with its firms and regulations (McGuire, Granovetter and Schwartz, 1993; Granovetter and McGuire, 1998). Nowadays, we could consider this industry as very stable and totally 'natural'. However, it may have taken other, radically different, institutional forms. It is impossible to explain its actual state by using the notion of efficiency; other factors must be introduced – in particular, networks of personal relations. Individuals mobilising financial, technical and political resources through their social and professional networks drove the industry in some directions rather than others, with substantial historical contingency and path dependency throughout the process. Here again, network analysis must be applied to understand the causal factors of institutional formation. For Granovetter, institutions may be defined as 'congealed social networks'.

Granovetter's works deal mainly with 'horizontal' relations, and the authority he considers is mainly 'weak' and symmetrical. This is clear in the case of job seeking, in which two networks symmetrically interfere: employee's and employer's. It is all the more important that Granovetter always puts the emphasis on the socially structured aspects of the networks, in order to highlight the reciprocal dependency and choices of actors.

---

[18] This is the idea, well known in economics, of a 'path-dependent process' (see, e.g., David, 1985; Arthur, 1988, 1989).

So, we are led to go beyond the formal symmetry of contractors, and to consider 'strong' authority in intertwined social interactions.

Bourdieu and 'political embeddedness'

We first present a number of theses, rather similar to Granovetter's, developed by the French sociologist Bourdieu, particularly in his recent work *Les structures sociales de l'économie* (2000). In this book, as in most others, Bourdieu offers an analysis that may be considered 'economic sociology' (although Bourdieu himself does not call it that). Indeed, the subject belongs to the domain of the most conventional economic analysis – the production and selling of individual houses – but is nevertheless analysed by means of sociological concepts.

Bourdieu starts with the following, essential assumption: any practice – in particular those studied by economists – is 'immersed' (*immergée*) in the social order. We must consider every economic practice as a 'total social fact', in the sense of the anthropologist Marcel Mauss: '[T]he social world is entirely present in every "economic" action' (Mauss, 1995, p. 13). Also, it is necessary to 'mobilise all the available knowledge on the different dimensions of social order, that is, in bulk, the family, State, school, trade unions, associations, and so on – and not only banks, firms and the market' (p. 12). This concept of 'immersion' is closely related to that of embeddedness. Some consequences are rather similar: the analysis of any economic action is impossible if we stay strictly at an individual level. We must take social considerations into account.

Another point of convergence is Bourdieu's use of the concept of 'social capital', a concept that he developed during the 1960s in his early works in ethnology in Kabily and Béarn (Bourdieu, 1958, 1963; Bourdieu et al., 1963; Bourdieu and Sayad, 1964). He went back to it in a more recent work, explicitly referring to Granovetter: 'Social capital' is 'all the actual or potential resources which are linked to possession of a *continuous network of relations* more or less institutionalised' (Bourdieu, 1980a, pp. 2 and 12, our italics). We can see here that Bourdieu shares with Granovetter the idea that it is impossible to understand any economic practice if one neglects to connect the analysis of interpersonal relations and the overall structure of social networks. This definition of social capital is grounded in the strategies developed by individuals or groups, and cannot be considered per se as a socially useful commodity.[19]

---

[19] Bourdieu insists on the global components of social relations, and states that it is most often artificial and unfruitful to oppose individualistic and holist methodologies. We have here an example of this attitude: he does not analyse social capital at a 'holistic' level.

However, other points allow us to introduce 'strong' authority, as well as important differences with Granovetter. In his analysis of economic phenomena, Bourdieu uses a theoretical system based on five main concepts, central to all his sociology. They are: *habitus, cultural capital, social capital, symbolic capital* and the *field.* We cannot develop all these concepts here, and focus on just two of them: the *field* and *habitus.*

Briefly, fields are structured spaces of positions (Bourdieu, 1980b, pp. 113–16). Examples are the political, philosophical, religious and, of course, economic fields. They all share invariant rules of functioning. Every field is defined by specific stakes and interests. A field exists only if there are people ready to play the game or to engage in the struggle – that is, people who see the specific stakes and interests of the field in question and who know its rules. The structure of the field is a state of the distribution of specific capital accumulated in past struggles – a distribution that determines future strategies.

A very important and specific point in Bourdieu's analysis is the deeply conflictual functioning of fields. Social fields are fields of forces and of struggles, conducted in order to transform or maintain these forces. The central object of struggle is capital or, more precisely, all the different varieties of capital, which are the specific stakes of the different social fields. However, the struggle requires an agreement between opponents on what is worth struggling for: 'People taking part in the struggle contribute to the reproduction of the game, in contributing – more or less, according to the field – to produce the belief in the value of stakes' (p. 115). The result is an unequal repartition of capital. So, in every field, there are dominant and dominated people.

This idea of domination is the social equivalent of 'strong' authority in more limited interactions: an asymmetric ranking relationship, reproduced daily. But – this is the second point we wish to underline – Bourdieu clearly separates himself from Granovetter, whom he criticises as an 'interactionist': '[The interactionist conception] reduces the structure of strength relations [*rapports de force*] constitutive of the field to a set of simple interactions without any transcendence to the individuals engaged at a moment' (p. 241). The interactionist vision is unable to take into account something other than the 'influences' exerted directly by one individual on another by some kind of 'interaction'. On the contrary, the structural concept takes into account these effects, which happen independently of every interaction. Indeed, 'the structure of the field, defined by the unequal distribution of capital – that is specific weapons (or trumps) – weighs, independently of every direct intervention or manipulation, on the set of agents engaged in the field; the worse position these agents have in this distribution, the smaller *space of possibilities* they possess' (2000, p. 238).

The dominant group is composed of the agents who have such a position in the field; the structure plays in their favour; and they exert a pressure on others by their weight in the structure, and not by direct intervention. Bourdieu does not deny the economic efficiency of networks in the functioning of the economic field (although he prefers to speak of the efficiency of social capital). But the position of an agent in the structure of the field is the main factor of his economic practices and of the strength of his 'network'. With the concept of the *field*, and in particular with that of *the structure of the field*, Bourdieu introduces strength relations – or, in other words, power relations – into the whole set of social interactions.

This second key concept allows us to get back to interpersonal relations and to some form of indeterminacy and freedom: the concept of *habitus*. Defined as a 'second nature', *habitus* is an incorporated set of individual behaviours, which depend on objective meanings socially created and relevant for someone in a specific social position and engaged in a specific practice. It is to be found in languages, in objects and in procedures, and it is relevant for understanding sexual as well as gift or exchange behaviours. This socially built form of spontaneity differs according to each person's position in the social structure.

Two remarks mitigate the over-deterministic tone of this analysis, placing everyone back in a constraining political context. First, a person dominated in a specific field (e.g. the economic) can be dominating in another one (e.g. the cultural). We may go further: the accumulation of different kinds of capital may become pointless in many circumstances, because their value and uses do not take place in a unified world but in a heterogeneous one.

Secondly, actors can innovate: 'The agents, although they are produced by the structure, make and make again the structure, and even can, under some structural conditions, transform it more or less radically' (Bourdieu, 1985, p. 173). Here, again, we find the game on the game, as analysed above.

5. Conclusions

Our short comparative inquiry leads to a few methodological remarks about the economic analysis of interpersonal relations.

First, the importance of the 'vertical' dimension of human relations is emphasised – i.e. power, authority and influence. This importance may be directly true, as when a face-to-face relation is established between two agents placed in an unequal social or hierarchical position. But, probably more importantly, it also holds indirectly, as when interpersonal relations take place among equals or peers engaged in some kind of dependency, as is the case for a group of salaried people in a workshop. Neglecting this dimension may lead to underestimating, overestimating or even misunderstanding the solidarity/egoism manifested by economic actors.

Secondly, it shows how some economic conceptualisations made steps towards the introduction of this 'vertical' dimension in an enlarged framework. This is the case of the model of 'gift giving' presented by Akerlof, which combines feelings, norms of reciprocity and a sense of honour with more conventional (maximising) behaviour. Such an enrichment, although it has an ad hoc flavour, is a remarkable example of an economic reinterpretation of a sociological case study.

Thirdly, we believe that the dialogue between economics and sociologists must be deepened in order to escape some typical limitations and drawbacks of current economic analyses of interpersonal relations.

If we focus on the most general enrichment strategy within the conventional framework, we can identify it as 'psychological revisionism': the 'humanisation' of *Homo œconomicus*, accomplished by simply adding new arguments to a utility function. This additive strategy may reveal itself as misleading, as an example taken from sociology makes clear. We briefly recall here the earlier encounter between sociology and interpersonal feelings: the 'human relations school'. From the 1930s to the 1960s authors such as Elton Mayo, Douglas McGregor, Abraham Maslow and Frederick Herzberg developed analyses stressing the importance of human feelings in understanding workers' behaviour. The contributions of this 'school' were two-sided: on the one hand, clear enrichment of the motives taken into account, and the identification of a new range of behaviours; on the other, a highly normative agenda, presented as a number of prerequisites for correctly managing organisations in a 'humanistic' way. These prescriptions soon appeared unsuccessful, and the organisational questions remained unattacked. As Friedberg remarks (1993, p. 37), the methodological aspect remained rather underdeveloped, and the proposed change may be summarised by a simple addition: beyond economic stimuli, affective stimuli.

Friedberg goes on to show that similar problems, and similar dead-ends, may threaten the more recent attempts of 'non-orthodox economists', such as Akerlof, Harvey Leibenstein and Amitai Etzioni, when they enlarge the neoclassical framework and introduce a wider set of motivations. In his view, their reasoning remains 'reductionist', and hides the plasticity and contingency of human behaviour, which is simultaneously free and constrained by the changing contexts of situations. This warning is to be taken seriously. The risk of undue 'psychologisation' is important: attempts to postulate human nature – i.e. a set of stable parameters – can be seized out of their context and presumed to allow forecasting. Sociologists manage the risk not by eliminating feelings but by developing analyses of behaviour combining the 'vertical' as well as the 'horizontal' aspects of human relations, and taking into account the social context structuring the resources controlled by actors. Perhaps this earlier experience of sociologists can be of some use for today's economists?

Fourthly, this leads us to our last methodological suggestion: the need explicitly to take into account the structure of social positions, the context of exchanges as well as their political nature, in modelling economic interpersonal relations. To do this, more drastic changes in methodology are needed, and would involve at least the introduction of procedural rationality and satisficing behaviour. Beyond these points, evolutionary options such as path dependency, the importance of history, and changes in preferences could also be considered. This may indicate that it is worth attempting to explore the span of methodological options outside the framework of strict methodological individualism. This question remains open, and we would like to suggest that another exercise would be fruitful for economists: reading sociologists!

ACKNOWLEDGEMENTS

We warmly thank our referees, who helped us to improve this chapter. Inevitably, though, we remain responsible for its content.

12　Interpersonal relations and economics: comments from a feminist perspective

Julie A. Nelson

1.　Introduction

Intelligent discussion of the importance for economics of interpersonal relations is far overdue.[1] This volume makes some substantial progress in opening up this critical area. As pointed out in a number of the chapters, 'economic man' – assumed to be autonomous, rational and self-interested – is a caricature of human nature. Theories based on this image sorely neglect human interdependencies, human emotions and the importance of social networks and institutions.

The pitfalls for economists entering this field, however, are many. One tempting – but, I believe, ultimately unsatisfactory – approach is to try to fit interpersonal relations within the pre-set taxonomies and methodological biases of mainstream contemporary economic thought. Another unsatisfying alternative is to treat interpersonal relations as radically 'other' – romanticising the subject and portraying it as a 'soft' area of research focused on harmony and good feeling, in stark contrast to the subject matter of standard, 'hard' economics. A third is to see interpersonal relations as primarily composed of politicised relations among opportunistic agents, bringing in issues of power but otherwise maintaining assumptions of self-interest. All these approaches, I believe, tend to distort the general class of phenomena beyond recognisability.

---

[1] This process has been going on for decades in some of the other disciplines. Psychologists and philosophers of moral development, for example, got a wake-up call concerning their reliance on theories emphasising autonomy and reason in 1982. In that year Carol Gilligan's path-breaking *In A Different Voice* put forth the thesis that concerns about responsibility in particular relationships – that is, about how one's decision would affect one's partner, children, friends, community – are very important, along with general rules and principles, in guiding mature ethical thinking. Gui and Sugden's definition of the term 'interpersonal relations' as referring to 'forms of human interaction in which the identity of the participants *as particular human beings* has affective or cognitive significance', is, for example, very reminiscent of feminist philosopher Seyla Benhabib's (1987) much-cited contrast between 'concrete' (particular) and 'generalised' (anonymous) others, in her discussion of Gilligan's work.

In my comments, I would like to point out where I see some of the contributions to this volume – sometimes subtly – falling into these traps, as well as where I see more satisfying analysis coming forth. My decades of work as a feminist economist are highly relevant to this task. After all, interpersonal relations with their emotionally expressive components have traditionally been stereotyped as 'feminine' and associated most centrally with home, family and intimacy, in clear counterpoint to the 'masculine' realms of firms and markets, assumed to be characterised by impersonal, rational and instrumentally oriented activities. Challenging this dichotomy within economics means challenging many basic assumptions about human nature and economic methodology.[2]

2.   Relationships are constitutive

While appreciating the fresh ground broken in this area by Gui (chapter 2), I would question whether the idea of 'relational goods' being produced by the 'encounters' of people goes far enough. Who, in fact, is doing the producing? My fear is that – despite the many steps taken in this volume towards a greater recognition of truly interpersonal relations – the image of a pre-existing, independent agent may still sometimes lurk in the background. Through an encounter, in Gui's terms, the agent can consume enjoyments and acquire human and social capital. But, in spite of Gui's explicit rejection of reductionism elsewhere in his contribution, I suggest that his use of the rhetoric of production, enjoyment and acquisition does not go far enough. This rhetoric does not in itself directly challenge the image of pre-existing agents: encounters might be seen as something that agents simply *do*, coming out on the other side of the encounter with greater utility or capital, but fundamentally unchanged.

An alternative view is that we are, in fact, in very large degree constituted by our relationships. That is, instead of an image of pre-existing agents going out in the world and partaking in encounters as consumers and acquirers, this alternative view suggests that we are continually *created and shaped by* the encounters in which we participate. In order to not deny an element of individuality and free will, of course, it is best to say that individuals and social orders are *mutually* constituting. Our social interactions form our capacities, preferences and usual modes of response to stimuli, at the same time as our individual choices influence our social surroundings. Gui's approach does not necessarily preclude

---

[2] For a sampling of the feminist economic literature, see Ferber and Nelson (1993, 2003).

such an interpretation, but, given his choice of words, the constitutive aspect is not emphasised.

Sugden's idea of a model 'in which people's tastes evolve over time' – violating the usual assumption of exogenous preferences – moves in this direction (chapter 3). His emphasis on the role of emotions in interpersonal relations is also appropriate: we may affect each other most profoundly through emotional channels. As philosopher Martha Nussbaum has put it, '[E]motions are…holes, so to speak, in the walls of the self' (1995, p. 367). It is through the vulnerabilities created by affective response that we have in*fluence* – literally, we in-*flow*, or 'get under another's skin'.

In contrast, I find Hargreaves Heap's attempt to take interpersonal relations into account to be too timid, as regards taking us beyond traditional economic notions. Hargreaves Heap repeatedly states that interpersonal relations are constitutive of the person; however, conversion of attention to the regard of others into a 'concern for self-esteem' (chapter 9) casts the topic back into an essentially individualistic mode. Others seem to exist, in this portrayal, only as 'the mirror' (chapter 9, quoting Adam Smith) that reflects us back on ourselves. Were it so, each person would remain solitary, like Narcissus, staring into his own reflection in the pond.

If, as I argue, an interpersonal encounter can change our preferences, the way we think about things, our values, our motivations, our emotional constitution, the way we see the world, or our ability to learn – then Gui's agent 1 doesn't necessary leave the encounter as agent 1 but, rather, leaves as agent 1´ instead. For example, a student who leaves an encounter with a professor with greater factual knowledge can be said to leave with higher human capital. But a student who leaves such an encounter inspired to learn, with a new direction in life and a greater depth of understanding and concern (or perhaps, unfortunately, the opposite: burned out and depressed) will, understandably, probably characterise the experience as 'life-changing'.

Two areas of human life, both ignored by standard economics (and both, not just coincidently, associated in intellectual study with women), particularly illustrate encounters in this constitutive sense.

The first is the area of early childhood development. All too often, in economic and political theory, scholars have followed the advice of Thomas Hobbes, who wrote, 'Let us consider men…as if but even now sprung out of the earth, and suddenly, like mushrooms, come into full maturity, without all kind of engagement to each other' (cited in Benhabib, 1987). Yet humans do not just spring out of the earth. The activities of gestating and giving birth to new humans are performed by women, and – by tradition – so was the raising of children to adulthood.

It is well known in child development research (Center for Career Development in Early Care and Education, 2000) that people

who are warm, responsive, and engage in one-to-one relationships have positive effects on children's learning. For the preschool child, the 'subjects' are all combined and integrated into a whole and learned simultaneously. Brain development research suggests that the strongest element for successful teaching at any level is the ability to form relationships and the ability to be responsive.

Relationships are, in every sense of the word, formative. It will be important to follow up on Sugden's references to brain research and research on child development, if the role of interpersonal relations and affect in human behaviour is to be adequately theorised in economics.

The second area is the theory of consumption, also briefly mentioned by Sugden (chapter 3). Yet Sugden writes only that manufacturers 'anticipate' and 'predict' evolving tastes. He does not mention that manufacturers try to influence tastes actively, through marketing research and the devotion of an extraordinary volume of resources to advertising. Gender is significant in this omission, for two reasons. First, the presumably malleable consumer who is the target of marketing research has traditionally been envisaged as female – the traditional homemaker who allocated much of the family consumption budget (Catterall, Maclaran and Stevens, 2000). Second, the field of consumer economics has traditionally been perceived as a more 'feminine' field of practice than economics proper, and, in fact, employed a number of women trained in economics in the first half of the twentieth century. One of the most glaring gaps in mainstream economic analysis is surely the lack of attention to the massive effects of marketing campaigns on the *formation* of preferences, many of which work by implicitly promising the consumer improved interpersonal relations (e.g. better sexual relations and/or higher social status). Marketing campaigns are also constitutive to the extent that they encourage the formation of particular moral as well as aesthetic values. The area of consumption is one that a relational approach to economics could begin to unpack.

3.   Families and power

Running through several of the chapters in this book is an acknowledgement that – in contrast to economists' treatment of human behaviour in firms and markets – behaviour within families has usually been exempted from assumptions of impersonality and instrumental interest. Sugden notes this, while Kolm (chapter 8) associates families with 'good social relations' characterised by gift giving and reciprocity.

Feminists beg to differ, on several points.

While marriage and family life may have seemed 'uneconomic' to most men, when compared to monetised market activities, the historical exclusion of many women from paid labour made these very much *economic* issues to them! Exclusion from paid labour – or, at least, from labour paid sufficiently high enough to support themselves (let alone themselves and their children) – meant that, for women in some economic and social classes, access to financial support could be gained only by partnering with a male breadwinner. This is not to deny that families also have personal and emotive aspects, but simply to point out that the salience of their economic aspects depends very much on the perspective from which they are viewed.

The notion that family relations are always good social relations is much undercut by feminist research on the uses of power within families, and particularly on the widespread phenomenon of domestic violence.

Taking a step away from such romanticising of interpersonal relations, Gazier and This Saint-Jean (chapter 11) rightly warn us about concentrating too much on positive reciprocity and altruism. They argue that, in addition to the 'horizontal' relations of people who are similar in power, we need also to look at 'vertical' relations, characterised by differences in power. However, I believe that, by defining power purely as the gaining of advantage over someone else, Gazier and This Saint-Jean's analysis leaves in the shadow another very significant arena of human interpersonal relations.

In order to explain this point, a typology of relationships that I have begun to develop elsewhere might be helpful.[3] The image of the 'separative' self is that of a person as radically individual and active – that is, at the non-relational, autonomous extreme. *Homo œconomicus* or the Hobbesian 'mushroom man' are cases in point. The image of a 'soluble' self is that of a person as radically self-less and passive – that is, at the highly relational, dependent extreme. For example, women were at one time completely 'soluble' legal persons, who disappeared, for all purposes related to the law, into their husbands upon marriage.

Working only with these two possibilities, the only possible relations among persons are these.

(1) *Separative–separative (arm's-length):* when separative selves interact with other separative selves, such interactions must be purely external; the action of one party cannot have any effect on the other's inviolable constitution.

---

[3] See Nelson (2003). See also Nelson and England (2002).

(2) *Soluble–soluble (merger):* when soluble selves interact with other soluble selves, the relation must be one of complete merger; the individuals must be completely melded into one unit.

(3) *Separative–soluble (domination):* when a separative self interacts with one or more soluble selves, the result is a strict hierarchy; the soluble selves take orders from and support (albeit invisibly) the separative self, who is perceived as autonomous, active and in control.

The separative–separative (arm's-length) image of relationships is, of course, the one underlying the neoclassical image of purely impersonal market exchange. Research into incorporating consideration of interpersonal relations into economics works within this model inasmuch as many economists neglect the constitutive aspects of relations. For example, many have entered this field of research because of the 'anomalous' experimental findings of 'too much' cooperative behaviour. They often seek to explain these anomalies from within a model of separative, self-interested persons (or, if that fails, of self-interested genes) (Ben-Ner and Putterman, 1998c; Manski, 2000; Bardsley, chapter 4, this book).

However, the soluble–soluble (merger) image is – quite arguably – of equal importance in neoclassical economic thinking. Implicit in the phrase 'the consumer chooses' when referring to a household, or in the phrase 'firms maximise profit', is the assumption that all the people who make up the household or the firm have melded themselves into one decision-making unit. Sugden's idea of 'team thinking' can perhaps be characterised similarly as introducing social behaviour through a merger image, though at least in that case the assumption is made explicit.

Assumptions of either completely arm's-length or completely merged relations can be methodologically convenient. When all agents are assumed to be separative, they can be treated as the billiard ball units of classical mechanics, having no interaction other than external bumping and jostling. When all agents are assumed to be soluble they can then, in complementary fashion, be easily bound up into one smooth and tidy billiard ball.

Both assumptions, I suggest, have a somewhat mythical nature, being very much analytical constructs rather than descriptions of real-world relations. Even in financial markets, for example (often pointed to as the epitome of arm's-length transactions), economic sociologists have found evidence of considerable affectively laden interpersonal interaction (Cetina and Bruegger, 2002).

The image of separative–soluble (domination) relationship is the one developed by Gazier and This Saint-Jean (chapter 11): one party (separative) influences another (soluble) to change his behaviour to the first party's advantage. This image of relationship is (alas) far more realistic that those of purely arm's-length or merger. However, contrary to these authors' impression that the growing economic literature on interpersonal relations generally considers only their *positive* side, my own impression has been the opposite. One of the main agendas of 'new institutionalist' economics, for example, has been to get beyond reliance on pure models of separative–separative exchange in order to take into account the use in firms of 'a different organizing principle – that of hierarchy – whereupon authority is used to effect resource allocations' (Williamson, 1991). Other theorists of organisational behaviour similarly seem to emphasise the controlling and conflictual aspects of human relations (e.g. Nohria, 1992).

If the separative and soluble images are the only possibilities for thinking about personhood, then the possible typology of relations is limited to these three: arm's-length (separative–separative), merger (soluble–soluble) and domination (separative–soluble). Yet I detect in many of the chapters in this book a desire to push further – to find ways of analytically approaching relations of positive reciprocity and care, as well.

For this, something beyond these images is necessary. I have suggested elsewhere an image of *individuals-in-relation*.[4] That is, while the separative image recognises human individuality without recognising relation, and the soluble image recognises relation without recognising individuality, the image of individuals-in-relation recognises that people are *both* individually unique and socially constituted. With the recognition of individuals-in-relation, a fourth relational possibility opens up.

(4) *Mutuality:* when individuals-in-relation treat each other with respect and consideration, the relation is supportive of the positive formative process of each; in relations of mutuality, people have mutual respect and mutual constitutive influence.

Within this category, two variants can be distinguished.

(4a) *Symmetric mutuality:* mutuality between similarly situated persons.

Such a definition covers a number of the behaviours talked about within this volume. For example, when discussing joint contributions to a public good, the implicit assumption is that all agents are autonomous 'citizens', who simply decide how much to contribute. A free-rider would be characterised as someone attempting to subvert *symmetric*

---

[4] See Nelson (1996). Similar ideas appear in many parts of the feminist literature – e.g. Mackenzie and Stoljar (2000).

mutuality into *domination*, by taking advantage of the contributions of others. Many of what Gazier and This Saint-Jean call 'horizontal' relations – relations of positive reciprocity, trust, etc. between citizens of similar power – obviously fall into the category of symmetric mutuality. The second possibility is, however, much neglected by scholars.

(4b) *Asymmetric mutuality:* mutuality in relations characterised by unequal power, status, ability or resources.

At first this may seem an impossibility: we are accustomed to thinking of *either* a horizontal relation of citizens in a democracy *or* a vertical relation of hierarchy and domination. The idea of *asymmetric* mutuality suggests that respect and consideration can exist even within 'vertical' relations. When Gazier and This Saint-Jean define power as the gaining of advantage over someone else, they have not considered that 'vertical' relations can be characterised only by *power over*, but also by *power to*.

The relation of a parent and child, for example, is quite obviously one of inequality in power. It may, in some cases, be characterised primarily by domination. But it may, in other cases, be characterised by mutuality, with the parent using his greater power *to* buy food, decide when to cross the street or treat a cut finger in ways that are supportive of the growth of the child. Meanwhile, the presence of the child is what causes the development of the adult's identity as a parent – including, perhaps, the development of skills and feelings that a childless adult could not even imagine.

One caveat should be kept in mind, however. Since dyadic relationships are only part of larger webs of relationships (as Gazier and This Saint-Jean rightly point out), mutuality should not be given an unambiguously positive valence. Mutuality may exist *within* a group in such a way that it aids in that group's domination *of others*. A tight-knit family may put the interests of its own children above larger social interests, for example, or camaraderie among soldiers may make the efforts of an invading army more effective. While it may well be the case that learning mutual respect and consideration 'at home' – in one's earliest and most basic relations – is a *necessary* condition for carrying it to a larger scale, it is clear that mutuality at one level does not automatically carry over to other levels of social organisation.

4.   Economics and care

While a healthy parent–child relation is one example of a relationship of asymmetric mutuality, there is no reason to believe that this sort of relationship stops at the household door. A good political leader has

258   *Julie A. Nelson*

the power *to* effect beneficial change; a good nurse has the power *to* aid the recovery of a helpless patient; a good social worker or therapist has the power *to* help straighten out troubled lives; a good professor has the power *to* contribute to the learning of less experienced students. In such relations, the power is asymmetric, but the more powerful actor uses his or her power for the benefit of the weaker party. We may, in shorthand, call these relations of *care*.

A crucial issue in examining such interpersonal relations is the issue of authenticity: do the leaders, nurses, etc. *really* care, in an emotive sense, or are they merely feigning concern about the well-being of those in their charge in order to receive some kind of reward? Anyone who has considered putting a young child into day care or a parent into a nursing home understands the salience of this question. What will happen after you leave, the doors close and the person is left alone with your loved one? In caring work, interpersonal relations are not just incidental to the job. A healthy ability to form positive relationships is an absolutely vital characteristic of the work itself. The chapters by Hargreaves Heap and by Borzaga and Depedri touch on the topic of how such relationships play out when interwoven with more typically 'economic' – that is, financial – concerns.

Hargreaves Heap (chapter 9) cites the work of Bruno Frey, one of the few economists who has looked at the relation of extrinsic motivations (such as monetary reward) and intrinsic (inner) motivations. Frey's work, however, is incompletely explained in that chapter.

One of Frey's points is that extrinsic rewards for work can 'crowd out' intrinsic rewards. This is the disturbing case if you are looking for paid care for a helpless loved one; the 'crowding out' story suggests that someone doing caring work 'for the money' will provide less 'real' care. Frey points out, however, that this case is not inevitable but, rather, occurs *under certain identifiable conditions*. The major characteristic of these conditions is that the individuals involved perceive the external intervention to be *controlling*, and thus impairing of their own feelings of self-determination and self-esteem, and their desire for self-expression (1997, pp. 17–18). In the terms of the current chapter, this would be a case where the terms of employment signal to the care giver that he is in the underdog position in a domination (separative–soluble) relation vis-à-vis his employer.

On the other hand, Frey notes, '[e]xternal interventions *crowd in* intrinsic motivation if the individuals concerned perceive it as supportive' (p. 18, emphasis in the original). That is, extrinsic interventions that are perceived as acknowledging the workers' own motivations and skill tend to *foster* their self-esteem and sense of freedom. In the terms of the current chapter, this would be a case where the employment relations signal to a care giver that he is in a situation of mutuality (of persons-in-relation) with his employer, even if the unidirectional flow of money makes the relations somewhat asymmetric.

Hargreaves Heap does not mention this possibility, instead using the term 'crowding in' to refer to a case in which extrinsic incentives are absent, with the result that intrinsic motivations are enhanced.[5] He thus concludes that in order to avoid undermining the intrinsic value of an activity one must make sure that 'the payment is relatively low' (chapter 9, pages 203–4). Frey's notion of the possible *supportive* crowding in of intrinsic motivations *by* positive external rewards is neglected.

A closer examination of the interplay of money and other motivations, and of larger social networks, might offer some insight into Borzaga and Depedri's finding that high pay does *not* seem to be an important factor making employees loyal to community care service organisations, while those who intend to leave 'are mainly dissatisfied with pay and career opportunities' (chapter 6). A naive interpretation of this empirical result might suggest that low pay – the norm in such occupations – is in fact (as argued by Hargreaves Heap) giving the correct incentive structure.[6] That is, it may appear at first sight that 'real carers', who do the work for its intrinsic reward (i.e. do not report that the pay of the job is an incentive to stay), are staying in the job, while 'greedy people' (who want higher pay and better career advancement) are leaving. This should not be accepted at face value.

It would have been interesting to gather, in this study, data on the family financial situations of the workers in the community service organisations. If the situation in Italy is anything like the situation in the United States (a country with which I am more familiar) I would expect to find that many of the 'stayers' in community service organisations are married women with a financially successful spouse. Historically, caring work in nursery schools, primary schools and hospitals has been cross-subsidised by the more financially remunerative work of workers' husbands. Another subsidy came from the willingness of some women to live on poverty wages – nuns, in many cases, or young single women waiting to get married. Some of these patterns continue today.

---

[5] In one single case Frey does use the term 'crowding in' in the same way as Hargreaves Heap (Frey, 1997, p. 91). However, Frey returns to using the term in the sense he had previously established (pp. ix, 11, 24) immediately after this example (pp. 91–2).

[6] Paula England has, in fact, found in an econometric study that occupations involving what she calls 'nurturance' tend to have lower predicted wages, after controlling for sex, the human capital demands of the job, and other job characteristics (England, 1992, ch. 3).

On the other hand, women who need to support themselves and their families find that the financial sacrifices of the job are beyond what they can afford. US scholar Kathy Modigliani found many of the subjects in her study of child care workers expressing the sentiment 'I love my job but I'm about to leave it' (1993). That is, there are many people who are strongly motivated by an internally generated desire to care for children, but who eventually 'burn out' as a result of the financial strain and the sense of disrespect they feel for their work.

Far from extinguishing caring motivations, in such a case a higher wage for caring work could increase the flow of 'real care' by making it *possible* for highly intrinsically motivated people *to continue to care*. There is no need to suppose that higher wages would lead only to problems of adverse selection. That is, while higher wages would probably encourage some non-caring people to try to enter caring jobs 'for the money', a possibly more important effect would be that higher wages would also support 'real carers' in doing their work and staying in their jobs. There is no way to tell which of these wage effects would predominate in the absence of empirical evidence, and no way to judge the impact on the quality of care without knowing how well other forms of quality control (such as observation of the worker's performance) work in sorting out carers from non-carers (Nelson, 1999).

Rather than see economic and relational interests as opposed, more sophisticated views of human nature and motivations can get beyond the naive idea of equating financial interests with selfishness. My hope is that new explorations of the relation of interpersonal relations and economics, such as the current volume, will greatly expand our ability to make sense of the economics of the caring professions, and of the caring and relational aspects of many other jobs.

5.   A note on methodology

In centring the discipline around easily mathematically formalised notions of individual autonomy and rational choice, economists gained *precision*, but at an extremely high price in terms of *accuracy*. As discussed above, images of separative–separative or soluble–soluble relations make it easy to apply concepts borrowed from classical mechanics, with its notions of laws and its use of formal equations. Bruni's chapter in this book (chapter 10) outlines admirably how *methodological* choices lay behind the erasure of relational phenomena in economic thinking.

Thus modelling exercises such as those by Pelligra (chapter 5), in the contribution by Antoci, Sacco and Vanin (chapter 7) and in the studies reviewed by Bardsley (chapter 4) should be evaluated carefully. At the end of the day, the question has to be: has the formalisation added to our understanding of relational phenomena? Or have we merely forced novel phenomena to take on a form we can address with standard tools, leaving out any aspects that may be methodologically inconvenient (no matter how important)? I believe that, in some cases, formal modelling can be enlightening. However, the *hegemony* of the use of formalism as a criterion for what counts as 'economic analysis' has, I think, had unambiguously negative consequences for economics. If economics aspires to be a science in the sense of a useful means for inquiry (instead of a pseudo-science, based on false analogies to outdated notions of physics), economists will need to be open to a larger methodological toolbox.

6.   Conclusions

Few, if any, real-world economic relations are characterised by the purely arm's-length relations or purely merged relations assumed in neoclassical theory. Extending economic thought to include the analysis of interpersonal relations of domination and of mutuality (both symmetric and asymmetric) will greatly strengthen our ability to understand the way that societies organise themselves to provide for human survival and flourishing.

Since this point is often misunderstood, I must stress that the main point of feminist analysis is *not* to reinforce the idea that women might be essentially 'more relational' than men. It is, instead, to show how standard scholarly analysis in many fields has reflected a particular set of masculine biases in definition, assumptions and methodology that systematically exclude those activities and characteristics that historically and culturally have been *stereotypically associated* with women. To the extent that future research about economics and interpersonal relations may continue to romanticise family life, or concentrate on issues of dominance and hierarchy to the neglect of mutuality and care, or restrict itself to narrow methodological recipes, it may reinforce old gender-based biases. To the extent that these old, gender biases are transcended, I expect to see truly path-breaking and important insights arising from the continued development of research in the areas of economics and interpersonal relations.

13 Economics and interpersonal relations: ruling the social back in

Louis Putterman

Humans are social animals. Being animals we are biological organisms imbued with the drive to maintain ourselves by consuming food and sheltering ourselves from the elements. Being social, we are physically, intellectually and emotionally interdependent. We are born helpless and need others' nurturing. We are born at all because our parents are moved by desires for intimate relations. We are cared for because they are endowed with the drive to nurture us and with tendencies to bond to each other to facilitate such nurturance. We learn to think – to converse with ourselves mentally, using words – only by interacting *with one another*, using languages that are the products of millennia of such interactions. Our senses of self emerge in our early encounters with others, and we construct identities by comparing ourselves with others and apprehending our places in a social order. How odd that we should ever have thought up a social science that gives short shrift to social interactions!

About twelve thousand years ago our ancestors, who had recently begun to fashion more elaborate tools, started to exploit their environments in new ways. The old lifestyles of hunting and gathering gradually gave way to new ones based on agriculture and animal husbandry. As technological progress fed population growth, more differentiated divisions of labour came into being and the intimate band gave way to the more complex village and to still larger societies and polities. Little by little, the self-sufficiency of the band gave way to specialisation and trade. Along with specialists in tool making, metal working, battle and administration, there arose specialists in doing business, and eventually specialists in thinking about things.

At first, thinkers were specialised to thinking, in general, not to thinking about any one thing only. But intellectual activity was no exception to the trend towards specialisation. As early as the fifth century before the Common Era treatises were being written about economics and politics. By the late nineteenth century the social sciences were further separating themselves from the physical and biological, and from each other. By the mid-twentieth century, macroeconomics and microeconomics were distinct fields. By the end of the twentieth century a general equilibrium theorist could scarcely talk to an applied health economist, an expert on industrial organisation or a specialist in open economy macroeconomics.

Commenting on the division of labour in industry, Adam Smith wrote in the late eighteenth century: '[t]he understandings of the greater part of men are necessarily formed by their ordinary employments. The man whose whole life is spent in performing a few simple operations...has no occasion to exert his understanding. [...] He generally becomes as stupid and ignorant as it is possible for a human creature to become' (1976/1776, pp. 781–2). Is this the fate, too, of the intellectual specialist? At least some have argued that it indeed has been so for economics. In 1985 journalist Robert Kuttner wrote that '[d]epartments of economics are graduating a generation of *idiot savants*, brilliant at esoteric mathematics yet innocent of actual economic life'.[1] In 2000 a group of critics of mainstream economics launched a *Post-Autistic Economics* newsletter.

Economics is about how humans satisfy their material needs using limited resources. But it has always been more social than technological in character. The questions of how food can be wrested from the earth, shelters be constructed, clothing made, and so forth are technological ones that are the stuff of agricultural science, engineering and other arts, not the concerns of economics. What economists study are interactions among people – in commerce, in organisations of production, in operating governments and making public decisions.

So why do we need to add social interaction back into economics? The answer, I think, is twofold. First, although economics is already about social interaction, it (ironically) treats such interaction in a de-socialised way – that is, as if the social interaction itself could be understood as a mechanical matter, without reference to humans' social and emotional natures. This has worked passably well, and has even aided progress in certain domains. But, clearly, it leads to unsatisfactory results in others – when studying, for example, the relationship between employer and employee and the resulting behaviour and satisfaction in the workplace, as Borzaga and Depedri document in chapter 6. Second, economics has been understood as a study of people interacting to satisfy their *material* wants and needs. Ruling the meeting of material wants and needs 'in' and the meeting of social and emotional wants and needs 'out' of the subject matter of economics has worked for some purposes but has

---

[1] Quoted from Colander and Klamer (1987).

been an inefficient strategy when material and social goods – or bads – are joint products, as in Gui's useful diagram, figure 2.1, in his chapter. A fine meal consumed alone, one consumed among people whose company one enjoys and one consumed with people one would rather not be among are quite different things, even if the food, the money price, the table setting and the service are identical. Much consumption and accumulation of goods and wealth is done for social reasons (gaining prestige, avoiding shame, attracting the opposite sex) rather than material ends, or with a mix of both kinds of objectives in mind. Goods with differing abilities to impart utility (an ice cream cone in summer and an ice cream cone in winter) are different goods, even in the most conventional theory of the consumer, so the social dimensions of consumption can be ignored only where tolerable as an approximation.

One of the strengths of economics as a discipline has been that it has never contented itself with asking small questions only – the sort that Joan Robinson once derided with a reference to the price of apples in terms of oranges – but has always raised big questions as well, such as whether our economic arrangements (sometimes summarised under the heading of 'the price system') maximise our well-being subject to our preferences, resources and technological knowledge. Clearly, that question can't be answered satisfactorily without paying some attention to the social dimensions of and the social spillovers from economic life. As Sugden argues persuasively in his chapter, 'On any plausible definition of the subject matter of economics, the value created in interpersonal relations is a matter of economic significance.'

The underlying justification for building the edifice of theoretical welfare economics was that it might provide guidance for making economic policy (even if that were to be a policy of leaving well enough alone, or *laissez-faire*). General equilibrium theory tried to spell out the conditions under which decentralised decision making would support socially optimal outcomes. Where optimal outcomes would not obtain, for instance because of external social costs or the existence of market power, remedies could be identified and advocated. By adding to an asocial depiction of economic reality key aspects of the association between economic activity and interpersonal relations, we can hope to provide improved policy guidance.

Consider, for example, the question of how a company's employees are paid. Without taking into account relevant psychological and social dimensions, economic theorists tend to argue against profit sharing, against the compression of wage differences and against the use of above-market-efficiency wages that can't be backed by termination threats. Instead of such devices, conventional economic arguments advocate creating as close an association between pay and individual performance as can be made feasible by supervision and monitoring. But the result of intensive monitoring and highly differentiated wages might be both a higher cost for such effort as is obtained, and less satisfaction overall. Thus, we may well be able to improve welfare by basing policy advice on an economic model augmented by the relevant social considerations (say, of the inclination to engage in mutual monitoring, or of reciprocity towards a trusting employer and resistance towards an untrusting one), much as advice in the environmental sphere is improved by incorporating the possibility of externalities into models that assume them away.

Much of this is not new. Thirty years ago, for example, Oliver Williamson, Michael Wachter and Jeffrey Harris (1975) suggested that an employer needs to consider the effects that intensive supervision and frequent evaluations can have on the 'atmosphere' of the employment relationship. Although the next decade and a half saw the development of principal–agent and other formal but asocial models that made concepts such as 'atmosphere' seem unrigorous to many economists, awareness of the social dimension has never died out entirely. With the continuing growth in the ranks of academic economists and in the number of outlets for the publication of their research, economics has never been entirely captured by simplifying formalism.

An additional and quite powerful dynamic, of late, has been the acceptance and impact of the experimental method, reflected also in several chapters in this book. At first, experiments were treated suspiciously by those economists who viewed 'asking people what they think' as the furthest thing from positive science and who considered choices in the laboratory to be more akin to survey responses than to data on purchases and sales in natural settings. But a funny thing happened as game theorists, searching for ways out of the conundra posed by multiple equilibria, competing equilibrium concepts, and so on, took an interest in the experimental method. When enough of these 'high priests of economics' (Leijonhufvud, 1973) took experiments seriously, the method began to become respectable. And with this came a willingness, in some quarters at least, to consider the possibility that behaviours that don't maximise profits or monetary payoffs may be common enough, and different enough from those otherwise expected, to require attention.

In the ultimatum game,[2] for example, standard economics says that the proposer will give the responder the smallest positive amount

---

[2] One individual is given the chance to propose how a sum of money is divided between himself and another. If the responder doesn't accept, neither gets anything.

permitted, since the latter will rationally prefer something to nothing, and the proposer will then get the maximum amount that can be assured to him. Experiments showed differently: proposers typically sent 40 or 50 per cent of the amount to be divided. The proposers could still be trying to earn as much as possible, it was pointed out, but could be anticipating that responders would reject small offers. Only half of the world, the responders, had to be 'irrational' (that is, to care about something beyond their own payoffs) to explain what was happening! Although some calculations indeed supported the hypothesis that proposers were at least approximately maximising their payoffs given the observed probabilities of rejection at each offer level, modifying the game by taking away the responders' right to veto the division – creating the so-called 'dictator game' – failed to eliminate, although it succeeded in reducing somewhat, positive offers.

Contributions to a public good or group effort have been another area in which predictions based on the assumption of payoff-maximising individuals have not performed well. As discussed in Bardsley's chapter, experimental subjects contribute substantial amounts to a public good when rational payoff maximisers would contribute nothing. Although the amounts contributed tend to decline with repetition if richer forms of interaction are ruled out, this is not the case when subjects can communicate with each other, when they can extract monetary punishments from one another at a cost to themselves, and when more cooperative individuals are isolated or can isolate themselves from less cooperative ones.[3] All these results can be interpreted as suggesting that some form of reciprocity or other preference distinct from own payoff maximisation is present among some participants, while the heterogeneity of preference may help explain why contributions tend to decline in mixed groups.

But, as the chapters by Bardsley and Pelligra also illustrate, even the replication of most results that appear anomalous in terms of a theory of atomistic payoff maximisation fail to clinch fully any particular theory of interpersonal preference or behaviour. Consider again that half of the world that appeared to care about fairness, the responders in ultimatum games. Rejecting small offers in real life could build a reputation that

---

[3] On communication, see the sources cited by Sally (1995) and the more recent papers by Brosig, Weimann and Ockenfels (2003) and by Bochet, Page and Putterman (forthcoming); on punishment, see Fehr and Gächter (2000), which has already been replicated by several teams of researchers; on the manipulation of group composition by the experimenter, see Gunnthorsdottir, Houser, McCabe and Ameden (2002) and Ones and Putterman (2004); and on the endogenous formation of cooperative groups, see Page, Putterman and Unel (forthcoming).

would do one good, in the long run, so even responders might not be anything but payoff maximisers – payoff maximisers who were simply acting normally in the abnormal environment of a laboratory one-shot game. And, whereas dictators tended to give 30 per cent of their endowments in the first dictator games, despite the absence of a second-mover veto, offerings fell considerably when experimenters assured subjects that third parties, including the experimenter, would not know how they had behaved.[4]

This is not to say that I find the evidence for social preferences unconvincing. Consider the fact that subjects tend to contribute more to a public good when the marginal return to contributing, always less than what one gets by keeping one's money, rises from smaller values in the direction of unity. The most parsimonious explanation of this is that many subjects get utility from contributing but that the amount of utility they get varies from one subject to another, so that, as the pecuniary cost of contributing falls, more and more subjects find contributing better than not doing so.

Rather than to reject social preferences, my purpose in raising caveats is to suggest that, while empirical research – including use of the experimental method – will play a central part in the research that is needed, it will always require the complement of a theoretical framework to guide the questions asked and to help make sense of the results obtained. My own preferred framework (sketched out in Ben-Ner and Putterman, 1998b) treats the preference sets of human actors as products of the coevolution of human genes and human cultures. I'll spare the reader any further recitation except to say that there is no escaping the evidence that we humans are the evolved products of the terrestrial biosphere, and that no biologist has yet come forth with an argument as to how natural forces would have moulded us into the perfectly rational, perfectly selfish and perfectly asocial creatures that the most simplified and orthodox economic models have taken us to be.

In embarking on the task of restoring the social to economics, we should not delude ourselves, Pollyanna-like, that this will be a romp among the daisies, adding to cold heartless economics no more than warm fuzzies and the milk of human kindness. For example, we can include in the objective functions of economic actors social as well as material goods. Just as a piece of bread is not itself the ultimate good

---

[4] See Forsythe, Horowitz, Savin and Sefton(1994), Hoffman, McCabe, Shachat and Smith (1994), Eckel and Grossman (1996) and Bolton and Ockenfels (1998). Lower dictator sending in double-blind treatments is not universal, though; see Ben-Ner, Putterman, Kong and Magan 2003.

sought – we seek, rather, the bread's ability to satisfy hunger and perhaps to generate some enjoyment in the process – so specific human interactions may not be our ultimate goods either but, rather, instruments towards the satisfaction of our ultimate needs for belonging, recognition, love, sexual relations, and even (in some instances) to make ourselves into objects of fear, or of envy, and so on. Intrusions of the relational on the economic include not only the reciprocity and trust that make commerce possible where unalloyed self-interest could not tread, but also such things as the interruption of commercial rationality to pursue forms of intercommunal bloodletting that the calculus of material rewards would rule out. In these matters as much as when choosing between apples and oranges, we must expect to find actors who negotiate trade-offs, who sacrifice one relational good for another and who exploit one relational good to achieve another or to achieve a material end. When the disciplinary barrier between economics and social relations comes down, we will be face to face with ugly as well as with beautiful facts.

Not only will it not all be pretty; it will also not be easy (there *was* parsimony in the decision to sweep these concerns under the rug at an earlier stage in the building up of economics as a discipline). As we ask the ultimate questions of well-being, we will have to grapple with methodologically and philosophically difficult questions. Because the preferences of individuals, which economics makes the basis for its scales of welfare, must ultimately be recognised as being themselves shaped by social environments, we'll need to have debate about what standards of well-being and human flourishing can be applied with objectivity. We may have devised, for example, systems of property rights and exchange that are extraordinary engines of progress in raising levels of material well-being, but how shall we judge whether their impetus to make us want more and newer material things, and to devalue our leisure or our autonomy or the collegiality at work, are making us better off overall?

One nightmare of the humanist is that those economists who see all of life in terms of maximising flows of goods and services and all human motivation as material incentives will remake the world in the image of *Homo œconomicus*, weaning us all from the aforementioned milk of human kindness to abundant but less nourishing synthetics. Because humans are social beings and have yet to replace the genes they evolved with by blueprints of their own design, I doubt that we need to worry too much that our natures will change. We may do ourselves much harm by adopting, out of ignorance of our natures, recommendations that suit *Homo œconomicus* better than they do ourselves. But the robustness of our sociality – including the quest for what Sugden (following Adam

Smith) calls 'fellow-feeling' – is not in doubt. I may find it sad that the overfed citizens of rich countries spend huge sums of money to pamper their house pets while people go hungry elsewhere on the globe, but I don't overlook the fact that the pet care industry, like personal introduction services, the cosmetics industry, fashion, the marketing of pop culture icons, health clubs, equipment to tighten the abdominal muscles, and even an extravagant funeral industry, are not random creations of advertisers but all reflect on what are basically social needs of the human heart. We will still need to understand our social natures to understand our economic behaviours in the future just as much as in the past. And what better time to get started.

Envoi

This book embodies an effort to confront openly the challenge that interpersonal relations present for economics, in the conviction that the 'relational' and the economic realms should not continue to be studied and managed separately. The contributions that are collated here, although diverse in method and flavour, all attempt to cross the disciplinary hiatus that persists between these two realms in spite of the links that bind them together in the real world. Far from exhausting the field, they offer some first answers to the main emerging questions, and at the same time provide a sample of what can be done.

We think that this effort is worth its while, not so much for what we may have achieved (others must judge that) but because of what is at stake. Referring back to the analogy between the natural and the social environment that we developed in the introduction, there are reasons for thinking that in the relational field, just as in the environmental, disasters have been and are being provoked by inadvertent or careless economic decision making. The new category of 'relational poor', living in social isolation in the middle of cities inhabited by hundreds of thousands of people, or the frequency of the psychological illnesses reportedly caused by mismanaged rapports in the workplace, are illustrations of this point. However, the same analogy also gives us grounds for optimism that attitudes can change quite quickly, that the public can become aware of the need to account for a previously ignored input to the economic system, and that – given such awareness – practices can evolve, both from above and from below.

Such a transformation requires changes in ideas; and one of those changes is a change in the messages, explicit or implicit, that society receives from economic theory. We see this volume as a contribution to that transformation.

BENEDETTO GUI
ROBERT SUGDEN

270

References

Abrams, Burton A., and Mark D. Schmitz 1984. 'The crowding out effect of government transfers on private charitable contributions: cross-sectional evidence', *National Tax Journal* 37: 563–8.

Adam, J. S. 1963. 'Wage inequalities, productivity, and work quality', *Industrial Relations* 3: 9–16.

1965. 'Inequity in social exchange', in Berkowitz (ed.), *Advances in Experimental Social Psychology*. New York: Academic Press.

Adam, J. S., and W. E. Rosenbaum 1964. 'The relationship of worker productivity to cognitive dissonance about wage inequalities', *Journal of Abnormal and Social Psychology* 69: 19–25.

Adelman, Mara B., Aaron C. Ahuvia and Cathy Goodwin 1994. 'Beyond smiling: social support and service quality', in Rust and Oliver (eds.), *Service Quality: New Directions in Theory and Practice*. Newbury Park, CA: Sage, 139–71.

Adelman, Mara B., Malcolm R. Parks and Terrance L. Albrecht 1987. 'Beyond close relationships: social support and weak ties', in Albrecht and Adelman (eds.), *Communicating Social Support*. Newbury Park, CA: Sage, 126–47.

Akerlof, George A. 1982. 'Labor contracts as partial gift exchange', *Quarterly Journal of Economics* 97(4): 543–69.

1984. *An Economic Theorist's Book of Tales*. Cambridge: Cambridge University Press.

1997. 'Social distance and social decisions', *Econometrica* 65(5):1005–27.

Akerlof, George A., and Rachel Kranton 2000. 'Economics and identity', *Quarterly Journal of Economics* 115(3): 715–53.

Allen, W. David 2000. 'Social networks and self-employment', *Journal of Socio-Economics* 29: 487–501.

Almond, Stephen, and Jeremy Kendall 2000. 'Taking the employee's perspective seriously: an initial UK cross-sectoral comparison', *Nonprofit and Voluntary Sector Quarterly* 29(2): 205–31.

Andreoni, James 1988a. 'Privately provided public goods in a large economy – the limits of altruism', *Journal of Public Economics* 35: 57–73.

1988b. 'Why free-ride? Strategies and learning in public goods experiments', *Journal of Public Economics* 37: 291–304.

1990. 'Impure altruism and donations to public goods: a theory of warm glow giving', *Economic Journal* 100: 464–77.

1998. 'Towards a theory of charitable fund-raising', *Journal of Political Economy* 106: 1186–213.

Antoci, Angelo 1996. *Negative Externalities and Growth of the Activity Level*. Report no. 9308, Ministero dell'Istruzione, dell'Università e della Ricerea research project on non-linear dynamics and application to economic and social sciences, University of Florence.

Antoci, Angelo, and Stefano Bartolini 1997. *Externalities and Growth in an Evolutionary Game*. Discussion Paper no. 10, Department of Economics, University of Trento.

2004. 'Negative externalities, defensive expenditures and labour supply in an evolutionary context', *Environment and Development Economics* 9(5): 591–612.

Antoci, Angelo, Pier Luigi Sacco and Paolo Vanin 2002. *Participation, Growth and Social Poverty: Social Capital in a Homogeneous Society*. Paper presented at the 54th International Atlantic Economic Society in Washington, DC, 12 October.

2005. 'Social capital accumulation and the evolution of social participation', *Journal of socio-Economics*, forthcoming.

Aoki, Masahiko 1984. *The Co-operative Game Theory of the Firm*. Oxford: Oxford University Press.

Aristotle 1980. *Nichomachean Ethics*. Oxford: Oxford University Press.

Arrow, Kenneth 1974. *The Limits of Organization*. New York: Norton.

1999. 'Observations on social capital', in Dasgupta and Serageldin (eds.), *Social Capital: A Multifaceted Perspective*. Washington, DC: World Bank, 3–5.

Arthur, W. Brian 1988. 'Self-reinforcing mechanisms in economics', in Anderson, Arrow and Pines (eds.), *The Economy as an Evolving Complex System*. Reading, MA: Addison-Wesley, 9–31.

1989. 'Competing technologies, increasing returns and lock-in by historical events', *Economic Journal* 99: 116–31.

Asch, Solomon E. 1951. 'Effects of group pressure upon the modification and distortion of judgements', in Guetzkow (ed.), *Groups, Leadership and Men*. Pittsburgh, PA: Carnegie Press.

Ash, Colin 2000. 'Social self-interest', in Gui (ed.) *Annals of Public and Cooperative Economics*, special issue on 'Economics and interpersonal relations' 71(2): 261–83.

Axelrod, Robert 1984. *The Evolution of Cooperation*. New York: Basic Books.

Bacharach, Michael 1993. 'Variable universe games', in Binmore, Kirman and Tani (eds.), *Frontiers of Game Theory*. Cambridge, MA: MIT Press, 255–75.

1999. 'Interactive team reasoning: a contribution to the theory of cooperation', *Research in Economics* 53: 117–47.

Bacharach, Michael, Gerardo Guerra and Daniel Zizzo 2001. *Is Trust Self-Fulfilling? An Experimental Study*. Mimeo, Bounded Rationality in Economic Behaviour Unit, University of Oxford.

Baier, Annette 1986. 'Trust and antitrust', *Ethics* 96: 231–60.

1994. *Moral Prejudices*. Cambridge, MA: Harvard University Press.

Baker, James 1987. 'Trust and rationality', *Pacific Philosophical Quarterly*, 68: 1–13.

Bardsley, Nicholas 2000. 'Control without deception: individual behaviour in free-riding experiments revisited', *Experimental Economics* 3: 215–40.

Barkema, Harry G. 1995. 'Do top managers work harder when they are monitored?', *Kyklos* 48: 19–42.

Baron, Hans 1955. *The Crisis of the Early Italian Renaissance.* Princeton, NJ: Princeton University Press.

1988. *In Search of Florentine Civic Humanism: Essays on the Transitions from Medieval to Modern Thought.* Princeton, NJ: Princeton University Press.

Baron, Jonathan 1998. 'Trust: beliefs and morality', in Ben-Ner and Putterman (eds.), *Economics, Value and Organisation.* Cambridge and New York: Cambridge University Press, 408–18.

Bartolini, Stefano, and Luigi Bonatti 1997. *Negative Externalities as the Cause of Growth in a Neoclassical Model.* Discussion Paper no. 9, Department of Economics, University of Trento.

2004. *Social Capital and its Role in Production: Does the Depletion of Social Capital Depress Economic Growth?* Quaderni di Dipartimento no. 421, Department of Economics, University of Siena.

Becker, Gary S. 1965. 'A theory of the allocation of time', *Economic Journal* 75 (299): 493–517.

1975. *Human Capital: A Theoretical and Empirical Analysis with Special Reference to Education.* New York: Columbia University Press.

1981. *A Treatise on the Family.* Cambridge, MA: Harvard University Press.

1991. 'A note on restaurant pricing and other examples of social influence on prices', *Journal of Political Economy* 99(5): 1109–16.

1996. *Accounting for Tastes.* Cambridge, MA: Harvard University Press.

Bénabou, Roland 1996. 'Equity and efficiency in human capital investment: the local connection', *Review of Economic Studies* 63: 237–64.

Benhabib, Seyla 1987. 'The generalized and the concrete other: the Kohlberg–Gilligan controversy and moral theory', in Meyers and Kittay (eds.), *Women and Moral Theory.* Totowa, NJ: Rowman and Littlefield, 154–77.

Benn, Stanley 1978a. 'The problematic rationality of political participation', in Benn, *Political Participation.* Canberra: Australian National University Press, 1–22.

1978b. 'The problematic rationality of political participation: rejoinder', in Benn, *Political Participation.* Canberra: Australian National University Press, 61–8.

Ben-Ner, Avner, and Louis Putterman 1998a. 'Preface', in Ben-Ner and Putterman (eds.), *Economics, Values and Organisation.* Cambridge and New York: Cambridge University Press, xv–xxvi.

1998b. 'Values and institutions in economic analysis', in Ben-Ner and Putterman (eds.), *Economics, Values and Organisation.* Cambridge and New York: Cambridge University Press, 3–69.

Ben-Ner, Avner, Louis Putterman, Fanmin Kong and Dan Magan 2004. 'Reciprocity in a two-part dictator game', *Journal of Economic Behavior and Organization* 53: 333–52.

Ben-Porath, Yoram 1980. 'The F-connection: families, friends, and firms and the organization of exchange', *Population and Development Review* 6(1): 1–30.

Berger, Peter L., and Thomas Luckmann 1966. *The Social Construction of Reality: A Treatise in the Sociology of Knowledge*. New York: Anchor Books.

Bergstrom, Theodore, Lawrence Blume and Hal Varian 1986. 'On the private provision of public goods', *Journal of Public Economics* 29(1): 25–49.

Bernheim, Douglas B., and Oded Stark 1988. 'Altruism within the family reconsidered: do nice guys finish last?', *American Economic Review* 78: 1034–45.

Bikhchandani, Sushil, David Hirschleifer and Ivo Welch 1998. 'Learning from the behavior of others: conformity, fads, and informational cascades', *Journal of Economic Perspectives* 12: 151–70.

Binmore, Kenneth G. 1992. *Fun and Games*. Lexington, MA: D. C. Heath.

1994. *Game Theory and the Social Contract*. Cambridge, MA: MIT Press, Vol. I: *Playing Fair*.

1998. *Game Theory and the Social Contract*. Cambridge, MA: MIT Press, Vol. II: *Just Playing*.

Bitner, Mary J., Bernard H. Booms and Mary S. Tetreault 1990. 'The service encounter: diagnosing favorable and unfavorable incidents', *Journal of Marketing* 54(1): 71–84.

Blume, Lawrence E., and Steven N. Durlauf 2001. 'The interactions-based approach to socioeconomic behavior', in Durlauf and Young (eds.), *Social Dynamics: Economic Learning and Social Evolution*. Washington, DC: Brookings Institution Press; Cambridge, MA and London: MIT Press, Vol. IV, 15–44.

Bochet, Olivier, Talbot Page and Louis Putterman (forthcoming). 'Communication and punishment in voluntary contribution experiments', *Journal of Economic Behavior and Organization*.

Bogart, William T., and Brian A. Cromwell 2000. 'How much is a neighborhood school worth?', *Journal of Urban Economics* 47: 280–305.

Bohnet, Iris, and Bruno S. Frey 1999. 'The sound of silence in prisoner's dilemma and dictator games', *Journal of Economic Behavior and Organization* 38(1): 43–57.

Bolton, Gary E., and Axel Ockenfels 1998. 'Strategy and equity: an ERC-analysis of the Güth–van Damme game', *Journal of Mathematical Psychology* 42: 215–26.

2000. 'ERC: a theory of equity, reciprocity and competition', *American Economic Review*, 90: 166–93.

Borjas, George J. 1995. 'Ethnicity, neighborhoods, and human-capital externalities', *American Economic Review* 85(3): 365–90.

Bornstein, Gary, and Meyrav Ben-Yossef 1994. 'Cooperation in intergroup and single group social dilemmas', *Journal of Experimental Social Psychology* 30: 52–67.

Borzaga, Carlo (ed.) 2000. *Capitale umano e qualità del lavoro nei servizi sociali: un'analisi comparata tra modelli di gestione*. Rome: Fondazione Italiana per il Volontariato.

Bourdieu, Pierre 1958. *Sociologie de l'Algérie*. Paris: PUF.

1963. 'La société traditionnelle: attitude à l'égard du temps et conduite économique', *Sociologie du travail* 1 (January–March): 24–44.

1980a. 'Le capital social', *Actes de la recherche en sciences sociales* 31: 2–3.

1980b. *Questions de sociologie*. Paris: Editions de Minuit.

2000. *Les structures sociales de l'économie*. Paris: Seuil.

Bourdieu, Pierre, Alain Darbel, Jean-Pierre Rivet and Claude Seibel 1963. *Travail et travailleurs en Algérie*. Paris: Editions Mouton.

Bourdieu, Pierre, and Abdelmalek Sayad 1964. *Le déracinement, la crise de l'agriculture traditionnelle en Algérie*. Paris: Editions de Minuit.

Bowles, Samuel 1985. 'The production process in a competitive economy: walrasian, neo-hobbesian and marxian models', *American Economic Review* 75(1): 16–36.

1999. '"Social capital" and community governance', *Focus* 20(3): 6–10.

Bowles, Samuel, Jeffrey Carpenter and Herbert Gintis 2001. *Mutual Monitoring in Teams: The Effects of Residual Claimancy and Reciprocity*. Working paper, Middlebury College, Middlebury, Vermont.

Bowles, Samuel, and Herbert Gintis 1988. 'Contested exchange: political economy and modern economic theory', *American Economic Review* 78(2): 145–50.

1990. 'Contested exchange: new microfoundations for the political economy of capitalism', *Politics and Society* 18(2): 165–222.

1993. 'The revenge of Homo economicus: contested exchange and the revival of political economy', *Journal of Economic Perspectives* 7(1): 83–102.

2000. 'Walrasian economics in retrospect', *Quarterly Journal of Economics* 115 (4): 1411–39.

Braithwaite, Valerie, and Margaret Levi (eds.) 2002. *Trust and Governance*. New York: Russell Sage Foundation Publications.

Brandts, Jordi, and Arthur Schram 2001. 'Cooperation and noise in public goods experiments: applying the contribution function approach', *Journal of Public Economics* 79: 399–427.

Brennan, Geoffrey 1996. 'Selection and the currency of reward', in Goodin (ed.), *The Theory of Institutional Design*. Cambridge: Cambridge University Press, 256–75.

Brennan, Geoffrey, and Loren Lomasky 1985. 'The impartial spectator goes to Washington', *Economics and Philosophy* 1: 189–211.

Brennan, Geoffrey, and Philip Pettit 2000. 'The hidden economy of esteem', *Economics and Philosophy* 16: 77–98.

Brewer, Marilyn B. 1989. 'Ambivalent sociality: the human condition', *Behavioural and Brain Sciences* 12: 699.

Brewer, Marilyn B., and Roderick M. Kramer 1984. 'Effects of group identity on resource use in a simulated Commons dilemma', *Journal of Personality and Social Psychology* 46: 1044–57.

1986. 'Choice behaviour in social dilemmas: effects of social identity, group size and decision framing', *Journal of Personality and Social Psychology* 50: 543–9.

Brosig, Jeannette, Joachim Weimann and Axel Ockenfels 2003. 'The effect of communication media on cooperation', *German Economic Review* 4(2): 217–42.

Bruni, Luigino 2002. *Vilfredo Pareto and the Birth of the Modern Microeconomics*. Cheltenham: Edward Elgar.

Bruni, Luigino, and Francesco Guala 2001. 'Pareto and the epistemological foundations of rational choice', *History of Political Economy* 33: 21–49.

Bryan, James H., and Mary A. Test 1967. 'Models and helping: naturalistic studies in aiding behaviour', *Journal of Personality and Social Psychology* 6: 400–7.

Burlando, Roberto, and John D. Hey 1997. 'Do Anglo-Saxons free-ride more?', *Journal of Public Economics* 64: 41–60.

Camerer, Colin 2003. *Behavioral Game Theory*. Princeton, NJ: Princeton University Press.

Cancian, Francesca M. 1975. *What are Norms?* Cambridge: Cambridge University Press.

Cartwright, Nancy 1999. *The Dappled World: A Study of the Boundaries of Science*. Cambridge: Cambridge University Press.

Casson, Mark 1991. *The Economics of Business Culture*. Oxford: Clarendon Press.

Catterall, Miriam, Pauline Maclaran and Lorna Stevens 2000. *Marketing and Feminism: Current Issues and Research*. London: Routledge.

Cauley, Jon, and Todd Sandler 1980. 'A general theory of interpersonal exchange', *Public Choice* 35: 587–606.

Center for Career Development in Early Care and Education 2000. *Briefing Booklet: Advance Reading for Sept. 14, 2000*. Wheelock College, Boston.

Cetina, Karin Knorr, and Urs Bruegger 2002. 'Global microstructures: the virtual societies of financial markets', *American Journal of Sociology* 107(4): 905–50.

Chadwick-Jones, John K. 1986. 'Social exchange, social psychology and economics', in MacFadyen and MacFadyen (eds.), *Economic Psychology: Intersections in Theory and Applications*. Amsterdam: North-Holland, 249–67.

Chaminade, Thierry, and Jean Decety 2003. 'Neural correlates of feeling sympathy', *Neuropsychologia*, special issue on 'Social cognition' 41(2): 127–38.

Chillemi, Ottorino, and Benedetto Gui 1997. 'Team human capital and worker mobility', *Journal of Labor Economics* 15(4): 567–85.

Cialdini, Robert B. 1993. *Influence: Science and Practice*. New York: HarperCollins.

Cialdini, Robert B., Carl A. Kallgren and Raymond R. Reno 1991. 'A focus theory of normative conduct', *Advances in Experimental Social Psychology* 24: 201–34.

Clotfelter, Charles T. 1985. *Federal Tax Policy and Charitable Giving*. Chicago: University of Chicago Press.

Coate, Stephen, and Martin Ravallion 1993. 'Reciprocity without commitment: characterization and performance of informal insurance arrangements', *Journal of Development Economics* 40(1): 1–24.

Cohen, Don, and Laurence Prusak 2001. *In Good Company: How Social Capital Makes Organizations Work*. Boston: Harvard Business School Press.

Colander, David, and Arjo Klamer 1987. 'The making of an economist', *Journal of Economic Perspectives* 1(2): 95–111.

Coleman, James S. 1988. 'Social capital in the creation of human capital', *American Journal of Sociology* 94(supplement): 95–120.

1990. *Foundations of Social Theory*. Cambridge, MA and London: The Belknap Press of Harvard University Press.

Collard, David 1978. *Altruism and Economy*. Oxford: Martin Robertson and Co. Ltd.

Commons, John R. 1934. *Institutional Economics: Its Place in Political Economy*. London: Macmillan.

Connolly, Laura S. 1997. 'Does external funding of academic research crowd out institutional support?', *Journal of Public Economics* 64: 389–406.

Connolly, Sara, and Alistair Munro 1999. *Economics of the Public Sector*. London: Prentice Hall Europe.

Conrad, Joseph 1998 [1909]. *Under Western Eyes*. On-line edition: www.bibliomania.com.

Cooper, Russel, and Andrew John 1988. 'Coordinating coordination failures in Keynesian models', *Quarterly Journal of Economics* 103(3): 441–63.

Corneo, Giacomo 2001. *Work and Television*. Discussion Paper no. 376, Institute for the Study of Labor, Bonn.

Corneo, Giacomo, and Olivier Jeanne 1999a. 'Segmented communication and fashionable behavior', *Journal of Economic Behavior and Organization* 39: 371–85.

1999b. 'Social organization in an endogenous growth model', *International Economic Review* 40(3): 711–25.

Cornes, Richard, and Todd Sandler 1984. 'Easy riders, joint production and public goods', *Economic Journal* 94: 580–98.

1986. *The Theory of Externalities, Public Goods and Club Goods*. Cambridge: Cambridge University Press.

Cowan, Robin, William Cowan and Peter Swan 1997. 'A model of demand with interactions among consumers', *International Journal of Industrial Organization* 15: 711–32.

Cox, Donald, and Mark R. Rank 1992. 'Inter-vivos transfers and intergenerational exchange', *Review of Economics and Statistics* 74(2): 305–14.

Croson, Rachel T. A. 1996. *Contributions to Public Goods: Altruism or Reciprocity?* Working Paper no. 96–08–01, Wharton Risk Management and Decision Processes Center, University of Pennsylvania.

Dasgupta, Partha 1988. 'Trust as a commodity', in Gambetta (ed.), *Trust: Making Cooperative Relations*. Oxford: Basil Blackwell, 49–72.

Dasgupta, Partha, and Ismail Serageldin (eds.) 1999. *Social Capital: A Multifaceted Perspective*. Washington, DC: World Bank.

David, Paul A. 1985. 'Clio and the economics of QWERTY', *American Economic Association Papers and Proceedings* 75(2): 332–7.

Davis, Douglas D., and Charles A. Holt 1993. *Experimental Economics*. Princeton, NJ: Princeton University Press.

Davis, John 2003. *The Theory of the Individual in Economics: Identity and Value*. London: Routledge.

Dawes, Robyn M., and Richard H. Thaler 1988. 'Anomalies: cooperation', *Journal of Economic Perspectives* 2: 187–97.

Dawes, Robyn M., Jeanne McTavish and Harriet Shaklee 1977. 'Behaviour, communication and assumptions about other people's behaviour in a Commons dilemma situation', *Journal of Personality and Social Psychology* 35: 1–11.

de Mello, Luiz 2000. 'Can fiscal decentralization strengthen social capital?', in Working Paper wp/00/129, International Monetary Fund, 1–31.

Demsetz, Harold 1988. 'The structure of ownership and the theory of the firm', in Demsetz (ed.), *Ownership, Control and the Firm*. Oxford: Basil Blackwell, 187–201.

Descartes, René 1965. 'Works', in Adam and Tannery (eds.), *Oeuvres de Descartes*. Paris: Vrin, 13 volumes.

de Waal, Frans 1996. *Good Natured: The Origins of Right and Wrong in Humans and Other Animals*. Cambridge, MA: Harvard University Press.

DiPasquale, Denise, and Edward L. Glaeser 1999. 'Incentives and social capital: are homeowners better citizens?', *Journal of Urban Economics* 45: 354–84.

Disney, Richard, Alissa Goodman, Amanda Gosling and Chris Trinder 1998. *Public Pay in Britain in the 1990s*. Commentary no. 72, Institute for Fiscal Studies, London.

Diwan, Romesh 2000. 'Relational wealth and the quality of life', *Journal of Socio-Economics* 29: 305–40.

Djajic, Slobodan, and Ross Milbourne 1988. 'A general equilibrium model of guest-worker migration', *Journal of International Economics* 25: 335–51.

Dufwenberg, Martin, and Uri Gneezy 2000. 'Measuring beliefs in an experimental lost wallet game', *Games and Economic Behavior* 30: 163–82.

Dufwenberg, Martin, and Georg Kirchsteiger 1998. *A Theory of Sequential Reciprocity*. Discussion Paper no. 37, University of Tilburg, Netherlands.

Durlauf, Steven N. 2002. 'Bowling alone: a review essay', *Journal of Economic Behavior and Organization* 47(3): 259–73.

Dustmann, Christian 1997. 'Return migration, uncertainty and precautionary savings', *Journal of Development Economics* 52(2): 295–315.

Easterlin, Richard 2002. *Happiness in Economics*. Cheltenham: The International Library of Critical Writings in Economics, Edward Elgar.

Eckel, Catherine, and Philip Grossman 1996. 'Altruism in anonymous dictator games', *Games and Economic Behavior* 16: 181–91.

Economist, The 2002. 24–30 August: 50.

Edgeworth, Francis Ysidro 1967 [1881]. *Mathematical Psychics*. London: Kegan. 1970 [1891]. *Papers Related to Political Economy*. New York: Burt Franklin, 3 volumes.

Edwards, Richard, David M. Gordon and Michael Reich 1982. *Segmented Work, Divided Workers*. Cambridge: Cambridge University Press.

Edwards, Richard, and Arthur MacEwan 1970. 'A radical approach to economics: basis for a new curriculum', *American Economic Review* 60(2): 352–63.

Einarsen, Stal 1999. 'The nature and causes of bullying at work', *International Journal of Manpower* 20(1–2): 16–27.

Elster, John 1983. *Sour Grapes: Studies in the Subversion of Rationality*. Cambridge: Cambridge University Press.
1989. *The Cement of Society*. Cambridge: Cambridge University Press.

England, Paula 1992. *Comparable Worth: Theories and Evidence*. New York: Aldine de Gruyter.

Fafchamps, Marcel, and Bart Minten 2002. 'Returns to social network capital among traders', *Oxford Economic Papers* 54(2): 173–206.

Falk, Armin, and Urs Fischbacher 1998. *A Theory of Reciprocity*. Discussion paper, University of Zurich.

2001. 'Distributional consequences and intentions in a model of reciprocity', *Annales d'économie et de statistique* 63–64: 111–30.

Fehr, Ernst, and Urs Fischbacher 2002. 'The impact of non-selfish motives on competition, cooperation and incentives', *Economic Journal* 112: C1–33.

Fehr, Ernst, and Simon Gächter 1998a. 'How effective are trust- and reciprocity-based incentives?', in Ben-Ner and Putterman (eds.), *Economics, Values and Organisation*. Cambridge and New York: Cambridge University Press, 337–63.

1998b. 'Reciprocity and economics: the economic implications of Homo reciprocans', *European Economic Review* 42: 845–59.

2000. 'Cooperation and punishment in public good experiments', *American Economic Review* 90(4): 980–94.

Fehr, Ernst, Simon Gächter and Georg Kirchsteiger 1997. 'Reciprocity as a contract enforcement device', *Econometrica* 65(4): 833–60.

Fehr, Ernst, and Klaus M. Schmidt 1999. 'A theory of fairness, competition and cooperation', *Quarterly Journal of Economics* 114: 817–68.

Ferber, Marianne A., and Julie A. Nelson (eds.) 1993. *Beyond Economic Man: Feminist Theory and Economics*. Chicago: University of Chicago Press.

(eds.) 2003. *Feminist Economics Today: Beyond Economic Man*. Chicago: University of Chicago Press.

Ferrara, Francesco 1934 [1849–51]. *Lezioni di economia politica*. Bologna: Zanichelli, 2 volumes.

Festinger, Leon 1957. *A Theory of Cognitive Dissonance*. Stanford, CA: Stanford University Press.

Fine, Ben 2001. *Social Capital versus Social Theory: Political Economy and Social Science at the Turn of the Millennium*. London: Routledge.

Fischbacher, Urs, Simon Gächter and Ernst Fehr 2001. 'Are people conditionally cooperative? Evidence from a public goods experiment', *Economics Letters* 71: 397–404.

Flap, Henk, and Beate Volker 2001. 'Goal-specific social capital and job satisfaction: effects of different types of networks on instrumental and social aspects of work', *Social Networks* 23: 297–320.

Foa, Uriel G. 1993. 'Interpersonal and economic resources', in U. G. Foa, Converse, Törnblom and E. B. Foa (eds.), *Resource Theory: Explorations and Applications*. San Diego: Academic Press, 13–30.

Folbre, Nancy, and Julie A. Nelson 2000. 'For love or money – or both?', *Journal of Economic Perspectives* 14(4): 123–40.

Fontaine, Philippe 1997. 'Identification and economic behavior: sympathy and empathy in historical perspective', *Economic and Philosophy* 13: 264–8.

Forsythe, Robert, Joel L. Horowitz, N. E. Savin and Martin Sefton 1994. 'Fairness in simple bargaining experiments', *Games and Economic Behavior* 6: 347–69.

Fox, Jonathan, and John Gershman 2000. 'The World Bank and social capital: lessons from ten rural development projects in the Philippines and Mexico', *Policy Science* 33: 399–419.

Frank, Robert H. 1985. *Choosing the Right Pond: Human Behaviour and the Quest for Status*. Oxford: Oxford University Press.

1988. *Passions within Reason: The Strategic Role of the Emotions*. New York: Norton.

1991. 'Positional externalities', in Zeckhauser (ed.), *Strategy and Choice*. Cambridge, MA: MIT Press, 25–47.

1997. 'The frame of reference as a public good', *Economic Journal* 107(6): 1832–47.

Frankfurt, Harry Gordon 1971. 'Freedom of the will and the concept of a person', *Journal of Philosophy* 68: 5–20.

Freeman, Richard B. 1997. 'Working for nothing: the supply of volunteer labor', *Journal of Labor Economics* 15(1): S140–66.

Frey, Bruno S. 1997. *Not Just for the Money: An Economic Theory of Personal Motivation*. Cheltenham, UK, and Lyme, NH: Edward Elgar.

1998. 'Institutions and morale: the crowding-out effect', in Ben-Ner and Putterman (eds.), *Economics, Values and Organisation*. Cambridge, New York: Cambridge University Press, 437–60.

Friedberg, Erhard 1993. *Le pouvoir et la règle*. Paris: Seuil.

Frijters, Paul 2000. 'The sale of relational capital through tenure profiles and tournaments', *Labour Economics* 7: 373–84.

Frohlich, Norman, and Joe Oppenheimer 1998. 'Some consequences of e-mail vs. face to face communication in experiment', *Journal of Economic Behavior and Organization* 35: 389–403.

Gächter, Simon and Ernst Fehr 1999. 'Collective action as social exchange', *Journal of Economic Behavior and Organizaion* 39: 341–69.

Gambetta, Diego (ed.) 1988. *Trust: Making and Breaking Cooperative Relations*. Oxford: Basil Blackwell.

1993. *The Sicilian Mafia: The Business of Private Protection*. Cambridge, MA: Harvard University Press.

Geanakoplos, John, David Pearce, and Ennio Stacchetti 1989. 'Psychological games and sequential rationality', *Games and Economic Behavior* 1(1): 60–79.

Geary, Robert Charles 1950. 'A note on "A constant-utility index of the cost of living"', *Review of Economic Studies* 18: 65–6.

Genovesi, Antonio 1963. *Autobiografia e lettere*. Milan: Feltrinelli.

1973 [1766]. *Della diceosina o sia della filosofia del giusto e dell'onesto per gli giovanetti*. Milan: Marzorati.

Gérard-Varet, Louis-André, Serge-Christophe Kolm and Jean Mercier-Ythier (eds.) 2000. *The Economics of Reciprocity, Giving and Altruism*. London and New York: Macmillan and St. Martin's Press.

Geschiere, Peter 1995. 'Working groups or wage labour? Cash crops, reciprocity and money among the Maka of southeastern Cameroon', *Development and Change* 26(3): 503–23.

Gibbons, Robert 1998. 'Incentives in organizations', *Journal of Economic Perspectives* 12(4): 115–32.

Gilbert, Margaret 1989. *On Social Facts*. London: Routledge.

Gilligan, Carol 1982. *In A Different Voice: Psychological Theory and Women's Development*. Cambridge, MA: Harvard University Press.

Gintis, Herbert 1976. 'The nature of labor exchange and the theory of capitalist production', *Review of Radical Political Economy* 8(2): 36–54.

Glaeser, Edward L., David Laibson and Bruce Sacerdote 2002. 'The economic approach to social capital', *Economic Journal* 112: 437–58.

Glaeser, Edward L., David Laibson, José A. Sheinkman and Christine L. Soutter 2000. 'Measuring trust', *Quarterly Journal of Economics* 65: 811–46.

Glaeser, Edward L., Bruce Sacerdote and José A. Sheinkman 1996. 'Crime and social interactions', *Quarterly Journal of Economics* 111: 507–48.

Glaeser, Edward L., and José A. Sheinkman 2000. *Non-market Interactions*, Working Paper 8053, National Bureau of Economic Research, Cambridge, Massachusetts.

Goffman, Erwing 1961. *Encounters: Two Studies in the Sociology of Interaction.* Indianapolis: Bobbs-Merrill.

Good, David 1988. 'Individuals, interpersonal relations and trust', in Gambetta (ed.), *Trust: Making and Breaking Cooperative Relations.* Oxford: Basil Blackwell, 31–48.

Goodfriend, Marvin, and John McDermott 1995. 'Early development', *American Economic Review* 85(1): 116–33.

Gossen, Hermann Heinrich 1981 [1854]. *The Laws of Human Relations.* Cambridge, MA: MIT Press.

Granovetter, Mark 1973. 'The strength of weak ties', *American Journal of Sociology* 78(6): 1360–80.

1974. *Getting a Job: A Study of Contacts and Careers.* Cambridge, MA: Harvard University Press.

1978. 'Threshold models of collective behavior', *American Journal of Sociology* 83(6): 1420–43.

1985. 'Economic action and social structure: the problem of embeddedness', *American Journal of Sociology* 91(3): 481–510.

1990. 'The old and the new economic sociology: a history and an agenda', in Friedland and Robertson (eds.), *Beyond the Marketplace: Rethinking Economy and Society.* New York: Aldine de Gruyter, 89–112.

1992. 'Economic institutions as social constructions: a framework for analysis', *Acta Sociologica* 35: 3–11.

2000. *Au delà du marché.* Paris: Desclée de Brouwer.

Granovetter, Mark, and Patrick McGuire 1998. 'The making of an industry: electricity in the United States', in Callon (ed.), *The Law of Markets.* Oxford: Blackwell, 147–73.

Grilo, Isabel, and Jacques F. Thisse 1999. 'Engouement collectif et concurrence', *Revue Economique* 50(3): 593–600.

Gui, Benedetto 1988. 'Eléments pour une definition d'économie communautaire', *Notes et documents de l'institut international Jacques Maritain* 19/20, 32–42.

1996. 'On relational goods: strategic implications of investment in relationships', *International Journal of Social Economics* 23(10/11): 260–78.

2000a. 'Beyond transactions: on the interpersonal dimension of economic reality', in Gui (ed.), *Annals of Public and Cooperative Economics,* special issue on 'Economics and interpersonal relations' 71(2): 139–69.

2000b. 'Economics and interpersonal relations: introduction', in Gui (ed.), *Annals of Public and Cooperative Economics*, special issue on 'Economics and interpersonal relations' 71(2): 133–8.

(ed.) 2000c. *Annals of Public and Cooperative Economics*, special issue on 'Economics and interpersonal relations' 71(2).

Gunnthorsdottir, Anna, Daniel Houser, Kevin McCabe and Holly Ameden 2002. *Disposition, History and Contributions in a Public Goods Experiment*. Unpublished manuscript, Department of Economics and Economic Science Laboratory, University of Arizona.

Güth, Werner 1995. 'An evolutionary approach to explaining cooperative behavior by reciprocal incentives', *International Journal of Game Theory* 24: 323–44.

Güth, Werner, Peter Ockenfels and Markus Wendel 1997. 'Cooperation based on trust: an experimental investigation', *Journal of Economic Psychology* 18 (1): 15–63.

Hammer, Michael 1995. *The Reengineering Revolution*. London: HarperCollins.

Hammond, Peter J. 1975. 'Charity: altruism or egoism?', in Phelps (ed.), *Altruism, Morality and Economic Theory*. New York: Russell Sage Foundation Publications, 115–31.

Hansmann, Henry 1980. 'The role of nonprofit enterprise', *Yale Law Journal* 89 (5): 835–901.

1986. 'A theory of status organizations', *Journal of Law, Economics, and Organization* 2(1): 119–30.

1989. *Politics and Markets in the Organization of the Firm*. Inaugural lecture for the Sam Harris Professorship, Yale Law School, New Haven, Connecticut.

Hardin, Russell 1993. 'The street-level epistemology of trust', *Politics and Society*, 21(4): 505–29.

2001. *Trust and Trustworthiness*. New York: Russell Sage Foundation Publications.

Hargreaves Heap, Shaun 1989. *Rationality in Economics*. Cambridge: Cambridge University Press.

1997. *When Norms Influence Behaviour: Expressive Reason and its Consequences*. Paper prepared for the Freiberg Symposium on 'Abandoning the hypothesis of omniscience in economics', 9–10 January 1997.

Hargreaves Heap, Shaun, Martin Hollis, Bruce Lyons, Robert Sugden and Albert Weale 1992. *The Theory of Choice*. Oxford: Basil Blackwell.

Harsanyi, John 1955. 'Cardinal welfare, individualistic ethics and interpersonal comparisons of utility', *Journal of Political Economy* 63: 309–21.

Harvey, James S. 2002. 'The trust paradox: a survey of economic inquiries into the nature of trust and trustworthiness', *Journal of Economic Behavior and Organization* 47(3): 291–307.

Hausman, Daniel 1998. *Fairness and Trust in Game Theory*. Mimeo, London School of Economics.

Helper, Susan, Elliot Bendoly and David I. Levine 1999. *Employee Involvement and Pay at U.S. and Canadian Auto Suppliers*. Working Paper no. 71, Institute of Industrial Relations, University of California, Berkeley.

Herzberg, Frederick 1966. *Work and the Nature of Man*. Cleveland and New York: The World Publishing Company.

Hicks, John R., 1939. *Value and Capital*. Oxford: Oxford University Press.

Hicks, John R., and Roy G. D. Allen 1934. 'A reconsideration of the theory of value', *Economica* 1: 52–76; 196–219.

Hirsch, Fred 1976. *Social Limits to Growth*. Cambridge, MA: Harvard University Press.

Hirschleifer, David 1995. 'Social influence, information cascades and fads', in Tommasi and Ierulli (eds.), *The New Economics of Human Behaviour*. Cambridge: Cambridge University Press.

Hirschleifer, Jack 1978. 'Natural economy versus political economy', *Journal of Social and Biological Structures* 1: 319–37.

Hirschleifer, Jack, and John G. Riley 1992. *The Analytics of Uncertainty and Information*. Cambridge: Cambridge University Press.

Hobbes, Thomas 1965 [1651]. *Leviathan*. Reprinted with an essay by W. G. Pogson Smith. Oxford: Clarendon Press.

Hoffman, Elizabeth, Kevin McCabe, Keith Shachat and Vernon Smith 1994. 'Preferences, property rights, and anonymity in bargaining games', *Games and Economic Behavior* 7: 346–80.

Hoffman, Elisabeth, Kevin McCabe and Vernon L. Smith 1996. 'Social distance and other-regarding behavior in dictator games', *American Economic Review* 86(3): 653–60.

Hollander, Heinz 1990. 'A social exchange approach to voluntary cooperation', *American Economic Review* 80(4): 1157–67.

Hollis, Martin 1998. *Trust within Reason*. Cambridge: Cambridge University Press.

Hollis, Martin, and Robert Sugden 1993. 'Rationality in action', *Mind* January: 1–34.

Homans, George C. 1954. 'The cash posters', *American Sociological Review* 19: 724–33.

Hont, Istvan, and Michael Ignatief 1983. *Wealth and Virtue: The Shaping of Political Economy in the Scottish Enlightenment*. Cambridge: Cambridge University Press.

Horsburgh, H. J. N. 1960. 'The ethics of trust', *Philosophical Quarterly* 10: 343–54.

Hume, David 1978 [1739]. *A Treatise of Human Nature*. New York: Oxford University Press.

2001 [1751]. *An Enquiry Concerning the Principles of Morals*. Project Gutenberg, on-line edition, www.gutenberg.net/etext06/8echu10h.htm.

Hurley, Susan L. 1989. *Natural Reasons*. New York: Oxford University Press.

Hutcheson, Francis 1971 [1725]. 'An inquiry into the original of our ideas of beauty and virtue', in *Collected Works of Francis Hutcheson*. Hildesheim, Germany: Olms, Vol. I.

Iannaccone, Laurence R. 1992. 'Sacrifice and stigma: reducing free riding in cults, communes, and other collectives', *Journal of Political Economy* 100(2): 271–91.

Independent 2002. 16 May: 9.

Ireland, Norman 1994. 'On limiting the market for status signals', *Journal of Public Economics* 53: 91–110.

Isaac, R. Mark, and James M. Walker 1988. 'Communication and free-riding behaviour: the voluntary contributions mechanism', *Economic Inquiry* 26: 585–608.

1998. 'Nash as an organising principle in the voluntary provision of public goods: experimental evidence', *Experimental Economics* 1: 191–206.

Isaac, R. Mark, James M. Walker and Susan H. Thomas 1984. 'Divergent evidence on free-riding: an experimental investigation of possible explanations', *Public Choice* 43: 113–49.

Jap, Sandy, and Erin Anderson 1998. *Vilification: Dysfunctional Dynamics in Interorganizational Collaborations*. Working Paper 99/06/MKT, INSEAD, Fontainebleau, France.

Jevons, William Stanley 1879. *The Theory of Political Economy*. London: Macmillan, 2nd edn.

Johnson, Paul A., and Jonathan Temple 1998. 'Social capability and economic growth', *Quarterly Journal of Economics* 113(3): 965–90.

Jones, Karen 1996. 'Trust as an affective attitude', *Ethics*, 107: 4–25.

Jones, Stephen R. G. 1984. *The Economics of Conformism*. Oxford: Basil Blackwell.

Jussim, Lee 1986. 'Self-fulfilling prophecies: a theoretical and integrative review', *Psychological Review* 93: 429–45.

Kahneman, Daniel, and Amos Tversky (eds.) 2000. *Choices, Values, and Frames*. Cambridge: Cambridge University Press.

Kant, Immanuel 1991 [1797]. *The Metaphysic of Morals*, [translated by Gregor]. Cambridge: Cambridge University Press.

Kelley, Harold H. 1986. 'Personal relationships: their nature and significance', in Gilmour and Duck (eds.), *The Emerging Field of Personal Relationships*. Hillsdale, NJ: Lawrence Erlbaum Associates, 3–19.

Keser, Claudia 1996. 'Voluntary contributions to public goods when partial contribution is a dominant strategy', *Economics Letters* 50: 359–66.

Khanna, Jyoti, John Posnett, and Todd Sandler 1995. 'Charity donations in the UK: new evidence based on panel data', *Journal of Public Economics* 56: 257–72.

Kirman, Alan 1997. 'The economy as an evolving network', *Journal of Evolutionary Economics* 7: 339–53.

Klein, Benjamin, Robert G. Crawford and Armen A. Alchian 1978. 'Vertical integration, appropriable rents, and the competitive contracting process', *Journal of Law and Economics* 21(2): 297–326.

Kolm, Serge-Christophe, 1981a. 'Altruisme et efficacité': le sophisme de Rousseau', *Social Science Information* 20: 293–344.

1981b. 'Efficacité et altruisme: le sophisme de Mandeville, Smith et Pareto', *Revue Economique* 1: 5–31.

1983. 'Altruism and efficiency', *Ethics* 94: 18–65. [Reprinted in Zamagni (ed.), *The Economics of Altruism*. Cheltenham: Edward Elgar.]

1984. *La bonne économie: la reciprocité générale*. Paris: Presses Universitaire de France.

1996. *Modern Theories of Justice*. Cambridge, MA: MIT Press.

1998. *Justice and Equity*. Cambridge, MA: MIT Press, [English translation of *Justice et équité*, 1971].

2000. 'The theory of reciprocity', in Gérard-Varet, Kolm and Mercier-Ythier (eds.), *The Economics of Reciprocity, Giving and Altruism*. London and New York: Macmillan and St. Martin's Press, 15–141.

2005. 'Reciprocity: its scope, rationales, and consequences', in Gérard-Varet, Kolm and Mercier-Ythier (eds.), *Handbook on the Economics of Giving, Reciprocity and Altruism*. Amsterdam: NorthHolland, ch. 2.

Kramer, Roderick M., and Lisa Goldman 1995. 'Helping the group or helping yourself? Social motives and group identity in resource dilemmas', in Schroeder (ed.), *Social Dilemmas: Perspectives on Individuals and Groups*. Westport, CT: Praeger, 49–67.

Kramer, Roderick M., and Tom R. Tyler (eds.) 1995. *Trust in Organisations: Frontiers of Theory and Research*. Thousand Oaks, CA: Sage.

Kranton, Rachel E., and Deborah F. Minehart 2001. 'A theory of buyer–seller networks', *American Economic Review* 91(3): 485–508.

Kreps, David M., Paul Robert Milgrom, John Roberts and Robert Wilson 1982. 'Rational cooperation in the finitely repeated prisoner's dilemma', *Journal of Economic Theory* 27: 245–52.

Kurz, Mordecai 1978. 'Altruism as an outcome of social interaction', *Journal of Public Economics* 36: 369–86.

1979. 'Altruism equilibrium', in Balassa and Nelson (eds.), *Economic Progress, Private Values, and Policy*. Amsterdam: North-Holland, 177–200.

Laband, David N., and Bernard F. Lentz, 1998. 'The effects of sexual harassment on job satisfaction, earnings, and turnover among female lawyers', *Industrial and Labor Relations Review* 51(4): 594–607.

Lalonde, Richard N., and Randy A. Silverman 1994. 'Behavioural preferences in response to social injustice: the effects of group permeability and social identity salience', *Journal of Personality and Social Psychology* 66: 78–85.

Lane, Christel, and Reinhard Bachmann (eds.) 1998. *Trust Within and Between Organisations*. Oxford: Oxford University Press.

Lea, Stephen E. G., Roger M. Tarpy and Paul Webley 1987. *The Individual in the Economy*. Cambridge: Cambridge University Press.

Ledyard, John O. 1995. 'Public goods: a survey of experimental research', in Roth and Kagel (eds.), *The Handbook of Experimental Economics*. Princeton, NJ: Princeton University Press, 111–81.

Leibenstein, Harvey 1979. 'A branch of economics is missing: micro-micro theory', *Journal of Economic Literature* 17(2): 477–502.

Leijonhufvud, Axel 1973. 'Life among the econ', *Western Economic Journal* 11: 327–37.

Ley, Eduardo 1997. 'Optimal provision of public goods with altruistie individuals', *Economics Letters* 54(1): 23–7.

Liebrand, Wim G. B., R. W. T. L. Jansen and V. M. Rijken, 1986. 'Might over morality: social values and the perception of other players in experimental games', *Journal of Experimental Social Psychology* 22: 203–15.

Liebrand, Wim G. B., Henk A. M. Wilke, Rob Vogel and Fred J. M. Wolters 1986. 'Value orientation and conformity', *Journal of Conflict Resolution* 30: 77–97.

Liu, Michel 1981. 'Technologie, organisation du travail et comportement des salariés', *Revue française de sociologie* 22: 205–21.

Loewenstein, George 2000. 'Emotions in economic theory and economic behavior', *American Economic Review* 90(2): 426–32.

Macaulay, J., and L. Berkowitz (eds.) 1970. *Altruism and Helping Behavior.* New York: Academic Press.

Mackenzie, Catriona, and Natalie Stoljar (eds.) 2000. *Relational Autonomy: Feminist Perspectives on Autonomy, Agency, and the Social Self.* New York: Oxford University Press.

Macneil, Ian R. 1987. 'Relational contract theory as sociology: a reply to Professors Lindenberg and de Vos', *Journal of Institutional and Theoretical Economics* 143: 272–90.

Mailath, George, and Andrew Postlewaite 1990. 'Workers versus firms: bargaining over a firm's value', *Review of Economic Studies* 57(3): 369–80.

Malthus, Thomas Robert 1966 [1798]. *Essay on the Principle of Population.* London: Macmillan.

1986 [1820]. 'Principles of political economy', in Wrigley and Souden (eds.), *The Works of Thomas Robert Malthus.* London: W. Pickering, Vol. V.

Manski, Charles F. 2000. 'Economic analysis of social interactions', *Journal of Economic Perspectives* 4(3): 115–36.

Marglin, Stephen 1974. 'What do bosses do? The origins and functions of hierarchy in capitalist production', *Review of Radical Political Economics* 6(2): 60–112.

Margolis, Howard 1982. *Selfishness, Altruism and Rationality: A Theory of Social Choice.* Cambridge: Cambridge University Press.

Marshall, Alfred 1927 [1919]. *Industry and Trade.* London: Macmillan.

1946 [1890]. *Principles of Economics.* London: Macmillan.

Marx, Karl 1906 [1867]. *Capital: A Critical Analysis of Capitalist Production.* London: Engels, Sonnenschein & Co.

1994 [1857–8]. *Grundrisse: Foundations of the Critique of Political Economy,* reprinted (the first three sections) in Hausman (ed.), *The Philosophy of Economics.* Cambridge: Cambridge University Press, 119–42.

Masclet, David, Charles Noussair, Steven Tucker and Marie-Claire Villeval 2003. 'Monetary and nonmonetary punishment in the voluntary contributions mechanism', *American Economic Review* 93(1): 366–80.

Mauss, Marcel 1995. *Sociologie et anthropologie.* Paris: PUF.

McGuire, Patrick, Mark Granovetter and Michael Schwartz 1993. 'Thomas Edison and the social construction of the early electricity industry in America', in Swedberg (ed.), *Explorations in Economic Sociology.* New York: Russell Sage Foundation Publications, 213–46.

Meade, James E. 1973. *The Theory of Economic Externalities: The Control of Environmental Pollution and Similar Social Cost.* Leiden, Netherlands: Nijhoff.

Ménard, Claude 1990. *L'économie des organisations.* Paris: La Découverte.

1994. 'Organizations as coordinating devices', *Metroeconomica* 45(3): 224–47.

References 287

Menchik, Paul L., and Burton A. Weisbrod 1987. 'Volunteer labor supply', *Journal of Public Economics* 32(2): 159–83.

Menger, Carl 1871. *Grundsätze der Volkswirtschaftslehre.* Vienna: Braumüller.

Michael, Robert T., and Gary S. Becker 1973. 'On the new theory of consumer behavior', *Swedish Journal of Economics* 75: 378–96.

Mill, John S. 1848. *Principles of Political Economy.* London: John W. Parker.

1897 [1836]. *Early Essays.* London: George Bell and Sons.

Miller, Nancy J. 2001. 'Contributions of social capital theory in predicting rural community inshopping behavior', *Journal of Socio-Economics* 30: 475–93.

Mirowski, P. 1999. 'Review of *A Beautiful Mind*, by S. Nasar', *Economics and Philosophy* 15: 302–7.

Mirvis, Philip H., and Edward J. Hackett 1983. 'Work and workforce characteristics in the nonprofit sector', *Monthly Labour Review* 106(4): 3–12.

Misztal, Barbara A. 1996. *Trust in Modern Societies.* Cambridge: Polity Press.

Mocan, Naci H., and Deborah Viola 1997. *The Determinants of Child Care Workers' Wages Compensation: Sectoral Difference, Human Capital, Race, Insiders and Outsiders.* Working Paper 6328, National Bureau of Economic Research, Cambridge, Massachusetts.

Modigliani, Kathy 1993. *Child Care as an Occupation in a Culture of Indifference.* Dissertation, Wheelock College, Boston.

Mosca, Manuela, Marco Musella and Francesco Pastore 2003. *Compensation Mechanism and Firm Performance in Italy's Nonprofit Sector.* Mimeo, Faculty of Economics, University of Naples 'Federico II'.

Moscovici, Serge 1985. 'Social influence and conformity', in Gardner and Aronson (eds.), *The Handbook of Social Psychology.* New York: Random House, Vol. II, 347–412.

Moss, M. K., and R. A. Page 1972. 'Reinforcement and helping behavior', *Journal of Applied Psychology* 2: 360–71.

Nelson, Julie A. 1994. 'I, thou, and them: capabilities, altruism, and norms in the economics of marriage', *American Economic Review* 84(2): 126–31.

1996. *Feminism, Objectivity, and Economics.* London: Routledge.

1999. 'Of markets and martyrs: is it OK to pay well for care?', *Feminist Economics* 5(3): 43–59.

2003. 'Separative and soluble firms: androcentric bias in business ethics', in Ferber and Nelson (eds.), *Feminist Economics Today: Beyond Economic Man.* Chicago: University of Chicago Press, 81–99.

Nelson, Julie A., and Paula England 2002. 'Feminist philosophies of love and work', *Hypatia: A Journal of Feminist Philosophy* 17(2): 1–18.

Ng, Yew-Kwang 1975. 'Non-economic activities, indirect externalities, and third-best policies', *Kyklos* 28(3): 507–25.

Nicole, Pierre 1675. *Essais de morale.* Paris.

Nohria, Nitin 1992. 'Introduction: is a network perspective a useful way of studying organizations?', in Nohria and Eccles (eds.), *Networks and Organizations: Structure, Form, and Action.* Boston: Harvard Business School Press, 1–22.

Normann, Richard 1984. *Service Management: Strategy and Leadership in Service Business.* Chichester: John Wiley and Sons.

Nussbaum, Martha C. 1986. 'The vulnerability of the good human life: relational goods', in *The Fragility of Goodness: Luck and Ethics in Greek Tragedy and Philosophy*. Cambridge and New York: Cambridge University Press, 343–72.

Olson, Mancur 1965. *The Logic of Collective Action*. Cambridge, MA.: Harvard University Press.

Ones, Umut, and Louis Putterman 2004. *The Ecology of Collective Action: A Public Goods and Sanctions Experiment with Controlled Group Formation.* Working Paper no. 2004–01, Department of Economics, Brown University, Providence, Rhode Island.

Orbell, John M., Robyn Dawes, and Alphons van de Kragt 1988. 'Explaining discussion-induced cooperation', *Journal of Personality and Social Psychology* 54(5): 811–19.

O'Reilly, Charles A., and Jeffrey Pfeffer 2000. *Hidden Value: How Great Companies Achieve Extraordinary Results with Ordinary People.* Boston: Harvard Business School Press.

Orléan, André 1995. 'Bayesian interactions and collective dynamics of opinion: herd behavior and mimetic contagion', *Journal of Economic Behavior and Organizations* 28: 257–74.

   1998. 'Informational influences and the ambivalence of imitation', in Lesourne and Orléan (eds.), *Advances in Self-organization and Evolutionary Economics*. Paris: Economica, 39–56.

Ortmann, Andreas, Kathleen M. Hansberry and John M. Fitzgerald 1997. *Voluntary Contributions to a Public Good when Partial Contribution is a Dominant Strategy*. Discussion paper, Bowdoin College, Brunswick Maine.

Ostrom, Elinor 1990. *Governing the Commons: The Evolution of Institutions for Collective Action*. Cambridge: Cambridge University Press.

   2003. *Reciprocity and Trust*. New York: Russell Sage Foundation Publications.

Oswald, Andrew 1997. 'Happiness and economic performance', *Economic Journal* 107: 1815–31.

Page, Talbot, Louis Putterman and Bulent Unel (forthcoming). 'Voluntary association in public goods experiments: reciprocity, mimicry, and efficiency', *Economic Journal*.

Paldam, Martin 2000. 'Social capital: one or many? Definition and measurement', *Journal of Economic Surveys* 14(5): 629–53.

Palfrey, Tom R., and Jeffrey E. Prisbey 1996. 'Altruism, reputation and noise in linear public goods experiments', *Journal of Public Economics* 61: 409–27.

Pantaleoni, Maffeo 1889. *Principii di economia pura*. Florence: Barbera. [English translation: 1898. *Pure Economics*. London: Macmillan.]

   1925. *Erotemi di economia*. Bari, Laterza, 2 volumes.

Paquè, Karl Heinz 1982. *Do Public Transfers 'Crowd Out' Private Charitable Giving? Some Econometric Evidence for the Federal Republic of Germany*, Working Paper no.152, Kiel University.

Pareto, Vilfredo 1896–7. *Cours d'économie politique professé à l'Université de Lausanne*. Lausanne: Rouge, 2 volumes.

   1900a. 'Sunto di alcuni capitoli di un nuovo trattato di economia politica del Prof. Pareto', *Giornale degli economisti* 10: 216–35; 511–49.

1900b. 'Sul fenomeno economico: lettera a Benedetto Croce', *Giornale degli economisti* 21: 139–62.

1909. *Manual d'économie politique*. Geneva: Librairie Droz. [English translation: Pareto, 1971.]

1916. *Trattato di sociologia generale*. Florence: Barbera. [English translation: 1963 [1935]. *The Mind and Society: A Treatise on General Sociology*. New York: Dover.]

1966 [1898]. 'Comment se pose le problème de l'économie pure', *Oeuvres complètes* 9. Geneva: Droz.

1971 [1906]. *Manual of Political Economy*. New York: Kelley.

1980 [1897]. 'Il compito della sociologia fra le scienze sociali', *Rivista italiana di sociologia* July: 45–54.

1984. 'Letters to Maffeo Pantaleoni', *Oeuvres complètes* 28, Vol. II. Geneva: Droz.

Parfit, Derek 1984. *Reasons and Persons*. Oxford: Clarendon Press.

Pelligra, Vittorio 2002. 'Fiducia r(el)azionale', in Sacco and Zamagni (eds.), *Complessità relazionale e comportamento economico*. Bologna: Il Mulino, 291–335.

2003. *Trust and Economics: Theoretical and Experimental Investigations*. Ph.D. thesis, University of East Anglia, Norwich.

2004. 'The not-so-fragile fragility of goodness', in Porta and Bruni (eds.), *Handbook of Happiness in Economics*. Cheltenham: Edward Elgar.

Pettit, Philip 1995. 'The cunning of trust', *Philosophy and Public Affairs* 24(3): 202–25.

Phelps, Edmund S. 1975. *Altruism, Morality and Economic Theory*. New York: Russell Sage Foundation Publications.

Pigou, Arthur C. 1920. *Economics of Welfare*. London: Macmillan.

Pocock, John Greville Agard 1975. *The Machiavellian Moment: Florentine Political Thought and the Atlantic Republican Tradition*. Princeton, NJ: Princeton University Press.

Polanyi, Karl 1944. *The Great Transformation*. [French translation: 1983. *La grande transformation: aux origines politiques et économiques de notre temps*. Paris: Gallimard.]

Prescott, Edward C., and Michael Visscher 1980. 'Organizational capital', *Journal of Political Economy* 88(3): 446–61.

Preston, Anne E. 1989. 'The nonprofit worker in a for-profit world', *Journal of Labor Economics* 7(4): 438–63.

Preston, Stephanie D., and Frans B. M. de Waal 2002. 'Empathy: its ultimate and proximate bases', *Behavioral and Brain Sciences* 25(1): 1–20.

Putnam, Robert D. 1993a. *Making Democracy Work: Civic Traditions in Modern Italy*. Princeton, NJ: Princeton University Press.

1993b. 'The prosperous community: social capital and public life', *American Prospect* 4(13): 35–42.

1995. 'Bowling alone: America's declining social capital', *Journal of Democracy* 6(1): 65–78.

2000. *Bowling Alone: The Collapse and Revival of American Community*. New York: Simon and Schuster.

Pyke, Frank, Giacomo Becattini and Werner Sengenberger (eds.) 1990. *Industrial Districts and Inter-Firm Co-operation in Italy*. Geneva: International Institute for Labour Studies.

Rabin, Matthew 1993. 'Incorporating fairness into game theory and economics', *American Economic Review* 83(5): 1281–302.

Raffaelli, Tiziano 2002. *Marshall's Evolutionary Economics*. London: Routledge.

Reynaud, Jean-Daniel 1997. *Les règles du jeu*. Paris: Armand Colin.

Rizzolatti, Giacomo, Leonardo Fogassi and Vittorio Gallese 2001. 'Neurophysiological mechanisms underlying action, understanding and imitation', *Nature Reviews: Neuroscience* 2: 661–70.

Robbins, Lionel 1932. *An Essay on the Nature and Significance of Economic Science*. London: Macmillan.

   1933. 'Introduction', in Wicksteed, *The Common Sense of Political Economy*. London: Routledge.

Rose, Richard 1998. *Getting Things Done in an Anti-Modern Society: Social Capital Networks in Russia*. Social Capital Initiative Working Paper no. 6, World Bank.

Rotemberg, Julio J. 1994a. 'Human relations in the workplace', *Journal of Political Economy* 102(4): 684–717.

   1994b. *Prices, Output and Hours: An Empirical Analysis Based on a Sticky Price Model*. Working Paper 4948, National Bureau of Economic Research, Cambridge, MA.

Rothschild, Michael, and Lawrence J. White 1995. 'The analytics of pricing of higher education and other services in which customers are inputs', *Journal of Political Economy* 103(3): 573–86.

Rousseau, Denise M. 1995. *Psychological Contracts in Organisations: Understanding Written and Unwritten Agreements*. Thousand Oaks, CA: Sage.

Sacco, Pier Luigi, and Paolo Vanin 2000. 'Network interaction with material and relational goods: an exploratory simulation', in Gui (ed.), *Annals of Public and Cooperative Economics*, special issue on 'Economics and interpersonal relations' 71(2): 229–59.

Sacco, Pier Luigi, Paolo Vanin and Stefano Zamagni 2005. 'Altruism and beyond: the economics of human relationships', in Gérard-Varet, Kolm and Mercier-Ythier (eds.), *Handbook on the Economics of Giving, Reciprocity and Altruism*. Amsterdam: North-Holland, ch. 3.

Saijo, Tatsuyoshi, and Hideki Nakamura 1995. 'The spite dilemma in voluntary contribution mechanism experiments', *Journal of Conflict Resolution* 39: 535–60.

Sally, David 1995. 'Conversation and cooperation in social dilemmas: a meta-analysis of experiments from 1958 to 1992', *Rationality and Society* 7(1): 58–92.

   2000. 'A general theory of sympathy, mind-reading, and social interaction, with an application to the prisoner's dilemma', *Social Science Information* 39: 567–634.

   2001. 'On sympathy and games', *Journal of Economic Behavior and Organization* 44: 1–30.

Saxon-Harrold, Susan, and Jeremy Kendall 1995. *Dimensions of the Voluntary Sector*. Tonbridge: Charities Aid Foundation.

Schiff, Maurice 1999. *Labor Market Integration in the Presence of Social Capital.* Development Research Group, World Bank.

2002. 'Love thy neighbor: trade, migration and social capital', *European Journal of Political Economy* 18(1): 87–107.

Schmid, A. Allan 2000. 'Affinity as social capital: its role in development', *Journal of Socio-Economics* 29: 159–71.

Schram, Arthur, and Joep Sonnemans 1996. 'Why people vote: experimental evidence', *Journal of Economic Psychology* 17: 417–42.

Schumpeter, Joseph A. 1997 [1952]. *Ten Great Economists: From Marx to Keynes.* London: Routledge.

Schwartz, T. 1982. 'What welfare is not', in Miller and Williams (eds.), *The Limits of Utilitarianism.* Minneapolis: University of Minnesota Press.

Scott, Alan 1990. *Ideology and the New Social Movements.* London: Allen and Unwin.

Searle, John R. 1995. *The Construction of Social Reality.* London: Penguin.

Sefton, Martin, Robert S. Shupp and James M. Walker 2002. *The Effect of Rewards and Sanctions in Provision of Public Goods.* Discussion paper, Centre for Decision Research and Experimental Economics, University of Nottingham.

Sefton, Martin, and Richard S. Steinberg 1996. 'Reward structures in public goods experiments', *Journal of Public Economics* 61: 263–87.

Sen, Amartya 1977. 'Rational fools: a critique of the behavioral foundations of economic theory', *Philosophy and Public Affairs* 6: 314–44.

1987. *The Standard of Living.* Cambridge: Cambridge University Press.

Shields, Michael A., and Stephen W. Price 2002. 'Racial harassment, job satisfaction and intentions to quit: evidence from the British nursing profession', *Economica* 69: 295–326.

Simon, Herbert A. 1951. 'A formal theory of the employment relationship', *Econometrica* 19: 293–305.

1978. 'Rationality as process and as product of thought', *American Economic Review*, Papers and Proceedings 68: 1–16.

Slovic, Paul, Melissa L. Finucane, Ellen Peters and Donald G. MacGregor 2002. 'Rational actors or rational fools: implications of the affect heuristic for behavioral economics', *Journal of Socio-Economics* 31(4): 329–42.

Smelser, Neil J., and Richard Swedberg 1994. 'The sociological perspective on the economy', in Smelser and Swedberg (eds.), *Handbook of Economic Sociology.* Princeton, NJ: Princeton University Press, 3–26.

Smith, Adam 1976 [1759]. *The Theory of Moral Sentiments.* Oxford: Clarendon Press.

1976 [1776]. *An Inquiry into the Nature and Causes of the Wealth of Nations.* Oxford: Clarendon Press.

Sobel, Joel 2002. 'Can we trust social capital?', *Journal of Economic Literature* 40 (1): 139–54.

Sober, Elliott, and David Sloan Wilson 1998. *Unto Others: The Evolution and Psychology of Unselfish Behavior.* Cambridge, MA: Harvard University Press.

Solow, Robert 1999. 'Notes on social capital and economic performance', in Dasgupta and Serageldin (eds.), *Social Capital: A Multifaceted Perspective.* Washington, DC: World Bank, 6–9.

Sousa-Poza, A., and A. A. Sousa-Poza 2000. 'Taking another look at the general job-satisfaction paradox', *Kyklos Review* 53(2): 135–52.

Steinberg, Richard 1985. 'Empirical relations between government spending and charitable donations', *Journal of Voluntary Action Research* 14: 54–64.

1991. 'Does government spending crowd out donations? Interpreting the evidence', *Annals of Public and Cooperative Economics* 62(2): 591–617.

Stigler, George J., and Gary S. Becker 1977. 'De gustibus non est disputandum', *American Economic Review* 67(2):76–90.

Stiglitz, Joseph E. 1988. *Economics of the Public Sector*. New York: Norton.

Stimson, Robert J., and John Minnery 1998. 'Why people move to the "Sunbelt": a case study of long-distance migration to the Gold Coast, Australia', *Urban Studies* 35(2): 193–214.

Stone, Richard 1954. 'Linear expenditure systems and demand analysis: an application to the pattern of British demand', *Economic Journal* 64: 511–27.

Sugden, Robert 1982. 'On the economics of philanthropy', *Economic Journal* 92: 341–50.

1984. 'Reciprocity: the supply of public goods through voluntary contributions', *Economic Journal* 94: 772–87.

1986. *The Economics of Rights, Cooperation and Welfare*. Oxford: Basil Blackwell.

1993. 'Thinking as a team: towards an explanation of non-selfish behavior', *Social Philosophy and Policy* 10: 69–89.

1998. 'Normative expectations: the simultaneous evolution of institutions and norms', in Ben-Ner and Putterman (eds.), *Economics, Values and Organisation*. Cambridge and New York: Cambridge University Press, 73–100.

2000a. 'Team preferences', *Economics and Philosophy* 16: 175–204.

2000b. 'The motivating power of expectations', in Nida-Rümelin and Spohn (eds), *Rationality, Rules and Structure*. Dordrecht: Kluwer, 103–29.

2002. 'Beyond sympathy and empathy: Adam Smith's concept of fellow-feeling', *Economics and Philosophy* 18(1): 63–87.

Swaney, J. 1990. 'Common property, reciprocity, and community', *Journal of Economic Issues* 24(2): 451–62.

Swedberg, Richard 1997. 'Vers une nouvelle sociologie économique: bilan et perspectives', [translated into French] 'Sociologie économique' *Cahiers internationaux de sociologie* 103 (July–December): 237–63.

Szompka, Pjotr 1999. *Trust: A Sociological Theory*. Cambridge: Cambridge University Press.

Tinel, Bruno 2000. *Origines et fonctions de la hiérarchie: trente ans de débats, 1968–1998*. Ph.D. thesis, University of Lyon 2.

Titmuss, Robert 1970. *The Gift Relationship*. London: Allen and Unwin.

Toffler, Alvin 1980. *The Third Wave*. New York: William Morrow & Co.

Tomer, John F. 1987. *Organizational Capital: The Path to Higher Productivity and Well-Being*. New York: Praeger.

Topa, Giorgio 2001. 'Social interactions, local spillovers and unemployment', *Review of Economic Studies* 68(2): 261–95.

Tuomela, Raimo 1995. *The Importance of Us*. Stanford, CA: Stanford University Press.

Turner, Jonathan H. 1999. 'The formation of social capital', in Dasgupta and Serageldin (eds.), *Social Capital: A Multifaceted Perspective*. Washington, DC: World Bank, 94–146.

Tyler, Tom R., and Peter DeGoey 1995. 'Collective restraint in social dilemmas – procedural justice effects and social identification effects on support for authorities', *Journal of Personality and Social Psychology* 69: 482–97.

Uhlaner, Carole J. 1989. 'Relational goods and participation: incorporating sociability into a theory of rational action', *Public Choice* 62: 253–85.

van Dijk, Frans, and Frans van Winden 1997. 'Dynamic of social ties and public good provision', *Journal of Public Economics* 64(3): 323–41.

von Neumann, John, and Oskar Morgenstern 1964 [1944]. *Theory of Games and Economic Behaviour*. New York: John Wiley and Sons.

Walker, James M., Roy Gardner and Elinor Ostrom 1990. 'Rent dissipation in limited access common pool resource environments: experimental evidence', *Journal of Environmental Economics and Management* 19: 203–11.

Weber, Max 1956 [1922]. *Wirtschaft und Gesellschaft*. [French translation: 1970, *Economie et société*. Paris: Plon. English translation: 1968, *Economy and Society*. New York: Bedminster Press.]

Weimann, Joachim 1994. 'Individual behaviour in a free-riding experiment', *Journal of Public Economics* 54: 185–200.

Weisbrod, Burton A. 1983. 'Nonprofit and proprietary sector behavior: wage differentials among lawyers', *Journal of Labor Economics* 1(3): 246–63.

Wicksteed, Philip H. 1906. 'Review to Pareto's *Manuale di economia politica*', *Economic Journal* 16: 814–18.

1914. 'The scope and method of political economy in the light of the "marginal" theory of value and distribution', *Economic Journal* 24: 772–96.

1933 [1910]. *The Common Sense of Political Economy*. London: Routledge.

Williamson, Oliver E. 1991. 'Introduction', in Williamson and Winter (eds.), *The Nature of the Firm: Origins, Evolution, and Development*. New York and Oxford: Oxford University Press, 3–17.

1993. 'Contested exchange versus the governance of contractual relations', *Journal of Economic Perspectives* 7(1): 103–8.

1996. *The Mechanisms of Governance*. Oxford: Oxford University Press.

Williamson, Oliver E., Michael L. Wachter and Jeffrey E. Harris 1975. 'Understanding the employment relation: the analysis of idiosyncratic exchange', *Bell Journal of Economics* 6: 250–78.

Winch, Donald 1978. *Adam Smith's Policy*. Cambridge: Cambridge University Press.

Wit, Arjaan P., and Henk A. M. Wilke 1992. 'The effect of social categorisation on cooperation in three types of social dilemmas', *Journal of Economic Psychology* 13: 135–51.

Wittgenstein, Ludwig 1953. *Philosophical Investigations*. Oxford: Basil Blackwell.

Zahn-Waxler, Carolyn, Barbara Hollenbeck and Marian Radke-Yarrow 1984. 'The origins of empathy and altruism', in Fox and Mickely (eds), *Advances in Animal Welfare Science*. Humane Society of the United States.

Zahn-Waxler, Carolyn, Marian Radke-Yarrow, E. Wagner and M. Chapman 1992. 'Development of concern for others', *Developmental Psychology* 28: 126–36.

Zak, Paul J., and Stephen Knack 2001. 'Trust and growth', *Economic Journal* 111: 295–321.

Zamagni, Stefano 1995. *The Economics of Altruism*. Cheltenham: Edward Elgar.

1999. 'Social paradoxes of growth and civil economy', in Gandolfo and Marzano (eds.), *Economic Theory and Social Justice*. London: Macmillan, 212–36.

Index